THE
Media & Morality

Contemporary Issues
Series Editors: Robert M. Baird
Stuart E. Rosenbaum

Other titles in this series:

THE
Media & Morality

EDITED BY
Robert M. Baird, William E. Loges, Stuart E. Rosenbaum

Prometheus Books

59 John Glenn Drive
Amherst, New York 14228-2197

Published 1999 by Prometheus Books

03 02 01 00 99   5 4 3 2 1

Library of Congress Cataloging-in-Publication Data

The media and morality / edited by Robert M. Baird, William E. Loges, Stuart
    E. Rosenbaum.
        p.   cm. — (Contemporary Issues)
    Includes bibliographical references.
    ISBN 1–57392–681–7
    1. Mass media—Moral and ethical aspects. I. Baird, Robert M.,
1937–   . II. Loges, William E. III. Rosenbaum, Stuart E. IV. Series:
Contemporary Issues (Amherst, N.Y.)
P94.M353   1999
175—dc21   98–50669
                                                                CIP

Contents

PART II: ENTERTAINMENT MEDIA AND ETHICS

Chapter Four: Entertainment Media and Ethics: The Terrain

Chapter Five: The Controversy over Content

Chapter Six: Entertainment Media and Ethics: Toward Solutions

PART III: LOOKING TO THE FUTURE

Chapter Seven: New Challenges to the Media

Introduction

As he eulogized his sister, Diana, Princess of Wales, in 1997, Earl Spencer spoke of the media as evil. This appraisal was born of his belief that "paparazzi," freelance photographers whose pictures of celebrities are purchased by a variety of media outlets, had caused Diana's death. Whether the media had caused her death in an immediate, literal sense by causing the automobile accident in which she died, or in a more indirect sense by forcing upon her a lifestyle that included speeding in a heavily armored limousine, the earl's indictment was generally accepted as reasonable, if not fully proven.

Evil media? By what standards of conduct can the mass media be evaluated and found so wanting that they become evil? In this volume we outline and illustrate some of the areas in which the mass media are presented with ethical issues. In two main sections, devoted to journalism and entertainment, respectively, we assemble articles by people who have thought about the ethical implications of ordinary and extraordinary practices of the mass media. Each main section begins with articles that introduce the broad contours of the ethical terrain occupied by journalists and entertainers. Then, particular cases of media behavior are examined, including issues related to Princess Diana's death. We conclude each section with suggestions some have offered for better ways of going about the business of mass media, either as journalists or as entertainers.

WHAT ARE MEDIA?

"Media" in this volume are understood as means of communication that tend to be highly centralized in their production and widely distributed in their dissemination. For instance, we exclude books because although there is a handful of publishers that dominate the book industry, authors and smaller publishing houses are scattered all over the country, and there is less professionalization in authorship. Compare books to television. Production of television shows is highly concentrated in Hollywood, and the training and capital needed to produce a television show is considerably greater than that needed to write a book. A book can be considered successful if it is sold to five thousand readers. Television shows are regularly canceled if they reach "only" 10 million viewers. In network television's prime time, a Neilsen rating of 5, which indicates viewership of roughly 5 million households, is considered an embarrassing catastrophe for its producer. The worst shows can attract twice that many viewers on a regular basis.

Why do such media bear special consideration from an ethical perspective? The answer to this question lies in the two characteristics that define them. First, their wide distribution gives them special influence over the lives of their audiences, and even over the lives of people who are not in their audiences. Second, the pervasiveness of the mass media allows them to influence what we think about and what we consider important. Scholars of communication call this "agenda setting." Does agenda setting have a moral dimension? Well, ask yourself if you'd consider the subject of your family's dinner table conversation to be free of any ethical or moral implication. Would discussing homosexuality be as acceptable as discussing the merits of various automobiles? Would discussing the techniques of mass homicide (as practiced, say, in a *Die Hard* film) be as acceptable as discussing hair styles? If a stranger entered your home and sat at the table and, without forcing you to do anything, continuously said things like "Let's talk about sex" or "Let's talk about Princess Diana," would you not consider it relevant to question whether it was appropriate for this person to raise such subjects? The ability to influence our conversations, and even the subject of our thoughts, is a form of power. Not everyone has equal ability to do this, and those with disproportionate ability to do so are properly subject to ethical evaluation of their decisions.

The concentration of the production of mass media content also raises ethical questions. Professions are by nature exclusionary. The various guilds and unions that organize camera operators, writers, actors, and others involved in Hollywood television and movie production exist in part to guard access to such occupations and guard their members' jobs and working conditions. Not just anyone can be a Hollywood television writer. The massive corporations that dominate the financing of television and movie production do not exist as public services. They guard their shareholders' interests by financing programming they believe will be profitable. Not just anyone can appear in prime time. The professionalization of media in a country devoted to the principle of free speech means that, at least for some of the means of communication, the freedom to speak is unevenly distributed. The technical nature of these media may make this inequity inevitable, but that fact does not relieve such inequity of the need to face ethical evaluation. If the ability freely to use the forums provided by television, radio, and newspapers is concentrated in a few hands, whose hands are they? What do those concentrated few intend to say to us? How do they weigh the impact on us of what they choose to say? Is everything they choose to say of equal moral standing? It seems unlikely that a paparazzi photo of Princess Diana is of equal ethical weight to a photo of death camp inmates in Bosnia.

The ethical point, then, is that when media are overwhelmingly pervasive in their distribution, their ability to dominate our agenda is monumental. Their impact on audiences may be profound, and it cannot be presumed that their audiences have altogether chosen that impact for themselves. Furthermore, when media are highly centralized in their production, the decision-making processes of any one "content provider" become momentous in their implications.

TO WHOM ARE THE MEDIA ETHICALLY RESPONSIBLE?

If the mass media are subject to ethical evaluation, where does one begin in performing that evaluation? In an article included in Part I, James Carey notes that in most professions ethical obligations are bounded by relationships between clients and practitioners. Lawyers and architects have their clients, doctors their patients, and teachers their students. But to whom are the media's professionals obligated? Carey argues that the public is clearly the "client" of journalists, but he knows that others can lay claim to a client's privilege in their relationship with the news media. Stockholders, for instance, might argue that if serving the public interest harms the bottom line, a publisher or producer is behaving irresponsibly as a guardian of the stockholders' property. Advertisers might argue that journalism that diminishes the size of the audience hurts them and decreases the value of the time or space they have paid for. Is it ethical for journalists to have disdain for such claims?

Carey does not address entertainment, but it is important to ask his question about entertainment media, too: who is the client? Is it the audience? Should program producers and station managers refuse to make or distribute programs (or commercials) that might harm audiences? This question is often rejected by media professionals as both condescending (it makes audiences seem like children—although some audiences *are* children) and threatening to First Amendment freedoms. Is the advertiser the client? Certainly the commercial media seem less willing to harm advertisers than to harm audiences, as an hour of Saturday morning television will confirm. Since it is generally advertisers who pay the bill, they seem to have a solid claim to client status.

The reason professionals' ethics are evaluated for the extent to which they look after their clients' interests is that professionals typically possess unique skill and knowledge, and their clients are generally incapable of knowing if the lawyer, doctor, or engineer is performing competently until it's too late. This principle is the same with the media. If a public is poorly informed by journalists, the public may not know this until the consequences of being poorly informed are upon them. One way, then, to decide who is the client most entitled to the protection of an ethical media is to see who is *least* powerful among those to whom the media are related: audiences, sponsors, governments, and stockholders.

Relationships between the media and others are sometimes called dependency relations, because parties to the relationships depend on access to one another's resources to accomplish important goals. An imbalance of goals and resources can create an opportunity for one party to influence another. For instance, compare the plight of Princess Diana with that of another victim of media attention, Richard Jewell. Diana's goals sometimes led her to seek media attention, or to take advantage of the attention she was getting regardless of her goals. Diana's resources—her beauty, money, and experience as a public figure—allowed her to influence the media to some extent even as the media influenced her in return. Richard Jewell, however, had no goals the media could help him attain outside those any private person might have. But as a suspect in a high-profile crime (the Olympic Park bombing during the 1996 Summer Olympics in Atlanta), he became a resource craved by the media. He had nothing to trade in order to affect the treatment the media gave him. He had no money, no glamour, no experience to draw upon.

Weaker partners in a dependency relation deserve the protection of stronger partners. The ethics of the strong are sometimes the *only* protection of the weak. For mass media, the audience members are the weak partners. Their main power is to withdraw from the relationship entirely ("just turn the TV off!"), which deprives them of any opportunity to reach any goals for which the media would be helpful. Advertisers can properly claim that they should be treated fairly by the media that take their money, but if they are not treated fairly they have alternative venues for ads. (They can also increase expenditures to buy the influence they feel they should have.) Politicians have unmediated ways to reach their constituents, or alternatives to mass media (such as the Internet, mass mailings, and public speeches). But for most people who want to know something about their representatives in government that those representatives don't *want* them to know—or at least choose not to tell them—the media are the only source for this information. Most people's access to drama, music, sports, and other entertainment is also —for better or worse—bounded by the media. Most audience members have more goals than they have resources, and those goals are not easily abandoned if an audience member feels ill served.

The authors in this volume explore relationships between the media and the subjects of press attention, audiences, and advertisers and attempt to define the obligations of the media in these relationships. In most cases the assumption is that the greatest risk is harm to audiences, or to the public. A theme that appears consistently in these essays is the tension between guarding the public and remaining profitable. The corporations that own the media protest that too much attention to the well-being of their audience (perhaps at the expense of advertisers or the government) will threaten the very existence of commercial media. Can the media be expected to fall on the sword of ethics? Would we accept this reasoning from other professionals? If an engineer protests that building a safe bridge would cost too much, and she'd make more money by building a bridge that is potentially unsafe, would we accept this as good "professional" judgment? If college professors are distracted from their teaching by opportunities to make money in private consulting, should their students simply shrug and accept whatever they are given? We generally reject such thinking as unethical.

IS ANYONE AT RISK?

But we now must ask ourselves one last question: is anyone really at risk from the behavior called into question by these authors? Even if the audience deserves ethical treatment from the media, are the media really so capable of harming audiences that ethics should play a large role in choices made by media professionals? If we accept that Richard Jewell was harmed by the media, must we accept that the people who read stories about him were harmed? Has a generation of children raised on slasher movies, gangsta rap, and Howard Stern become a horde of perverts and criminals? In the absence of evidence of harm, the media may claim (as professional basketball players do), "no harm, no foul."

Newton Minow and Craig LaMay (article no. 27) argue that the nature of television advertising is harmful, or at least deceptive, to children. They also assert that treating children as audiences available for sale to advertisers is irresponsible and a threat to children's interests. Scott Stossel describes the ideas of George Gerbner, who spent thirty years cataloging the extremes of violence in American television, and the harm Gerbner believes is done to American culture by the excesses he documents. Presidential commissions into the causes and effects of violence in the 1960s and 1970s have documented in various ways how portrayals of violence in the media can lead to violence in real life.

But research into the effects of media has always been controversial. Is it true, as Minow and LaMay claim, that "we all know what the public interest is: it is the best interests of our children"? Would people without children agree? Suppose the public interest is a healthy economy or maximum personal liberty? Does this conception of the public interest contradict the emphasis on children claimed by Minow and LaMay? In fact, in debates about federal regulation of the media, some have argued that protecting children cannot be our primary aim in regulation, lest we end up with media whose content is suited only to children. Other interests, this line of argument contends, must be allowed at least occasionally to take precedence over those of children.

Scholars involved in the study of violence and the media have noted that politics frequently becomes intermingled with social science. Politicians may see advantages in appearing to protect a vulnerable public, especially children, and thus may exaggerate any perceived danger. The FCC is a political body, not a group of disinterested judges, and its policies are often responses to ideological cues from the executive branch that do not result from impartial review of scientific literature. The first amendment covers all print media and is being extended to the Internet; thus legislation to identify and regulate printed material considered harmful has come under strict Supreme Court scrutiny. Debating and passing such legislation has become as much a matter of political grandstanding as it is of practical public policy.

As Stossel points out, there is enough evidence by now of moderate causal connections between exposure to televised violence and real-life violent behavior by children for us to take the connection for granted.[1] This finding, in fact, is consistent with common sense. If we accept the principle that the vulnerable party in a relationship deserves protection, then the debate about public policy to improve the quality of children's media should be couched in ethical terms as Minow and LaMay do— as opposed, for instance, to partisan political or economic terms.

Gerbner's arguments about the impact of media on adults' culture are more subtle and more complex from an ethical standpoint. Do adults need protection from their own tastes in media fare? Would it be reasonable for politicians to make policy that curbs the predilection of media audiences for lowbrow entertainment, such as *The Jerry Springer Show* and erotica? Economists can make elegant arguments for the beneficial economic effects of a free market, but must we treat the health of the economy as our highest priority if, as Gerbner claims, our culture is suffering?

Alternatives to existing media structures are presented in chapters three and six. Each of these chapters follows one in which particular indictments against journalism and entertainment media are introduced. For instance, chapter two reviews journalists' "feeding frenzies" around three recent news events: the death of Princess Diana, the investigation of Richard Jewell in the wake of the Olympic Park bombing in Atlanta, and the investigations of the sex life of President Bill Clinton. Chapter three begins with a discussion of alternatives to the feeding frenzy in the Clinton case, but this discussion—mostly among professional journalists—largely presumes that traditional principles of journalistic integrity sufficiently guide future practice. The subsequent articles in chapter three contemplate an approach to journalism that may offer an alternative to treatments of the news that produce "feeding frenzies." In many ways this alternative challenges some of the oldest canons of the profession of journalism, including the principle that the reporter's personal point of view be undetectable in the story. A reader might ponder two things: (1) is "public journalism" likely to solve any of the problems described in chapters one and two, and (2) is the cure worse than the disease (i.e., might the "solution" make the problem worse)?

These questions are reasonable only if one believes that harm can come to some people, if only the very young, from the content and practices of the mass media. Once the potential for harm is accepted, ethics *requires* raising such questions. If the content and practices of journalists can harm, then the content of all media, from the *New York Times* to *The Mighty Morphin Power Rangers,* must be addressed in ethical terms. The purpose of this book is to introduce readers to some of the ways the ethical analysis of the media takes place, and to prepare readers to conduct such analyses themselves. As the final section of the book indicates, the need for creative moral analysis is intensified by new developments in the media, particularly by their going more and more "on line." We believe the essays in this collection will prepare readers to enter the media market better prepared to make choices that reflect sound moral judgment. In this way a free market might become a vehicle for protecting, and even enhancing, our culture.

NOTE

1. See F. M. Christensen, "Elicitation of Violence: The Evidence," in R. M. Baird and S. Rosenbaum, *Pornography: Private Right or Public Menace?* (Amherst, N.Y.: Prometheus Books, 1998), pp. 259–82.

Part I

JOURNALISM
AND ETHICS

Chapter One

Journalism and Ethics:
The Terrain

Needed: A More Ethical Press

John C. Merrill

As we begin to consider the philosophical foundations of journalism ethics, we should first look at the present state of the press and at why there is concern. What are the main problem areas in relations between the public and the media? Numerous surveys in recent years have shown that the public has little faith in, or respect for, the press. Actually, as Michael J. Robinson and Norman Ornstein (1990, 34) have pointed out, it is not so much that the people dislike the press (they seem to have affection for it in a general sense), but that, in increasing numbers, they do not believe it.

Professor Charles Self (1988, 17) of Texas A&M University examined the reasons for public distrust of the media and of the journalists working for them. He found that there are four main reasons for the credibility gap:

1. Insensitivity, arrogance, and generally bad behavior by journalists
2. Inaccuracies, incompleteness, and generally poor professional practices
3. Disagreements over the kinds of news used and over news judgment
4. Disagreements over the task of news in the lives of readers

Originally published in John C. Merrill, *Journalism Ethics: Philosophical Foundations for News Media* (New York: St. Martin's Press). Copyright © 1997 by St. Martin's Press, Inc. Reprinted with permission of Bedford/St. Martin's Press, Inc.

Certainly there are many other reasons, some perhaps as important as these, for the public's loss of faith in the press. If the main purpose of the mass media is to water the roots of democracy by helping to create a knowledgeable and sensitive electorate, then the overabundance of sleaze, rumor, gossip, sensation, superficiality, and arrogance does not bode well for responsible journalism. Leo Bogart (1995, 1–2), writing about the media's relationship to democracy, notes that the situation does not look too promising. He writes: "A sober look at how media work in today's world suggests that they remain vulnerable to manipulation— by political authorities motivated by ideological zeal or crude self-interest, or by economic forces that limit their resources, their variety and their integrity. They are not inevitably an agent of democracy."

A common theme in the public's criticism of the media is that the concept of freedom has gotten out of hand and that the media push all sorts of irresponsible information in the name of freedom of the press. Responsible journalism, not free journalism, is increasingly proposed by would-be media reformers. As we will see in the following section, the old ideas of the Enlightenment philosophy are increasingly being questioned.

A PROBLEM: ENLIGHTENMENT LIBERALISM

The new communitarians (who stress social responsibility) believe that the basic cause for the public's current distrust of the press is that journalism is still mired in the Enlightenment's liberal ideas of individualism and libertarianism. The public sees only inconsistency in media practices; it sees no core of virtuous agreement and no shared sense of responsibility among journalists. Thus, the public begins to doubt whether there are any common ethical standards in journalism. It seems, to the public, that all journalism is relative and that the press is following John Stuart Mill's belief that the "only freedom which deserves the name is that of pursuing our own good in our own way" (Merrill, 1994, ch. 16).

Communitarian critics of the modern American press see such Enlightenment liberalism (or libertarianism) as an individualist mindset that is counterproductive to a meaningful ethics and that deprecates the spirit of cooperation and community progress. Michael Sandel (1984, 1), for one, bemoans the relativism found in liberalism and asks: "Why should toleration and freedom of choice prevail when other important values are also at stake?"

Stephen Holmes (1993), discussing liberalism and its enemies, provides a good look at writers who echo Sandel's perspective. Holmes points out that although liberalism's opposition to interference with the individual's life is well entrenched in the Western mind, the opposition to liberalism is also a tradition. It is represented, he says, by such modern figures as Sandel, Joseph de Maistre, Leo Strauss, Alasdair Mac-Intyre, Amitai Etzioni, and Christopher Lasch. These *antiliberals* (communitarians) stress the social nature of human beings and view liberalism as atomistic, that is, regarding each person as a separate, self-contained entity. The antiliberals also emphasize that values are absolute; many of them put stress on God and the supreme value of religious authority, and in so doing, they are critical of liberalism for its moral relativism and secularism.

Holmes, who teaches political theory at the University of Chicago, shows that the great liberal writers, such as John Locke, Adam Smith, and John Stuart Mill—men who significantly influenced Western journalism—were insightful and well-balanced thinkers who did not make the kind of errors attributed to them by the antiliberals. They were not, for example, so extreme in their individualism as to ignore or deny the importance of a person's living in society and relating to other people. The idea that human beings can be fully human only as members of tightly knit social groups goes back at least to the philosophy of Plato. Today this notion has been influentially represented by late-twentieth-century writers such as Robert Bellah and Alasdair MacIntyre.

One truth ignored in such communitarian critiques of liberalism, contends Holmes, is that many cohesive social groups are evil, and if individualism means standing apart from such groups, then individualism can be quite a good thing. Reporters who, due to their individual consciences, refuse to go along with the group-mandated activities of their newspapers, are not necessarily wrong in ethics and may very well be right. At any rate, we see that the deep strain of individualism, although lessening, can still be found in American journalism and that it still results in a pluralism of ethical perspectives.

Journalist Michael J. O'Neill (1993, 193) points to the weaknesses of modern mass media (especially television) and fires this blast at journalists: "They should be looking past today's breaking news to discover the hidden pockets of misunderstanding, the undetected human tensions that will burst into the headlines tomorrow, next week, or a month or year from now." Reflecting the communitarian ethos, O'Neill stresses that journalism should be "preventive rather than merely reactive" (193-94), and he faults journalism for serving entertainment rather than thought:

> Immediate action and controversy are the dominant fare at most newspapers, and superficiality bathed in entertainment and fiction is the chief product of television. The media's mission to inform democracy would be better served if they redefined news to emphasize thought as well as action, harmony as well as conflict, explanation as well as exposure. . . . This kind of journalism would search out the causes of social breakdowns before they turn into the failures and violence which the TV shows now celebrate.

The popular British writer C. S. Lewis had very little good to say about the press. Normally calm and scholarly in his writing style, Lewis produced heat when he denounced the newspapers. James Heiser (1992, 51) quotes Lewis as writing these blunt words to a friend: "I never read the papers. Why does anyone? They're nearly all lies, and one has to wade thru such reams of verbiage and 'write up' to find out even what they're saying."

According to Heiser (52), Lewis's contempt for the press was due to his rejection of "wicked journalists"—people "who disseminate for money falsehoods calculated to produce envy, hatred, suspicion and confusion." Lewis believed that what little respect the press may have is due to the fact that many researchers rely on newspapers for their information. But this respectability of the press is perpetuated by circular logic: A researcher uses a particular newspaper because of its authority, but the reason that it is authoritative is because many scholars use it.

Lewis stated that "we must get rid of our arrogant assumption that it is the masses who can be led by the nose. As far as I can make out, the shoe is on the other foot." Lewis continued: "The only people who are really the dupes of their favourite newspapers are the *intelligentsia*. It is they who read leading articles [editorials]: the poor read the sporting news, which is mostly true" (Heiser, 53).

Television, perhaps even more than the press, provides a diet of sensation, sleaze, negativism, and superficial news coverage. S. I. and Alan R. Hayakawa (1993) discuss the weaknesses of the television medium—especially its limited and distorted picture of reality, which they call the "world through the keyhole." The authors describe television's "advocacy of individual gratification through romance and consumption of material goods" (147) and note that it is "not balanced by advocacy of thrift or of work."

There are, the Hayakawas say, a few excellent television shows (such as Robin MacNeil's series, *The Story of English*), but these "few bright moments on the small screen" are the exception. The authors conclude (154): "If humanity had used writing in the same limited way we use television, we would have created for ourselves little more than tabloid newspapers and comic books."

RECENT WARNINGS ON THE ETHICAL FRONT

The erosion of press believability extends to all media, but especially to television from which the people say they get most of their news. Robinson and Ornstein (1990) did show, however, that network anchors were rated as more believable than such nonjournalists at the time as Donald Trump, Mikhail Gorbachev, Johnny Carson, and George Bush. They also found that daily newspapers' believability had fallen a full sixteen points in five years. This problem of credibility is extremely important, especially to journalists. If their stories cannot be believed, then the whole of journalism is on a shaky foundation.

A 1994 survey conducted in eight Western democracies indicated a deep skepticism about the growing "tabloidization" of the news media. In Britain, for example, 23 percent of the people said that the press *hurts* democracy rather than helps it (Tucher and Bischoff, 1995, 161). And only 49 percent of the British respondents saw the press as good for democracy. The image or reputation of the press as a serious and helpful social institution seems to be dissolving everywhere in the world. Tabloidism is largely responsible for this, and, as was noted in 1995, if "that's what it takes to sell newspapers, the next Gallup poll will leave the journalists providing consolation for the car salesmen" (Tucher and Bischoff, 162).

The 1993 Gallup poll was bad enough. It found that less than a third of Americans believed that journalists had high ethical standards (Henry, 1993). In the same year, *USA Today* apologized for a "misleading" picture showing armed Los Angeles youth-gang members ready to retaliate if Los Angeles police officers were acquitted of beating Rodney King. The printing of the picture certainly did not help the media's image. Nor was it helped by other incidents, such as the rigged GM truck explosion aired by NBC News, also in 1993, or the television reporter and cameraman in Minnesota who admitted giving alcohol to a minor to illustrate a story on teenage drinking. In 1995, the circus atmosphere created by the press in the O. J. Simpson trial did little to help the media's image. Another media problem that year involved Connie Chung and Newt Gingrich's mother. During the taping of a CBS show, Chung had assured Newt Gingrich's mother that revealing Newt's opinion of Hillary Clinton ("she's a bitch") would be "between you and me." Chung betrayed this promise, and the story went international.

Many newspeople believe that such incidents have led to a new ethical awareness—even a moral renewal—among journalists across the country. For instance, Don Browne of NBC News has argued that the network's trauma over the GM controversy actually gave a boost to ethical concern in newsrooms everywhere (Henry, 1993, 54). His exact words: "Journalism will not be diminished but strengthened. Because we made one mistake on *Dateline NBC*, hundreds of mistakes will *not* be made elsewhere." But Henry (54) contends that news consumers have serious doubts about whether journalistic ethical concern has been enhanced.

Henry says that although individual journalists may have "highly developed ethical sensibilities," journalism as a whole—unlike law or medicine—has no licensing, no disciplining boards, and no generally accepted codes of behavior. He points out that such actions as undercover exposés of wrongdoing are acceptable by some media and forbidden by others. And, he adds, in most media nothing is automatically a firing offense (54). Editors, Henry notes, insist on dealing with every case individually, and this leads to a kind of permissiveness.

The press came under a torrent of criticism for overplaying and biasing the coverage of the 1993 siege and explosive attack near Waco, Texas, on the religious sect (Branch Davidians) led by David Koresh. Television coverage of this incident was considered particularly inflammatory. A "feeding frenzy" by the media? Many journalists believe such coverage is just that. Others, however, do not agree, believing stories of celebrities and titillating court cases are quite natural and expected by the audience. These journalists say that it is the public, not the press, who must take most of the blame for a "feeding frenzy," if such a frenzy in fact exists.

GUILT WITHIN THE PRESS

This "blame the public" type of rationalization notwithstanding, there is a growing sense of guilt within the media. Journalists' concern with their possible excesses was evident in a story (Quindlen, 1994) in which a number of media personalities were asked to express their opinions. Typical of the sins mentioned in the story were these comments by Jeff Greenfield and Lesley Stahl, who are television reporters, and Michael Kinsley, who is in both television and the print media:

GREENFIELD: [There] is the difficulty of insulating yourself from prurience. . . . I think what's happened now is that a lot of the most appalling stuff is right in your face—as easy to reach as a flick of the channel. You can turn off an evening news program and you're right into *Hard Copy* or *Montel* or *Sally Jessy* (28).

STAHL: I think what we're all dancing around is that journalism hasn't caught up with the technology we're using. You can throw a guy on the air live. You haven't any thought, in your own mind, about what you're going to do once he opens his mouth. We don't check anything out until it's out there. And once it's out there, the talk show hosts get it and the tabloids get it and then we say, "Oh, my God, we're being forced to run that" (31).

KINSLEY: What about the hypocrisy of the viewers and the readers? They say they don't like us; they're disgusted with the press for covering all this sleaze, and then they create a market for it. That's why it feeds the fire (53).

Whereas Kinsley is prone to shift the blame to the audience, another well-known broadcaster, Jim Lehrer of the *Newshour*, excoriates the contemporary press (1993, 3), saying he knows of no time in American history in which journalism has been practiced so poorly. He goes on to say: "Journalism in my opinion is being consumed before our eyes and ears by a form of arrogance that I believe, if it is not arrested and stopped soon, could undermine the whole point of the exercise."

Lehrer urges people not to "tolerate lousy, arrogant, snide journalism," to cease reading newspapers and watching television news programs that are irresponsible and arrogant. Paul H. Weaver (1994), a former Harvard political science professor, also severely censures the press and contends, like Lehrer, that the failings of the news business today seriously threaten American constitutional democracy. He, too, suggests a boycott of modern journalism in general by right-thinking citizens.

Other journalists have pointed to the arrogant and hypersensitive demeanor of the press. Howard Kurtz (1993, 33), a reporter for the *Washington Post*, writes: "Although news organizations make their living pointing fingers and hurling accusations, they are notoriously slow to fess up to their own mistakes. With varying degrees of stubbornness, stupidity, and arrogance, media executives often circle the wagons when their own actions come under scrutiny."

In 1994, at the onset of the O. J. Simpson case, the prestigious journal of Harvard's Nieman Foundation, *Nieman Reports*, published a special issue called "Ethics on Trial," in which many writers dealt with current ethical problems in journalism. The titles of a number of the articles show journalists' concern with ethical improvement: "Tonya Harding Orgy," "Michael Jackson Scandal," "TV Sitting on Stories to Improve Ratings," "Presuming They Know the Truth," "Indians Struggle on in Battle for Fairness," "Can Militant Minority Reporters Be Objective?" "The Ombudsman As Ethicist," "Who Cares about the Truth?" and "Surrender of the Gatekeepers."

This special issue of *Nieman Reports* on ethics was appropriately subtitled "Tabloid Trash and Flash Threaten to Corrupt the American Media." One of the authors, Katherine Fulton, a former North Carolina editor who now teaches at Duke University, had these harsh words to say about journalists: "Our [journalists'] performance has led to a deepening credibility problem, which in turn feeds the desire some people have to bypass mainstream journalism and search for other information sources. We're arrogant, we're ignorant, we're destructive. If citizens are disengaged from politics, cynicism is partly to blame. This litany from inside and outside the profession is familiar—and mostly ignored in the nation's newsrooms" (17).

Much of the media's arrogance may stem from a smug feeling of being protected by the First Amendment, from a recognition of their power, and from the fact that they have the last word in most controversies. Press power, of course, can be counterproductive to ethical action. Here is what Professor Ted J. Smith (1992, 30) of Virginia Commonwealth University says on this point:

> American democracy is founded on the idea that no group, no matter how enlightened or altruistic, should be able to exercise unrestrained power. Journalists constitute a tiny, homogeneous, and closed elite. They are also enormously powerful, thanks to an unplanned and unforeseen sequence of developments that placed them in control of the most effective means of communication in a mass democracy. As long as it was restrained by stringent professional norms of objectivity and balance, that power could be tolerated. Without those norms, it is intolerable.

Columnist William Safire (1994, 4A) has pointed out that the media too often treat public figures unfairly. He referred specifically to the 1994 Cardinal Joseph Bernardin case, in which the Roman Catholic prelate in Chicago was accused by Steven Cook of sexually molesting him years earlier. Cook, under hypnosis, had "recovered" memories of the supposed abuse. Four months later, Cook admitted his memory was not reliable and dropped the $10 million lawsuit. According to Safire, "the Bernardin episode raises acute ethical questions for lawyers and journalists." Although the lawsuit was "without a whisper of credible evidence to support it," the media treatment of it resulted in a "devastating assault on the character of a public man of high reputation."

Safire notes that "responsible journalism is not stenography" but requires judgment about the credibility of sources and claims. The media should have learned, writes Safire, in the heyday of Senator Joe McCarthy, "that it was not honest to keep reporting his charges without putting them in the context of his record." The Bernardin case, says Safire, suggests that the lesson must be relearned.

Other leading ethical controversies in recent years have centered on such press practices as tampering with quotes, omitting the names of sources, staging news photographs, impersonating someone to get a story, paying for interviews with newsmakers, intentionally biasing stories, and using sexist or racist language. American journalists have differing opinions about the rights and wrongs of these and the many other ethical problems found daily in their work.

Many journalists, though, believe the problem lies in the absence of a universal, absolute standard for the practice of journalism. This premise is, in fact, the driving force behind the communitarians, just as it was the underlying concern of the Hutchins Commission in its study of the American press a half century ago. We should look briefly at the commission's ideas about a responsible press; they have been resurrected in large part by the modern-day communitarians.

THE NEED FOR A RESPONSIBLE PRESS

Although the need for a more responsible press is increasingly expressed in our society, such a "need" has been discussed since the earliest days of the republic. The Founding Fathers talked about it after a rather scurrilous party journalism established itself in the new country. In every era, voices have cried out against press irresponsibility. Since World War II, such voices have had wide circulation and stimulated considerable dialogue and controversy, especially in academic circles. Prior to the 1950s, the American press focused almost exclusively on its freedom guaranteed by the First Amendment, but during the last five decades the emphasis has shifted to journalistic responsibility.

The principal agent in this shift of emphasis has been the report of the Hutchins Commission, which was published in 1947. Even though the majority of practicing journalists may not have encountered the Hutchins report firsthand, its concepts and criticisms have filtered into their world. Prior to the Hutchins report, many journalists and academicians had thought in terms of "responsibility," but no significant effort had been made to consider the concept as a serious theory parallel in importance to "libertarianism." Before 1947, if responsibility in journalism was considered at all, it was thought of as being automatically built into a libertarian press, or it was assumed that various media would interpret "responsibility" in their own ways. In other words, the many interpretations of responsibility were considered a sign not only of a free press but also of a responsible press.

Hutchins and his twelve commissioners thought differently. They saw a very clear danger in the restriction of communication outlets and general irresponsibility in many areas of American journalism. Consequently, their report offered the ominous warning that if the mass media persist in being irresponsible, "not even the First Amendment will protect their freedom from governmental control" (80).

The Hutchins Commission Revisited

Two main conclusions stood out in the Hutchins report: (1) that the press has a responsibility to society; and (2) that the libertarian press of the United States was not meeting its responsibility. Therefore, a need for a new journalistic theory (or emphasis) existed.

For a few years after the report came out, the majority of American publishers were angry about it and the authoritarian implications they read in (or into) it. By the mid-1950s, however, the issue had largely settled down, with journalists perhaps thinking that the best policy was to ignore the report. But the report did not go away. Its ideas gradually took root in journalism, as there was already a readiness to challenge the old ideas of individualism and pluralistic freedom.

The best researched and strongest worded book blasting the Hutchins Commission report was published in 1950 by Chicago journalist Frank Hughes. He criticized the report and the "arrogance" of the commission, its lack of members who were journalists, and its inherent authoritarianism. By 1956 the heat had largely disappeared from discussions of the Hutchins report. It was in that year that University of Illinois journalism professors Fred Siebert, Theodore Peterson, and Wilbur Schramm published their popular book, *Four Theories of the Press*. From this work the new "theory" of social responsibility made its way, largely unchallenged, into innumerable books, articles, speeches, classrooms, and academic theses and dissertations.

This new theory was depicted as an outgrowth of the libertarian theory, not just a change in emphasis. Its acceptance was aided by the common suspicion of, and dissatisfaction with, the libertarianism of *press-centered* journalism. Implicit in this trend toward social responsibility was the loss of faith in the Enlightenment concept that people (journalists included) are rational and quite capable of deciding what is responsible. Again, there was the Platonic idea that some arbiter, some authority, some group, or some kind of philosopher-king is needed to define how the media should be responsible. This incipient seed of monolithic responsibility is what has continued to disturb many media people, who retain a basic belief in pluralism and libertarianism.

The Hutchins Commission went beyond the libertarians in that it stressed what the press *should* do. In this way, it was beginning to plow a relatively new field in journalism: ethics. And, as journalism professor Edmund Lambeth (1992) has noted, the legacy of the Hutchins Commission persists. He states that many media leaders are "finding the nomenclature of 'social responsibility' irresistible," and "countless classrooms consider and some even memorize its injunctions" (7). Even though it may be true, as Lambeth says, that the commission's literature "contains little that would assist individual journalists in daily ethical judgments" (7), it did take a giant step away from libertarianism and thrust journalistic thinking into a different ("social" or "communitarian") direction.

Press Responsibility: The Requirements

The Hutchins Commission (20-29) came up with five requirements for the press if it is to be responsible to the society:

1. *The media should provide a truthful, comprehensive, and intelligent account of the day's events in a context which gives them meaning.* (Media should be accurate; they should not lie, should separate fact from opinion, should report in a meaningful way internationally, and should go beyond the facts and report the truth.)

2. *The media should serve as a forum for the exchange of comment and criticism.* (Media must be common carriers; they must publish ideas contrary to their own, "as a matter of objective reporting"; all "important viewpoints and interests" in the society should be represented; media must identify sources of their information for this is "necessary to a free society.")

3. *The media should project a representative picture of the constituent groups in the society.* (When images presented by the media fail to present a social group truly, judgment is perverted; truth about any group must be representative; it must include the group's values and aspirations, but it should not exclude the group's weakness and vices.)

4. *The media should present and clarify the goals and values of the society.* (Media are educational instruments; they must assume a responsibility to state and clarify the ideals toward which the community should strive.)

5. *The media should provide full access to the day's intelligence.* (There is a need for the "wide distribution of news and opinion.")

The Requirements: Some Questions

Few of us would deny the nobility of the spirit that underlies the requirements formulated by the Hutchins Commission. Some libertarians, however, might wince at the thought of these things being *required* in some way, which was the implication behind the commission's report. Nevertheless, the five media duties are generally consistent with journalistic ethics of any serious type. There are, however, some questions that thoughtful students might ask and discuss. Here are a few of them, keyed to the five requirements:

1. Can the media actually present a truthful account of the day's events, much less a comprehensive and intelligent one? And how can media put all these events into a meaningful context? Is this a completely unrealistic—even naive—requirement or expectation for the media?
2. Do not, and have not, the media always *to some degree* served as a forum for the exchange of comment and criticism? Just what did the commission mean by this requirement? Was it simply saying that the media should do more in this respect? How much comment and criticism is enough? What kind of comment and criticism should there be?

3. How can the media project a representative picture of the constituent groups in the society? It is doubtful that the media can *even identify* all the constituent groups, much less give a representative picture of them.
4. Is it not too much to ask of the press to present and clarify the goals and values of the society? Just what are such goals and values? Did the Hutchins Commission know exactly what these ideals were? There is obviously a wide diversity of social goals and values. Why should the press have to present and clarify them?
5. What is meant by "full access to the day's intelligence"? Does that mean that media have to tell everything? Just how much is enough for the commission? Does it mean that *every* medium has such a responsibility, or that *all media together* have that responsibility? If the commission means the latter, then is it assumed that every citizen be exposed to *all the media* so that they can get all the news?

GROWING MEDIA ETHICAL SENSITIVITY

In the years since the Hutchins Commission report, the American media have faced increasing criticism from individuals, groups, and government for their callousness, bias, unfairness, invasion of privacy, misrepresentations, and misplaced allegiances—all of which were mentioned in one way or another in the report. Journalists have long enjoyed bashing everything and everybody in sight; they are now beginning to get growing amounts of their own medicine.

Media people may well feel more important and powerful today than ever before. Celebrity journalism is common. Television political talk shows are giving journalists more public exposure. More and more media people are doing well on the lecture circuit. They are increasingly rubbing shoulders with the people who hold the seats of power and with the creative intellectuals. Historian Christopher Lasch (1995) proposes that journalism's ills are symptomatic of the arrogance pervading all professional elites. In an interview with Stephen Budiansky (1995, 47) Lasch states that as professionals are ever more removed from community ties and ordinary life, they develop a disdain for those they see as inferiors and manage to denigrate any genuine achievement or heroism. Budiansky quotes Lasch as saying that for the media "nothing is properly understood until it is exposed as corrupt, duplicitous or hypocritical."

As the media grow in power and as they cling to their "watchdog on government" role and other self-enhancing labels, they continue to indulge in what many people consider irresponsible or unethical practices. In their mad rush to meet deadlines and what they see as their prime responsibility "to let the people know," American journalists have long been pushing ethics into a small corner of their concern.

The journalistic love for constitutionally guaranteed press freedom has been a stimulant (or at least a defense) for many cases of questionable journalism. A few voices have, from time to time, warned journalists about carrying their freedom too far. One such voice is that of Walter Lippmann (1955, 97–100), who warned that the right of self-expression is "a private amenity rather than a public necessity." He noted further, echoing the spirit of the Hutchins Commission, that free expression has limits and that utterances should be true and significant. Lippmann proceeded to condemn unbridled freedom (which he called license) when it exploited the ignorance, and incited the passions, of the people. "Freedom," then, he wrote, "is such a hullabaloo of sophistry, propaganda, special pleading, lobbying, and salesmanship that it is difficult to remember why freedom of speech is worth the pain and trouble of defending it."

Toward a New Emphasis on Responsibility

Voices like Lippmann's seem to have set the stage for a growing concern. Journalists are bombarded from every side with ethical dilemmas, controversies, and questions and are hearing and reading more and more about their responsibilities. Some people have even suggested professionalizing journalism—having minimum entrance requirements, licenses, meaningful and forceful codes of ethics, and systems for removing recalcitrant and unethical practitioners. Ethics conferences abound, ombudsmen are increasing (albeit very slowly), critical press reviews (as in the *American Journalism Review*) note questionable media practices, and university courses in ethics proliferate. Despite this quantitative growth in concern, one may still wonder if the moral quality of the media is improving or if a monolithic concept of journalistic ethics is developing.

Many press people feel that talk of responsibility leads to obligations and duties and that these in turn tend to restrict press freedom. The journalists—especially those of the Enlightenment-libertarian persuasion—always get back to stressing *press freedom* and deemphasizing *press responsibility*. Perhaps what journalists should do is to recognize that press freedom can just as easily include the freedom to be positive as negative, and that it can include the freedom to be an ally or apologist for government as well as an adversary. In fact, when the press convinces itself that it is an adversary or watchdog on government, it restricts its own freedom by accepting a very limited role. This "adversary dogma," interestingly, is not even consistent with libertarian theory, and it would seem reasonable that journalists who talk about press freedom would not like being tied to this narrow role.

Communitarians, especially, fault the press for its negative and socially disruptive approach to news. Many journalists respond that the people want such an approach. How can journalists put their ethical "house" in order if they do not know that it is out of order? It appears that journalists, by and large, see themselves as a new breed of muckrakers, unearthing the unsavory aspects of society, the sensational and negative events. They also see themselves as a kind of permanent, relentless opposition to government. They must watch government carefully; they must protect the people from government excesses and crimes. At least, as the Hutchins Commission recommended, the media should try to give more reality to news coverage—good and bad, bright and dark, positive and negative, serious and entertaining. The media have the freedom as well as the responsibility to do this.

In many ways, the eighteenth-century French philosopher Jean-Jacques Rousseau was a forerunner of communitarianism, with its emphasis on social, rather than individual, concern. Freedom, for such thinkers, can be a dangerous thing and must be sacrificed to the social good. The philosopher Isaiah Berlin (1969, 189) clearly highlights Rousseau's relevance to the modern spirit of communitarianism: "Rousseau tells me that if I freely surrender all the parts of my life to society, I create an entity which, because it has been built by an equality of sacrifice to all its members, cannot wish to hurt any one of them; in such a society, we are informed, it can be nobody's interest to damage anyone else."

A BREAK WITH TRADITION?

It is not easy for American journalists to be self-surrendering in Rousseauistic fashion. Tradition-bound libertarians that they are, most journalists do not want any kind of consensus ethics. In spite of their growing institutionalization and corporate awareness, they are largely suspicious of social ethics or any group-imposed rules that might cause them to lose their sense of identity and freedom. The press is, for the most part, so protective of the traditional ideas of individualism and pluralism that it resists anything that might result in standardization or conformity, even codes of ethics and news councils.

Evidence exists, however, that things are changing. Journalists may be starting to see ethics as the best policy for long-term success. Across the country, people are talking about the use of anonymous sources, inaccurate quotes, unbalanced stories, shocking and even gruesome photographs, gossip masquerading as news, political bias in the news, and a large number of other questionable practices.

Communitarians, as we have seen, desire a change away from the individualism of the past. Charles Derber (1993, 75) has written that "America is ripe for a communitarian awakening" and that "rugged individualism" has had its day. Increasingly, voices are heard repeating the kind of message that Margot Adler (1993, 77) of National Public Radio expresses: "Communitarians believe that Americans have become so focused on individual rights that they have forgotten that responsibilities go with them. . . . While they are few in number and more academic than activist, the communitarians see themselves as a new social movement that recommits America to a sense of shared responsibilities for the common good."

Although most journalists probably know little about communitarianism, they are becoming more conscious of their social or community responsibilities. Increasingly they are asking themselves: Do we print the name of the rape victim? What about the name of the accused rapist? Do we really believe in full-disclosure reporting—in the people's right to know? What are our real responsibilities and to whom are they owed? Do the ends (such as getting the story) really justify the means? Any means? Which means? Questions such as these, and many others, are currently being taken seriously by journalists.

The spirit of individualism, however, is certainly not gone. As Robert Bellah and his coauthors (1986, 142) have pointed out, "individualism lies at the very core of American culture." John Locke's individualism, they propose, is still very much alive in American thought, and the Lockean position that the individual "is prior to society, which comes into existence only through the voluntary contract of individuals . . . trying to maximize their own self-interest" is still influential (143). But Bellah and his colleagues warn that individualism, if not wisely harnessed by a sense of community, can be quite destructive and can lead to a kind of relative and incohesive morality.

Despite some obvious instances of unethical activities, undoubtedly spawned from time to time by the runaway individualism of specific journalists, the press seems to have received a message: It needs to be responsible. It needs to care more about ethics. The question now is whether journalists will put their awareness into action, whether they will move from the discussion level of ethical awareness to the everyday habitual level of actually "doing" ethics.

The cynic may still say that "an ethical press" is an oxymoron. But there is evidence that journalists are trying to remedy their excesses and moral lapses and to warrant public trust. For a long time, the press has unabashedly pummeled the weaknesses of others and has set itself up as a paragon of virtue based solely on its own self-appraisal. Those days are over. The press itself is in the spotlight now, prompting journalists to clean up their ethical houses before exposing the dirt in the houses of others.

REFERENCES

Bellah, Robert N., et al. 1986. *Habits of the Heart: Individualism and Commitment in American Life.* New York: Harper & Row (Perennial Library).

Berlin, Isaiah. 1969. *Four Essays on Liberty.* London: Oxford University Press.

Bogart, Leo. 1995. "Media and Democracy." *Media Studies Journal* (summer).

Budiansky, Stephen. 1995. "The Media's Message." *U. S. News & World Report,* January 9.

Derber, Charles. 1993. "About Communitarians." *The Responsive Community* (fall).

Hayakawa, S. I., and Alan R. Hayakawa. 1993. "The Empty Eye." *ETC.* (summer).

Heiser, James. 1992. "C. S. Lewis As Media Critic." *The Intercollegiate Review* (spring).

Henry, William A., III. 1993. "When Reporters Break the Rules." *Time,* March 15.

Holmes, Stephen. 1993. *The Anatomy of Antiliberalism.* Cambridge: Harvard University Press,

Hughes, Frank. 1950. *Prejudice and the Press.* New York: Devin-Adair.

Hutchins Commission (Commission on Freedom of the Press). 1947. *A Free and Responsible Press.* Chicago: University of Chicago Press.

Kurtz, Howard. 1993. "Why the Press Is Always Right." *Columbia Journalism Review* (May-June).

Lambeth, Edmund. 1992. *Committed Journalism*. Bloomington: Indiana University Press.

Lasch, Christopher. 1995. *The Revolt of the Elites and the Betrayal of Democracy*. New York: Norton.

Lehrer, Jim. 1993. "Journalistic Arrogance." *Media Ethics Update*, vol. 6, no. 1 (fall).

Lippmann, Walter. 1955. *Public Philosophy*. New York: Mentor Books.

Merrill, John C. 1994. *Legacy of Wisdom: Great Thinkers and Journalism*. Ames: Iowa State University Press

Nieman Foundation. 1994. "Ethics on Trial: Tabloid Trash and Flash Threaten to Corrupt the American Media." *Nieman Reports*, vol. 48, no. 1 (spring).

O'Neill, Michael J. 1993. *The Roar of the Crowd: How Television and People Power Are Changing the World*. New York: Times Books.

Quindlen, Anna. 1994. "The Media: Out of Control?—A Freewheeling Exchange on the Intrusive, Prurient, Run-amok (but More Democratic) Press." *New York Times Magazine*, June 26.

Robinson, Michael, and Norman Ornstein. 1990. "Why Press Credibility Is Going Down (and What to Do about It)." *Washington Journalism Review* (January–February).

Safire, William. 1994. "Bringing Down the Nation's Public People." The *Columbia Missourian*, May 30.

Sandel, Michael J., ed. 1984. *Liberalism and Its Critics*. New York: New York University Press.

Self, Charles. 1988. "A Study of News Credibility." *International Communication Bulletin* 23, nos. 1-2 (spring).

Siebert, Fred, Theodore Peterson, and Wilbur Schramm. 1956. *Four Theories of the Press*. Urbana: University of Illinois Press.

Smith, Ted J. 1992. "Are We Betraying the Public Trust?" *Communicator* (December).

Tucher, Andie, and Dan Bischoff. 1995. "Scorned in an Era of Triumphant Democracy." *Media Studies Journal* (summer).

Weaver, Paul H. 1994. *News and the Culture of Lying*. New York: Free Press.

2

Journalists Just Leave:
The Ethics of an
Anomalous Profession

James Carey

There has been a remarkable upsurge of interest in professional ethics
in recent years. We should not assume such an interest is an unmixed
blessing. On the positive side, there has been a surprising reawakening
of political philosophy, a reawakening which, if it needs a date, can be
traced to the publication in 1961 of H. L. A. Hart's *The Concept of Law*
or John Rawls's *The Theory of Justice* a decade later. This interest in politics and justice has spilled over to a reexamination of the ethical foundations of the professions: their role in advancing or frustrating justice
and a genuinely democratic politics. This interest, in turn, can be
traced, as with so much in our recent history, to the Vietnam War and
to the social upheavals surrounding it, upheavals which forced us to
rethink in the concrete the foundations of justice and democratic politics. We have, then, plenty of good reasons for being interested in professional ethics.

We have some bad reasons as well. Conferences . . . [on professional
ethics] seem to me often little more than thinly disguised excuses for
warding off attacks on the professions, for asserting the rhetoric of
ethics into a void where little ethical conduct or concern in fact exists.
The professions have come under widespread attack in recent years,
characterized as a problem rather than a solution, and one of the defensive reactions to these attacks is the conference: a ritual which serves less

From *Ethics and the Media,* ed. Maile-Gene Sagen, 1987, a publication of Humanities
Iowa (formerly Iowa Humanities Board), a state affiliate of the National Endowment
for the Humanities.

to explore the actual ethics of the professions than to celebrate the presumably positive role of the professions in American life. The ritual is driven on the academic side by intellectuals looking for a subject, any subject, of presumed social relevance so that one philosopher can declare that professional ethics is a subject that exists only because there is a market for it. "Just as failed pop singers end up in the Catskills, failed metaphysicians end up in professional ethics."

I share some of this skepticism concerning professional ethics. It is too often an arena for professors looking for a subject of research and professions looking for a defense of the indefensible. In the case of journalism the subject of ethics is too often a response not to the actual conduct of journalists but to the so-called crisis of credibility of the press, a crisis which occupies pride of place at virtually every professional gathering these days. The loss of credibility by the press is seen as prelude to the abandonment or radical reinterpretation of the First Amendment and the decline in the prerogatives, prestige, and power of the press. Put this way, the problem of professional ethics reminds one of an old saw: "there are no professions; there are only vested interests."

Much of what passes for a discussion of journalism ethics—gifts, junkets, conflicts of interest, free press, fair trial, pretrial publicity, the Janet Cooke case,★ sensationalism, unattributed sources—seem to me to be beside the point. I do not underestimate the difficulty of these dilemmas but discussion of such problems takes the practice and craft, indeed the entire structure of professional life, as a given. The ethics of journalism often seems to be a cover, a means of avoiding the deeper question of journalism as a practice in order to concentrate on a few problems on which there is general agreement, though of course the flesh, as usual, is weak. As a current East European joke has it, they are a means of "signaling left and turning right."

Given these reservations, I want to conceive my argument on a broad scale and begin with a caveat or two. I open by confessing my respect for and allegiance with journalism as a craft. While much I say will sound critical of journalism, as if I'm biting the hand that in one way or another has fed me much of my adult life, I do not want such criticism misconstrued. I have learned more about ethics hanging about with journalists after hours than I have in the halls of the academy. Jour-

---

★Janet Cooke was a reporter for the *Washington Post* when she won a Pulitzer Prize in 1981 for a story titled "Jimmy's World," about an eight-year-old heroin addict. Soon after receiving the prize, Cooke confessed to having created Jimmy as a composite of a variety of children and situations she had observed. She returned the Pulitzer Prize and resigned when her admission became public. (Eds.)

nalists, as a class, are among the most thoughtful and reflective of people concerning the ethics of their enterprise—at least when you can talk to them in private. The source of such ethics is not journalism, however. Such ethics as they possess come from their private lives, from the communities—ethnic, religious, neighborly—in which they have grown up and the real conflict is between these primordial sources and the conditions under which they must work. I agree with William Buckley that I would rather be governed by the first one hundred names in the Boston phone directory than by the Harvard faculty, though I would prefer the staff of the *Boston Globe* to either. If the subject of journalism ethics is a primitive one, it is rather more developed than the subject of academic ethics. If journalism ethics hasn't been thought by the professors of philosophy, academic ethics hasn't been thought or practiced by anyone. I will have hope for the subject of professional ethics when the academy turns its light of analysis inward, when it takes its own ethical problems seriously. Whatever critical notes are struck in this presentation, then, should be interpreted in the larger context of my generally positive attitudes toward the press and journalism and my rather more dubious attitudes about university life. But more than that, I suggest we avoid turning this into another kind of ritual in which our coming together is little more than an excuse for bashing the press and thereby comparing journalists, implicitly and unfavorably, with the law, medicine, and the academy. Indeed, much of what seems wrong with American life is that its elites are internally divided, continually competing over the distribution of prestige, rather than honestly facing the general systemic weakness which afflicts all our professions and all our institutions, journalists and the press no more and no less than all the others. Finally, I want to make this argument in as straightforward a manner as possible without recourse to jargon and technical language. To some degree the strongest and most honorable of the ethical imperatives of journalism is the requirement to make things clear and I will try to take that injunction seriously.

PART I

I take my title, "Journalists Just Leave," from Arthur Caplan, the associate director of the Hastings-on-Hudson Institute. That institute was formed, if memory serves, some twenty years ago to deal with the ethical consequences of advances in medical technology, with the ethical dilemmas surrounding abortion, euthanasia, organ transplants, etc. Early on the institute broadened its concerns from the ethics of medicine to the ethics of nursing, law, business, the military, social work, and, eventually, journalism. The institute has had some success in all these areas but found that journalists were the most resistant to ethical discourse of all the professions. (The only group that was comparable in this regard was politicians.) Art Caplan in an agitated moment summarized the success and frustration of the institute this way: "We have doctors come to Hastings and when they leave create a journal on medical ethics; we have lawyers come and when they leave create study groups, academic programs and sections of professional organizations devoted to the subject; we have nurses in and when they leave they create radical professional organizations; we have social workers in and when they leave they may not do much but they at least feel guilty. But we have journalists in and *journalists just leave*. Nothing happens." A pebble is dropped in the professional pond but nary a ripple spreads out from the meeting itself. The question that perplexes the Hastings Institute is why is it that journalists just leave, why are journalists resistant to ethical discourse? Why are they so obviously uncomfortable in the sessions at Hastings, at least compared to other professional groups? I want to try, first of all, to answer this query from the Hastings staff, to set out some of the reasons why journalists just leave.

First, neither journalists nor philosophers know how to talk about journalism ethics and, as a result, conversation on the topic is merely evasive and dispiriting. They can be forgiven. Nothing of real consequence has ever been written about journalism ethics. The only major philosopher to write seriously on the topic is the late George Herbert Mead and only in one essay on the aesthetics of the news. In the work of Mead's colleague, John Dewey, you can find remarks about journalism and public communication, but he never faced the subject directly or gave it much thought. The most cited recent work in professional ethics, Alan Goldman's *The Moral Foundations of Professional Ethics,* ignores journalism entirely, except for an aside or two. This avoidance of journalism on the part of philosophers stems, I believe, from the absence of a serious body of literature or tradition on which to draw and, more to the point, that journalism has no obvious foundation. Philosophers somehow feel that for a profession to warrant serious ethical and philosophical treatment it must have a purpose, a foundation; it must in some sense be grounded in a universal value. What is the purpose or foundation of law? Justice. What is the purpose or foundation of medicine? Health. But what, pray tell, is the purpose or foundation of journalism? To ask the question is to trigger bemused smiles from all at the conference table. Someone will eventually claim that the purpose or foundation of journalism is "the Truth." Well, that purpose is hardly distinctive to journalism and can hardly serve as the basis of a distinctive professional ethics. Telling the truth is rather like doing what our mothers always told us to do. Truth is a general human obligation and that is about how journalists understand it. But journalists are likely also to be a little skeptical about high-minded professors declaiming about "the Truth." A lifetime in police stations, the courts, the emergency rooms of hospitals, and the anterooms of political assemblies will leave one more than a little uncomfortable thinking one is exactly living a life of the truth. It will also make one more than a little skeptical about justice, health, social welfare, and the presumed foundations of the other professions. Moreover, some journalists remember that the most high-minded of their breed, the late Walter Lippmann, declared a half century ago that journalism had nothing to do with the truth.

In *Public Opinion* Lippmann argued there could be no relationship between news and truth because we no longer lived in a concave democracy: a self-contained democracy of the small town. News cannot bring together the world outside and the pictures in our heads when we live in an international community. We have interests in everything everywhere and we cannot rely on our experience in the local and immediate world to serve as a guide to the larger one. Lippmann went on to argue that news can approach the truth only when there is an adequate statistical machinery of record—when the world can be reduced to a table. Otherwise, news is merely a signal, a "blip," an alarm that something is happening out there. But journalism cannot give us a reliable way of finding out the truth about the world. From Lippmann's standpoint, there is an inevitable divide between news and truth, and this divide disables the philosophers.

If you abandon truth as the grounding of journalism, what do you have left? Bud Benjamin, the CBS producer who conducted the internal audit of the network's handling of the Westmoreland affair,*

---

*General William C. Westmoreland was overseer of U.S. military operations during the Vietnam War. In 1982 CBS aired a documentary titled *The Uncounted Enemy: A Vietnam Deception* that alleged that Westmoreland and others had covered up details regarding the true strength of enemy forces. Westmoreland sued CBS for libel, and in the 1984 trial it appeared that the evidence favored CBS. But just before the jury was given the case, Westmoreland abruptly withdrew his suit and settled for a mild statement of correction from CBS. (Eds.)

declared at a recent meeting that journalism ethics had three foundations: accuracy, accuracy, accuracy. True enough, and only those who have never typed a news story underestimate the problem of accuracy. But accuracy hardly sounds like a serious philosophical problem; it hardly sounds like the basis upon which to erect a professional ethics. Accuracy sounds rather like getting the person's age right, the name spelled correctly, the street and number in accordance with the phone book: getting, in short, the facts in order. Accuracy is important, not always easy to achieve, and there is a constant temptation to fudge the facts. But if accuracy is the foundation of journalism ethics, we hardly need conferences let alone monographs on the subject.

Let me gloss this matter in a slightly different way. To most journalists ethics smacks of a certain highmindedness and, therefore, a state of mind of which journalists are rather suspicious. Journalists knew all about the "hermeneutics of suspicion," though they hardly called it that, long before the phrase passed into the literature of social science. Journalism is part of the low life of the country; it begins in the jail house and the courts. Early on journalists develop, as a necessary protective covering, a certain cynicism about human motives and little in their experience dissuades them from such a view. When journalists go looking for human motives, they normally find self-interested ones and rather quickly come to the view that social life is pretty much a matter of whose ox gets gored. Tell a journalist that someone is acting out of a love of justice or honor, or beauty, or truth and his eyes are likely to glaze over. This is not the noblest of views but it is not so easy to shed. As a result, journalists are not likely to take seriously discussions of the truth, even in relation to their own craft, though they may have to feign such an interest on ceremonial occasions.

A second reason journalists just leave is that they react to ethics the way the *New York Times* reacted to the National News Council: ethics as an invasive tyranny, the first step down the path of control and regulation by the state. Ethics, in this view, is the Trojan Horse, out of which will march the petty bureaucrats and enslavers to overwhelm the unarmed editorialists.

The tradition of freedom of the press in America is almost exclusively negative: "Congress shall make no law. . . ." The language of ethics by contrast is almost inevitably a language of duty, of obligation, of responsibility and reciprocity. Ethics constitutes a moral vocabulary of human relations and such a vocabulary sounds suspiciously opposed to freedom of expression as journalists have understood such freedom. The language of objectivity and value neutrality leads journalists to think of ethics as a subjective and dangerous matter and even a little "wimpy" and unmanly: tender-minded rather than tough-minded. Ethics also seems to be the benign and well-intentioned opening to a horror story—censorship, regulation, and governmental interference—and consequently inimical not only to the interests of the press but to a free society generally.

I can again gloss this matter in a slightly different way. Louis Hartz, the late professor of history at Harvard, has a wonderful crack to the effect that in "America law feeds on the corpse of philosophy." Ethics is a philosophical discourse; freedom is a legal one. Freedom feeds, in a way, on the corpse of ethics. As a result, all philosophical and ethical questions are converted into legal questions, questions of the interpretation of the First Amendment. The First Amendment, in other words, sets the outer limit, the boundary, for the discussion of ethics. It is the First Amendment, not ethics, that is the source of the norms of professional practice but the First Amendment is solely concerned with removing restrictions from the press, not imposing duties or obligations. To raise any ethical question with journalists is to invite the response that the First Amendment is being violated in even considering the issue.

There is a third reason why journalists just leave. There is an old saw that doctors bury their mistakes and lawyers hang them, to which I might add that academics sequester them in private classrooms and social workers in client booths. Journalists, unfortunately, publish their mistakes. They make a public record which can be easily reconsulted. As a result, they are an unusually vulnerable social group, and consequently cautious in public discussions of their work. I am always astounded that at public gatherings I am somehow responsible for all the problems of journalism, and everything that has been published and televised that day, beginning with the student newspaper and ending with CBS. The law school dean is not responsible for *All the President's Men,* the business dean for Robert Vesco, or the engineering dean for the fact that nothing works anymore. But, because journalism is a public activity—shared in common, easily accessible, not so hard to criticize, not so difficult to understand, very hard to mystify—journalists are unusually vulnerable to criticism and that makes them unusually wary about public discussions of their craft. More than that, journalists are not very good at taking criticism. Nothing in the conditions of their work prepares them for it. Despite being public figures, on some accounts the archetype of the public man or woman, they are not very comfortable in the public arena. As Edward R. Murrow said in an oft-quoted line, "journalists not only have thin skins, they have no skins."

Journalists react defensively and with hostility to the mildest rebuke. As an example, Roger Tartarian, thirty-four years with the UPI, ten years as editor-in-chief, retired to teach at Fresno State University. He was given the Elijah Parish Lovejoy Award by Colby College and in his acceptance speech he argued against shield law for journalists and cameras in the courtrooms. These are not exactly radical notions among journalists. Nonetheless, *Editor and Publisher* headlined its report of the speech "Former UPI Editor Opposed to Press Rights." Subsequent letters to the editor attacked Tartarian as an apostate, an academic turncoat who was endangering the First Amendment. Journalists react as if all criticism of the press must be suppressed in the name of the First Amendment, even if the criticism is conventional wisdom among journalists themselves.

A final sense in which journalism is ethically irregular is that our models of professional ethics have been derived from the examples of doctors, lawyers, and ministers: independent practitioners who serve an individual client. The models in professional ethics are the lawyer in private practice serving a known client facing a problem of justice, the doctor in the office with a sick patient, the priest in the confessional with a moral problem on the other side of the curtain. Journalists, on the contrary, have always worked for organizations: originally family businesses, then corporations, increasingly conglomerates. They always have been hired hands rather than independent practitioners. And who is the client of the journalist? The public? Well, it is easy to say, but what is the public? The public is not as vividly particular as a person in trouble: a defendant in the dock, a patient on the operating table, a sinner in moral confusion. Well, perhaps the community is the client. This may be true in Boone, Iowa, but unlikely in New York City or Chicago; unlikely perhaps in a town as big as Iowa City. It is the fact that journalists are employees and that there is no clarity in the relationship of the journalist and the client that makes the ethical obligations of journalists so difficult to puzzle through. The public is there, but the public is not part of the working culture of a journalist. Someone is out there, undefined, someone who shows up in a letter to the editor, who may even call once or twice, but is not a vivid, continuous, understandable presence that the client is to the other professions.

Journalists, to come back to the first part of this dilemma, have always been employees of organizations, and they have little control over the terms of their employment or the conditions of their work. They have never been protected by essentially medieval traditions such as academic freedom or the privileged communication of the doctor, lawyer, or priest. Freedom of the press is a legal right grounded in the modern idea of property. As the old saying goes, freedom of the press extends only to those who own the presses. Moreover, journalism has been until recent times a vehicle of upward mobility for the working class and for the lower middle class. The impulse to ethics in journalism, and in journalism education, was less a high-minded sense of the republic, than the need to assert social control over the reporter, to deflect trade unions, and to make working-class journalists into sober, responsible, working men and women who would not question the prerogatives of ownership and management. It is sobering to remind ourselves that journalism education did not begin because university presidents believed the subject and the craft deserved the imprimatur of the academy but rather that presidents were having trouble controlling the political and moral radicalism of the staff at the student newspaper. The first journalism professors were advisors—read censors—to the student paper instructed to make students ethical—read docile. The now vast academic enterprise of journalism education came about because way back when some university president decided he had to exercise social control over the student newspaper. It was not so different in the case of the press generally. The development of journalism ethics was often an attack on the style of the bohemian reporter, and the sensational interests and styles of the working class and the immigrant. In this sense ethics reflected status and class conflict between middle-class owners and readers and working-class reporters rather than a high-minded attempt to articulate a satisfying moral code. As a result, journalism ethics ignores, when it does not deliberately mask, the deeper problems of the ethics of property, ethics governing the acquisition, use, and disposal of property that under the Constitution partakes of a public trust. I know how contentious this argument is, but we must face the contradiction. The fundamental practices of journalism are justified on the basis of private property and capitalist imperatives: the need to compete for and build audiences, to protect stockholders, to take advantage of opportunity costs, to beat back competitors within the industry, and to ward off others from without. While no one denies these facts, or wishes necessarily a different arrangement, the press nonetheless insists upon a special position in the corporate community because it is a private business imbued with a public trust. The real responsibility for this public interest, however, is saddled on the lowest level of its employees: those who have the least control over the conditions of work and the greatest insecurity. Arguments about journalistic ethics are almost exclusively concerned with the conduct of reporters and editors and not with the ethics of ownership and property. The fundamental ethical problems of journalism originate at the deepest level of ownership but are "solved" at the level of the reporter and editor. For all practical purposes, reporters are professionals subject to professional ethics but owners are not.

PART II

A catalogue of reasons does not an argument make, and so I would now like to change the lens and refocus the problem. The god term of journalism, the be-all and end-all, the term without which the entire enterprise fails to make sense, is the public. Insofar as journalism is grounded, it is grounded in the public; insofar as journalism has a client, the client is the public. The press justifies itself in the name of the public: it exists, or so it is regularly said, to inform the public, to serve as the extended eyes and ears of the public, to protect the public's right to know, to serve the public interest. Ethics in journalism originates in and flows from the relationship of the press to the public. The public is totem and talisman; the object of ritual homage and, rather too often, a semantic crucifix engaged to ward off modern vampires.

The public is also the deepest and most fundamental concept in the entire liberal tradition. Liberal society is grounded in the notion of a virtuous public. For John Locke, to be a member of the public was to accept a calling. But for all the ritual incantation of the public in the rhetoric of journalism no one quite knows any longer what the public is or where one might find it or even whether it exists any longer. There is no better witness to these matters than the most cited journalist of his generation, Walter Lippmann. In 1914 Lippmann published *Drift and Mastery*, a book whose very title tells us of the mood of the year. The country, the entire Western world, is at drift: things are out of control, the Great War is about to commence. How were we to avoid drift and regain mastery; how was the course of human events to be brought back under human control? During the war Lippmann went to work for Woodrow Wilson, provided the first draft of the Fourteen Points on which the peace settlement was to be based, and later attended the negotiations at Versailles. Like so many others, he was disappointed by the outcome of the negotiations and the subsequent failure of the League of Nations. He wrote as follows of the chaotic scene at Versailles:

The pathetically limited education of officials at the conference, trained to inert and pleasant ways of life, prevented them from seeing or understanding the strange world before them. All they knew, all they cared for, all that life meant to them, seemed to be slipping away to red ruin. And so in panic they ceased to be reporters and began bombarding the chancelleries at home with gossip and frantic explanation. The clamor converged on Paris and all the winds of doctrine were sent whirling about. Every dinner table, every lobby, almost every special interview, every subordinate delegate, every expert advisor was a focus of intrigue, bluster, manufactured rumor. The hotels were choked with delegations representing, pretending to represent, hoping to represent every group of people in the world. The newspaper correspondents struggling with this illusive and all-pervading chaos were squeezed between the appetites of their readers for news and the desire of the men with whom the decisions rested not to throw the negotiations into a cyclone of distortion.

Lippmann's book *Public Opinion,* published in 1922, the founding book of modern journalism, was an extended reflection on his experience at Paris and Versailles. His conclusion was a dour one. You will not get out of drift and achieve mastery by relying on the public or the newspapers. There is no such thing as informed public opinion, and therefore, that opinion cannot master events. Voters are inherently incompetent to direct public affairs. "They arrive in the middle of the third act and leave before the last curtain, staying just long enough to decide who is the hero and who is the villain." He concludes: "The common interest in life largely eludes public opinion entirely and can be managed only by a specialized class. I set no great store on what can be done by public opinion or the action of the masses." The road away from drift and toward mastery was not through the public, not through public opinion, not really through the newspaper. The only hope lay in taking the weight off the public shoulders, recognizing that the average citizen had neither the capacity, nor the interest, nor the competence to direct society. Mastery would come only through a class of experts, a new order of samurai, who would mold the public mind and character: men and women dedicated to making democracy work for the masses whether the masses wanted it or not.

Lippmann, in effect, takes the public out of politics and politics out of public life. In a phrase of the moment, he depoliticizes the public sphere. Lippmann turned the political world over to private and specialized interests, albeit interests regulated by his new samurai class. Lippmann wrote, of course, in the heyday of science, when science was taken to be the exemplar of a culture as a whole. He assumed that scientists were a transcendent class, without interests and objectives: philosopher kings of the new world.

> The burden of carrying on the work of the world, of inventing, creating, executing, of attempting justice, formulating laws and moral codes, of dealing with the technic and the substance, lies not upon public opinion and not upon government but on those who are reasonably concerned as agents in the affair. Where the problems arise, the ideal is a settlement by the particular interests involved. They alone know what the trouble really is.

What is the role of the journalist and journalism in the state of affairs Lippmann envisaged? It is not to tell the truth, for, as I mentioned earlier, journalism has nothing to do with the truth. News is a blip on the social radar, an early warning system that something is happening. Otherwise, journalists primarily serve as conduits for relaying truth arrived at elsewhere: by the experts—scientists in their laboratories, bureaucrats in their bureaus. Journalists are symbolic brokers who translate the arcane language of experts into a publicly accessible language for the masses. They transmit the judgments of experts and thereby ratify decisions arrived at by that class—not by the public or public representatives. Beyond that the chief function of news was publicity. News kept the experts honest; it prevented them from confusing the public interest with the private interest, by exposing them to the hot light of publicity. Lippmann had more faith in publicity than in the news or an informed public: "The great healing effect of publicity is that by revealing man's nature, it civilizes them. If people have to declare, publicly, what they want and why they want it, they won't be able to be altogether ruthless. A special interest openly avowed is no terror to democracy; it is neutralized by publicity."

The message of *Public Opinion* never quite got through, so a few years later he published it again, under the title of *The Phantom Public*. Here is the judgment of that book: "the accepted theory of popular government, resting on the belief that there is a public that directs the course of events is simply wrong. Such a public is a phantom." For Lippmann the problem of politics was to select the right elites, to put them in control of the instruments of information, to train them in the new sciences and to create a press that will keep the hot light of publicity on such elites so that they would not act as ruthlessly as they might otherwise.

One person got the message of Lippmann's deeply pessimistic and anti-democratic books. John Dewey reviewed *Public Opinion* and called it "the greatest indictment of democracy yet written." Lippmann has been accepted as the exemplar of the journalists' craft and has been one of the formulators of the ideology of modern journalism. Yet, his work is an attack on the public, on the concept that provides the only hope for grounding an ethics of journalism. The revelations of Ronald Steel that Lippmann spent his life as consort of the powerful and advisor to heads of state has tarnished his reputation, but it has not dislodged the patrician view of journalism that Lippmann not only described but advocated.

We have inherited and institutionalized Lippmann's conception of journalism and the ethical dilemmas of journalism flow directly from that conception. We have our new order of samurai but they turn out to be what David Halberstam acidly described as "the best and the brightest." We have a scientistic journalism devoted to the sanctity of the fact and objectivity, but it is one in which the hot light of publicity invades every domain of privacy. We have a journalism that is an early warning system but it is one that keeps the public in a constant state of agitation or boredom. We have a journalism that reports the continuing stream of expert opinion, but, because there is no agreement among experts, it is more like observing talk show gossip and petty manipulation than bearing witness to the truth. We have a journalism of fact without regard to understanding through which the public is immobilized and demobilized and merely ratifies the judgments of experts delivered from on high. It is above all a journalism that justifies itself in the public's name but in which the public plays no role except as an audience: a receptacle to be informed by experts and an excuse for the practice of publicity.

PART III

Journalism ethics as currently understood is a purely negative enterprise. It attempts to remove or ameliorate the faulty practices of journalists, practices which lead to unfairness or damage the credibility of the press. I do not wish to discourage this undertaking. Journalists ought to be accurate, ought to recognize the rights of the accused, ought to respect the legitimate domain of privacy, ought to avoid sensationalism, ought to avoid conflicts of interest. They ought, in short, to practice the well-known ethical imperatives that are part of the civilization at large: that we honor the Golden Rule, tell the truth, keep our promises, and confess our sins. But none of this will solve the real problems of journalism. In fact, those problems cannot be solved; they can only be dissolved into a new set of practices, a new way of conceiving what journalism is and how one ought to go about it.

In other words, the removal of bad practice from journalism as it currently exists leaves that journalism wholly intact. The real problem of journalism is that the term which grounds it, the public, has been dissolved, in part, by journalism. Journalism only makes sense in relation to the public and public life. Therefore, the fundamental ethical problem in journalism is to reconstitute the public, to bring it back into existence. How are we going to do that?

Alas, my questions outrun my answers. I do not know how to restore the public to a vital role in American politics and American journalism. I can only ask that we at least consider how we might do it. I do know that we have inherited a deeply flawed self-understanding of journalism of the kind promoted by Walter Lippmann. We have to root out that self-understanding and develop a new vocabulary, a new metaphor with which to think and practice journalism. I cannot describe that vocabulary in a few moments—perhaps I couldn't in a few hours—but I can point to a direction or two such a rethinking must take.

We have inherited, to reduce it all to a few words, a journalism of the expert and the conduit, a journalism of information, fact, objectivity, and publicity. It is a scientific conception of journalism: it assumes an audience to be informed, educated by the journalist and the expert. In their different ways, the methods of the journalist and the expert guarantee the truth and sanction the practices of the press. I would suggest we throw out this vocabulary and think of journalism, instead, as a record, a conversation, and as an exercise in poetry and utopian politics.

The first thing to remember about journalism is that it derives its name from the French word for "day" and is, therefore, a daybook, a diary, a collective and public diary that records public occurrences of the day. The importance of journalism is less that it disseminates news and information and more that it is one of the primary instruments through which the culture is preserved and recorded and, therefore, available to be reconsulted. This was Jefferson's basic justification for freedom of the press: the newspaper produced, compared to human memory or manuscript, a virtually indestructible record of the significant events in community life. We have to return, in other words, to a journalism of record.

Second, journalism ought to be conceived less on the model of information and more on the model of a conversation. Kenneth Burke has a wonderful series of lines somewhere that goes about as follows: "Life is a conversation. When we enter it it is already going on. We try to catch the drift of it. We leave before it's over." Journalists are merely part of the conversation of our culture; one partner with the rest of us—no more and no less. This is a humble role for journalism—or it seems so at first blush—but in fact what we need is a humble journalism. Lippmann was right. Journalism can't tell the truth because no one can tell the truth. All journalism can do is preside over and within the conversation of our culture: to stimulate it and organize it, to keep it moving and to leave a record of it so that other conversations—art, science, religion—might have something off which they can feed. The public will begin to reawaken when they are addressed as a conversational partner and are encouraged to join the talk rather than sit passively as spectators before a discussion conducted by journalists and experts.

Finally, we ought to think of journalism not as an outgrowth of science and the Enlightenment but more as an extension of poetry, the humanities, and political utopianism. What would journalism look like if we grounded it in poetry, if we tried to literalize that metaphor rather than the metaphor of objectivity and science? It would generate, in fact, a new moral vocabulary that would dissolve some current dilemmas. I have no way of magically summoning such a vocabulary into existence, but we might get closer to it if we went back to the beginnings of journalism, to the relations between journalism and the novel, and to the first of the great political journalists, Samuel Johnson. In *A Journey to the Western Islands,* the first great travel book, Johnson and his companion Boswell come to the town of Bamff in Scotland. Johnson was no great lover of the Scots and he didn't think much of their towns. He describes in economical but telling detail the crude houses of Bamff and the rather bad carpentry of the Scots. They didn't know how to make windows or properly lead glass and as result their homes smelled badly and were distinctly unpleasant places in which to be a guest. As he goes on in this vein, a hitch suddenly appears in his voice: "These diminutive observations seem to take something away from the dignity of writing and are never communicated but with hesitation and with a little fear of abasement and contempt." Johnson paused as he found himself using the great instrument of writing to discuss the low life—the appearance and smell of Scottish houses—and he was embarrassed. Writing was for the contemplation of God and the higher virtues and here he was putting it to vulgar ends. Despite the embarrassment he goes on and makes a plea for the importance of petty things: "It must be remembered that life consists, not of a series of illustrious actions or elegant enjoyments. The greater part of our time passes in compliance with necessities in the performance of daily duties, in the removal of small inconveniences, in the procurement of petty pleasures, and we are well or ill-at-ease as the mainstream of life glides on smoothly or is ruffled by small obstacles and frequent interruption." Again, Johnson hitches his voice and comes to the defense of a democratic journalism:

> The true state of every nation is the state of its common life. The manners of the people are not to be found in the schools of learning or palaces of greatness where national character is obscured or obliterated by travel or instruction, by philosophy or vanity, nor is public happiness to be estimated by the assemblies of the gay, or the banquets of the rich. The great mass of nations is nether rich nor gay; they whose aggregate constitutes the people are found in the streets and the villages and the shops and the farms and from them, the people, collectively considered, must the measure of general prosperity be taken; as they approach to delicacy, a nation is refined. As their conveniences are multiplied, a nation, at least a commercial nation, must be denominated wealthy.

That is the first great plea in our language for a democratic journalism of the common life. Johnson is the first to utter what is really the great ethical imperative of journalism: to comfort the afflicted and to afflict the comfortable. But you can neither afflict nor comfort if publicity, objectivity, factuality are your only concerns.

Science could at one time serve as the exemplification of our culture and the scientist could at one time be our hero. The sciences did enormous and important work in securing the foundations of liberal democracy and it is not surprising that journalism should take science as its model and try, in however degenerate a form, to imitate it. But that age is over.

Today, the most important parts of our culture are in the arts, in poetry, in political utopianism, in the humanities. We should not shrink from this new metaphor. Social life is, after all, the succession of great metaphors. The metaphor which has governed our understanding of journalism in this century has run into trouble. Conferences such as this are merely testimony to our troubles. The ethics of journalism will not move forward until we actually re-think, re-describe, re-interpret what journalism is: not the science or information of our culture but instead its poetry and conversation.

3

Ethics as a Vehicle for Media Quality

Andrew Belsey and Ruth Chadwick

QUALITY AND THE MEDIA

The social psychologist Urie Bronfenbrenner once wrote that "the only safe way to avoid violating principles of professional ethics is to refrain from doing social science research altogether" (Bronfenbrenner, 1952, 453; quoted in Barnes, 1979, 5). Such an option is not open to the journalist. Although the nature of the media might change, probably with the enhancement of the role of electronic media at the expense of traditional print, it is a reasonable assumption that the media are here to stay. Given the importance of the media to society as a whole, how then can the quality of the media be protected and promoted? Is quality assurance in the media a matter of professional ethics?

The media are important to society because of their close connection with democracy (see Lichtenberg, 1990; Keane, 1991). It is generally agreed that free media are a necessary condition of a democratic society.[1] A democracy is an association of citizens who participate in a wide range of social processes, obviously including the political. Democratic political participation requires an informed citizenry, and one of the roles of the media is to enhance the level of participation by providing the information, opinion, comment, and debate on a wide

European Journal of Communication © 1995 SAGE (London, Thousand Oaks, Calif., and New Delhi), Vol. 10(4): 461–73. Reprinted by permission of the publisher and authors.

range of social and political issues. (Clearly, the media are not alone in having a democratic role, but are building on the work of, for example, the education system.) However, although in fulfilling their democratic role the media require freedom, this is not sufficient. There is also the issue of the quality of the information and opinion that the media make available to the public. "Diversity" is often put forward as the watchword here, especially as far as the circulation of opinion is concerned.

Although this sounds like a commonplace of much modern democratic theory, it is not without its problems. It could be argued in particular that there is a conflict between the theory of the role of the media in a democratic society, and the market ideology which dominates political and economic practice in the world today, including those parts of the world, especially Western Europe, North America, and Australasia, normally assumed to be the paradigms of a democratic approach to social and political organization. According to this dominant ideology, the media and their contents are commodities, subject to the laws of supply and demand just like any other product, and as such should be outside the sphere of state regulation.

Where deregulation and market forces predominate, there are two possible approaches to the question of media quality. The first would rule out the question altogether, as representing an unwarrantable intrusion of nonmarket forces into the free market. The second approach is slightly more sophisticated, reinterpreting questions of quality in terms of the satisfaction of consumer preferences, as measured by sales and audience figures. Thus the best newspaper would be the one with the largest sales, the best television channel the one with the largest number of viewers, etc. In other words, "quality" would be decided by the market.

Whether either of these approaches is a satisfactory response to the question of media quality is debatable. The first refuses to recognize the question at all, while the second avoids the question by a quantitative redefinition of "quality." Both approaches, by adopting an over-narrow idea of regulation, assume wrongly that regulation is necessarily hostile to the media, and thus fail to notice that the idea of regulation, as a constitutional or legal framework within which the media operate, is neutral in itself. The consequences of regulation in practice depend on the particular content of the framework in some particular state and jurisdiction. Some contents can be highly positive, as can be argued in the case of the First Amendment to the American Constitution, where the legal guarantee of a free press permits journalists to focus on questions of quality in the ethical sense (see Klaidman and Beauchamp, 1987; Belsey, 1995). Other contents can be highly negative, as can be argued in the case of

British libel law, where both uncertainty and the possibility of a draconian outcome have a severely inhibiting effect on investigative journalism and editorial comment (see Robertson and Nichol, 1992, 102–103).

Furthermore, at a more fundamental level the whole market approach can be criticized not just for ignoring questions of quality but for failing to deliver democratic media at all. John O'Neill, for example, has criticized the supposed connection between a free market and a free press, arguing that "the market inhibits the dissemination of information and diverse opinion required of a democratic society" (O'Neill, 1992, 15). A narrow range of ownership and control in the media results in an unduly narrow output, one that reflects the interests of those with ownership and control.

The market approach does not face up to the problem that a democracy cannot be indifferent to questions of media quality. No set of media institutions, even if free by market standards, is likely to assist in achieving democratic expectations unless the question of quality is faced. It is clear that inaccurate news, biased discussions, and manipulative opinion pieces will not serve the ends of democracy.

The question of media quality remains, then. But before directly addressing it, it is worthwhile briefly drawing attention to a distinction that has already been mentioned and will recur in various guises in this essay, the distinction between positive and negative aspects of quality assurance. This distinction accords fairly well with common sense. In general terms it is the distinction between what the media should and should not do, between what should and should not appear in the media. The positive aspect of media quality is concerned with the media's contribution to democracy through the dissemination of information and opinion in terms of range, depth, diversity, etc. The negative aspect of media quality is concerned with what should be avoided: manipulation, exploitation, obscenity, pornography, for example.

It appears that there could be two approaches to the question of media quality in the terms outlined: the legal and the ethical. Which, then, is the best route to follow for quality assurance, the legal route or the ethical route? Or do they both lead to the same goal?

THE LEGAL ROUTE TO MEDIA QUALITY

The legal route to media quality has both positive and negative aspects. The positive aspect, however, rather than addressing the question of quality directly, can instead be thought of as providing an enabling framework, within which good journalism can be practiced. The obvious example, already mentioned above, is the First Amendment to the American Constitution, which lays down that "Congress shall make no law . . . abridging the freedom of speech, or of the press." Another important example is freedom of information legislation, which not only makes information available but, ideally, by so doing encourages an atmosphere of openness and debate about political and social issues. A legal framework which guarantees press freedom and promotes the free flow of information is serving not just the ends of good journalism but also the ends of democracy.

The negative aspect of the legal route to media quality concerns the prohibition or restriction of what may be published, and introduces a concomitant panoply of police action, criminal or civil proceedings, injunctions, writs, sanctions, penalties, and other legal processes. Although this tends to conjure up images of a police state, even democratic countries have laws which restrict or regulate the media in some ways, although they differ in extent and often reflect accidents of history and tradition. It seems that there will be an inverse proportional relationship between the negative aspect and the positive aspect of media law: a country with a legal guarantee of press freedom and freedom of information legislation will have few laws restricting the media. Conversely, a country with no statutory press freedom and no freedom of information will have fewer inhibitions about restricting the media, and here, unfortunately, the United Kingdom provides an example, with its considerable battery of legislation on official secrecy, confidence, contempt of court, race hatred, blasphemy, obscenity, defamation, and many other matters.[2] In such a system media freedom exists in the interstices of the legal framework, though of course the interstices are much larger than in totalitarian states.

Is the legal route a necessary part of quality assurance in the media? Clearly, yes, both the positive and negative aspects assist in promoting media quality. Admittedly some of the possible range of negative legal restrictions are highly controversial—blasphemy, for example, or the severely restrictive British law on official secrecy. But some legal restriction on the publication of libel, pornography, or racist material is compatible with media quality and with democracy—the problem is where to draw the line, how to frame legislation that rules out the genuinely objectionable without stifling justifiable circulation of information or expression of opinion. But the issue is perhaps clearer if the negative restrictions are balanced by a commitment, enshrined in legislation, to a positive framework which has the task of promoting rather than hindering the contribution of the media to a democratic polity.

But however necessary and however desirable, the legal route to media quality will not be sufficient. Neither legal rights for journalists, nor legal restrictions on the media, will in themselves produce good journalism. Quality in the media requires an additional route, the ethical.

THE ETHICAL ROUTE TO MEDIA QUALITY

No legal framework guarantees ethical behavior in any area of life, though the law does provide an arena in which some forms of behavior are encouraged and some discouraged. There will be (dis)incentives in the form of sanctions and penalties, but ultimately a society depends on the sense of morality and responsibility of its members. This is how it ought to be in a democracy. Similarly, neither the negative nor the positive aspects of the legal route will guarantee media quality. Unless media professionals have a sense of morality and responsibility too, the quality will be lacking. But in relation to the media there is an important interplay between law and ethics. To put the point simply: too many legal prohibitions and restrictions force journalists to concentrate on what they can get away with in legal terms, and thus distract their attention away from matters of ethics. This has a distorting and a trivializing effect on the output of the media, to the detriment of quality.[3] Conversely, giving legal rights and freedoms to journalists places them under an obligation to pay attention to the ethical issues of their profession. As Klaidman and Beauchamp put it in their influential discussion of media ethics, "freedom from legal constraints is a special privilege that demands increased awareness of moral obligation" (Klaidman and Beauchamp, 1987, 12).

This is because a legal right to publish does not mean that it is morally right to publish. Even when the law is satisfied there are still ethical questions in areas such as obscenity, character assassination, privacy, confidentiality, deception, sexism, and homophobia. Journalists need to select from the mass of possible information what should be included and what should not, and judgments about what is important, significant, trivial, or tasteless are, basically, ethical judgments. Similarly, judgments about presentation are also ethical, inasmuch as they raise issues of sensitivity and taste on the one hand, and sensationalism and vulgarity on the other. All these ethical issues can be summed up in the concept of professional competence, as this requires not just a command of technical skills but also the ability to deploy moral qualities (Klaidman and Beauchamp, 1987, 12). Thus, for example, a commitment to truth-telling, often put forward as constitutive of journalism (and therefore basic to journalistic competence), requires honesty, integrity, tenaciousness, and no doubt other ethical qualities, too, on the part of the journalist.

One interesting and important way of spelling out further what is involved in this ethical notion of competence in the media is by referring to Klaidman and Beauchamp's prescription for journalism in terms of virtue and the virtues: every journalist the "virtuous journalist" (Klaidman and Beauchamp, 1987). The virtuous journalist will display a commitment to many virtues, including fairness, accuracy, honesty, integrity, objectivity, benevolence, sensitivity, trustworthiness, accountability, and humor. More important, though, than a list of specific virtues is virtue: the virtuous journalist is one who has a virtuous character, one who therefore has a disposition to act virtuously not only in familiar but also in novel situations. It is in this sense that the competent journalist is the virtuous journalist and is also the journalist with a commitment to quality.

In such a way, then, can ethics be a vehicle for media quality. As before, it is a vehicle which can travel the ethical route in two ways, a positive aspect emphasizing the ethical requirements for maintaining quality in the media (the virtues, like truth-telling), and a negative aspect emphasizing the prohibitions (the corresponding vices, such as lying).

THE ETHICAL ROUTE VIA A CODE OF PRACTICE?

The ethical route to media quality requires a commitment by individual journalists and other media practitioners to certain ethical principles and standards—a commitment which may be conveniently expressed by the notion of the "virtuous journalist." But should this commitment be further demonstrated by adherence to an ethical "code of practice," incorporating the various principles and standards?

While not essential, such an approach has advantages. It joins journalism with other occupations that have promulgated codes of practice, and is one of the moves which demonstrate an aspiration to move beyond mere occupation to professional status. Adherence to a code brings journalists together as professionals recognizing common aims and interests and accepting responsibilities to the public. Adherence to a code thus shows a collective public commitment to acknowledged ethical principles and standards, rather than a purely solitary conscientiousness about ethical matters. Putting ethical principles and standards into a published code is a convenience, announcing to both professionals and the public that there is a commitment to quality and to the standards of behavior and practice necessary to achieve quality.

An ethical code of practice will have both positive and negative aspects, detailing what is required and what is prohibited. Both aspects clearly have a contribution to make to media quality. A code of practice for the media, for example, could require journalists to be honest and accurate in all matters, to be impartial and objective in reporting news, to publish corrections, to offer a right of reply, to protect the identity of confidential sources. It could also, presumably, prohibit deception, harassment, invasions of privacy, doorstepping the victims of traumatic events, exploiting children, buying the stories of criminals. It is noticeable that these prohibitions tend to be much more specific than the positive requirements.

However, a code of practice could be seen as having functions other than just listing the requirements and prohibitions. First, a code could have a disciplinary function, linking breaches of requirements and prohibitions with sanctions. A code could also have an educative function, in that it would teach what was expected of a journalist and would both state and encourage the standards of competence and the underlying thinking that constitute journalism as professional practice. Related to this a code could also have a "utopian" function, which would be a statement of the ideals and aspirations of the profession, going beyond a list of requirements and prohibitions. In the case of a code for the media, such ideals could go back to First Amendment aspirations, linking press freedom with the requirements of democracy. (For further discussion of codes see Belsey and Chadwick, 1992; Harris, 1989, 1992.)

An Example: The Press Complaints Commission's Code of Practice

Examination of the Code of Practice of the (British) Press Complaints Commission (PCC) can throw some light on the advantages and disadvantages of attempting to encapsulate avowedly ethical conduct in a code. But first, the history of the PCC Code is illuminating on the issue of the relationship between legal and ethical regulation of the media. The Press Complaints Commission is a nonstatutory body, consisting largely of newspaper and periodical editors but with an independent chairperson and other members. Its code is an attempt at self-regulation, precisely to avoid further restrictive legislation. The British press has in recent years shown what the government regarded as an unhealthy disregard for its authority, in that the press took a considerable interest in the *Spycatcher* case and other matters involving the security and intelligence services, matters that the government regarded as its secrets.[4] When the press went on to take an even more unhealthy interest in the sex lives of prominent figures—many of them senior establishment politicians or even ministers—the government took this as an opportunity to try to rein in what it regarded as the excesses of the media through such mechanisms as a statutory regulatory body for the press and privacy legislation.[5] The problem was that such mechanisms would threaten to reach beyond the main immediate offenders, the tabloid newspapers, to inhibit serious and responsible investigative journalism, and so far the solution has eluded the drafters of possible legislation.[6] But the press responded—without great enthusiasm, it must be admitted—to the threat of further restrictive legislation with an attempt to "put its own house in order" (the politicians' favorite cliché in the circumstances) by creating the PCC and the self-imposed Code of Practice.[7]

The code is fairly brief, occupying only two sides of paper, and consists of a preamble followed by eighteen clauses:

1. Accuracy;
2. Opportunity to reply;
3. Comment, conjecture, and fact;
4. Privacy;
5. Listening devices;
6. Hospitals;
7. Misrepresentation;
8. Harassment;
9. Payment for articles;
10. Intrusion into grief or shock;
11. Innocent relatives and friends;
12. Interviewing or photographing children;
13. Children in sex cases;
14. Victims of crime;
15. Discrimination;
16. Financial journalism;
17. Confidential sources;
18. The public interest.

The text of the code immediately suggests one problem with such codes, as little thought appears to have gone into making it well ordered, with a coherent theoretical base. There is very little attempt to state what its basis or purpose is, or to demonstrate that the clauses are individually necessary and jointly sufficient to achieve whatever the aims of the code are. It does not explicitly mention such obvious virtues as truth-telling and objectivity, for example, and it is more concerned with the way in which material is gathered than with how it is presented to the public, although both these aspects of journalism are considered to some extent.

The preamble does offer a few hints at an underlying purpose when it says:

> All members of the press have a duty to maintain the highest professional and ethical standards. In doing so, they should have regard to the provisions of this Code of Practice and to safeguarding the public's right to know.

Here the reference to the public's right to know does indicate the connection between the media and democracy, but the point is left vague and unexplained, as is the link between the right to know and the earlier reference to professional and ethical standards.

The code is no clearer or better at explanation when it says: "While recognizing that this [i.e., following the code] involves a substantial element of self-restraint by editors and journalists, it is designed to be acceptable in the context of a system of self-regulation." The syntax of this statement is somewhat obscure, but it appears to involve a considerable element of circularity, or what is popularly called tautology. As a result, the code is left floundering, with no substantial basis to fall back on. A clearer statement of basis and principle would be more helpful, especially if it also enabled the user or reader of the code to see how each particular clause was developed in a coherent way from the foundation.

The clauses themselves, a mixture of positive requirements and negative prohibitions, are not presented in any obvious sequence but are just a series of unconnected dos and don'ts, which can be summarized as: do be accurate; do apologize for mistakes; do offer a right of reply; do distinguish between fact and comment; do protect the identity of confidential sources—but don't invade privacy or harass people, especially if hospital patients, victims, or children are involved; don't eavesdrop; don't misrepresent; don't pay witnesses in court cases or criminals; don't be sexist or racist; don't profit from inside knowledge if you are a financial journalist.

There are two further problems with the clauses as they appear in the code. The first is vagueness and generality, and as a result many of the prescriptions would need further interpretation or elaboration before they could actually be put into effect. An apology is required "whenever appropriate"; a "fair" opportunity for reply should be given; approaches to victims of traumatic events should be made "with sympathy and discretion"; and so on.

The second further problem is that exceptions to some of the other clauses are built into clause 18. Thus privacy is not totally protected, nor are eavesdropping, misrepresentation, harassment, and payments to witnesses and criminals totally banned, provided there is a public-interest defense for breaches of the provisions of the relevant clauses. The public interest is defined in terms of detecting crime and serious misdemeanor, protecting public health and safety, and preventing the public from being misled by individuals or organizations. Once again, there is a lot of scope for further interpretation and elaboration.

However, just because criticisms can be made of the code, it does not follow that it is without value. Such a code also has many advantages. First, it offers journalists some guidance in areas that are going to be problematic in their practice, and the individual requirements and prohibitions are, in themselves, perfectly sound. Even though some of the clauses cannot be acted on without further interpretation, the code does at least draw the attention of journalists to the type of situation in which some care and reflection would be desirable. It might even stimulate journalists to become interested in ethical problems and to seek further interpretation through reflection and mutual discussion—and by such a process to improve the code itself.

The code also has the advantage of making a public declaration of attachment to maintaining high ethical standards in professional practice and to serving the public interest. This is particularly important when the code is considered in its historical and political context. Of course, given this context many members of the public will greet the code with a degree of cynicism, believing that it was introduced merely to avoid further restrictive legislation and that the press is unlikely to make any great efforts to live up to its provisions.

The third advantage of the code is that it does include a disciplinary function which might have some success in combating the cynicism of the public. The sanctions that a self-regulatory system can bring to bear are not great, but the preamble of the code does speak of the PCC "enforcing" the Code of Practice. The main sanction is that any publication found by the PCC to have breached the code is required to print the critical adjudication in full with due prominence. This, and the related sanction of bad publicity for the offender, shows that the PCC's system of self-regulation amounts to operating a "shame" culture within which the media feel obliged to act with higher ethical standards.

The fourth advantage is that the code as part of a system of self-regulation, even if backed by only weak sanctions, is surely better than statutory regulation. Self-regulation is preferable in a democracy—or perhaps this should be put more strongly: self-regulation is a necessary part of a society which hopes to call itself democratic.

ETHICS AND MEDIA QUALITY

An examination of the PCC Code shows some of the problems in taking the ethical route to media quality via a code of practice. A code which consists of a series of positive and negative rules cannot cover every case or every type of case. Life in general throws up novel situations which are ethically problematic, and it is these which create the most serious problems for everyone, and professionals in their practice are no exception. Journalists already know (it is to be hoped) that they should not use deception in gathering ordinary material, but what should they do if they think they have come across a serious case of corruption? A code might help, but what is more important are the principles and standards on which a code ought to be based.

A well thought out, well constructed, and ethically sound code, one that is clearly based on a coherent set of moral principles, is likely to be more successful in doing what a code ought to do: to produce in journalists internalized competence, including competence in the ethical sense, or in other words (since the language of virtue is helpful here) a virtuous character, one that has a disposition to act virtuously in the journalistic sense which includes a commitment to quality. It will also be a bonus that such a journalist will have a greater likelihood of coping with problems that are ethically novel.

It is the virtuous disposition which is necessary, not the code. A good, properly based code can be useful, but the code itself is merely a convenient way of conveying the principles and standards with which it should be informed. It is principles and standards that form the ethical route to quality in the media, and it is explicit and reflective acknowledgment of the ethical route that offers the best chance for quality assurance, if this is regarded as an issue separable from quality itself.

There are still many areas that require further exploration and explanation in media ethics. There is first the requirement for principles soundly based in ethical theory, and second the application of these principles to actual issues and cases in the practice of journalism. Third, there is the issue of how the application of ethical principles is to promote media quality, and, finally, the question of the role of an explicit code of practice in achieving the desired level of ethical competence and quality in journalism. The ethical route to media quality is, therefore, still something of a rocky path, but through further ethical reflection and discussion there is hope that it can become easier to travel.

NOTES

1. We do not examine this claim here, but for a critical review see Curran (1991).

2. A comprehensive overview and discussion of British media law is provided by Robertson and Nichol (1992); see also Article 19 (1991). For an account of recent developments from the point of view of the media, see Stephenson (1994).

3. This point and some of the following discussion draws on arguments elaborated in more detail in Belsey (1995).

4. For critical accounts of the conflicts over the British Official Secrets Act, see Ewing and Gearty (1990, esp. ch. 5) and Thornton (1989, esp. ch. 2). For further background on this issue see Hooper (1987).

5. See Stephenson (1994) for a discussion of the recent build-up of pressure for privacy legislation.

6. . . . Stephenson (1994) offers a defense of a (possibly augmented) system of self-regulation.

7. The code has been revised since its first appearance. The current version is Press Complaints Commission (1994).

REFERENCES

Article 19. 1991. *Freedom of Expression and Information in the United Kingdom.* London: Article 19, The International Centre against Censorship.

Barnes, J. A. 1979. *Who Should Know What: Social Science, Privacy and Ethics.* Harmondsworth: Penguin.

Belsey, Andrew. 1995. "Ethics, Law and the Quality of the Media," pp. 89–103, in Brenda Almond, ed., *Introducing Applied Ethics.* Oxford: Blackwell.

Belsey, Andrew, and Ruth Chadwick. 1992. "Ethics and Politics of the Media: The Quest for Quality," pp. 1–14, in Andrew Belsey and Ruth Chadwick, eds., *Ethical Issues in Journalism and the Media*. London: Routledge.

Bronfenbrenner, U. 1952. "Principles of Professional Ethics: Cornell Studies in Social Growth," *American Psychologist* 7: 452–55.

Curran, J. 1991. "The Liberal Theory of Press Freedom," pp. 277–94, in J. Curran and J. Seaton, *Power without Responsibility: The Press and Broadcasting in Britain*. London: Routledge.

Ewing, K. D., and C. A. Gearty. 1990. *Freedom under Thatcher: Civil Liberties in Modern Britain*. Oxford: Oxford University Press.

Harris, Nigel G. E. 1989. *Professional Codes of Conduct in the United Kingdom: A Directory*. London: Mansell.

Harris, Nigel G.E. 1992. "Codes of Conduct for Journalists," pp. 62–76, in Andrew Belsey and Ruth Chadwick, eds., *Ethical Issues in Journalism and the Media*. London: Routledge.

Hooper, D. 1987. *Official Secrets: The Use and Abuse of the Act*. London: Secker and Warburg.

Keane, John. 1991. *The Media and Democracy*. Oxford: Polity.

Klaidman, S., and Tom L. Beauchamp. 1987. *The Virtuous Journalist*. New York: Oxford University Press.

Lichtenberg, J., ed. 1990. *Democracy and the Mass Media*. Cambridge: Cambridge University Press.

O'Neill, J. 1992. "Journalism in the Market Place," pp. 15–32, in Andrew Belsey and Ruth Chadwick, eds., *Ethical Issues in Journalism and the Media*. London: Routledge.

Press Complaints Commission. 1994. *Code of Practice*. London: Press Complaints Commission.

Robertson, G., and A. Nichol. 1992. *Media Law*, 3d ed. Harmondsworth: Penguin.

Stephenson, H. 1994. *Media Freedom and Media Regulation: An Alternative White Paper*. Birmingham: Association of British Editors, Guild of Editors and International Press Institute.

Thornton, Peter. 1989. *Decade of Decline: Civil Liberties in the Thatcher Years*. London: National Council for Civil Liberties.

4

Sleaze Journalism?
It's an Old Story

Adam Goodheart

The American press is once again at risk —grave risk!—of abandoning its proud tradition of sobriety, fairness and impartiality. Or so say most of the people who are paid to fill air time and column inches with that sort of pronouncement.

What seems to be the problem is something referred to as "the 24-hour news cycle" or "the feeding frenzy" or, more simply, "Matt Drudge."★ Reporters and editors, we're told, care less about being right than about being first, scandalmongers spread rumors and falsehoods, any crackpot with a strong opinion and a little money can make himself heard, and no one in the press exhibits the slightest respect for the dignity of high public office. Thanks to the Internet, round-the-clock television news, and other new media, such wild anarchy may represent the future of American journalism, the pundits warn.

Their prediction could well come true. But if it does, it will represent not a break from the traditions of American journalism, but a return to them.

For most of our history, Americans didn't get their news from the David Brinkleys and the Walter Lippmanns. They got it from the Matt Drudges.

When Alexis de Tocqueville toured the United States in 1831 and

★Matt Drudge is publisher of the *Drudge Report,* an on-line gossip column that became notorious for breaking the Monica Lewinsky story in January 1998.

1832, he had high praise for the role of newspapers in sustaining demo-cratic government. "We should underrate their importance if we thought they just guaranteed liberty," he wrote. "They maintain civi-lization."

What sort of press was it that impressed Tocqueville so favorably? It was the press of the Jacksonian era, a time when politicians' sex lives (real or fictitious) were regularly exposed by the partisan opposition, when one newspaper assured its readers that the president's mother "was a common prostitute, brought to this country by the British soldiers," and when the president, like several of his predecessors, responded by bribing editors to support him.

Today's commentators, many of them products of institutions like the *Harvard Crimson* and the Columbia School of Journalism, look down their noses at Mr. Drudge, a former grocery-store clerk without a college degree who peddles gossip on the Internet. But Mr. Drudge actually belongs to a venerable tradition. Joseph Pulitzer was a penni-less immigrant; Horace Greeley dropped out of school at fifteen to work in a print shop.

Like Web pages now, newspapers were cheap to set up in the nine-teenth century. And objectivity was almost unheard of. Scandal sheets with names like *Truth's Advocate* and *Monthly Anti-Jackson Expositor* sprang up in moments of political crisis, only to vanish, as evanescent as electrons, once they had outlived their usefulness.

The 24-hour news cycle—which Hillary Rodham Clinton has blamed for the brushfire spread of gossip—also has a history that long antedates the Internet and the Cable News Network. Until the 1920s, each major city often had more than a dozen fiercely competitive morning and evening newspapers. A paper like *The Philadelphia Evening City Item* appeared in as many as twelve editions each day.

Journalism didn't truly become a respectable profession until after World War II, when political journalism came to be dominated by a few big newspapers, networks, and news services. These outlets cultivated an impartiality that, in a market with few rivals, makes good sales sense. They also cultivated the myth that the American press had always (with a few deplorable exceptions, of course) been a model of decorum.

But it wasn't this sort of press that the framers of the Bill of Rights set out to protect. It was, rather, a press that called Washington an incompetent, Adams a tyrant, and Jefferson a fornicator. And it was that rambunctious sort of press that, in contrast to the more genteel Euro-pean periodicals of the day, came to be seen as proof of America's republican vitality.

When Charles Dickens's fictional hero Martin Chuzzlewit stepped off the steamer from England in the 1840s, the first sight he saw at quayside was a motley crowd of newsboys:

> "Here's this morning's *New York Sewer!*" cried one. "Here's this morning's *New York Stabber!* Here's the *New York Family Spy!* Here's the *New York Private Listener!* Here's the *New York Peeper!* Here's the *New York Plunderer!* Here's the *New York Keyhole Reporter!* Here's the *New York Rowdy Journal!*"

The *Rowdy Journal*'s star correspondent turns out to be a scruffy character called, in the best Dickensian fashion, Mr. Jefferson Brick. (One imagines Dickens could also have made good use of "Matt Drudge.") It was the perfect name for a reporter, because in Dickens's day, the news wasn't delivered in a deferential whisper—it arrived like a rude democratic missile crashing through a windowpane.

For better or for worse, we now seem to be returning to the brickbat days of journalism. It will all be quite Dickensian, to be sure—but perhaps a bit Tocquevillean as well.

Chapter Two

Journalism's Feeding Frenzy

The Jewell Case

5

Going to Extremes

Alicia C. Shepard

Three days after the bombing at Centennial Olympic Park, Christina Headrick, an intern at the Atlanta *Journal and Constitution,* drove to security guard Richard A. Jewell's apartment in northeast Atlanta.

Her assignment was to stake out Jewell, the man hailed for discovering the bomb and evacuating hundreds of people from the area. The paper had heard that law-enforcement authorities were beginning to have doubts about Jewell's story, and her mission was to watch what he did and check out who came or left his apartment. When she arrived at the apartment complex she spotted three cars, all occupied by men in sunglasses watching Jewell's apartment. By the pool, other men had their binoculars trained on the same target.

Headrick called in several times to report that Jewell—who had been treated as a hero during an interview with Katie Couric only hours before—was clearly under surveillance.

Headrick's discovery, buttressed by the fact that the FBI had interviewed one of Jewell's former employers that morning and by off-the-record information from several law enforcement sources, led the Atlanta *Journal* to tear up its afternoon Olympics special edition on July 30[, 1996]. The new banner story proclaimed that Jewell had become "the focus of the federal investigation" in the bombing that killed one person and injured 111 others.

This article originally appeared in *American Journalism Review,* October 1996. Reprinted by permission of *American Journalism Review.*

The new edition hit the streets around 4:30 P.M. Half an hour later, a CNN announcer was reading the *Journal* story aloud on the air. The networks led with the development that night. The next day, almost all major newspapers—with the notable exception of the *New York Times*—carried stories about Jewell's suspect status on page one, above the fold.

A day later, the public knew more about Jewell's life than most people know about their own neighbors. Jewell, thirty-three, was publicly psychoanalyzed as a victim of the "hero syndrome," a condition in which a person creates a dangerous, life-threatening situation and then comes to the rescue. The security guard was tagged a police "wannabe."

"This much was clear: He had a driving desire, even a need, to be a cop," concluded *Boston Globe* reporters Brian McGrory and Bob Hohler in a profile of Jewell on July 31.

The unattributed 378-word *Journal* story naming Jewell as a suspect before he had been detained, arrested, charged, or indicted triggered a media frenzy. The prominent play and exhaustive, often unflattering, detail that characterized the coverage left the widespread impression that law-enforcement officials had swiftly nabbed the culprit behind the terrible Olympic tragedy. But were the media being manipulated by authorities? And in their zeal to respond quickly to a competitive, high-interest story, did the media go too far, inalterably tarnishing Jewell in the process?

"The news media's focus on the background and character of the suspect at this stage of the investigation is entirely out of line," says Deni Elliott, an ethics professor at the University of Montana. "Unless news organizations can provide some good reason why we need to have this information, which is a violation of his privacy, at this stage it's illegitimate to give out this information."

Says *Village Voice* media critic James Ledbetter, "I don't mean to portray any of this as an easy call in an extraordinarily competitive environment." But, he adds, "there's a way in which you can report that he's a suspect that doesn't constitute the massive character assassination and invasion of privacy that happened to him. There's a world of difference in reporting he's a suspect and camping out at his apartment, writing detailed profiles, and having psychologists on the air talking about him."

While many struggled over the issue of how best to handle the story, it was an easy call at the *Journal and Constitution,* says managing editor John Walter. The paper has a policy of not basing stories solely on anonymous sources, and it didn't do so in this case. While unnamed sources were used, says Walter, the paper also had physical evidence that the FBI was focusing on Jewell.

"Our sources led us to the path that we better pay attention to Richard Jewell," Walter says. The paper had received a tip that an administrator at Piedmont College in Demorest, Georgia, where Jewell had worked as a security guard, had called the FBI. On the morning of July 30 FBI agents went to the college to follow up. A *Journal and Constitution* reporter tagged along and talked to those at the college the agents had interviewed.

"We challenged ourselves," says Walter. "If the FBI is doubting his story, what are they doing about it? The answer was they are physically interviewing the people who phoned in the tip, and they are surveying his apartment. By day's end, they were interviewing him again. We watched all this."

While Headrick was driving to Jewell's apartment, police reporter Kathy Scruggs and Olympics security reporter Ron Martz were working their sources.

"I had no idea what Christina was doing," Martz says. "Neither of us knew what Kathy was doing. Then Christina called back and said there are all these guys out there and it's pretty obvious he's under surveillance.

"At the same time," he continues, "Kathy comes back and says she's gotten from her sources that Jewell is the prime suspect. Then I confirmed that Jewell was the primary guy being looked at with some of the sources I've developed over two years. Then a decision was made to put the story on the streets."

Adds Metro editor Mike King, "We were quickly able to develop information independently of one another. That, on top of what we were witnessing was happening to [Jewell], led us to believe that it was something worthy of reporting."

And it was a development in a case King calls "one of the biggest stories since Sherman marched through Atlanta." The Atlanta *Journal and Constitution* was the hometown paper; it felt tremendous responsibility and pressure. How could it not print that Jewell was considered a suspect at the very moment he was basking in a hero's glow? Wouldn't that have been withholding information from readers?

And so the story was published in the Atlanta *Journal* "Extra," a 40,000-circulation street sales paper specially created for the Olympics. The paper did not—as was widely reported—put out a special edition solely to report that Jewell was considered a suspect; it did revamp the "Extra."

"I don't think we did [Jewell] wrong . . . ," says Martz. "We did not say he was guilty. We said the FBI was investigating him, and that was very obvious from the fact that they were questioning him and had a search warrant for his apartment."

Martz says the paper was in a no-win situation. "If we'd gotten beaten, we'd have been the laughing stock of the industry," he says. "We are the only newspaper in town. But since we broke the story naming the suspect, it seems like a lot of people are coming back questioning why we did it. There's some sour grapes. I get the sense that certain members of the media are trying to justify to bosses why they'd gotten beaten."

Atlanta lawyer G. Watson Bryant Jr. was near Centennial Olympic Park when he saw the headline in the "Extra": "FBI Suspects 'Hero' Guard May Have Planted Bomb." Bryant was stunned. The lawyer had been a friend of Jewell's from the days a decade ago when they worked for the same government agency and played video games together at lunchtime. Jewell already had sought his friend's legal advice when someone suggested that the newly minted celebrity write a book.

Bryant knew things would quickly snowball. He desperately tried to track down his friend, who at the time was being interrogated by the FBI. After Bryant found Jewell, he went to the suspect's home, only to be confronted by a throng of shouting, shoving journalists.

"You can't imagine what it was like going into [Jewell's] parking lot after the Atlanta *Journal* story appeared," says Bryant. "My guess was there were two hundred, maybe three hundred people out there. I couldn't get up to his apartment."

Not long after the *Journal* hit the streets, CNN anchor Bob Cain made a dramatic announcement: "The Atlanta *Journal-Constitution* in a special edition today identified a security guard named Richard Jewell as the prime suspect in the Atlanta bombing," Cain said. He then read the story verbatim.

Earl Casey, managing editor for domestic news, says CNN already knew that Jewell was a suspect but didn't feel it had enough confirmation to go with the story on its own.

Once CNN weighed in, the story was officially in play. The development, said CNN correspondent Charles Zewe, speaking live from the Olympic site at 8:06 P.M., "has literally shot through this park."

The pop psychology was soon to follow. Later that night CNN correspondent Art Harris said Jewell was considered a suspect because he fit the profile of a lone bomber. And CNN was hardly alone in pursuing this story line. "This profile generally includes a frustrated white man who is a former police officer, member of the military or police 'wannabe' who seeks to become a hero," wrote Scruggs and Martz in the Atlanta paper.

How should the Richard Jewell story be handled? That was the raging debate that Tuesday night in newsrooms across the country. Not only hadn't Jewell been arrested or charged, he hadn't been identified as a suspect by anyone on the record. But this was a huge story, a tragic incident marring a sporting event that, as it does every four years, had the world mesmerized.

The sheer number of journalists in Atlanta—about 15,000—made naming Jewell "almost inevitable," says Bob Steele, an ethics specialist at the Poynter Institute for Media Studies. "You had more journalists there than at any other event in history. You had a landscape where terrorism was a concern for everybody, especially in light of the TWA crash.* And you certainly had a competitive situation. Although competition is not an ethical value, it's a professional value. And you had an unusual character in Mr. Jewell."

Wire services quickly transmitted the *Journal*'s story, and reporters began trying to confirm it with their own sources. Although the FBI was publicly saying it was eyeing a number of suspects, bureau personnel were privately steering reporters toward Jewell. That Jewell was a suspect appeared irrefutable. But how to write the story and where to play it were quandaries for editors at newspapers and television stations nationwide.

"We discussed not naming him or putting it inside," says Pam Maples, national editor of the *Dallas Morning News*. "But his name was all over TV. His face was all over TV. When people watch CNN, the next morning they want to read more in the newspaper." The paper played its story about Jewell as a suspect on the front page above the fold.

"The story got beyond individual control," Maples says. "The responsibility of the newspaper is, if you're going to do the story, you have to be as careful and responsible as you can. We still have not run a story about the 'hero complex' and what that is. We have one ready to go if he's charged."

By the time the Jewell story broke, *Los Angeles Times* Atlanta correspondent Eric Harrison had already written a story on the reopening of Centennial Olympic Park and the status of the investigation for the

---

*On July 17, 1996, as the Atlanta Olympics were getting underway, TWA Flight 800 from New York to Paris exploded in midair shortly after takeoff. Early FBI statements suggested that a terrorist bomb, perhaps connected to the Olympics, was responsible. After an exhaustive months-long investigation, the FAA and the FBI attributed the crash to mechanical failure. (Eds.)

next day's paper. "There was some feeling we should downplay the Jewell angle and not include it in the lead and deal with it in the body [of the story] without screaming it out," he says. "That's how I felt."

But the story ran on the front page. Jewell was the lead.

At the *Seattle Times*, it was a trickier call. The paper has written guidelines stating suspects should not be named until they are charged. "We make exceptions," says Greg Rasa, who was filling in as national editor when Jewell surfaced as a suspect, "if there's a smoking gun situation or a person is apprehended in the midst of a crime in a public place." Two points of view were expressed at the paper's news meeting: Why have a policy if you don't follow it? Or, won't we appear foolish for being the only medium in the country not to name Jewell? "The second camp won," says Rasa.

Washington Post reporter William Booth says he felt it was crucial to salt the *Post*'s coverage with cautionary notes. "We tried to write a straight news story and emphasize the man hadn't been charged and hadn't been arrested," he says. "In the subsequent story, we said the FBI keeps saying it has other leads and other suspects. We included that. It was a story that gave me pause and continues to give me pause."

Booth and fellow *Post* reporter Thomas Heath included information that raised doubts about Jewell's involvement. They noted that if Jewell had placed the bomb, he had put his own life in jeopardy since he was near the device, and that it wasn't physically possible for him to have placed the bomb and to have made the call about the bomb to 911. (ABC also made the latter point on its evening broadcast.) The *Post* reporters pointed out Jewell spoke with a strong Southern drawl, whereas investigators said the caller had no regional accent.

Booth says he feels it's incumbent upon the media to stay with the story and not simply move on to other things, as reporters often do. "When I was talking to my editor, I said, 'If this is not the guy, we have to come back and do a substantial story and not run it on A9.' "

CBS anchor Dan Rather also took pains to point out on July 30: "It's important to note that Jewell has not been charged."

At ABC, Kathryn Christensen, executive producer for the evening news, says the network fretted about identifying Jewell. "We had several sources with Mr. Jewell's name," she said on a *Nightline* special report in late August. "We had decided all day we were not going to name him unless he was arrested or charged." But as soon as other news organizations named him, says Christensen, "it validated our information." The network used the name.

This prompted anchor Ted Koppel to ask, "Are we all prisoners of the lowest common denominator?" In effect, Koppel was pointing out how the media, more often than not, now feel justified in reporting something if it has appeared in another medium first—even if it's a supermarket tabloid.

While numerous news organizations led with the story, there was one prominent exception: the *New York Times*. Reporter Kevin Sack wrote a story that focused more on the media than on Jewell's status as a suspect. The story ran inside the B-section, with a front page refer.

"We had a very animated discussion on how to handle the story," says *Times* national editor Dean Baquet. "Nobody in the room thought it was a front page story. The animated subject was how to write it. . . . The only discussion was whether you write a straight-ahead lead and attribute it to the Atlanta *Journal-Constitution* or whether to write it as a media story. I was arguing for a lead that put it on the Atlanta *Constitution* and then described how thin the stuff was."

He lost, but came to agree that executive editor Joseph Lelyveld and managing editor Gene Roberts were correct in their belief that it should be treated as a remarkable media event rather than as a breakthrough in the bombing investigation.

"Everybody was going nuts," Baquet says. "If you want to make the argument that a newspaper has to remain even and coolheaded and try to put things in perspective, this was the case. You want to be the one place that's a little bit measured, even if you appear slow."

The Jewell case not only dramatizes the pitfalls of editorial decision making in a highly charged atmosphere, it also spotlights the delicate, symbiotic relationship between the news media and law enforcement. Journalists are hungry for information about high-profile investigations that only the investigators have. On a competitive mega-story like the Olympic bombing, journalists aren't always as skeptical as they should be of information whispered by FBI agents and police officers.

"I think there's a very significant issue and a broader issue than Richard Jewell, and that deals with the media and law enforcement," says *Boston Globe* ombudsman Mark Jurkowitz. An important question, he says, is when a reporter learns from a police source that someone is a suspect, is that enough to justify a story?

Law-enforcement officers confirmed Jewell was a suspect in the bombing—but which law enforcement officers, and what their motives were, remain a mystery.

"You can argue whether it's morally right for the FBI on the one hand to say, 'We are not going to ever identify suspects,' " says Jim

Stewart, a CBS reporter who covers the Justice Department, "while on the other hand privately assuring people, 'Yes, this guy does look promising,' which has been going on in this case."

(On August 8[, 1996], Stewart reported that the FBI was preparing its first-ever public apology to Jewell because it had found "no definitive evidence linking Jewell to the crime." The FBI had not apologized as of *AJR's* [*American Journalism Review*] press time, nor had Jewell been charged.)

Since the FBI and the Atlanta police held all the cards, most of the media accepted their off-the-record comments as gospel and reported them anonymously. The story unfolded with such speed largely because the FBI said it was so. If the story had come from elsewhere, it's unlikely it would have mushroomed so rapidly. Were any journalists questioning the FBI? Why wouldn't the FBI say on the record that Jewell was a suspect?

"We should have asked what was the probable cause" to suspect Jewell, Stewart said on *Nightline*. And when the question was finally asked, he says, "we got very weak answers."

FBI spokesman Jay Spadafore's typical response to questions about Jewell was, "He's not been charged with a crime, and it's not appropriate for us to comment. Our guidelines don't permit us to make on-the-record comments to reporters on pending cases. I can say we have a number of suspects in this case."

But the name of only one suspect became public knowledge: Richard Jewell.

"When law enforcement makes a mistake, there's no attempt at accountability . . . ," says *Village Voice* media critic Ledbetter. "If you report skeptically, you are not going to continue to get access. Why would the FBI or the Georgia Bureau of Investigations or the Atlanta Police Department want to leak to someone who's going to report that it's possibly not true or the press is being manipulated?"

Ethics professor Elliott believes the press let the public down. "The news media know they were being used and exploited in this case, and are in many cases where law enforcement ends up feeding them juicy tidbits," she says. "The news media have failed to provide context. What I mean is, provide explanations why law enforcement may give reporters information that they normally wouldn't be getting at this stage. What's the motivation of law enforcement here?"

One reason might be public relations. If officials quickly identified a suspect, crowds at the Olympics could stop worrying about pipe bombs under their seats. "There is that possibility it was a PR thing," says Steele of the Poynter Institute. "If law enforcement floated his name to release the pressure they were feeling from the public or to appease Olympic officials, that's clearly wrong."

Mike Littwin, a columnist with Baltimore's *Sun* who wrote about the press's rough treatment of Jewell, says, "The FBI was leaking the story to calm the population or make the guy crack. It was a story that went out of control. But the story was so irresistible. Hero on the *Today* show, then it's leaked out that he's a suspect."

Says Jewell's attorney Bryant, "What's amazing to me is if you contrast the TWA bombing to this case. I can't think of a single leak that's come out of the TWA case."

A case not unlike Jewell's is that of Robert Wayne O'Ferrell, who has a $20 million lawsuit pending against the federal government stemming from a 1989 incident in which an Alabama federal judge and a Georgia civil rights attorney were killed by mail bombs. O'Ferrell, a junk dealer in Enterprise, Alabama, was a leading suspect although he was never charged.

According to O'Ferrell's attorney, William Gill, the FBI searched his client's warehouse on January 22, 1990—after alerting the news media. O'Ferrell says the FBI hounded him until November 7, 1990, when another suspect was indicted. "I gave them almost three years to apologize and they never did . . . ," he says. "I kind of feel the FBI are doing to that fellow Jewell what they did to me."

In the end, O'Ferrell lost his business and his home. His wife of twenty-three years divorced him, and he ended up in the hospital with a bleeding ulcer and $10,000 worth of medical bills.

Since the Jewell case, O'Ferrell, fifty-three, has become something of a media darling, telling his story to *48 Hours, Dateline NBC, Nightline,* and dozens of newspaper reporters. "I want people to know what the government can do to hurt people," he says. "It ain't only me. It's Jewell. It's Waco. It's Ruby Ridge."

One night in late August [1996] my telephone rang. It was G. Watson Bryant Jr., Richard Jewell's lawyer, whom I'd been calling almost every day. I was trying to interview him, but he wanted to interview me about journalism. "I've got the Society of Professional Journalists' Code of Ethics here," he said. "Is it anything journalists pay attention to? Is it respected?"

After I said it was, he continued, "According to this ethics code, the news media [should] guard against invading an individual's right to privacy. Does anybody follow this stuff? For God's sake, he [Jewell] and his mother can't even take the dog for a walk without seeing themselves in the news the next day."

Bryant says he feels certain that Jewell has been wronged, but he's not sure whom to sue and for what. So much has been written and broadcast. Bryant's brother searched for Jewell's name on the Internet three weeks after the bombing and got 10,000 references.

"We have a bigger problem going through all this stuff than the FBI does in going through all the stuff from the bombing," Bryant says. "You couldn't turn on the television after this thing broke and not see people analyzing Richard Jewell, and what does the FBI have against him and who is he? Digging up all this stuff in his past that, when cast one way, makes him look like he did it."

Bryant assails the *Journal and Constitution* for saying that his client fit the profile of a lone bomber because he'd approached the paper seeking publicity.

The paper later acknowledged that a spokesman for the firm that hired Jewell for the Olympics had suggested the Jewell interview. CNN's managing editor, Earl Casey, says Jewell didn't contact CNN. In fact, he says, his network made "twenty to thirty approaches to draw Mr. Jewell out."

So what, if anything, should the media have done differently in handling the "news" that Jewell was considered a suspect? It's a question that news organizations around the country are asking themselves—and it remains a valid question regardless of whether Jewell is charged. The *Village Voice's* Ledbetter and others suggest printing or airing such information but downplaying it until charges are filed—and dispensing with the pop psychological profiles until legal action is taken.

Richard Jewell's life no doubt was changed irrevocably by the orgy of national publicity as well as the television stakeout of his apartment that continued daily for at least a month, making Jewell, in effect, a hostage of the media. But news organizations frequently mention the names of suspects before they are charged, then forget about them. At least the world will know the outcome of the investigation of Richard Jewell.

Perhaps the saga will be one of those seminal events that triggers a full-scale examination by the press of how it does its business. Perhaps it will lead to a more cautious approach to using law enforcement leaks, even in the context of a competitive story.

The key question, says *Boston Globe* ombudsman Mark Jurkowitz, is this: "Are we going to have harder and faster rules about printing the names of suspects before they are charged?"*

---

*To date, no settlement has been reached with the Atlanta *Journal and Constitution* or Piedmont College. (Eds.)

6

Journalists, the FBI, and the Olympics Bomb*

Lou Hodges et al.

A few days after a bomb exploded at the Olympic Games in Atlanta, the Atlanta *Journal-Constitution* published an extra edition that named one suspect who, among others, was under investigation. News organizations throughout the nation reported the story within hours. Reporters followed investigators' every move as they searched the named suspect's property for clues that might link him to the bombing.

Before becoming a suspect his name had become a household word. He was the first to discover the bomb and he helped move the crowd away from it, perhaps saving lives. Publicity (which he sought aggressively) made him a hero and put him very much in the public eye.

He became a suspect because he was thought to fit the profile of a person who needs attention so badly that he creates a crisis in which to perform "heroic" acts. The dramatic transition from hero to villain was too much for the press to resist.

The newspaper published the story even though it had received information only from an anonymous source and despite the fact that the named suspect had not been arrested, charged, or even detained.

Journal of Mass Media Ethics, Volume 11, Number 4, pp. 246–56. Copyright 1996 by Lawrence Erlbaum Associates, Inc.

*The *Journal of Mass Media Ethics* publishes case studies in which scholars and media professionals outline how they would address a particular ethical problem. Some cases are purely hypothetical, but most are from actual experience in newsrooms, corporations, and other agencies. . . .

I wrote the following case from a wide variety of print and broadcast sources.

Other news organizations reacted immediately by reporting the *Journal-Constitution*'s publication of the extra edition. After all, the story was "already out."

One month after the investigation began, no solid evidence has been found to link the suspect with the crime. A polygraph expert tested him and concluded "he didn't do it." The FBI exonerated him October 26, 1996.

The case raises a number of ethical questions. (a) At what point in a criminal investigation should journalists identify suspects? After an arrest? After specific charges have been filed? (b) What is the motive of law enforcement for releasing names of suspects under investigation? Is the press being used to promote special interests? (c) Can the justification that the story is "out there" stand up to critical ethical scrutiny? (d) Should the law's presumption of innocence until guilt is proven in a court of law apply in journalism as well as in law? (e) If it turns out that he did not plant the bomb, and if his reputation is ruined, who must bear the blame? Is any restitution possible? (f) What ethical standards should journalists use in deciding cases involving the reporting of crime and the criminal justice system? (g) What ethical standards should law-enforcement officials follow in protecting the interests of suspects under investigation?

COMMENTARY #1

The guideline is straightforward and observed routinely in newsrooms across the country: A suspect in a criminal case is not identified until after he or she has been arrested and charged in court.

There are several important reasons for the standard this guideline conveys. It recognizes that law enforcement agencies and the courts alone have the responsibility for determining whether there is sufficient evidence to charge a suspect. It maintains the fundamental role of the press in reporting the actions of police and the courts. It protects the press from authorities who may be serving their own agendas when they leak the identity of a suspect. And it recognizes that police agencies often are unreliable sources that, when challenged in a lawsuit, deny or forget or insist they cannot disclose identities.

The guideline for identifying criminal suspects is similar to others that news organizations have established and followed. Among these are an editorial reluctance to name victims of rape or to identify juvenile suspects.

Even when news organizations have failed to follow the guideline, the courts have declined to hold them accountable against claims of harm to the reputation and privacy of individuals.

In a Michigan case from the 1980s, David Rouch was arrested in the rape of a seventeen-year-old girl who was babysitting for his former stepchildren at his ex-wife's house. The local newspaper, the *Battle Creek Enquirer & News,* reported that he was arrested and charged with the rape. In fact, he was arrested briefly, then released and never charged. The newspaper did not follow up until almost a year later on the fact that he had not been charged.

Rouch sued the newspaper for libel, claiming that the story on his arrest was false. He won a $1 million jury award in Calhoun County Circuit Court. The verdict was overturned by the Michigan Supreme Court. The U.S. Supreme Court refused to review the case.

The Michigan Supreme Court's decision recognized that, as a matter of constitutional law, the press cannot be sanctioned for publishing what is substantially true. The court also suggested that reliance on police reports would not constitute negligence in any event.

The tradition of self-imposed restraints on publishing and the history of court decisions favorable to the press in reporting on law enforcement provide an important context for examining the coverage of Richard Jewell as a suspect in the bombing at Centennial Olympic Park [on] July 27[, 1996].

The decision by the editors of the Atlanta *Journal-Constitution* to identify Jewell was made under extraordinary circumstances: an international event being covered by 15,000 journalists; intense media competition; the pressure of being the hometown paper for the Olympics; a bombing that created widespread feelings of terror, especially in light of the TWA crash; the fear that if someone else got the story, the newspaper would be either ridiculed or accused of withholding information from the public, or both.

This was professional rationale absent apparent ethical considerations. Perhaps the story can be justified as an exception to the commonly used guidelines on identifying suspects because the bombing was such a special circumstance. And perhaps, at the end of the day, most editors would have made the same call as those in Atlanta.

The report that Jewell was the FBI's suspect was true. Still the rationale for reporting it might have been more rigorously tested by considering these factors posed by the situation, as well as their ethical consequences:

- Does the FBI have an agenda or a motive in leaking Jewell as the suspect?
- Is the FBI making this a public event as a way of calming the public or responding to pressure to come up with a suspect?
- Is the FBI acting out of character to volunteer to reporters that Jewell is the prime suspect?
- Is the FBI willing to go on the record by saying Jewell is the suspect and explaining why?
- Does the FBI have verifiable evidence that justifies making Jewell its prime suspect?
- How crucial is the identity of a suspect today?
- To what level of protection is Jewell entitled, based on what is known about him?
- Would putting Jewell's name in the newspaper under these circumstances tend to erode the presumption of innocence?
- Can a decision to identify the suspect be justified, if it turns out that he eventually is cleared?
- What are the legal risks of publishing his name?
- In a lawsuit, will the FBI stand by the information it now wants to make public?

After Jewell was cleared by the FBI in October, a federal magistrate ordered the release of sealed court documents related to the investigation. These papers revealed that the FBI had no evidence linking him to the bombing—news that has prompted journalists to replay the scenario and ask: Had this been known, would the press have acted differently? And, what if the press had reported only that the FBI was investigating "a suspect" without naming him or providing information that would enable him to be identified?

Striking such a balance would have given the authorities a chance to pursue their investigation, would have suggested to the public that the investigation was moving ahead, and would have protected the suspect until a decision about formally charging him had been made.

Robert H. Giles

COMMENTARY #2

(*Ed. note:* Following Justice Department exoneration of the suspect on October 26, 1996, three people at the Poynter Institute decided to reflect on the ethical implications of the whole case. Here are their reflections.)

JOANN BYRD: I would like to pose two questions, and take a first shot at them. First: What lessons can journalists draw from the coverage of this investigation and of Richard Jewell? Second: Next time, what alternatives should we consider?

I think the main lesson is that law enforcement people may be wrong. This is only one of the recent cases when journalists went even further than law enforcement in our presumption that police suspicions were right. To make the point, think of how different the coverage would have been if we had presumed from the start that the FBI's focus on Jewell was wrong: We would have pressed the FBI about other suspects every day. We would have gone to sources—including previous employers—who had good experiences with Jewell. We would have done our best to reconstruct his alibi, and to give attention to his lawyers and his mother and anyone else who would provide a different picture of him.

In this case, I would look for a way to describe the person without using the name, or so much detail that the person can be identified. If there are enough security guards, the report could have been that the FBI was focusing on a security guard.

I have not heard a story yet that could not be told in different ways. We can, and should, keep the public informed. But we can do that in ways that are less harmful. In the future, I would have us take a deep breath and make a list of all the options, and then choose one that gets people the most information at the lowest cost.

BOB STEELE: You're right, Joann, in suggesting that journalists must guard against being manipulated by our sources, particularly those whose power is so great. I sure wish news organizations had applied a higher level of skepticism to those law enforcement sources who originally suggested Jewell had become the focus of the investigation. Given the seriousness of the allegations, journalists had a great responsibility to insure fairness to Mr. Jewell when his name surfaced as a suspect instead of as a hero.

Journalists should have pushed their sources to offer more substance as to why Jewell was now being targeted as a bad guy instead of being praised as a hero. At the same time, I believe it was inevitable that news organizations would go with the story once law enforcement used a search warrant to investigate Jewell directly. While I respect the alternative you suggest of using the term "security guard" instead of Jewell's name, I do not believe that works in this case.

First, since Richard Jewell already was a key figure in the bombing story, it was likely many people would put two and two together and presume an "unnamed security guard" was indeed Jewell.

Second, leaving Jewell's name out could be unfair to other security guards at the Olympics who might become the suspect in the minds of some.

Third, and perhaps most important, this development of Jewell as a suspect demanded a high level of specificity to meet accuracy standards. The absence of specifics could create rumors that would only compound an already tense situation fueled by fears of terrorists on the loose.

News organizations had a responsibility, I believe, to report that Jewell was being investigated. They just did a poor job of reporting that story in the days and weeks that followed. In too many instances Jewell was depicted in words and visuals as someone sinister. Stories focused on relatively small-scale mistakes he made in the past, suggesting his less than stellar background was the foundation for terrorist behavior. Video, often in slow motion, showed him shuffling across the parking lot of his apartment or lurking near his doorway, suggesting a man who was troubled and in trouble. Headlines and teases too often implied guilt, emphasizing the "hero turned villain" angle. Accuracy and fairness were shortchanged.

The watchdog was wearing blinders.

KEITH WOODS: Bob, I agree that the release of Jewell's name was not only an inevitability, but a responsibility. The problem is that some of the watchdogs we unleashed turned out to be rabid.

The Jewell case points up the distinction between journalism that we must do and journalism that is optional. Both may do harm, but only some of it is unavoidable.

An anxious world needed to know as soon as we did that there was a suspect, a viable suspect, in the bombing case. Richard Jewell was that man.

It was his misfortune that he had been elevated to hero status, creating the rich irony and drama that make a story sell. But no matter what the competitive or commercial motivations might have been for giving that information to the public, the media had to tell that story, name included, for reasons of truth-telling, fairness, and accuracy. That is the mandate of a free press.

Optional journalism is not covered in that mandate. Under the optional umbrella falls the placement of a story, the tone of the storyteller, the framing of the story. Declaring that Jewell "fit the profile" of a bomber went way beyond the media mandate. Describing him as all but a maladjusted mama's boy, as one print story did, is not what the First Amendment demands of journalists.

Exploring, then exposing, his personal life through the lens of those searching for a murderer is an option that the media can employ at will. In the Jewell case, it was employed prematurely, recklessly, and with disastrous and now embarrassing results.

This new pseudopsychology journalism that we have seen emerge in the past decade is anathema to informed, reasoned public discourse. It is sophisticated rumor-mongering. It encourages quick judgment and mob mentality. Worst of all, it happens every day in smaller, less dramatic ways, when the lives of "suspects" are investigated and explicated by journalists single-mindedly seeking facts to validate the accusations.

We gnash our teeth and wring our hands over Richard Jewell, but I worry about those many less public people who are bitten each day by rabid watchdogs.

Poynter Institute, Online/Ethics
Bob Steele, Keith Woods, Joann Byrd.

COMMENTARY #3

On November 8,[1996], the publisher of the Atlanta *Journal-Constitution* said, "It was not illegal, immoral, or unethical to publish the story about the FBI's investigation of Richard Jewell." Not illegal, okay. But whether it was immoral or unethical to publish that story on July 30 naming him as a suspect in the Atlanta bombing requires an examination of the details and sequence of events. The newspaper's refusal since then to offer an apology or acknowledge any responsibility for the ignominy that befell Jewell, even after an unusual letter from the FBI removing him from its target list, makes for even tougher questions about the ethics of journalism and the mirror-image ethics of law enforcement. And all the media involved in trashing Jewell need to ask themselves if a little more institutional restraint in the future might not help restore a modicum of public confidence in the press.

On July 30, relying on unnamed sources, the newspaper ran an extra edition with this breathtakingly cowardly headline:

FBI suspects "hero" guard may have planted bomb

Within minutes, the electronic media jumped on the newspaper's bandwagon, and Richard Jewell's life imploded. Eighty-eight days after the *Journal's* extra edition branding him as the suspect, the FBI wrote a letter to Jewell's lawyer stating that "Jewell is not considered a target of the federal criminal investigation" and "Barring any newly discovered evidence, this status will not change."

What we don't know is who the original source was and what the source said to the reporter. A recording of that conversation would give us a better grip on who was using whom, on who was the prostitute and who was the john. But a fair guess is that the FBI source (or a state agent in contact with the FBI), who should not have been talking, wanted his or her pal at the paper to know that the feds were about to get their man, that they had enough for a search warrant, and that it was only a matter of time—no guarantees, of course, but darn near certain—that Jewell was about to be nabbed. The source also undoubtedly wanted anonymity.

Was the decision to publish the story, which looks so wrong in hindsight, defensible? Probably. Newspapers presumably value speed, truth, fairness, and good judgment in their stories. The identity of the Atlanta bomber would be newsworthy by any standard; the identity of suspects is also fair game if the suspicion is strong enough for the story to be fair to the suspect. The Atlanta newspapers want to be first with the news in their own city. A reporter can wait for an arrest or an indictment, by which society brands someone a suspect, but the same conclusions can be drawn, with enough support, before those events. For the story to be fair, the source had to be reputable, and had to tell the reporter enough to separate Jewell from the ranks of other potential suspects. Given the fact that search warrants were executed the next day, one can conclude that the FBI had made the decision to move aggressively against Jewell, and the timing makes it look like that information was shared with the newspaper. The next day's searches would have been newsworthy, as an event, and would have been covered by every media outlet at the Olympics. So identifying Jewell as a suspect a day early probably passes rudimentary ethical scrutiny.

But rudimentary standards shouldn't be enough for a newspaper that brags, on its Website, about the four Pulitzers it has won. The details we lack will tell us if the paper really did what a great and responsible newspaper should have done. Simple inquiries would have enabled the reporter to judge whether the FBI had done its job, or was looking for help from the paper, or both. Did the reporter ask if there were any eyewitnesses? Did the FBI have hard evidence, forensics, photos, or videos that pointed toward Jewell? Did the source say only that Jewell was a "focus" of the investigation? Focus can change as quickly as a twist on those bazooka-like lenses the cameramen kept aimed at Jewell and his family. Did the reporter know enough about federal criminal investigations to ask if Jewell was a "target" or a "subject" not just the "focus"? *Target* and *subject* are terms of art in federal criminal practice, indicating degrees of suspicion—roughly, targets are almost certain to be charged, subjects are being looked at for potential involvement, and everybody else is a mere witness. If the answers to these questions were "no," if Jewell wasn't a "target" yet, the paper was probably premature or inaccurate or both in reporting the FBI's "suspicions." If the reporters or editors didn't know to ask these questions, they were treading in water over their heads. Note that the FBI's letter to Jewell used the "target" lingo: News accounts of the letter seem largely devoid of any explanation of the significance of this term.

If running the story is defensible, however, the decision to run it as headlines in an extra edition is harder to explain. For my money, that headline alone shows that the paper on that day placed the value of speed—wanting to be first—over all the other values which make for admirable reporting and editing. Options were available—waiting for the next edition, waiting for the search to occur, running the FBI's "suspicions" as routine stuff somewhere other than the front page. Something like "the FBI's investigation even includes scrutiny of Richard Jewell's actions," in the middle of a calm story in the next regular edition would have been fairer (and, in retrospect, more accurate) than the headline that ran.

The newspaper's actions, of course, begat even worse conduct on the part of many other media organizations. Abandoning any pretense of independence, the broadcast media rushed to replicate the *Journal-Constitution*'s story just because it was "out there." Those editors, like Geneva Overholser at the *Washington Post*, who ran cautionary commentaries early in August, deserve medals for their perspicacity.

Whether the FBI would have wanted suspicions about Jewell out so early is a related question. The interests of the government in speed, truth, fairness, and good judgment are not unlike the newspapers'. No investigative interest is served when innocent people are tarnished, and the rules that apply to criminal cases reflect concern for personal privacy. Those rules were violated by the leaks in this case. But publication of leaks often produces other leads, and can precipitate motion in any case. Particularly in cases as intense as the Atlanta bombing, coming right on the heels of the TWA explosion, the rush for immediate answers—led by reporters' insistent questions—produces hasty and regrettable decisions to bend the rules. The agents on the case are undoubtedly discouraged by the delay caused by their leaks and by their focus on Jewell. Even worse, now, must be the delays caused while other investigators investigate the investigators for the source of the leaks.

The investigators' errors in leaking the story were ultimately ame-liorated, to some extent, by the FBI's letter telling Jewell he is no longer a target. That unusual act is a rare example of government officials ac-cepting responsibility—in a moral and ethical sense—for their actions.

By contrast, the newspapers and networks have not shown the same remorse. The media are playing by the strict rules and laws that govern them, not the more substantial ethical concerns that inform laws and rules. Hordes of lawyers must have scrubbed every comment and fortified all the stonewalling, including the comments by the *Journal-Constitution's* pub-lisher. The story may not have been libelous (although reasonable people might differ), and it might not have violated minimal standards of journal-ists' rules, and it might be the best sort of damage control to never, ever admit you were wrong. But no one can doubt that Richard Jewell has been treated unfairly and harmed by the journalistic excesses he has endured.

What could or should the media do, regardless of risk or rules, to try to restore some of Richard Jewell's peace, not only out of a sense of fairness to Jewell but also out of concern for the media's own reputa-tion? For Jewell, how about an extra edition of the Atlanta paper on Christmas, or Jewell's birthday, saying "Suspicions Were Wrong—Jewell Cleared"? How about Tom Brokaw going to Jewell's house, on TV, to apologize to Jewell and his mother for the weeks of agony? Actions like that would at least show some humanity, a characteristic journalists are generally perceived to lack.

The media's position has also changed now that their coverage has become the story. While the FBI is investigating the leaks and surely has "suspicions" and suspects, the newspaper knows with absolute certainty the source and accuracy of the leaks. Now that's newsworthy. (Other news outlets may be hounding that story, unless news organizations spare each other the attention they bestowed on Jewell.) One option available to the paper is to name the source, and describe the conversa-tions, so the public would have the details needed to better understand how the story appeared. Such a disclosure would violate the paper's confidentiality with its source, and might expose it to a lawsuit from the source. (Remember Dan Cohen and the *Minneapolis Star Tribune?**)

---

*Dan Cohen worked for an advertising agency hired by a candidate for Minnesota governor in 1982. Cohen, on condition of anonymity, offered the Minneapolis news-papers documents demonstrating prior arrests (in 1969 and 1970) of an opposition can-didate for lieutenant governor. The *Star Tribune* published the details of the arrests, but named Cohen as its source, violating their promise of anonymity. Cohen sued the newspaper successfully, and in *Cohen v. Cowles Media Co.,* the U.S. Supreme Court ruled that promises of anonymity are legally binding. (Eds.)

Over the long haul, however, "outing" the source just this once might strike a principled balance between the paper's short-term interests and litigation risks versus long-range need to be perceived as fair, reliable, and responsible to its readers and its sources.

"Do unto others" is a simple, maybe trite, ethical rule. But it is a rule that ought to inform the press's behavior. Had all the media followed it earlier, some of Richard Jewell's embarrassment could have been avoided or reduced. As for the original source, the *Journal-Constitution,* considering the Golden Rule now might at least make an apology easier to utter.

Benjamin L. Bailey

COMMENTARY #4

For a long time distinctions between rumor, allegations, and hard news about individual misbehavior have haunted the press. "Today's news" easily becomes tomorrow's error, and no item in a "Corrections" box or any counter-story the next day will often undo the damage to personal reputation that some mere accusations inflict. Ethical theory and libel law may honor "intention" along with resulting harms, but journalists are likely to shy away from both classic tests: "We just report what is out there."

To be sure, careful reporters and editors, chained to dailiness, have to be the first to distinguish between "truth" and "the news." It takes time to get at an account of many human events at a level deserving the name of truth. That is why historians feed on journalism's achievements in writing the first draft of history, but in full awareness that first drafts are often simply to be thrown away. The historian and the courts have similar responsibility here: to defer judgment until all possible evidence is in.

Such deference is a sophisticated human social norm, however, and it takes a sophisticated public to lay aside the thought, "Wasn't he the one accused of . . ." in favor of the thought, "innocent until proven guilty." The principle is therefore all the more important in a democratic society, whose free press has to be countered with other arenas of freedom. The courts are one of those arenas.

A first rule in the medical profession, ancient inheritance from Hippocrates, is "Do no harm." It is a hard rule for the press to follow, even that part of it committed to only news that is "fit to print." Are pretrial criminal accusations fit to print? Or pretrial civil suits? Yes: if reported in all deference to the as-yet-unascertained validity of claims on either side; and if left to the courts' sober inquiry. The press is a proper countervailing power vis-à-vis the courts. But court reporting should be the soberest reporting of all, and probably put on the back pages; the line between holding harmless and doing harm is often a sensational front page headline.

The ethical problem here concerns not only the injury that can be done to the eventually declared innocent of the land. The problem is achieving a due balance between skepticism and trust toward what passes as daily news. For five hundred years *print* has acquired a lingering permanence in the accumulation called "public record." Recently the *New York Times* reported on the protests of certain residents of Panama who feel falsely characterized and only vaguely disguised in the newest novel of John le Carré, set in that country. A local resident comments sadly, "The responsibility of the novelist transcends the novel. The images they transmit are what posterity thinks a country really is. Unfortunately for us, the image painted here is one that is ugly, unreal, and unjust."[1] Fiction the news itself may turn out to be, but once it has been framed in headlines, permanent damage can easily result. Functional public truth is what the public believes. I think of the Scopes trial, made famous in both the satirical reports of H. L. Mencken and the fiction of *Inherit the Wind*,[2] each more influential in shaping an enduring public reputation of William Jennings Bryan than fairer revisiting of the event by Garry Wills's *Under God*[3] will manage to change. Some fictions are more powerful than the facts, including fictions that began as news.

The selling of papers and TV ads will always be an inducement to journalists to portray the possible as an actual, even when a breath of suspicion is enough to blow a reputation away. On the side of us readers and viewers lies responsibility for giving our accused neighbors the benefit of our agnostic doubts. On the side of journalists lies equal responsibility for nourishing that doubt, for curbing our common temptations to voyeurism and believing the worst about our neighbors. To be considered innocent until proven guilty is a precious rule for public moral life. It is a specification of what it means to love one's neighbor as a fallible human like oneself.

Donald W. Shriver Jr.

NOTES

1. L. Rohter, "In the Land of the Big Ditch, le Carré's 'In Hot Water,' " *New York Times,* November 19, 1996, p. A4.

2. J. Lawrence and R. Lee, *Inherit the Wind* (New York: Random House, 1955).

3. G. Wills, *Under God: Religion and American Politics* (New York: Simon & Schuster, 1990).

The Diana Case

7

Journalism after Diana

Lance Morrow

When I was a boy growing up in Washington, I mixed the martinis at our house on N Street—precocious brat—and got to listen to my journalist parents and their journalist friends batting around scandalous gossip about the late Truman or early Eisenhower administrations: the item, for example, about the famous senator who could not give a speech without a twelve-ounce glass of bourbon to steady himself, and about the night someone got the senator loaded at the Shoreham and had a redheaded woman who looked just like his wife (the great man was too drunk to tell) lead him to a hotel room and get him undressed, whereupon a photographer burst in and took a picture of both of them naked on the bed. For what use, exactly?

The assembled journalists soaked up the gossip and martinis and did not publish the story, any more than they wrote about another popular subject in those days, Mamie Eisenhower's supposed lonely boozing.

Later I worked a couple of summers as a Senate page and took a sort of Dickens urchin's pride in knowing what I thought was the secret stuff. I knew, for example, which senators kept "cough medicine" bottles full of vodka in their desks and nipped at them on the Senate floor.

My boss in the Democratic cloakroom was Bobby Baker, Lyndon Johnson's protégé from North Carolina, a hillbilly version of Sammy Glick, with a Wildroot pompadour and pleated silk ties—later indicted

Reprinted from *Columbia Journalism Review,* November/December 1997. © 1997 by *Columbia Journalism Review.*

for tax evasion. Bobby Baker entertained us on Monday mornings with stories about the blonde he had seen "Jack" with on F Street on Saturday night—Baker making curvy va-va-voom hourglass motions with both hands, and winking. Jack, of course, was Jack Kennedy of Massachusetts, the golden boy on crutches (he'd just had another back operation). Jack's adventures, along with those of Senator George Smathers of Florida, Jack's roguish and magnificently tailored buddy, fascinated the ragamuffin pageboys. I would repeat the stories to my parents, to impress them that, at age thirteen, I was an insider too.

My father had covered the White House for the *Philadelphia Inquirer* during Franklin Roosevelt's last term, and was of course complicit in the gentlemen's agreement among White House reporters and photographers that suppressed the fact that the president was crippled, bound to a wheelchair, and had to be lifted in and out of cars by Secret Service men.

Some kindred complicity (or possibly mere inattention) years later allowed Wilbur Mills of Arkansas, chairman of the House Ways and Means Committee—the man who had to approve much of the legislation that went through Congress, and therefore one of the most powerful public servants in the republic—to stay drunk for several years (by his own later account) without the public getting wind of it. Only his famous synchronous swimming in the Tidal Basin with stripper Fanne Foxe, "the Argentine Firecracker," one night in 1974 brought his alcoholic untidiness to light.

All of that was long ago and far away. We live in a different universe, as the journalistic post-mortems after the death of Princess Diana remind us. We have gone, it seems, from being the courtiers, the scribbling butlers of power (souls of discretion or clueless sycophancy) to being, as Earl Spencer said in Westminster Abbey, assassins on motorbikes—princess-killers.

When exactly did American journalism start to change over from the old standard? Bay of Pigs, 1961? Dallas, 1963? Gulf of Tonkin, 1964? Tet, 1968? Watergate, 1972–74? Rock Hudson's death from AIDS, 1985? The answer, of course, is that the entire culture has changed dramatically in the last thirty or forty years, and journalistic practice with it. The overall evolution, or devolution (depending on your point of view), can be traced from Franklin Roosevelt's invisible wheelchair long ago to press speculation now about Bill Clinton's "distinguishing mark." We have come a long way.

But journalists retain, presumably, their editorial free will—meaning the power to say yes or no on a story. The Diana phenomenon is another of those occasions for earnest and even penitential introspection (like, in a very different way, Spiro Agnew's 1970 speech, written by William Safire, about the press: "nattering nabobs of negativism, the effete corps of impudent snobs"). Have we, in our carnivorous careerism (to use Spiro's voice), erased the necessary line between the public and private? Or how exactly do we draw the line now? Have we sufficiently understood and honored a distinction between what might be called public privacy (the private lives of public figures) and private privacy (the private lives of people who deserve to be considered private figures)? Should we revert now to some overall status quo ante of reticence?

As if we could. You cannot begin this discussion without a caveat or two. Journalists are incurably self-important, even narcissistic. For some reason (an uneasy conscience?), we always agonize about our "role," though it is not clear that such spiritual exercises result in better behavior or higher standards on the street. (By the way, it might be a useful display of humility, that neglected virtue, if we stopped calling ourselves "journalists" and went back to saying we are "reporters.")

Further: the paparazzi who chase down celebrities on motorbikes or shove cameras into famous people's faces hoping to provoke a punch are comparatively few and do not represent the craft as a whole. They are the *shifta* of journalism, the profession's renegade poachers of ivory and rhino horn. The distinguished photographer Neil Leifer, who shot for *Sports Illustrated* and *Time* for thirty-five years, insists that "such people are not journalists. It is ridiculous to give them the dignity of the title and then to beat our breasts about 'what's wrong with journalism?'"

Yes, the hypocritical mainstream press publishes the paparazzi's shots, and then condemns the jackals who took them. (It is a bit of a sophomore's irony to keep saying so, however.) Yes, we should have better taste, should resist the lowest common denominator, and should set about defining deviancy up again.

But the disappearing line that is most troubling in the Diana story is not the line between public and private; rather it is the line between journalists and the subjects we are covering. What worries me more than the individual outrage against privacy, however tragic the result, is the tendency, especially among magazines and television shows, to abandon the traditional journalistic attitude of skepticism and instead to indulge themselves in inundations of uncritical gush—a massive wave of Barbara-ism.

That wave was far worse news for the practice of journalism than the familiar paparazzi intrusions. Has there ever been a more noisome display of grief-pandering, simultaneously self-important and venal? "I guess it's safe to say that [Diana and I] were friends," Barbara Walters began on ABC, setting a ghastly and unprofessional tone of self-congratulatory pseudo-intimacy. As the "Bright Young Things" said years ago in Evelyn Waugh's *Vile Bodies,* it was "too, too sick-making."

The occasion of Diana's funeral was sorrowful and harmless, but any journalist, at the end of the twentieth century, should be made vaguely uneasy by any mass display of intense, irrational emotion. A number of observers did not entirely buy into the global grief; even if they felt private sorrow over Diana's death, they considered it a professional duty to wonder about the sources and dynamics of such dramatic mass emotion. But too many journalists, instead of analyzing the phenomenon, bent themselves to manipulating it and turning it to profit.

Tina Brown's *New Yorker* distinguished itself for mawkishness. *Time,* on the other hand, did a more restrained job and sold 1,200,000 newsstand copies of its Diana commemorative issue; a respectable newsstand sale of *Time* is, say, 180,000 (full disclosure: I work for *Time* as a contributor and wrote a somewhat skeptical essay for that issue). It would be childish to be shocked—shocked!—to find that the media made a lot of money off Diana's death. After all, *Life* made a lot of money covering World War II.

But at a time when boundaries are vanishing between news and entertainment, between fact and fiction, subjective coloration and objective reality, between celebrity movie star and celebrity journalist, and all vivid news seems to form almost instantly into global folklore, reporters need to refresh their skepticism and to harden their eyes and their hearts a little, even when such skepticism or hardness seems to go against human nature, against the individual impulse to weep.

The press too often undertakes the role of a third-rate dramatist—even of a pornographer: it tends to sanctify (as with Diana, borne off to eternity on a tide of teddy bears and flowers and a quaver of Elton John, floated to her Avalon on the lake); or else to demonize, or in any case to pry and slaver over, the darker details, as with the Marv Albert case.*

O. J. Simpson upped the journalistic ante and lesser fare is bound to disappoint. The night that Marv Albert pleaded guilty, television was awash with the sort of interviews and commentary (on the network news, on *Larry King,* on *Geraldo,* on *Crossfire* and a dozen other shows) one might have expected in the midst of an international crisis. Yet here was merely a well-known sports announcer (not really a celebrity; most women, for example, did not recognize Marv Albert until all this happened) brought to court for some vividly sleazy private misbehavior.

---

*Marv Albert was a popular sportscaster employed by NBC Sports for, among other things, coverage of the NBA. In 1997 he was accused of sexual assault, the lurid details of which filled tabloids for weeks. After two days of damaging trial testimony, Albert pleaded guilty to a misdemeanor charge of assault and battery. (Eds.)

Every era has its Fatty Arbuckle case (though in the Arbuckle case, which involved a popular Hollywood comedian who was host to a wild sexual party in 1921, a woman died). Chris Matthews, hosting CNBC's *Hardball,* aggressively defended his discussion of Albert's case by adducing the Watercooler Principle: if people are talking about it at the office around the watercooler, then it should be on the show. Some magazine editors call it the Dinner Party Principle.

If there were a world war going on right now, or an economic depression, the people at the dinner party would be discussing those. A hypothetical: it is October of 1962, at the height of the Cuban Missile Crisis, when millions around the world held their breath, expecting nuclear war. Suppose that just at that moment, the *New York Times* had obtained evidence confirming that the president, John Kennedy, had been having an affair with a woman named Judith Exner, who was also the girlfriend of a Mafia boss, Sam Giancana. It would have made an interesting story conference that morning at the *Times.* What priorities to put in place? Eight-column page-one banner on the possible nuclear holocaust? Two-column story below the fold on Exner? More likely: no story on Exner until (1) the crisis had passed, or (2) the world had been incinerated.

Stories of global moment tend to crowd out sleaze. Today, with global war and cold war long gone, with a surging economy for the moment, the proliferating media are suffering through a terrible substance famine. More and more competitive with one another, harassed by bottom-lining business offices, hungrier and hungrier for material, they are increasingly tempted to plunge profitably into the emotional goo (as with Diana) or else, as with Marv Albert, to elevate private pornographic moments (savage erotic bites! ladies' underwear!) to the status of public events. Marv's misadventures made the front page of the *Times,* below the fold, after he pleaded guilty.

What has happened to journalism?

In part, two answers: (1) The Exile of the Grownups, the remarkable disgrace of "elitism," and therefore the erosion of those standards that an older journalistic "elite" once enforced; and (2) what might be called The Multicultural *Faute de Mieux*: in a multicultural society where uniform standards of propriety and ethics are difficult to maintain or even to locate, editorial profiteers can cater, in the confusion, to the least common denominator.

But the two points immediately suggest their own countertruths: (1) If the old elite was so good, why was it so often subservient to power? An alert Washington press corps, for example, could have reduced Joseph R. McCarthy of Wisconsin to nonentity at least two years before Edward R. Murrow accomplished the job on CBS, after McCarthy's damage was done. And (2) do we really want the nation, and its media, to be run by a moral monopoly—the sort, say, that brought in Prohibition? Maybe not. Still, the media could use more taste and brains, and more respect for their audiences. The old elite, at its best, did not write or edit down. Those in charge today cannot seem to dumb down fast enough.

The press reflects the culture, and churns it through a Heisenberg spin cycle as well. The sleaze and stupidity abroad in the media advance chicken-and-egg* with a permeating trashiness in the society at large. Maybe both are, curiously, a function of boredom and directionlessness.

But journalism should not lose itself in its metaphysical perplexities. Good journalistic standards are not difficult to state—just tough sometimes when applied case by case. Journalists function best when they are mature and experienced and intelligent—and calm; when they keep their work as clear and simple as possible; when they keep their own egos out of the story; when they fall back upon decency and common sense if questions arise about whether to run a piece.

Is there a reason, beyond prurient interest, to make the private story public? The answer lies in the answer to another question: Is the private hurt that it might cause outweighed by the public need to know?

---

*"Which came first, the chicken or the egg?" is a children's riddle that demonstrates the frustration of mutual causality. In this context the author likens the puzzle of whether general social "trashiness" leads to "sleaze and stupidity abroad in the media," or vice versa, to the chicken/egg conundrum. (Eds.)

8

The Diana Aftermath

Jacqueline Sharkey

The Earl of Spencer's voice trembled slightly as he read a statement the day his sister, Princess Diana, died in an automobile accident. Initial press reports said the accident occurred as news photographers chased the car through the streets of Paris after midnight on August 31[, 1997].

"I always believed the press would kill her in the end. But not even I could imagine that they would take such a direct hand in her death as seems to be the case," Spencer said. "It would appear that every proprietor and editor of every publication that has paid for intrusive and exploitative photographs of her, encouraging greedy and ruthless individuals to risk everything in pursuit of Diana's image, has blood on his hands today."

New York Times columnist A. M. Rosenthal agreed. "Someday," Rosenthal wrote, "I believe, the words of Earl Spencer will hang in the private offices of publishers, network chiefs, and print and electronic editors worthy of any respect or trust."

The public, and some members of the press, denounced the photographers—and journalists in general—as "barracuda," "jackals," "piranha," and "vultures" feeding off celebrities.

Barbara Cochran, president of the Radio-Television News Directors Association, says it was impossible to "ignore how angry the public was" immediately after Diana's death.

"Numerous news directors have said to me that their photographers

---

This article originally appeared in *American Journalism Review,* November 1997. Reprinted by permission of *American Journalism Review.*

would be yelled at on the street," she says. Some passers-by accused photojournalists of "being responsible for killing Diana."

Following Diana's death, other issues involving the press emerged because of the public's lingering anger toward the news media. This hostility symbolizes what Nieman Foundation Curator Bill Kovach calls "an enormous disconnect" between the American people and the press that has "profound implications" for journalists' legal protections and privileges.

In addition, economic and technological developments made Diana's image such a marketing force that broadcast network news operations devoted more time in one week to her fatal accident than to any news event since the 1991 coup attempt against Soviet leader Mikhail Gorbachev, according to *The Tyndall Weekly,* a newsletter that monitors broadcast network news.

In the weeks since Diana's death, this confluence of controversies has led the American media to reexamine fundamental questions about their role, responsibilities, and relationship to the American people.

It is ironic that this soul-searching began as U.S. journalism organizations were already launching initiatives to explore what Sandra Mims Rowe, president of the American Society of Newspaper Editors, calls "the damaging erosion of our credibility with the public."

One impetus for these initiatives has been a series of public opinion polls during the last ten years that indicates many Americans have doubts about the news media's priorities and the ways in which they exercise their First Amendment rights.

A 1996 poll by the Center for Media and Public Affairs found that 80 percent of those surveyed thought the press ignored people's privacy; 52 percent thought the news media abused their press freedoms. More than 95 percent of respondents to an informal *USA Today* online survey thought the princess had been unfairly hounded by the news media, which confounded some journalists, given Diana's skill at using the press.

The day after the princess died, University of Southern California law professor and CNBC legal analyst Erwin Chemerinsky predicted that public outrage "will lead to attempts to restrict paparazzi in the United States and elsewhere."

During the next two weeks, French and British officials called for such laws, and a U.S. congressman introduced a bill to make some invasions of privacy a federal crime. California state lawmakers drafted legislation to create a "zone of privacy" in public places, change state defamation law, and establish a commission to examine paparazzi behavior.

These initial reactions could have troubling long-term ramifications for the U.S. press:

- Technology and corporate values are increasingly influencing the priorities of U.S. news media, which are competing in a global information marketplace, say some media analysts. The fact that Diana's death received more network news coverage than the landing of U.S. troops in Somalia is a clear sign of this.

- Proposed federal and state laws indicate that privacy rights are becoming more important than press rights to legislatures and the public. These measures are part of a growing movement by legislators and courts to control news-gathering practices in the name of privacy.

- The increasing intrusiveness of some photographers has led to renewed debate about licensing journalists.

- Reaction to the press—and calls for additional regulations in the wake of Diana's death—shows that public support for the First Amendment can be very fragile. This support for limiting press freedom makes it imperative that journalists understand the dynamic that exists between the American people and the press, and reevaluate their responsibilities to the public.

Some journalists and press analysts believe coverage of Diana's life and death reflect how entertainment values have replaced traditional news values in many U.S. newsrooms.

Print media found coverage of Diana so profitable, both before and after her death, that *Newsweek* media critic Jonathan Alter wrote, "Lady Di launched at least a thousand covers, and hundreds of millions of newspaper and magazine sales."

When Diana died, magazines such as *Time* and *Newsweek* scrambled to redo their covers and devote dozens of pages to stories about the princess. As reporters started to question what *Time* contributor Martha Smilgis called the "media gush" about Diana, *Time, Newsweek, People,* and *TV Guide* all published special commemorative editions.

Time's first issue about Diana's death had newsstand sales of about 850,000—650,000 more than normal. The commemorative edition sold about 1.2 million copies. They are the two largest sellers in the history of the magazine, according to managing editor Walter Isaacson.

Newspaper sales also rose. *USA Today*'s total circulation for the week after Diana's death was several hundred thousand above normal. The *Washington Post* sold more than 20,000 additional copies of its Sunday editions the day Diana died and the day after her funeral.

Television news ratings also increased. CNN reported "a dramatic surge in viewership," and the highest ratings ever for its Sunday night newsmagazine, *Impact,* which aired the night Diana died. More than 15 million people watched the August 31 *60 Minutes* devoted to the princess, according to Nielsen Media Research.

Television coverage of Diana's funeral was watched in more than 26 million households, Nielsen estimates. The week of September 15— two weeks after Diana died—broadcast networks devoted more time to the princess and the British monarchy than any other story, according to *The Tyndall Weekly.*

"We overdosed on Diana," says Steve Geimann, immediate past president of the Society of Professional Journalists.

Jeff Cohen, an attorney who is executive director of Fairness & Accuracy In Reporting (FAIR), agrees. He notes with irony that in a country that revolted against the British crown to form a democratic union, many people "can give you chapter and verse now on the infighting amongst British royalty," but "can't identify their representative to the U.S. Congress."

"They're getting facts that are utterly meaningless to them acting as informed citizens in a participatory democracy," Cohen says.

Some journalists, however, think the coverage was appropriate. Jeff Fager, executive producer of the *CBS Evening News,* says Diana's death had "huge political overtones," revealing the British people's animosity toward the monarchy, and involving top British and French officials in discussions of the accident investigation.

Maxwell E. P. King, [former] editor and executive vice president of the *Philadelphia Inquirer* . . . says the coverage "represented an important public catharsis about all sorts of different issues—about women and their place in society, about how the famous and their fans interact."

CNN editor-at-large Ed Turner points out that Diana's funeral enabled millions of Americans to share their grief, and "there aren't that many shared experiences that occur these days." In the early days of TV, "the nation sort of went through the same news stories together," Turner says, but technology has been "fracturing the viewing audience" by providing "a diversity of not only sources, but alternatives to news."

Critics, he says, don't take this diversity into account. Turner points out that CNN, unlike the broadcast networks, provides news twenty-four hours a day and has given the public extensive coverage of events in Russia, the Middle East, and Bosnia. "You think that's numbers? Wrong! It's a killer" for ratings, says Turner. "If at times we are excessive, in other ways, well, we paid our dues. . . . We're not tabloid all the time."

But several incidents during the coverage of Diana's death show

how difficult it can sometimes be to distinguish between the so-called tabloid and mainstream media.

Newsweek, Time, and other publications used photographs of Diana that some readers and journalists found intrusive, while captions talked about the pictures capturing intimate moments. Isaacson defends his magazine, saying *Time* used valid news photographs taken in public places, and rejected pictures by "stalking paparazzi invading people's privacy."

In the meantime, *National Enquirer* editor Steve Coz made a televised plea for news organizations to refuse to publish pictures of the injured princess and her dead companion. "We have refused to buy these pictures," Coz said, "and we're asking that the rest of the world press join us in shunning these photos."

Dana Kennedy, an *Entertainment Weekly* reporter, called Coz's comments "the worst hypocrisy," especially since the *National Enquirer's* cover the previous week had a headline that said, "Di Goes Sex-Mad— I Can't Get Enough!'"

However, journalists thought other news media also were hypocritical. *Time* columnist Margaret Carlson decried the practice of "tabloid-laundering, which is we take what the tabloids do and write about it, and that way get what we wouldn't write about originally into the magazine. And then we run pictures of the pictures to show how terrible the pictures are."

Newsweek seemed to do just that with two Alter stories. On September 8, his full-page spread about the media's celebrity obsession included a color picture of one cover of the British tabloid *The Sun,* published before Diana's death. The cover included a now famous photo of Diana, her swimsuit straps slipped down her arms, on a boat with her companion, Emad Mohamed "Dodi" al-Fayed. The headline: "Dodi's to Di For, World Picture Exclusive."

The next week, his article about Diana and the news media—in which the princess is quoted as calling paparazzi photography "face rape"—was accompanied by a blurry full-page picture of the princess, visibly upset, putting her hand in front of a camera lens.

Newsweek managing editor Mark Whitaker defends the pictures, saying, "You have to look at the context in which photographs are being used. When the subject of a legitimate news story is the paparazzi phenomenon, and you're running these pictures in a way that's used to illustrate . . . that news story, and not just to titillate people with exclusive photographs that have never been seen that you pay a lot of money for, then I think that that is still a defensible and legitimate use of the photographs." Alter believes the photos "are not a good example of tabloid laundering," because the motivation is to "illustrate a serious article," not a gossip-oriented feature.

But some readers were irate about the use of pictures they considered invasive. "I would never have expected to find such photos in your publication," wrote Allison Seale of Los Angeles to *Newsweek*. "Shame on you and shame on us all."

One reason the line between tabloid and mainstream media is fading is that the press is under mounting pressure to provide entertainment-oriented news, says longtime journalist Ben Bagdikian, author of *The Media Monopoly*.

Stockholders in major media corporations expect high profits, and entertainment products deliver them, he says. This puts news subsidiaries "under terrible pressure" to deliver reports that will boost the bottom line. "The value system of commercial television and of entertainment companies has made dangerous intrusions into the integrity of real news," says Bagdikian.

King says this has not happened with Knight-Ridder, which he says has "a very, very good level of awareness of news values." But he acknowledges that "some so-called news companies," which he declined to name, "don't reflect the most serious values."

U.S. News & World Report editor James Fallows believes corporate pressures are forcing more news organizations to produce entertainment-oriented reports, and says this is a "Faustian bargain." "In the short run it raises your audience," Fallows says, but "in the long run it threatens to destroy your business, because if the only way you make journalism interesting is by making it entertainment, in the long run people will just go to entertainment, pure and simple, and skip the journalistic overlay."

Meanwhile, despite the high ratings and circulation figures for stories about Diana, a *Wall Street Journal*/NBC News poll of more than two thousand people in mid-September showed 56 percent of respondents thought there had been too much coverage of Princess Diana's death.

Some news executives say such polls reveal a paradox about the public's relationship with the press. People respond to certain types of coverage, then criticize the press for providing it. However, other polls show the American people want the news media to provide them with information that is not only interesting, but important to their lives, regardless of ratings.

So does one lawmaker who proposed legislation to restrict the press following Diana's death. If journalism is simply a "profit-seeking, market-oriented enterprise," then the controversy about the news media's involvement with Diana "becomes a much bigger issue than who chased who into a tunnel," says California State Senator Tom Hayden. It's about whether entertainment has "taken root in the very heart of journalism" and become a "substitute for information."

The public's reaction to coverage of Diana's life and death, Hayden says, is "one of those moments along the way when we need to take an accounting."

Hayden is one of several lawmakers who, in the weeks after Diana died, drafted laws to limit access to public figures. On Capitol Hill, [the late] Rep. Sonny Bono (R.-CA) introduced a bill that could result in jail sentences and fines for anyone who "persistently" follows a person who "has a reasonable expectation of privacy and has taken reasonable steps to insure that privacy," for the purpose of obtaining "a visual image, sound recording, or other physical impression of the victim for profit in or affecting interstate or foreign commerce."*

In California, State Senate Majority Leader Charles Calderon has prepared draft legislation for a "Personal Privacy Act" that provides broad definitions for terms such as "intrusion" and would change the civil defamation law.

Hayden is drafting a "Paparazzi Harassment Act" that would enable courts to fine journalists engaging in behavior that was "threatening, intimidating, harassing, or causes alarm, harm or the potential of harm to any person who is the subject of media interest." Such behavior could be penalized even if it is unintentional. Publishers who know or have reason to know of such behavior also would be liable. Pursuit of a story "of meaningful public interest" would be a recognized legal defense, says Hayden.

The draft legislation also calls for creating a Commission of Inquiry into Paparazzi Behavior to evaluate the impact of new technology, such as long-range telephoto lenses, on privacy and trespass laws; to study "the growth, behavior, structure, funding and ethics of the paparazzi and tabloid journalism"; and to explore ways to "preserve and enhance freedom of the press while curbing abusive practices that threaten legitimate privacy and safety rights."

Miami Herald executive editor Douglas C. Clifton thinks these laws could be passed, "given the state everyone seems to be in" following Diana's death. He is concerned that "political figures will use this as an opportunity to further restrict press coverage of public events."

---

*Although revived in the 1998 legislative session after Rep. Bono's death in January 1998, the bill to protect celebrities was never brought to a vote. (Eds.)

Some journalists and attorneys are optimistic that such legislation won't be enacted because it is unconstitutional and unnecessary. "There are enough laws on the books already to protect the privacy of public figures," says Cohen of FAIR. These include criminal laws dealing with assault, stalking, and trespass, and civil remedies.

Hayden believes such laws are "insufficient." He compares these arguments to those used by opponents of sexual harassment laws, which he helped draft in California. "We heard all these same arguments—that women didn't need a specific sexual harassment statute, there was existing law," he says. But specific legislation was needed to deal with the unique circumstances surrounding date rape and domestic violence. Now, Hayden believes, special laws also need to be written to address the paparazzi's invasion of privacy.

Attorney Martin London disagrees. He argued, in a *New York Times* op-ed piece, that in 1973 he and other attorneys helped Jacqueline Kennedy Onassis get an injunction preventing photographer Ron Galella from approaching her or her children by asking a judge to apply principles in existing law "to the singular phenomenon of paparazzi." The injunction was tailored specifically to Onassis's situation. London urged other public figures to look to the court rather than the legislature for relief.

Some journalists believe the proposed laws would not stop the paparazzi. "Extremist photographers," says David R. Lutman, president of the National Press Photographers Association, believe "chancing arrest for breaking a minor law" is worth the risk, because they can make hundreds of thousands of dollars for a single picture. Lutman worries that the law will be used to stop other news photographers from pursuing legitimate stories.

Media analysts and attorneys also are concerned that the bills being considered by Congress and California lawmakers are the latest indication that privacy rights are superseding press rights. "It seems more and more in our society that we want the right to be left alone to trump the right to know," says Paul McMasters, the Freedom Forum's First Amendment ombudsman. "If that happens, democracy is in real danger."

The proposed laws are the latest in a series of moves by legislatures and the courts to cite privacy as a reason for restricting newsgathering techniques. Some states restricted access to drivers' license information after a stalker obtained actress Rebecca Schaeffer's address from the California motor vehicles department and killed her in 1989. The federal government passed a similar law in 1994.

Some news outlets originally supported the drivers' license laws, not realizing these measures don't protect people from stalkers, says Jane

Kirtley, executive director of the Reporters Committee for Freedom of the Press, but do provide governments with a rationale for declaring public records off-limits.

The courts also have moved to limit newsgathering. A federal judge in Pennsylvania granted an injunction last year prohibiting an *Inside Edition* team from following executives of a large health maintenance organization. The team was preparing a story on the large compensation packages paid to HMO executives. The judge ruled that "the right to gather the news is not absolute," and that a jury would probably agree the team was not trying to obtain information for journalistic purposes, but for "entertaining background for their TV exposé."

Although *Inside Edition* frequently is referred to as a "tabloid" television show, it has won several journalism awards from groups such as Investigative Reporters & Editors.

The Freedom Forum's McMasters is "very troubled" by the "trend for the public to want judges and now legislatures to take on a new job of being editors and reporters." If the trend continues, he says, "it will be a travesty for the public" because "when you put shackles on newsgathering operations, it's across the board. It doesn't just apply in one place. Because a law that perhaps is meant to help a future Princess Diana will be used and abused by an elected official to restrict the kind of coverage that might expose corruption or malfeasance."

Some media analysts worry that these initiatives could erode journalists' privileges as well as protections. Kovach of the Nieman Foundation expects that "rules and regulations that keep the press out, that restrict the press access both to institutions and to people in certain circumstances, are going to get a hell of a lot tighter."

Another development that jolted news organizations and their attorneys was the serious discussion of whether journalists—especially photographers—should be licensed.

Security consultant Gavin de Becker wrote in *USA Today* that "a person who chooses to earn money as a paparazzo should be required to obtain a permit, just like any street vendor. Permits could then be revoked for violations of the law. Paparazzi want to call this a profession, so let's regulate it." According to California State Senator Diane Watson, the legislature is "looking at" licensing professional photographers.

"That is completely out of bounds in a country that values a free press," says RTNDA [Radio and Television News Directors Association] president Cochran. She points out that the licensing system used by the British crown to stifle the press in the 1700s was one reason the First Amendment was written.

But some mainstream journalists have unwittingly helped fuel the licensing debate by struggling to distinguish themselves from colleagues who work for the so-called tabloid press. *USA Today* White House bureau chief Susan Page told CNN's Frank Sesno that she didn't think "the paparazzi who pursued this car are part of the press, frankly."

Katharine Graham of the *Washington Post* Co. wrote in an essay published in the *Post* and *Newsweek*, "One point we all have to keep clear is that the paparazzi are different from the news media. The problem the paparazzi present will not be solved by abridging press freedom."

But pushing the distinction too hard is not without peril, says CNN executive Ed Turner. "This characterizing as 'legitimate' or 'not legitimate' seems to me to be a dangerous sort of road to travel" because such statements imply that restrictions on "irresponsible" journalists might be acceptable.

Many members of the public already believe restrictions on the press are acceptable. A survey last year by the Center for Media and Public Affairs showed 53 percent of the three thousand respondents support licensing, and 70 percent favored court-imposed fines for inaccurate or biased reporting.

Some of these attitudes might result from ignorance. A 1997 Freedom Forum poll showed that 85 percent of respondents could not name press freedom as one of the five First Amendment freedoms. But others arise from anger and resentment. That poll, and others during the past five years, show that a majority of Americans believe that special interests, such as corporate media owners and advertisers, as well as pressures for profits, improperly influence the way news is gathered and presented.

People's perception that the news media don't "seem to be serving their needs very well" is often correct, says *Washington Post* ombudsman Geneva Overholser. "The trouble is that newspapers have become so profitable—profitable beyond any normal retailers' dreams—that the pressure on corporate executives to run them with an emphasis on the short term as opposed to the long term is just enormous." This means "the debate is between enormous profit expectations . . . and the community's need to know, which requires real investment."

Advertisers contribute to the problem. They used to be interested in newspapers' mass-market appeal, but now "think it's altruistic to service a wide readership," says Overholser. Advertisers want to attract wealthy, well-educated readers, so they want to place ads in sections where subjects aren't too controversial and have strong human-interest components, she says.

Broadcast, cable, and satellite media face similar pressures, which increase as they become subsidiaries in multinational conglomerates, some media analysts say. These corporations believe that "the marketplace sets the standard" for what is important, says Kovach. Executives look at a picture of Princess Diana and ask, "'What's the picture worth to us economically?' That has nothing to do with the journalistic value of it. It has to do with the uses they can put it to. All of those trends take journalism closer to entertainment values and further away from what I think are the values that justify the protection the First Amendment offers a free press."

Some news executives say not all corporations view information this way. *Time* magazine managing editor Isaacson says there "absolutely" is a wall between Time Warner's news and entertainment divisions. In the two years since he has been in his job, the magazine has done "fewer pure entertainment covers than were done in the seventies."

The press has a moral obligation to balance profits and public benefits, because it is the only business given explicit constitutional protection, says Lutman of the National Press Photographers Association. "It isn't necessarily our responsibility to give people what they want, it's to give them what they need." Those who put profitability ahead of public service "are betraying our profession."

When the public senses this betrayal, its support for the media's First Amendment protections and privileges begins to decline, SPJ's [Society of Professional Journalists] Geimann points out. This sets up a climate in which legislatures, judges, and juries feel justified in placing limits on the press. "We the press depend on the public support for all the rights and liberties that are built into the Constitution and the Bill of Rights. When the public support disappears, our rights and liberties disappear."

McMasters believes journalists must address the situation quickly, because "the global nature of news today presents some unique challenges to the First Amendment." As the American people gain access to news around the world via satellite television feeds and the Internet, they are questioning whether the restrictive laws of countries such as France and England do in fact lead to a more responsible press, he says. This is why "freedom of the press in the United States depends as much on how we fulfill our responsibilities as they do on how we exercise our rights."

Journalism organizations initiated several projects during the past year to focus attention on the media's responsibilities and to look for ways to restore public confidence in the press. The American Society of Newspaper Editors recently began a three-year project to examine how to increase the print media's credibility. The Society of Professional Journalists updated its code of ethics, adding a section on accountability, and is sponsoring ethics workshops at news organizations and professional conferences. The National Press Photographers Association plans to emphasize privacy issues during workshops and seminars.

CBS newsman Mike Wallace is leading a drive to establish a national news council that would consider complaints about the media. The Freedom Forum recently announced a major initiative to improve press fairness and freedom. The Nieman Foundation and the Project for Excellence in Journalism, funded by the Pew Charitable Trusts, have helped organize the Committee of Concerned Journalists, which hopes to clarify the purposes and principles that should guide the news media.

Several new programs involve public participation. The ASNE [American Society of Newspaper Editors] Journalism Credibility Project includes research partnerships with eight newspapers that will study credibility issues in their communities and implement solutions. The Freedom Forum's Free Press/Fair Press project will include town meetings and discussions with business leaders and minority groups.

The Committee of Concerned Journalists will hold public meetings as part of a "period of national reflection about journalism," says Nieman Curator Kovach, the committee chairman. The meetings will deal with issues such as "the meaning of news" at a time "when serious journalistic organizations drift toward opinion, infotainment and sensation," according to the committee's Statement of Concern. Any journalist can join the committee by signing its statement.

Doug Clifton of the *Miami Herald* believes that during such a period of reflection, a journalist should think about the First Amendment in terms of what it means to the American people. "They don't see us as defenders of their First Amendment freedom; they see us as protectors of a special legislation that permits us to make a profit," Clifton says.

McMasters has been surprised at how many journalists have "a real ignorance of what the First Amendment stands for," and how many do not understand the ethical responsibilities that come with the rights the press enjoys. "Journalists," he says, "sometimes are the First Amendment's worst enemy."

9

Without Skipping a Beat

Sinéad O'Brien

The hand-wringing over the excessive coverage of Princess Diana's death had barely begun when sportscaster Marv Albert, quite reluctantly, took center stage.

By now the pattern is a familiar one: The media massively overplay a story, generally one with tabloid or pop culture elements; they wallow in guilt and shame for allowing things to get so far out of hand; then, when the next Nancy Kerrigan/Tonya Harding or Lorena Bobbitt saga comes along, they start the process all over again.

But this time there was barely a cooling-off period.

Princess Diana was buried on September 6[, 1997]. "There was a time, immediately after the tragedy with Diana and the funeral, that journalists everywhere seemed to take an oath that for some period of time they would stay away from excessive, intrusive, sensational coverage of the private lives of public figures," says Marvin Kalb, director of the Joan Shorenstein Center on the Press, Politics, and Public Policy at Harvard University.

It proved to be a short period. Sportscaster Albert's sexual assault trial began in Arlington, Virginia, on September 22, and the frenzy began anew.

The trial, replete with lurid details about kinky sex, attracted the sixth largest amount of airtime on the nightly network newscasts during

This article originally appeared in *American Journalism Review*, November 1997. Reprinted by permission of *American Journalism Review*.

the week of September 22, according to *The Tyndall Weekly*. After Albert pleaded guilty and was fired by NBC, *USA Today* played the story at the top of page one on September 26, above a piece about the IRS pledging to clean up its act. The same day, the *Washington Post* ran three stories, one on page one, and a column about the scandal.

While tabloid-style journalism inundated the mainstream media, the actual tabloids were hardly caught napping. The *New York Post* treated the first day of the trial the way the *New York Times* covered the Persian Gulf War, with page after page of Albert copy. In one breathtaking stretch, it ran a sidebar on how attractive ABC's Peter Jennings was to women, and how much he liked them. The hook? Defense lawyer Roy Black had said in his opening argument that the woman who charged Albert with attacking her had bragged of relationships with a number of celebrities, including Jennings. (Jennings said he didn't know her.)

Some critics remain unconvinced that the trial of a sports announcer, who while well known to sports junkies is hardly an A-list celebrity, was cause to jettison the post-Diana restraint.

"A sportscaster bites a woman on the back and forces her to perform oral sex: This is the biggest story of the day?" asks *Los Angeles Times* media writer David Shaw. "We beat our breasts in public and say we're different from the paparazzi, but there'll be no changes. We enjoy it."

In today's fevered environment, the media may need it. "The Marv Albert story sort of took over the slot that now exists in much of the media for the tabloid frenzy," says *Washington Post* media writer Howard Kurtz. "It's hardly coincidental that the Marv story exploded just as Diana was fading."

Former *New Republic* media columnist William Powers cautions against citing the Albert affair as evidence of the "tabloidization" of news. "This was not a case of scurrilous whispers to a tabloid," he says. "It was shocking charges [against] a prominent person. We tend to lump stories of bad journalism with stories of seamy content. This wasn't bad journalism. It just happens to delve into sex and private doings."

Still, the episode illustrates the extent to which the boundaries have been pushed. "The Marv Albert trial shows when there's a clear temptation to go the route of kinky journalism, journalists—even the very best—can't quite resist," Kalb says.

The juxtaposition of the two stories seemed to shine a spotlight on the excessive nature of the Albert coverage. While many would argue that far too much ink and airtime ultimately were devoted to Diana's death and its aftermath, few would deny that the death of the much-admired princess, a figure with tremendous resonance for many people, was a major story.

Geneva Overholser, the *Washington Post*'s ombudsman and the former editor of the *Des Moines Register,* says she was "not uncomfortable with an enormous amount of Diana coverage. People were moved by her death. Whereas," she adds, "the sexual exploits of a sportscaster are not that compelling." Overholser says putting the Albert case on the front page is simply titillation and that she finds it hard to justify the mainstream media's presentation of the case as major news.

Bob Steele, an ethics specialist with the Poynter Institute for Media Studies in St. Petersburg, Florida, agrees. In the case of Diana, he says, "it was meaningful coverage with a phenomenal tragic element." But while the Albert story had newsworthy aspects, he adds, "the tone and degree were out of proportion."

Some media analysts see marketplace pressures fueling the growth of sensational coverage. "Partly because we're suffering shrinking market shares, news organizations . . . are under pressure to build ratings," says Tom Rosenstiel, director of the Project for Excellence in Journalism.

Adds Powers, "Generally the media is profit driven and picks up on stories people like to tell each other about." The competition among news outlets drives the media to play heavily what Powers calls "watercooler talkers."

The bottom line? "Any week some sleazy story will grab the lion's share of attention, whether it deserves it or not," Kurtz says. The dissipation of Diana stories "threatened to leave about seventy-two cable talk shows with nothing to talk about."

Even in such a tabloid-tinged age, the amount of tawdry detail from the Albert trial that found its way into news pages and onto the evening newscasts was astonishing. Graphic accounts of panty wearing (by Albert), toupee flinging, and back biting were enough to prompt one reporter forced to cover the trial to say, "It's ridiculous that this situation generated the kind of coverage it has."

The X-rated reporting turned off many readers and media critics. "The *Post* printed seamy details of [Albert's] sex life on the front page," Overholser says. "It was tawdry to me." Says Powers, "It was rather appalling language on the front page."

Brooke A. Masters, who covered the trial for the *Post,* defends her reporting. "There were plenty of things we didn't [print]," she says. "There were whole sections of testimony we didn't get into." Editors, she says, decided on how much detail to include after debating how much readers needed to know.

Mark Jurkowitz, the *Boston Globe*'s media writer, says that it was those kinky details that heightened media interest in Albert. Asserting that we are living in a culture that revels in the discomfort of others, he adds, "The sexual weirdness aspect made it a big story."

Real tabloids, like the *New York Post,* had a field day. It celebrated the trial's opening day with five pages devoted to "Ménage à Marv." The lead was chock full of the most salacious descriptions of Albert's sexual proclivities. But those descriptions quickly became fodder for the mainstream media.

"What was once the occasional waver into the tabloid gutter has been institutionalized for much of the media," says Kurtz. "We put our hearts in stories about trials because we can dress them up with legal terms and pretend they're socially redeeming. What we're really interested in is who's wearing the panties."

Not everyone played the story big throughout the trial. Interest crested at the dénouement, when the *Los Angeles Times,* for example, carried an Albert story on page one for the first time.

The Albert contretemps briefly became local news in Dallas when a surprise witness testified Albert had bitten her in a hotel room there. *Dallas Morning News* national editor Pam Maples calls the story a "talker," but says that a perfunctory question about whether to run something about it on the front page was rejected. "There was never a strong sentiment the story should be on page one," she says. It moved from sports to inside the A section when the trial began and got a page one refer toward the end.

Daisey Harris, acting national editor of the *Boston Globe,* says the paper covered the trial on page three of the A section. While Albert broadcast pro basketball games for NBC, he was long known as the voice of the New York Knicks and had a higher profile on the East Coast. "People here know him," Harris says.

At the *Milwaukee Journal Sentinel,* says assistant national editor Mark Ward, "we had direction for Marv Albert to play in sports." A page one skybox with a mug shot teased into sports the day after Albert's guilty plea, but, says Ward, "it was not A section news—it was sports news."

The *Los Angeles Times* relied on wire reports until a sports staffer wrote a front page story on the guilty plea. "It's hard to say if he's well known here," says national editor Norman Miller, but the surprise guilty plea and the fact that the story had evolved into a huge topic of conversation pushed it out front.

Despite some unsettling aspects of the coverage, some critics find merit in prominently covering the Albert case. Poynter's Steele says such stories have a place in the mainstream: "High-profile cases bring attention to issues that are undercovered."

Says Ralph Barney, editor of the quarterly *Journal of Mass Media Ethics,* "I'm not quite as uncomfortable with either Marv Albert or Diana as some would be. It provides me—as a private citizen—with valuable information."

The bad news is that the Albert extravaganza may have set a precedent. "An embarrassment has set into the industry," says Kalb. "When another Marv Albert comes along, it will be covered extensively. The media is incapable of ignoring it." Barney agrees. "I don't see this ceasing," he says. "That's probably the tragedy of this."

So how can the cycle be broken? "It will go on until such a time when the leadership of American journalism—anchors, editors, publishers—all say enough is enough," Marvin Kalb says. "I don't know when that will be."

The Clinton Case

10

Where We Went Wrong

Jules Witcover

In the sex scandal story that has cast a cloud over the president, Bill
Clinton does not stand to be the only loser. No matter how it turns out,
another will be the American news media, whose reputation as truth-
teller to the country has been besmirched by perceptions, in and out of
the news business, about how the story has been reported.

The indictment is too sweeping. Many news outlets have acted
with considerable responsibility, especially after the first few frantic days,
considering the initial public pressure for information, the burden of
obtaining much of it from sealed documents in legal proceedings and
criminal investigations, and the stonewalling of President Clinton and
his White House aides.

But the explosive nature of the story, and the speed with which it
burst on the consciousness of the nation, triggered in the early stages a
piranha-like frenzy in pursuit of the relatively few tidbits tossed into the
journalistic waters by—whom? That there were wholesale leaks from
lawyers and investigators was evident, but either legal restraints or
reportorial pledges of anonymity kept the public from knowing with
any certainty the sources of key elements in the saga.

Into the vacuum created by a scarcity of clear and credible attribution raced all manner of rumor, gossip, and, especially, hollow sourcing,
making the reports of some mainstream outlets scarcely distinguishable

Reprinted from *Columbia Journalism Review*, March/April 1998. © 1998 by *Columbia
Journalism Review.*

from supermarket tabloids. The rush to be first or to be more sensational created a picture of irresponsibility seldom seen in the reporting of presidential affairs. Not until the story settled in a bit did much of the reporting again begin to resemble what has been expected of mainstream news organizations.

The Clinton White House, in full damage-control mode, seized on the leaks and weakly attributed stories to cast the news media as either a willing or unwitting collaborator of sorts with independent counsel Kenneth Starr's investigation of alleged wrongdoing by the president. Attacking the independent counsel and his office was a clear diversionary tactic, made more credible to many viewers and readers by suggesting that the overzealous news business, so suspect already in many quarters, was being used by Starr.

Unlike the Watergate scandal of twenty-five years ago, which trickled out over twenty-six months, this scandal broke like a thunderclap, with the direst predictions from the start. Whereas in the Watergate case the word "impeachment" was unthinkable and not uttered until much later in the game, the prospect of a premature end to the Clinton presidency was heard almost at once. "Is He Finished?" asked the cover line on *US. News & World Report*. Not to be outdone, *The Economist* of London commanded, "If It's True, Go."

ABC News's White House correspondent Sam Donaldson speculated on *This Week with Sam and Cokie* on January 25 that Clinton could resign before the next week was out. "If he's not telling the truth," Donaldson said, "I think his presidency is numbered in days. This isn't going to drag out. . . . Mr. Clinton, if he's not telling the truth and the evidence shows that, will resign, perhaps this week."

After Watergate, it was said that the president had been brought down by two reporters, Bob Woodward and Carl Bernstein, and their newspaper, the *Washington Post,* and they were widely commended for it. This time, after initial reporting by Michael Isikoff of *Newsweek,* there was a major piling-on by much of American print and electronic journalism, for which they have been widely castigated. A *Washington Post* poll taken ten days after the story broke found 56 percent of those surveyed believed the news media were treating Clinton unfairly, and 74 percent said they were giving the story "too much attention."

The advent of twenty-four-hour, all-news cable channels and the Internet assured the story of non-stop reportage and rumor, augmented by repeated break-ins of normal network programming and late-night rehashes. Viewing and listening audiences swelled, as did newspaper and magazine circulation, accommodated by special press runs.

Not just the volume but the methodology of the reporting came in for sharp criticism—often more rumor-mongering than fact-getting and fact-checking, and unattributed appropriation of the work and speculation of others. The old yardstick said to have been applied by the *Post* in the Watergate story—that every revelation had to be confirmed by two sources before publication—was summarily abandoned by many news outlets.

As often as not, reports were published or broadcast without a single source named, or mentioned in an attribution so vague as to be worthless. Readers and listeners were told repeatedly that this or that information came from "sources," a word that at best conveyed only the notion that the information was not pure fiction or fantasy. As leaks flew wildly from these unspecified sources, the American public was left as seldom before in a major news event to guess where stories came from and why.

Readers and listeners were told what was reported to be included in affidavits and depositions in the Paula Jones sexual harassment case—information that supposedly was protected by a federal judge's gag order—or presented to independent counsel Starr. Leakers were violating the rules while the public was left to guess about their identity, and about the truth of what was passed on to them through the news media, often without the customary tests of validity.

In retrospect, it was sadly appropriate that the first hint of the story really broke into public view not in *Newsweek,* whose investigative reporter, Isikoff, had been doggedly pursuing for more than a year Paula Jones's allegations that Clinton had made inappropriate sexual advances to her when he was governor of Arkansas. Rather, it surfaced in the wildly irresponsible Internet site of Matt Drudge, a reckless trader in rumor and gossip who makes no pretense of checking on the accuracy of what he reports. ("Matt Drudge," says Jodie Allen, Washington editor for Bill Gates's online magazine *Slate,* "is the troll under the bridge of Internet journalism.")

Drudge learned that *Newsweek* on Saturday, January 17, with its deadline crowding in, had elected not to publish. According to a February 2 *Newsweek* report, prosecutors working for Starr had told the newsmagazine they needed a little more time to persuade former White House intern Monica Lewinsky to tell them about an alleged relationship she had with the president that had implications of criminal conduct.

Early Saturday morning, according to the same *Newsweek* report, the magazine "was given access to" a tape bearing conversations between Lewinsky and her friend Linda Tripp. But the *Newsweek* editors held off. Opting for caution of the sort that in earlier days was applauded, they waited.

The magazine also reported that publication was withheld because the tapes in themselves "neither confirmed nor disproved" obstruction of justice, because the magazine had "no independent confirmation of the basis for Starr's inquiry," and because its reporters had never seen or talked with Lewinsky "or done enough independent reporting to assess the young woman's credibility." If anything, such behavior if accurately described resonated with responsibility, although holding back also left *Newsweek* open to speculation by journalists that its action might have been a quid pro quo for information received.

Drudge, meanwhile, characteristically feeling no restraints, on Monday morning, January 19, jumped in and scooped *Newsweek* on its own story with a report that the newsmagazine had "spiked" it after a "screaming fight in the editors' offices" on the previous Saturday night. Isikoff later said "there was a vigorous discussion about what was the journalistically proper thing to do. There were no screaming matches."

Drudge was not without his defenders. Michael Kinsley, the editor of *Slate*, argued later that "the Internet beat TV and print to this story, and ultimately forced it on them, for one simple reason: lower standards. . . . There is a case to be made, however, for lower standards. In this case, the lower standards were vindicated. Almost no one now denies there is a legitimate story here." Kinsley seemed to harbor the crazy belief that had Drudge not reported that *Newsweek* had the story, the newsmagazine never would have printed it the next week, and therefore the Internet could take credit for "forcing" the story on the mainstream news media.

Newsweek, not going to press again until the next Saturday, finally put the story on its America Online site on Wednesday, January 21, after the *Washington Post* had broken it on newsstands in its early Wednesday edition out Tuesday night, under the four-column banner atop page one, CLINTON ACCUSED OF URGING AIDE TO LIE. The story was attributed to "sources close to the investigation." ABC News broadcast the gist of it on radio shortly after midnight Wednesday.

The *Los Angeles Times* also had the story in its Wednesday editions, but the *New York Times*, beaten badly by the *Post* on the Watergate story a quarter of a century earlier, was left at the gate again. The lead on its first story on Thursday, January 22, however, was a model of fact: "As an independent counsel issued a fresh wave of White House subpoenas, President Clinton today denied accusations of having had a sexual affair with a twenty-one-year-old White House intern and promised to cooperate with prosecutors investigating whether the president obstructed justice and sought to have the reported liaison covered up."

The story spread like an arsonist's handiwork. The *Washington Post* of Thursday reported from "sources familiar with the investigation" that the FBI had secretly taped Lewinsky by placing a "body wire" on Tripp and had got information that "helped persuade" attorney general Janet Reno to ask for and receive from the three-judge panel overseeing the independent counsel authorization to expand the investigation.

On that same Thursday, the *Times* identified Lucianne Goldberg, the literary agent who later said she had advised Tripp to tape her conversations with Lewinsky. But the *Washington Post* continued to lead the way with more information apparently leaked by, but not attributed specifically to, lawyers in the case, and in the Paula Jones sexual harassment lawsuit that had caught Lewinsky in its web.

On network television on Friday, taste went out the window. ABC News correspondent Jackie Judd reported that "a source with direct knowledge of" Lewinsky's allegations said she "would visit the White House for sex with Clinton in the early evening or early mornings on the weekends, when certain aides who would find her presence disturbing were not at the office." Judd went on: "According to the source, Lewinsky says she saved, apparently as a kind of souvenir, a navy blue dress with the president's semen stain on it. If true, this could provide physical evidence of what really happened."

That phrase "if true" became a gate opener for any rumor to make its way into the mainstream. Judd's report ignited a round of stories about a search for such a dress. Despite disavowals of its existence by Lewinsky's lawyer, William Ginsburg, stories soon appeared about a rumored test for tell-tale DNA by the FBI.

The *New York Post,* under the headline MONICA KEPT SEX DRESS AS A SOUVENIR, quoted "sources" as saying the dress really was "a black cocktail dress that Lewinsky never sent to the cleaners," adding that "a dress with semen on it could provide DNA evidence virtually proving the man's identity—evidence that could be admissible at trial." The newspaper also reported that "Ken Starr's investigators searched Lewinsky's Watergate apartment, reportedly with her consent, and carried off a number of items, including some clothing," which Ginsburg subsequently confirmed. He later said that the president had given Lewinsky a long T-shirt, not a dress.

The *Village Voice,* in a scathing retracing of the path taken by the ABC News report of a semen-stained dress, labeled Judd's account hearsay and noted it had nevertheless been picked up by other news organizations as if such a dress existed. Six days after the original ABC story, CBS News reported that "no DNA evidence or stains have been found on a dress that belongs to Lewinsky" that was "seized by the FBI from Lewinsky's apartment" and tested by "the FBI lab."

ABC the next day reported that "according to law enforcement sources, Starr so far has come up empty in a search for forensic evidence of a relationship between Mr. Clinton and Lewinsky. Sources say a dress and other pieces of clothing were tested, but they all had been dry cleaned before the FBI picked them up from Lewinsky's apartment." In this comment, ABC implied that there had been stains, and it quoted an ABC spokesperson as saying, "We stand by that initial report" of a semen-stained dress.

A close competitor for the sleaziest report award was the one regarding the president's alleged sexual preference. On Wednesday, January 21, the Scripps Howard News Service reported that one person who has listened to the Lewinsky-Tripp tapes said Lewinsky "described how Clinton allegedly first urged her to have oral sex, telling her that such acts were not technically adultery."

That night, on ABC News's *Nightline,* Ted Koppel advised viewers gravely that "the crisis in the White House" ultimately "may come down to the question of whether oral sex does or does not constitute adultery." The question, he insisted, was neither "inappropriate" nor "frivolous" because "it may bear directly on the precise language of the president's denials. What sounds, in other words, like a categorical denial may prove to be something altogether different."

Nightline correspondent Chris Bury noted Clinton's "careful use of words in the matter of sex" in the past. He recalled that in 1992, in one of Gennifer Flowers's taped conversations offered by Flowers in her allegations of a long affair with the then governor of Arkansas, she "is heard discussing oral sex with Clinton." Bury went on, "During this same time period, several Arkansas state troopers assigned to the governor's detail had said on the record that Clinton would tell them that oral sex is not adultery."

The distinction came amid much speculation about whether Clinton, in his flat denial of having had "sexual relations with that woman," might be engaging in the sort of semantic circumlocution for which he became notorious in his 1992 presidential campaign when asked about his alleged affair with Flowers, his draft status, smoking marijuana, and other matters.

The *Washington Post* on Sunday, January 25, reported on the basis of the Tripp tapes that "in more than twenty hours of conversations" with Tripp, "Lewinsky described an eighteen-month involvement that included late-night trysts at the White House featuring oral sex." The story noted in its second paragraph: "Few journalists have heard even a portion of these audio tapes, which include one made under the auspices of the FBI. Lewinsky herself has not commented on the tapes publicly. And yet they have been the subject of numerous news accounts and the fodder for widespread speculation." Nevertheless, it then added: "Following are descriptions of key discussions recorded on the tapes, information that the *Washington Post* has obtained from sources who have listened to portions of them."

The story went on to talk of "bouts of 'phone sex' over the lines between the White House and her apartment" and one comment to Tripp in which Lewinsky is alleged to have said she wanted to go back to the White House—as the newspaper rendered it—as "special assistant to the president for [oral sex]." The same story also reported that "Lewinsky tells Tripp that she has an article of clothing with Clinton's semen on it."

On television, these details led some anchors, such as Judy Woodruff of CNN, to preface some reports with the kind of unsuitable-for-children warning usually reserved for sex-and-violence shows like *NYPD Blue*. But comments on oral sex and semen may have been more jarring to older audiences, to whom such subjects have been taboo, than to viewers and readers from the baby boom and younger.

The tabloids were hard-pressed to outdo the mainstream, but they were up to the challenge. Borrowing from the *Sun* of London, the *New York Post* quoted Flowers in an interview saying "she reveals that Clinton once gave her his 'biblical' definition of oral sex: 'It isn't "real" sex.' " The headline on the story helped preserve the *Post's* reputation: GOSPEL ACCORDING TO BUBBA SAYS ORAL SEX ISN'T CHEATING.

Meanwhile, the search for an eyewitness to any sexual activity between Clinton and Lewinsky went on. On Sunday, January 25, Judd on ABC reported "several sources" as saying Starr was investigating claims that in the spring of 1996, the president and Lewinsky "were caught in an intimate encounter" by either Secret Service agents or White House staffers. The next morning, the front-page tabloid headlines of both the *New York Post* and the *New York Daily News* shouted CAUGHT IN THE ACT, with the accompanying stories attributed to "sources."

Other newspapers' versions of basically the same story had various attributions: the *Los Angeles Times* to "people familiar with the investigation"; the *Washington Post* to "sources familiar with the probe"; the

Wall Street Journal to "a law enforcement official" and "unsubstantiated reports." The *Chicago Tribune* attributed ABC News, using the lame disclaimer "if true" and adding that "attempts to confirm the report independently were unsuccessful." The *New York Times,* after considering publication, prudently decided against it.

Then on Monday night, January 26, the *Dallas Morning News* reported in the first edition of its Tuesday paper and on its Website: "Independent counsel Kenneth Starr's staff has spoken with a Secret Service agent who is prepared to testify that he saw President Clinton and Monica Lewinsky in a compromising situation in the White House, sources said Monday." The story, taken off the Internet by the Associated Press and put on its wire and used that night on *Nightline,* was retracted within hours on the ground that its source had told the paper that the source had been mistaken.

Then there was the case of the television talk-show host Larry King referring to a *New York Times* story about a message from Clinton on Lewinsky's answering machine—when there was, in fact, no such story. Interviewing lawyer Ginsburg the night of January 28, King told his guest that the story would appear in the next day's paper, only to report later in the show: "We have a clarification, I am told from our production staff. We may have jumped the gun on the fact that the *New York Times* will have a new report on the phone call from the president to Monica Lewinsky, the supposed phone call. We have no information on what the *New York Times* will be reporting tomorrow."

Beyond the breakdown in traditional sourcing of stories in this case, not to mention traditional good taste, was the manner in which a questionably sourced or totally unsourced account was assumed to be accurate when printed or aired, and was picked up as fact by other reporters without attempting to verify it.

For days, a report in the *Washington Post* of what was said to be in Clinton's secret deposition in the Paula Jones case was taken by the press as fact and used as the basis for concluding that Clinton had lied in 1992 in an interview on *60 Minutes.* Noting that Clinton had denied any sexual affair with Gennifer Flowers, the *Post* reported that in the deposition Clinton acknowledged the affair, "according to sources familiar with his testimony."

Loose attribution of sources abounded. One of the worst offenders was conservative columnist Arianna Huffington. She offered her view on the CNBC talk show *Equal Time* that Clinton had had an affair with Sheila Lawrence, the widow of the late ambassador whose body was exhumed from Arlington National Cemetery after it was revealed he had lied about his military record. Huffington, in reporting on the alleged affair, confessed that "we're not there yet in terms of proving it." So much for the application of journalistic ethics by journalistic amateurs.

With CNN and other twenty-four-hour cable outlets capable of breaking stories at any moment and Internet heist artists like Drudge poised to pounce on someone else's stories, it wasn't long before the Internet became the venue of first resort even for a daily newspaper. The *Wall Street Journal* on February 4, ready with a report that a White House steward had told a grand jury summoned by Starr that he had seen Clinton and Lewinsky alone in a study next to the Oval Office, posted the story on its World Wide Web site and its wire service rather than wait to break it the next morning in the *Journal*. In its haste, the newspaper did not wait for comment from the White House, leading [then–]deputy press secretary Joe Lockhart to complain that "the normal rules of checking or getting a response to a story seem to have given way to the technology of the Internet and the competitive pressure of getting it first."

The Web posting bore the attribution "two individuals familiar with" the steward's testimony. But his lawyer soon called the report "absolutely false and irresponsible." The *Journal* that night changed the posting to say the steward had made the assertion not to the grand jury but to "Secret Service personnel." The story ran in the paper the next day, also saying "one individual familiar with" the steward's story "said that he had told Secret Service personnel that he found and disposed of tissues with lipstick and other stains on them" after the Clinton-Lewinsky meeting. Once again, a juicy morsel was thrown out and pounced on by other news outlets without verification, and in spite of the firm denial of the *Journal* report from the steward's lawyer.

One of the authors of the story, Brian Duffy, later told the *Washington Post* the reason the paper didn't wait and print an exclusive the next morning was because "we heard footsteps from at least one other news organization and just didn't think it was going to hold in this crazy cycle we're in." In such manner did the race to be first take precedence over having a carefully checked story in the newspaper itself the next day.

[Former] White House press secretary Michael McCurry called the *Journal*'s performance "one of the sorriest episodes of journalism" he had ever witnessed, with "a daily newspaper reporting hour by hour" without giving the White House a chance to respond. *Journal* managing editor Paul Steiger replied in print that "we went with our original story when we felt it was ready" and "did not wait for a response from the White House" because "it had made it clear repeatedly" it wasn't going to respond to any questions about any aspect of the case.

Steiger said at that point that "we stand by our account" of what the steward had told the Secret Service. Three days later, however, the *Journal* reported that, contrary to its earlier story, the steward had not told the grand jury he had seen Clinton and Lewinsky alone. Steiger said "we deeply regret our erroneous report of the steward's testimony."

On a less salacious track, the more prominent mainstream dailies continued to compete for new breaks, relying on veiled sources. The *New York Times* contributed a report on February 6 that Clinton had called his personal secretary, Betty Currie, into his office and asked her "a series of leading questions such as: 'We were never alone, right?'" The source given was "lawyers familiar with her account."

The *Post*, "scrambling to catch up," as its media critic Howard Kurtz put it, shortly afterward confirmed the meeting "according to a person familiar with" Currie's account. Saying his own paper used "milder language" than the *Times* in hinting at a motivation of self-protection by the president, Kurtz quoted the *Post* story that said "Clinton probed her memories of his contacts with Lewinsky to see whether they matched his own." In any event, Currie's lawyer later said it was "absolutely false" that she believed Clinton "tried to influence her recollection."

The technology of delivery is not all that has changed in the reporting of the private lives of presidents and other high-ranking officeholders. The news media have traveled light years from World War II days and earlier, when the yardstick for such reporting was whether misconduct alleged or proved affected the carrying out of official duties.

In 1984, when talk circulated about alleged marital infidelity by presidential candidate Gary Hart, nothing was written or broadcast because there was no proof and no one willing to talk. In 1987, however, a *Newsweek* profile reported that his marriage had been rocky and he had been haunted by rumors of womanizing. A tip to the *Miami Herald* triggered the stakeout of his Washington townhouse from which he was seen leaving with Donna Rice. Only after that were photographs of the two on the island of Bimini displayed in the tabloid *National Enquirer* and Hart was forced from the race. Clearly, the old rule—that questions about a public figure's private life were taboo—no longer applied.

But the next time a presidential candidate ran into trouble on allegations of sexual misconduct—Bill Clinton in 1992—the mainstream press was dragged into hot pursuit of the gossip tabloids that not too many years earlier had been treated like a pack of junkyard dogs by their supposedly ethical betters. The weekly supermarket tabloid *Star* printed a long, explicit first-person account of Flowers's alleged twelve-year affair with Clinton. Confronted with the story on the campaign trail in New Hampshire, Clinton denied it but went into extensive damage control, culminating in his celebrated *60 Minutes* interview. With the allegations quickly becoming the centerpiece of his campaign, the mainstream press had no recourse but to report how he was dealing with it. Thus did the tail of responsible journalism come to wag the dog.

From then on, throughout Clinton's 1992 campaign and ever since, the once-firm line between rumor and truth, between gossip and verification, has been crumbling. The assault has been led by the trashy tabloids but increasingly accompanied by major newspapers and television, with copycat tabloid radio and TV talk shows piling on. The proliferation of such shows, their sensationalism, bias, and lack of responsibility and taste have vastly increased the hit-and-run practice of what now goes under the name of journalism.

The practitioners with little pretense to truth-telling or ethics, and few if any credentials suggesting journalistic training in either area, now clutter the airwaves, on their own shows (Watergate felon G. Gordon Liddy, conspiracy-spinner Rush Limbaugh, Iran-Contra figure Oliver North) or as loudmouth hosts and guests on weekend talkfests (John McLaughlin, Man Drudge).

In the print press and on the Internet as well, journalism pretenders and poseurs feed misinformation, speculation, and unverified accusations to the reading public. The measure of their success in polluting the journalism mainstream in the most recent Clinton scandal was the inclusion of Drudge as a guest analyst on NBC News's *Meet the Press*. The program also included Isikoff, the veteran *Newsweek* investigative reporter.

Playing straight man to Drudge, moderator Tim Russert asked him about "reports" that there were "discussions" on the Lewinsky tapes "of other women, including other White House staffers, involved with the president." The professional gossip replied, deadpan: "There is talk all over this town another White House staffer is going to come out from behind the curtains this week. If this is the case—and you couple this with the headline that the *New York Post* has, [that] there are hundreds, hundreds [of other women] according to Miss Lewinsky, quoting Clinton—we're in for a huge shock that goes beyond the specific episode. It's a whole psychosis taking place in the White House."

Drudge officiously took the opportunity to lecture the White House reporters for not doing their job. He expressed "shock and very much concern that there's been deception for years coming out of this White House. I mean, this intern relationship didn't happen last week.

It happened over a course of year and a half, and I'm concerned. Also, there's a press corps that wasn't monitoring the situation close enough." Thus spoke the celebrated trash-peddler while Isikoff sat silently by.

Such mixing of journalistic pretenders side by side with established, proven professional practitioners gives the audience a deplorably disturbing picture of a news business that already struggles under public skepticism, cynicism, and disaffection based on valid criticism of mistakes, lapses, poor judgment, and bad taste. The press and television, like the Republic itself, will survive its shortcomings in the Lewinsky affair, whether or not President Clinton survives the debacle himself. The question is, has the performance been a mere lapse of standards in the heat of a fast-breaking, incredibly competitive story of major significance? A tapering off of the mad frenzy of the first week or so of the scandal gives hope that this is the case.

Or does it signal abandonment of the old in favor of a looser regard for the responsibility to tell readers and listeners where stories come from, and for standing behind the veracity of them? It is a question that goes to the heart of the practice of a trade that, for all its failings, should be a bulwark of a democracy that depends on an accurately informed public. Journalism in the late 1990s still should be guided by adherence to the same elemental rules that have always existed—report what you know as soon as you know it, not before. And if you're not sure, wait and check it out yourself.

Those news organizations that abide by this simple edict, like a disappointed *Newsweek* in this instance, may find themselves run over by less scrupulous or less conscientious competitors from time to time. But in the long run they will maintain their own reputations, and uphold the reputation of a craft that is under mounting attack. To do otherwise is to surrender to the sensational, the trivial, and the vulgar that is increasingly infecting the serious business of informing the nation.

11

After Monica, What Next?

Neil Hickey*

- About six out of ten senior journalists give the press a high grade (A or B) for its coverage of the Bill Clinton/Monica Lewinsky White House scandal, but well over a third firmly believe the profession deserves a lowly C, D, or F for its performance.

- Only about a tenth of journalists plan to change the way they cover public officials' private lives as a result of the Lewinsky story.

- Almost two-thirds of journalists think that many promising and effective officeholders have been driven from public life by intense press scrutiny of their personal lives.

- But well over half disagree with the notion that journalists' own personal lives, including their sexual behavior, should be held to the same high moral standards as those applied to political officials.

Those are a few of the findings in a *Columbia Journalism Review* national poll of 125 senior journalists, the first in a new, continuing feature aimed at probing how print and electronic newspeople feel about major issues facing them in an increasingly turbulent period for the press.

The poll was conducted in conjunction with Public Agenda, a non-profit, nonpartisan research organization. It was confidential, but more

Reprinted from *Columbia Journalism Review*, November/December 1998. © 1998 by *Columbia Journalism Review*.

*Additional reporting was done by *CJR*'s assistant editor Nicholas Stein.

than four out of ten respondents agreed to followup telephone interviews to elaborate on their answers. Many others contributed brief essays to flesh out their answers.

While only 1 percent of journalists give their profession an outright flunking grade for handling the ten-month-long (so far) saga of Bill and Monica (not to mention Ken and Hillary), only 6 percent believe that journalists deserve the top grade. Tom Rawlins, senior editor of the *St. Petersburg Times,* marks the report card with a humble C, but blames cable television for "dragging all other coverage down." When people say they're angry at the media, he declares, what they often mean is that they're peeved at cable, which is "full of spin doctors shouting at each other." He calls cable news "Jerry Springer without the hairpulling." MSNBC is less a news channel than "a forum for lobbyists," he insists, and wonders why Tom Brokaw didn't resign when the network hired Geraldo Rivera. A pervasive lack of journalistic discipline allows biased pundits to prattle on for hours, Rawlins says. They're "professional manipulators of information, and we sit back and let them do that and don't hold them responsible."

Many respondents scolded their colleagues for misplaced priorities, pointing out that most news organizations have never devoted to foreign affairs, health care, the budget, or the military the same ardent coverage bestowed on the Lewinsky affair. James E. Shelledy, editor of the *Salt Lake Tribune,* claims that "competitive juices overtook common sense." He wonders: How many papers would have printed the entire Starr report if it had focused on Whitewater instead of sex, and contained the same allegations about perjury, witness tampering, and obstruction of justice? "Those issues, we are told, are the reasons we're supposed to be excited about all this, which is utter bullshit. Sex has driven this from the start. Sex and the Beltway's obsession with scandal."

Starr injected plenty of sex into the report in order to get it covered, Shelledy claims, and the media were eager, compliant partners in that objective. (He adds: "And we make fun of the tabloids who put a nude on page three.") Even though people gobble up this coverage, the press has sorely injured itself with the public, he feels sure, fostering the belief that "we don't have good priorities, that we're always looking for the sensational." The whole Clinton/Lewinsky tale "has taken the press into a new era, and it's not going to be pretty." His grade for the overall coverage: a feeble D.

Bill Endicott, deputy managing editor of the *Sacramento Bee,* says that if newspapers hadn't published the Starr report, they would have been accused of supporting the president. "When we did print it, people called us pornographers."

Why do so many people think the media have drastically overplayed this story? Bill Marimow, managing editor of the Baltimore *Sun,* says his hunch is that the unwelcome tonnage of salacious detail is what has made the public holler, "Enough already!"

Says Ron Thornburg, managing editor of the *Standard-Examiner* in Ogden, Utah: "Many believe that what politicians and journalists talk about in Washington has little connection with what's going on in ordinary people's lives." When the political discourse is so dominated by subjects that don't matter to them, he finds, readers and viewers either tune out or become irritated by the news they consume. They care more, says Thornburg, about crowded schools, public transportation, and local referenda. Still, he detected a subtle shift in that position, starting when the threat of a presidential impeachment became a real possibility.

Almost half of our sample is sure that the volume of Lewinsky coverage has been "about right," even though the public in huge numbers thinks otherwise. (A gluttonous 4 percent of our respondents has the view that the story has been underplayed.)

Making editorial decisions based on polls of reader interest is a losing game, according to Linda Lightfoot, executive editor of the *Advocate* in Baton Rouge, Louisiana. A journalist's job is to be totally focused on stories this important, she maintains, no matter what the public wants. "I don't think we should let people who are not concerned about important affairs dictate our coverage," she says. "The fact that a president of the United States might be impeached is extremely important, whether people are tired of hearing about it or not."

More than half the journalists we polled in conjunction with Public Agenda feel that people seeking public office have to accept that their most intimate secrets are likely to be exposed by enterprising reporters. But a surprisingly large segment—almost four out of ten—are extremely leery about such invasions of privacy. A number of journalists made important distinctions about when—and when not—to cover politicians' private lives.

Examples: office seekers who parade their families in television commercials, print ads, and during stump speeches and conduct righteous, "family values" campaigns are making themselves a fair target for investigative reports—especially if their personal standards don't match up with their public ones. Similarly: to avoid legitimate media scrutiny, candidates who loudly promise to run government on sound business principles, and others who evangelize against extramarital sex, had better be sure there are no bankruptcies or hot-sheet motel room trysts in their pasts.

That said, a consensus exists that the press should not invade any-one's privacy without cause. Says the *St. Petersburg Times*'s Rawlins: "Generally, the private lives of public officials should remain so." But a substantial majority of the poll sample draws the line at private behavior that affects public performance, and officials' ability to handle their jobs. "Just because somebody is elected to public office," says David Bauer, editor of the *Daily News* in Bowling Green, Ohio, "doesn't mean jour-nalists should hang out in his shower stall."

One editor declares that "few politicians are targeted without reason," and points to Wilbur Mills, Wayne Hayes, and Ted Kennedy, as well as to Bill Clinton. Many more, he suspects, escape. But always, the investigation "must be fair and above-board and the subject must be given a chance to respond. If we err at all, it should be on the side of kindness."

Some comments on when it's legitimate to probe private lives:

- David Hall, editor, the *Cleveland Plain Dealer*: "When private behavior contradicts public statements, or when a candidate or official tells voters how to behave in their private lives."

- Narda Zacchino, associate editor and vice president, the *Los Angeles Times*: "When the story is relevant to an officeholder's position and responsibilities. If a gay-basher turns out to be gay, that's relevant. If a politician spouts family-value rhetoric and has a secret second family, that's news."

- Phelps Hawkins, executive producer, news, New Jersey Net-work: "When there's clear potential impact on one's ability to do the job. Each successive level of inquiry must meet recurring tests of the public's need to know, following the core dictates of fair-ness and balance."

All of which leads to the nettlesome question: Should journalists' own private lives and secret foibles be ventilated in public the same way that public officials' often are? Should their morals be judged by the same high standards? Opinions vary:

- No, says Sharon Rosenhause, managing editor, news, *San Fran-cisco Examiner*: "We don't get elected, so we don't have to account for our policies or expenses."

- Yes, counters Richard Scott, news director, WPHL-TV, Philadel-phia: "If you put your byline in the paper, your voice on the radio, or your face on TV, you should be prepared to face the same scrutiny as any public official." That goes double for Jennings, Rather, and Brokaw, he insists, because they're bigger celebrities than most officeholders.

- No, insists Ralph Langer, editor and executive vice-president, the *Dallas Morning News*: Since public officials deserve privacy (unless their malefactions affect public policy), then journalists deserve the same deal.

- Yes, declares Victoria Jones, a producer at WHDH-TV, Boston: If the rules were the same, journalists "would be a lot more careful, a lot more thoughtful, and have more empathy. We've lost our ability to empathize, to be human."

While an overwhelming percentage of our sample insist they'll make no big changes in the way they treat public figures' private lives, the Lewinsky case clearly has initiated a wholesale reappraisal of news handling in newsrooms across America. Many journalists say they'll exercise much more restraint in passing along unverified reports, especially those from the Internet; and they'll be using far more discretion about the relevance of private details. In the words of one respondent: "It will make us more thoughtful and cautious." Another: "We must get better at what we do!"

But other journalists agree with the newspaper editor who declared: "I see no need for radical surgery in the press." A news director in Des Moines, Iowa, Bob Quinn of talk-radio WHO, says the reason he won't be altering coverage is that his audience tells him in their phone-in comments that the White House scandal is still the big "watercooler" story. "We know the audience is interested. They tell us that," he says. "Are we going to see more of these stories being covered in the future? You bet." "It's hard to put the genie back in the bottle," says David Busiek, news director of KCCL-TV, Des Moines, Iowa.

Taking a more cosmic view, Susan Ungaro, editor of *FamilyCircle,* thinks that the Clinton/Lewinsky drama has created "a real turning point for all media." In the future, will newspersons be driven, more so than ever, to swarm all over sensational stories in pursuit of circulation and ratings? She fears that may happen: "We should have the public interest and not the bottom line at heart or else all we can do is wait for a time when sex doesn't sell."

12

Spot News:
The Press and the Dress

Lawrence K. Grossman

"Of all the stories we reported involving the president and Monica Lewinsky, ABC was most vilified for our reports about the semen-stained dress," says ABC News Washington correspondent Jackie Judd. "Critics kept asking, 'where's the proof?' Most people think it was the story's 'yuk' factor that made us so unpopular, but there was more to it than that."

Here is an account of how the press covered the bizarre story of the semen-stained dress, which was more accurately reported than most critics have been willing to admit, and what that coverage reveals about the journalism in today's high-intensity, echo–chamber world of cyberspace.

Jackie Judd first reported the semen-stained dress story on ABC's *World News Tonight* on Friday, January 23[, 1998]: "Lewinsky says she saved, apparently as some kind of souvenir, a navy blue dress with the president's semen stain on it. If true, this could provide physical evidence of what really happened." Judd repeated her account later that night on *20/20*.

Surprisingly, in the first draft of her script, Judd had failed to mention anything about the dress, even though she had nailed down the basic facts from two trusted sources and had alerted her editors in New York to the story. Asked why she held back, Judd told me, "At that stage, only the third day into the Lewinsky scandal, I was still squeamish about putting a story like that on the air. It was all new territory for us."

Reprinted from *Columbia Journalism Review,* November/December 1998. © 1998 *Columbia Journalism Review.*

But Judd's editors persuaded her to revise her script and report the facts she had learned about the dress with President Clinton's semen stain still on it. The dress, they argued, would be "the smoking gun" that could contradict the president's denials and take the scandal out of the "he-said, she-said" cul-de-sac in which it seemed to be stuck.

Judd was not the first to go public with the story. That distinction went to cyber gossip Matt Drudge, who had posted his attention-getting scoop on the Internet two days earlier. On Wednesday, January 21, his heavily trafficked *Drudge Report* broke the news that Linda Tripp* had told investigators Lewinsky claimed she "kept the garment with Clinton's dried semen in it—a garment she allegedly said she would never wash." Drudge repeated the story the next morning in an interview on NBC's *Today* show.

However, it was Judd's January 23 report on ABC that was the first in the mainstream media to rely on the reporter's own sources, rather than on secondhand information from Drudge. Peter Jennings introduced Judd's report this way: "Today, someone with specific knowledge of what it is that Monica Lewinsky says really took place between her and the president has been talking to ABC's Jackie Judd."

Where Judd got the dress story has become a matter of tradecraft controversy. [In June 1998], in the premiere issue of *Brill's Content,* media critic Steve Brill accused Judd of basing her report on an untrustworthy, biased single source, Lucianne Goldberg, the self-confessed Clinton-hater. He wrote, "Although Judd would not comment on her source, Lucianne Goldberg told me that she herself is the source for this Jackie Judd report and for others that would follow." While Goldberg, a New York book agent, claimed to have given Judd the story, she denied to Brill that she had been the source for the Drudge scoop, even though in January she had bragged to the New York *Daily News*: "The dress story? I think I leaked that. . . . I had to do something to get [the media's] attention. I've done it. And I'm not unproud of it." Brill's article charged, "[W]hether it turns out that [the president] stained one dress or one hundred dresses, Judd's every utterance is infected with the clear assumption that the president is guilty at a time when no reporter can know that."

In her own defense, Judd insisted to me that she had adhered to ABC's two-source rule on the dress story. She got her information, she said, from two sources she knew well and considered to be reliable, a fact confirmed by ABC News senior vice president Richard C. Wald,

---

*Linda Tripp, former White House aide, secretly taped conversations she was having with former White House intern Monica Lewinsky.

who oversees the network's news standards. Judd says she had met Goldberg only once briefly, and "spoke to her only for thirty seconds or less." It was made clear that Brill was mistaken in his assertion that Goldberg was her source.

I asked Judd why, in her January 23 piece, both she and Jennings had referred to only a single source for the story, when now she says she had relied on two sources. "The first person who told me about the dress told it to me off the record on condition that I not use it," Judd replied. "Then I confirmed the story from another source who insisted on anonymity, but who did not say we couldn't run it. So, to be accurate, we cited only one source on *World News Tonight*."

Drudge, as was his custom, had cited no source for his story of January 21. But his revelation earned the former Hollywood gift shop clerk with no journalistic credentials an interview on *Today*, the number-one network morning news show. Most mainstream journalists disdain *The Drudge Report*. They consider it not a legitimate news outlet but a gossip sheet posted on the Internet, where anybody can report or expose anything as fact whether true or not. Nevertheless, with many scoops about recent scandals to his credit, Drudge has become a hot media property. The Fox News Channel has given him his own news-gossip show.

Introducing Drudge on *Today*, co-anchor Matt Lauer described *The Drudge Report* as "a media gossip page known for below-the-Beltway reporting." Lauer then asked his guest about his semen-stained dress story that had appeared on the Internet the day before. Said Drudge: "I have reported that there's a potential DNA trail that would tie Clinton to this young woman." Lauer asked Drudge if he had any confirmation. Drudge answered, "Not outside of what I've just heard, but I don't think anybody does at this point."

Another *Today* guest that morning was *Newsweek*'s Michael Isikoff, whose reporting on the president's sex scandals had earned him a consulting contract with NBC. Appearances by *Newsweek* staffers on television's rapidly expanding schedule of talk shows generate valuable publicity for the magazine, part of the high-decibel ricochet effect of today's nonstop multimedia environment. *Time* has even installed a small TV studio in its New York offices so its editors and reporters can appear on screen at the drop of a newsbreak.

Lauer asked Isikoff if he heard anything about the dress. An experienced journalist, Isikoff knew better than to speculate on network television: "I have not reported that, and I am not going to report that until I have evidence that it is, in fact, true," he said. "I've heard lots of wild things, as I am sure you have. But you don't go on the air and blab them."

Still, simply by appearing on NBC News's highly regarded *Today*, the stained-dress story immediately graduated from gossip to news, gaining a measure of credibility and legitimacy despite the fact that no mainstream journalist had yet verified it. At that point, NBC News had done none of its own reporting on the story or gotten any independent verification. Landing a guest who makes a bombshell revelation on an established show like *Today* is a ploy guaranteed to gain instant world-wide attention, as Drudge's interview certainly did.

The beauty of getting the guest to deliver the sensational news is that the network itself doesn't have to hold back and risk being scooped on the story until its own reporters and editors are satisfied that it is accurate. No one at the network has to spend time and money digging for facts. Even better, if the story turns out to be wrong, the network has an out: "Matt Drudge said it; we didn't. We were only doing our job trying to find out from him whether it was true." This can be a dubious practice, and lately it has become all too commonplace, especially on cable talk shows.

A story of that magnitude appearing on *Today* also creates a king-sized dilemma for the rest of the press. Editors ask themselves, "Now that it's been on *Today*, shouldn't we carry it? True, we have no verification ourselves, but neither does anybody else. The fact that *Today* carried the story is itself news. Besides, if we don't run it, you can bet other guys will." And so, before any reporter for the mainstream press had even checked the story out (Judd's piece on ABC did not appear until January 23, the day after Drudge's *Today* interview), the unsubstantiated gossip posted by Matt Drudge on the Internet had risen to the level of apparently credible news. NBC's Tom Brokaw calls this multimedia, echo-chamber effect, "the Big Bang theory of journalism." But is it journalism, or gossip-mongering on a worldwide scale?

On Thursday, January 22, while Drudge was dropping his bomb-shell on NBC's *Today*, Sam Donaldson was breaking an entirely different dress story on ABC's *Good Morning America*. Donaldson talked about a dress that, he said, the president had allegedly given Lewinsky as a gift. (Later on, the *New York Times* and many others were to confuse the gift dress with the semen-stained model.) "How do we know" about the gift? *Good Morning America* co-anchor Lisa McRee asked Donaldson. "Well," he replied, "I guess we don't know. We're talking about leaks." Donaldson's revelation on *GMA* is a textbook example of an un-sourced, unsubstantiated pseudo-fact, disseminated by a reporter play-ing catch up, that simply feeds the public's distrust of the news media.

Donaldson was repeating a story that had been posted on

Newsweek-on-Line the previous day. It said Lewinsky had been heard, on a tape in *Newsweek*'s exclusive possession, claiming that Clinton had given her a dress as a present. *Newsweek*'s Washington bureau chief Ann McDaniel repudiated this report two weeks later, explaining that the magazine's reporters had misinterpreted what they heard on the tape.

Other outlets would make a similar mistake. On Monday, January 26, for example, the *New York Times* reported, "People who have heard the tapes said Monica Lewinsky had reportedly claimed that Mr. Clinton gave her a dress and that it was later stained with semen." In fact, the claim was not on the tape and the dress that Lewinsky said had the stain was not the one the president allegedly gave her. The *Times,* the *Washington Post,* and the Baltimore *Sun,* among others, repeated that error on succeeding days. Did that story really come from "people who have heard the tapes," or did the reporters get it secondhand from *Newsweek*-on-Line, *GMA, Drudge,* or elsewhere and, as in the children's game Telephone, garble the information?

By Saturday morning, January 24, news of the *real* semen-stained dress hit the world and splattered in all directions. The garment, in print, on-air, and on cable, was the blockbuster story of the week. The New York *Daily News* blared on page one, SHE KEPT SEX DRESS. The *New York Post* bannered, MONICA'S LOVE DRESS. Many newspaper and broadcast accounts picked up a UPI story that reported as fact that Lewinsky had kept a dress with Clinton's semen, eliminating the detail that Lewinsky had only claimed to have such a dress.

Time and *Newsweek,* released on Sunday, January 25, carried almost identical reports about the dress, adding a few marginally different details of their own. *Time*: In an untaped conversation with Tripp, Lewinsky "allegedly held up a dress she claimed was stained with the president's semen and said, 'I'll never wash it again.'" *Newsweek*: "Lewinsky told Tripp that she was keeping, as a kind of grotesque memento, a navy blue dress stained with Clinton's semen. Holding it up as a trophy to Tripp, she declared, 'I'll never wash it again.' "

Neither of the newsmagazines, which appear to have gotten their quotes from the same anonymous leaker, gave any indication of the nature of the source. A month later *Time* wrote, its "source was someone close to Tripp that *Time* believes credible." *Newsweek*'s piece that week reported Lewinsky was given a dress by Clinton, although later the magazine said it was no longer sure there ever was a dress given to her by the president. *Newsweek,* however, did stand by its account that Lewinsky claimed she had the dress with Clinton's semen.

On Monday, January 26, the *New York Times* quoted Lewinsky's lawyer William Ginsburg dismissing press reports about the semen-stained dress: "I would assume that if Monica Lewinsky had a dress that was sullied or dirtied, she would have had it cleaned. I know of no such dress."

On Thursday, January 29, CBS News's Scott Pelley broke the story that the FBI had found no evidence on any of the clothes taken from Lewinsky's apartment. The next night on ABC, Judd, citing "law enforcement sources," said, "Starr so far has come up empty in a search for forensic evidence," explaining that the Lewinsky clothes the FBI tested had been dry cleaned. As it later turned out, dry cleaning had nothing to do with the absence of the semen stain; the FBI had tested the wrong garments. The *Washington Post* reported that President Clinton assured associates there was no such dress.

In the spring, the tale of the semen-stained dress fast lost credibility. Critics came forward in force. The *Toronto Star* wrote, "Take the notorious blue dress, the one said to have been stained with the president's 'residue.' Can anyone blame the public for not trusting wild and sometimes truly unbelievable daily news reports, no matter what medium?" A Cox News Service piece by Scott Shepard began, "The dress? It has vanished into the misty realm of yesterday's newspaper and last night's TV news broadcast." Shepard blamed "the well-traveled route of hearsay in today's brave new information world, where a few established 'facts' are repeated and mixed with speculation and allegations from unidentified sources." Kathleen Hall Jamieson, dean of the Annenberg School for Communications at the University of Pennsylvania, complained on PBS's *NewsHour with Jim Lehrer* about the press's lack of careful sourcing and confirmation, citing allegations about the semen-stained dress. "It turns out now that there may be no dress."

Longtime TV news producer Ed Fouhy, now at the Pew Center in Washington, D.C., deplored the apparent fact that "so many good journalists [were] spending so much time analyzing so little." *Los Angeles Times* contributing editor Robert Scheer wrote of the press performance, "It's sick. There was no blue dress and no semen stain, but America's mass media fell for the lurid tales." The *New York Times* columnist Frank Rich blasted the reports of "phantom semen stains."

Then, at the end of July, Lewinsky and special prosecutor Kenneth Starr finally agreed on an immunity deal. On *World News Tonight,* July 29, Judd, citing legal sources (plural this time), revealed that "as part of the immunity deal with prosecutors, Monica Lewinsky agreed to turn over evidence she claimed would back up her story that she had a sexual relationship with the president. The sources confirm that one piece of evidence is, in fact, the dress Lewinsky said she saved after an encounter with Mr. Clinton because it had a semen stain on it. Lewinsky's claim of the dress's existence was first reported by ABC News six months ago. The dress may provide Starr with forensic evidence of a relationship."

As Judd's script made clear, the beleaguered ABC News correspondent felt vindicated at last.

The next day, July 30, on CNN's *Inside Politics,* CNN White House correspondent Wolf Blitzer revealed the astonishing news that Lewinsky had given the stained dress to her mother, who, he said, hid it in her New York apartment for six months. According to Blitzer, when the president agreed to testify to the grand jury, he was unaware that Lewinsky would be turning over the dress with its physical evidence of their sexual relationship.

The blue dress with the president's semen stain existed after all. It was real. And it had returned to center stage.

That same day, like a recurring nightmare, an improbable connection was made between the dress and the O. J. Simpson murder case. Former Los Angeles police detective Mark Fuhrman, a key witness in the Simpson trial, appeared on MSNBC, the cable news channel that gained the dubious reputation of programming "All Monica, All the Time." Fuhrman revealed that he had been contacted the previous October by his one-time book agent Goldberg, who asked him how DNA could be extracted from a dress.

In their August 10 editions, both *Time* and *Newsweek* reported that Goldberg and Tripp had plotted to get their hands on Lewinsky's dress, take a swab of the stain if they could, and have it tested for semen themselves. Goldberg described their scheme, which sounded like a dark soap opera mystery: Tripp allegedly called Lewinsky and told her she was so broke she would like to come over to Lewinsky's apartment while Lewinsky was away to check out her wardrobe and borrow a dress. Would Lewinsky tell her doorman to let her in? Tripp's plan to get at the blue dress with the semen stain did not succeed. Lewinsky failed to respond, according to Goldberg. *Time* reported the Goldberg tale and concluded, "Tripp's associates say that story is not true." *Newsweek* credited "sources familiar with the investigation" for its account.

On August 4, the *New York Post* reported that Goldberg claimed to have declined an offer of $500,000 from the *National Enquirer* for a photo of Lewinsky wearing the infamous blue dress. Goldberg said the photo exists but since it was not in her possession, she had to turn down the offer. According to the *New York Post,* Goldberg said: "'This is not about money. This is about right and wrong,' . . . adding with a wicked chortle, 'Besides, I don't have it [the photo].' "

In hindsight, it is easy to be critical of those who beat up on the press for its "phantom dress" reports before the full story came out. It is also somewhat unfair. It is now clear that Matt Drudge's scoop on the dress turned out to be essentially accurate. So did the reports by Jackie Judd, Wolf Blitzer, and most other reporters. The issue here is not about how the press spread misinformation; when it came to the dress, the press got some things wrong, but the major facts right. Still, too many news organizations paid too little attention to basic rules of the trade in their hot pursuit of the story. In today's nonstop news environment, the real issue is: How can the press overcome the public's growing distrust, even when it gets the story right?

Many critics have complained that the press has been promiscuous in its use of anonymous sources. But those who urge the press to "Stop using anonymous sources," as former Poynter Institute president Robert J. Haiman did recently, are unrealistic. It was virtually impossible to find a firsthand source in the special prosecutor's office, the White House, or anywhere else willing to be quoted on the record. Reporters had no choice but to rely largely on anonymous leakers and spinners. The dress story could never have been reported by any news medium that held to the ideal journalistic standard of full disclosure.

Certainly, reporters try to persuade their sources to go on the record. But failing that, they should at least indicate the level of the sources' direct knowledge and the nature of their vested interest. People recognize that it is all too easy for anonymous sources with axes to grind to avoid accountability and therefore to lie, mislead, or exaggerate.

A study commissioned by the Committee of Concerned Journalists examined the reporting of the first six days of the scandal, in which the dress played a central role. It concluded that: "Nearly one in three statements (30 percent of what was reported) was effectively based on no sourcing at all by the news outlet publishing it." Also: "Four in ten statements (41 percent of the reportage), out of "the 1,565 statements and allegations contained in the reporting [of the scandal] by major television programs, newspapers, and magazines . . . were not factual reporting at all . . . but were instead journalists offering analysis, opinion, speculation, or judgment."

Those who practice journalism in the volatile new media age could do worse than abide by a few of the old-fashioned rules from a more leisurely time, before the arrival of the endless news cycle: When sources insist on anonymity, disclose enough about their connection with the story so the audience can judge both their trustworthiness and the story's. Take care to separate fact from speculation and reporting from commentary. In covering personal and private matters that go public, restraint and dignity are more credible than excessive and unseemly enthusiasm. Resist the rush to judgment; it's better for the audience to reach its own conclusions based on the facts. Above all, before going with anyone's gossip, no matter how explosive, check it out.

Recently, in a special message to journalists, Pope John Paul II stressed the need for still greater responsibility in the age of the Internet and other speedy information systems. The pope called on journalists to "transmit information while respecting truth, fundamental ethical principles, and personal dignity." It's advice from a credible source, and it's worth heeding.

13

Wag the Media

Don Hazen

Hyperobsessed media reports of Bill Clinton's alleged sexual relations with a twenty-one-year-old White House intern raise the age-old question: Does life imitate art or vice versa?

The art in this case is *Wag the Dog*, the biting, cynical satire about using Hollywood techniques and mass media to fake a war with Albania. The reason for fabricating the war: The president's sexual molestation of a Firefly Girl (read Girl Scout) in the White House. Look back a bit to the long-forgotten season before sex scandal hit and you'll find the media-as-villain trend really began with James Bond's triumphant return in *Tomorrow Never Dies*. The culprit: a power-crazed media mogul, à la Rupert Murdoch, who attempts to start a war to seal his monopoly over the global media system.

Fast forward to present: [In January 1998] the *Los Angeles Times* and other major media report that the United States is edging closer to military strikes against Iraq—the most serious threat of military action since the Gulf War—to force Iraqi president Saddam Hussein to complete the long-delayed destruction of his regime's deadliest weapons.

Hollywood, politicians, and the media have a long history of colluding to distract the public and make wars, which are generally good business for all three. For Clinton, confronting Iraq couldn't come too soon as the media barrage about his personal life is beginning to erode

This article originally appeared in *Media Culture Review*, Volume 98, January 29, 1998. Reprinted by permission of the author.

his public support. No matter if we go to war to distract the public and media from Clinton's troubles, the confluence of events in fact and fiction is putting the press in yet more of a disparaging light, with attitudes toward the press already at record lows. Public disgust with the media's current feeding frenzy and an almost complete breakdown in boundaries between news reporting and tabloids could do untold damage to the credibility of the news industry in the long run.

According to *Washington Post* media critic Howard Kurtz, "The furious, almost blinding pace of coverage of allegations of scandalous behavior in the White House has all but shattered traditional media standards and opened the floodgates to a torrent of thinly sourced allegations and unrestrained speculation." Said noted press critic and *U.S. New & World Report* editor James Fallows, the reporting has "gotten out of control."

WHEN JOURNALISTS WORE WHITE HATS

Remember back twenty years or so when we saw films like *All the President's Men* and *Under Fire?* Then, journalists were heroes, and the media —especially the *Washington Post*—were bulwarks against the excesses of power. Not any more. The mirror that is Hollywood, reflecting back the image of our culture, has a new vision of the media and it isn't pretty.

No place is the transformation of media to monster so complete as in *Tomorrow Never Dies*. Here the arch villain, Elliot Carver, kills his wife and plots a war between China and Britain just so his media empire can flaunt the scoop of the century, and give him paramount access to every television screen on earth. Bond is, of course, among the most infamous Brits around—think Rupert Murdoch and Robert Maxwell with better haircuts. Who ever thought of James Bond as a trained-to-kill media watchdog?

"It's my theory that they wanted an adversary for Bond that the public would really hate," speculated humorist Art Buchwald in his syndicated column. "Today's moviegoers are no longer intimidated by South American dictators or Russian generals. Recent surveys reveal that the public is scared silly by the media. So the producer decided to model the archvillain after a media mogul because he knew that the audience would really root for Bond to destroy him."

As critic Dana Bisbee writes, "Journalists are the new villains of pop culture." But there is much more to the public's feelings about the media than mere suspicion of the press. The public simply doesn't trust or believe what it sees, hears, and reads, and the media and Hollywood are actors in this drama.

THE LIBERATION OF TED KOPPEL

Sex stories do change things. You know there is new ground being broken when Ted Koppel opens *Nightline* saying, "It may, as you will hear later in the program, ultimately come down to the question of whether oral sex does or does not constitute adultery."

Nightline offered the theory that Clinton may think that intercourse is adultery, but fellatio just a casual Arkansas undertaking—which is why Clinton can issue those earnest denials with a straight face. We now have a situation where the lure of the tabloid is completely irresistible to all media everywhere, or as Frank Rich wryly noted in the *New York Times*, "All Monica, All the Time."

There no longer appears to be a line between Sally Jessy Raphael and network news. The Unabomber cops a plea, the pope is in Cuba,★ Arafat is at the White House, and where is the media? Focused on the president's zipper. When all three network anchors abandon the historic, unprecedented Castro-pope encounter and rush home for an unconfirmed sex story, we understand what the priority is. The MSNBC banner reads: "President in Crisis." CNN's special report: "Investigating the President." The First Lady comes out swinging on the *Today* show, and by the evening news poker-faced anchors are asking Rep. Dick Armey if he believes there is a "right-wing conspiracy" at work. Is this really a presidency in jeopardy, or is it the final abdication of truth to the power of spin?

Spin, after all, is the well-greased machine exposed so cunningly in Barry Levinson's *Wag the Dog*. Robert DeNiro's Connie Brean, the powerful, undercover presidential media-fixer with a lethal touch, is the living incarnation of this essential political tool. Coupled with Dustin Hoffman's self-centered, Robert Evans–type producer, the two pull off the ultimate in spin control. It's a perfect marriage of modern-day media handling and the best of Hollywood storytelling.

★Pope John Paul II made a historic trip to Cuba in January 1998.

MEDIA MONOPOLY GROWS UP

Depending on your vantage point, *Wag the Dog* is either a funny satire, or enervating cynicism that contributes to the very problem it is skewering. But no matter what your take, *Wag the Dog* represents a new level of understanding of our mediated world. Since today's giant global media conglomerates shape virtually every aspect of media reality through the seamless dynamics of synergy—owning the programming and the capacity to deliver it, in news, music, radio, television, movies, book, online and through various other sources of entertainment—virtually any reality is possible.

"You'll remember the picture fifty years from now, they'll have forgotten the war," says Brean. "Gulf War? Smart bomb falling down a chimney, 2,500 missions a day, one hundred days, one video of one bomb. And the American people bought that war. War is show business."

The film's behind-the-scenes media manipulations render the practicing news media and the president mere props in a larger game. It's no wonder that close to 90 percent of the public think media owners exercise too much control over the press. Nor should anyone be surprised when large numbers of Americans report that they feel powerless in a system they perceive is locked up by a hegemonic troika of corporate moguls, corrupt politicians, and wealthy media celebs formally known as journalists.

Politics may still be different than show business, but if *Wag the Dog* accomplishes one thing, it clearly shows how close these two worlds have become. Today we have a media system where major arms and nuclear manufacturers General Electric and Westinghouse own NBC and CBS; ABC is owned by Disney, America's largest entertainment operation and, historically, war is entertainment. Time Warner owns CNN, whose reputation was established and highest popularity achieved during the Gulf War. And now that MSNBC and Murdoch's Fox have entered the 24-hour news/talk show format, all aching for that mesmerizing moment when all America is again glued to the tube, do we doubt that there will be more war in our future?

Politicians, always looking to boost their popularity, will be no doubt ready to provide the synergy. Remember, two days after 241 Marines were killed in a terrorist truck bombing in Beirut, Ronald Reagan invaded Granada, a country with fewer than 100,000 people. Former presidential adviser Dick Morris was particularly revealing when he recently wrote: "In the aftermath of the Olympic bombing and the assault on the American base in Saudi Arabia, many of us at the White House longed for a clear adversary against whom to demonstrate the president's strength and decisiveness. We didn't in fact fabricate one as DeNiro and Hoffman do in the film, but that wasn't because we didn't want to. Unfortunately, neither the FBI or the CIA could pin the blame on a bombable enemy. So our dreams of a macho response went unfulfilled."

So are we ready for Gulf War II? Bombs may well drop, and in the meantime it looks like the hot-and-bothered White House press corps may not get its longed-for climax in the Monica Lewinsky story anytime soon. The relation of art to life in this case may actually put the dog firmly back in control of the wag: The public is watching with a wary eye, and it knows this unzipping won't soon be the undoing of the president. The question is: Does the media?★

★The August 1998 strikes by the United States on terrorist-related facilities in Afghanistan and Sudan provide more recent comparisons with *Wag the Dog*'s satire. (Eds.)

14

Cartoon

Dick Wright

Chapter Three

Journalism and Ethics:
Toward Solutions

15

What Do We Do Now?

Editors of the *Columbia Journalism Review*

Regardless of who ultimately wins or loses, regardless of who is judged right or wrong, regardless of the fate of William Jefferson Clinton—or Monica Lewinsky or Kenneth Starr—what will matter mightily to journalists are the long-lasting lessons that we learn from this lamentable and depressing affair.

However the scandal turns out, the press stands to lose in the court of public opinion. In a Pew Research Center poll of 844 people taken from January 30 to February 2[, 1998], nearly two-thirds said the media had done only a fair or poor job of carefully checking the facts before reporting this story; 60 percent said the media had done only a fair or poor job of being objective on the story and 54 percent thought the press put in another fair or poor performance in providing the right amount of coverage. "The rise of Clinton's popularity in the polls is in part a backlash against the press," said Andrew Glass, Cox Newspapers' senior correspondent. "One way the people can say that the press has been too critical is to tell the pollsters that they support Clinton."

If the president should fall, then those who jumped the gun, who ran with rumor and innuendo, who published or broadcast phony reports without eventual retraction, will falsely claim vindication and triumph. And if this president should persevere and prevail, many in the public will be convinced that the press and the independent counsel

Reprinted from *Columbia Journalism Review*, March/April 1998. © 1998 by *Columbia Journalism Review*.

were in some unholy conspiracy to persecute him. Remember that the Clinton controversy is only the latest in a string of stories—Diana, O. J., Versace*—that the press has been widely accused of exploiting. Says *Los Angeles Times* editor Michael Parks: "We're good at wretched excess, at piling on."

Parts of the press have gone wrong in reporting the White House crisis, [which] leads to these further conclusions:

- Competition has become more brutal than ever and has spurred excess. TV newsmagazines are now viewed by traditional print newsmagazines as direct competitors. Thus, says Michael Elliott, editor of *Newsweek International*, "The proliferation of TV news shows makes it harder for us to delay the release of a story." With the spread of twenty-four-hour all-news cable channels—CNN, MSNBC, Fox—there's pressure to report news even when there isn't any. In a remarkably prescient statement . . . to the Catto Conference on Journalism and Society, former TV newsman Robert MacNeil said: "I tremble a little for the next sizable crisis with three all-news channels, and scores of other cable and local broadcasters, fighting for a share of the action, each trying to make his twist on the crisis more dire than the next."

- The Internet has speeded the process and lowered quality by giving currency to unreliable reports. When a story is posted on the Internet, it races around the globe almost instantly. But the Internet has no standards for accuracy. Web gossipist Matt Drudge once claimed only an 80 percent accuracy rate—wholly unacceptable under any journalistic standards. Technology, long the journalist's great and good friend, has turned out to be a dangerous mistress. "The Internet is a gun to the head of the responsible media," says Jonathan Fenby, editor of the *South China Morning Post* in Hong Kong. "If you choose not to report a story, the Internet will."

- As journalism speeds up, there is less time to think, to ponder, to edit, to judge, to confirm, to reconsider. Never was there greater need for gatekeepers with sound and unimpassioned editorial judgment who refuse to be stampeded in the pressure of competition.

And never was there a better time to start examining what journalists can do, immediately, to improve and recapture public respect.

---

*The Italian designer Gianni Versace was shot to death outside his Miami Beach, Florida, mansion in July 1997. (Eds.)

A major step, surely, would be to resolve to make abundantly clear in the reporting of every fast-breaking or controversial story what is known fact and what is mere speculation—or better yet, to swear off disseminating speculation at all except as it can be fully attributed to a knowledgeable source. And to forgo cannibalizing the stories of other news outfits—whether mainstream or tabloid—and to refrain from merely retransmitting them on their face value, without independent reporting.

Clearly, every news organization needs to establish its own written guidelines for almost every conceivable coverage situation. Many already have them. In Britain, the BBC has a thick book containing policies for everything from covering elections to interviewing terrorists to determining when the people's right to know supersedes what may constitute invasion of privacy.

The BBC's dedication to the two-source rule caused anchorman Nik Gowing to fill forty excruciating minutes of airtime [in August 1997] awaiting confirmation by a *second* source of Princess Diana's death before broadcasting the news.

Journalists must more freely and fully admit—and quickly correct—their errors. More gross missteps were committed in the early stages of the Clinton scandal than in all of Watergate. Just one example: All of those "sightings" of the president in intimate situations with Ms. Lewinsky in the White House as reported, variously, by ABC News, the *Dallas Morning News,* and the *Wall Street Journal.* . . .

Newspersons must have the courage to stand up to their editors, news directors, and other bosses when the need arises—and refuse to take a story beyond where sound journalistic principles allow.

In short, the time has come for a thoughtful and uncompromising reappraisal—time to stand back and recall the fundamentals that once made the free press of America the envy of the world. We asked a sampling of journalists and media analysts for their views on what lessons the profession ought to learn from the Clinton scandal story, and where we go from here:

• **Walter Isaacson,** managing editor, *Time*
We're in a set of rooms where we've never been before. It's murky, and we keep bumping into the furniture. But this is a very valid story of a strong-willed prosecutor and a president whose actions have been legitimately questioned. Reporters must be very careful to stick to known facts, but not be afraid to cover the story. A case involving sex can be a very legitimate story, but we can't let our journalistic standards lapse simply because the sexual element makes everybody overexcited. One lesson is, in the end, you're going to be judged on whether you got it right, not just on whether you got it first.

• **Richard Wald,** senior vice president, ABC News

There are, at least, three lessons.

One: when you are dealing with the president and sex, you must be extremely precise in how you say what it is you think you know. When carefully phrased stories that we ran on ABC were picked up by other news organizations, nobody said: "ABC News reports they got the story from source A or source B." They simply reported it as fact. It then gets into the public vocabulary as fact rather than as allegation.

Two: People dislike the messenger but like the message. If you believe the polls, the public is annoyed with the media and doesn't want to hear about this story anymore. On the other hand, they're buying a lot of newspapers and driving up the ratings of twenty-four-hour news channels. If you believe surveys that ask people what they watch on TV, PBS is the highest rated network in the world. And ballet is huge.

Three: We all get tarred with the excesses of a few. Some TV news organizations rush onto the air with bulletins that don't mean anything. Some newspapers plaster stuff over page one that's really quite minor. Each tiny advance in the story is treated like a journalistic triumph. But the bulk of the reporting has been reasonable and in context.

• **Marvin Kalb,** director, The Shorenstein Center on the Press, Politics and Public Policy, Harvard University

Check the coverage of the O. J. trials, the Versace/Cunanan saga, Princess Diana's tragic death. With each burst of excessive, shallow, intrusive, and hardly uplifting electronic herd journalism, there has been the promise that next time it would get better. The new technology and the new economics have combined to produce a new journalism, which has bright spots but is marked by murky questions about ethics, slipping standards, and quality.

• **James Fallows,** editor, *U.S. News & World Report*

When this whole thing is over, we'll be wringing our hands in symposia and postmortem critiques. The trick would be to keep some of that retrospective view in mind while we're in the middle of covering the story. A year from now people will be saying:

—that we shouldn't have let this story blot out so much else of the news, as happened with O.J. and Diana and Flight 800.

—that we should have avoided some of the flights of fancy that come with ever-escalating hypothetical questions. ("If it is proven that Monica Lewinsky killed Vince Foster, then . . . ?")

—that we should have been more skeptical about single-source anonymous reports—and made the possible motive of leakers clearer to our readers.

—that we should have found some way to retain the proper function of editorial judgment, i.e., waiting to see when there is enough basis to publish a story—rather than just saying: "It's on the Internet, it's 'Out There.'"

—that we should have recognized that we're in a morally complex situation when it comes to dealing with leaks—one where we really need consider the inherent rights and wrongs.

The point is: why wait until next year before trying to let such concerns shape our coverage?

• **Anthony Lewis,** columnist, the *New York Times*

The serious press has an obligation to stand back and warn the reader about how thin is the basis for many of these stories. It's a disgrace what the papers are doing in terms of sourcing.

The obsession of the press with sex and public officials is crazy. Still, after Linda Tripp went to the prosecutor, it became hard to say we shouldn't be covering this. My criticism is in the way it was covered. In general, the press started out rather gullible as regards the Starr operation, and has caught up. The public's been way ahead.

• **William Marimow,** managing editor, the Baltimore *Sun*

When a story is sensitive and controversial, you don't go into print until you've done everything possible to interview people on both sides of the issue, until you understand their accounts of what happened. If you're going to report that "sources" said a White House butler saw the president and an intern in a "compromising situation," you ought to go to the ends of the earth to get the point of view of the butler, the president, the intern, and their attorneys.

• **Geneva Overholser,** ombudsman, the *Washington Post*

Again and again, readers complained about how much we in the press have been reporting from anonymous sources that just seems like gossip. And that is, in fact, inexcusable. We aren't clear enough [in our reports] about the possible motivations of these sources. It's not that we can't have anonymous sources, but each one costs us something in credibility.

And we're too loose with language. One story quoted a source as saying that in her written proffer Monica Lewinsky had "acknowledged" having sex with the president. But she may have "asserted" it rather than "acknowledged" it. We can't use language that hangs somebody before the facts are out.

The *Washington Post* conceded that one of its articles was based on sources who had heard the [Lewinsky-Tripp] tapes, not on a hearing of the tapes by the reporter. Yet there were quotes around the president's alleged words to Lewinsky—"You must deny this." Here's an *anonymous* source *paraphrasing* a woman who is *characterizing* the words of the president to her on tapes made without her knowledge.

• **Deni Elliott,** director, Practical Ethics Center, University of Montana and professor in the university's philosophy and journalism departments

In the Monica Lewinsky stories in the February 16[, 1998,] *Newsweek,* there are at least thirty instances in which information is either not attributed, or attributed to anonymous sources, or attributed to other news organizations.

News organizations have not differentiated between different kinds of leaks. Leaks of grand jury testimony create information that ought not be disclosed unless it can be explained that the information is so important that the leak is justified. Grand juries have great latitude and are supposed to operate secretly because of that latitude. If information looks like grand jury testimony but is not, the reader should be informed, or readers will be led to believe you can't trust in grand jury secrecy.

• **Peter Prichard,** president, Freedom Forum, former editor, *USA Today*

One big lesson: never let hypercompetition take precedence over good news judgment. And be alert to the possibility that you're being manipulated. Also: one anonymous source on any story is simply not enough. The speed of news cycles these days has resulted in errors, but generally the coverage has been good. Newspapers have done a better job than television.

• **Thomas E. Patterson,** Bradlee Professor of Government and the Press, Harvard's John F. Kennedy School of Government

It's not hard to identify the standards we ought to have, it's just hard to get everybody on board. It's going to take real leadership—strong voices, editors, reporters who are willing to stand up to management.

There isn't much real self-criticism among journalists. There has been a flurry of it in the current scandal because so many stories were so outrageous. But where is the same kind of scrutiny the press gives everyone else—really hammering away? These flurries blow over and six months later they're forgotten. Journalists have to say, "Here's an example of the kinds of things we don't do"—and then don't do it. And if journalists do do it, someone must tell them, "You're violating the standards of your profession. Stop it."

• **Anthony Marro,** editor, *Newsday*

Before self-examination moves into self-flagellation, let's look at the lessons here:

With the blur that results when television viewers can switch from the

CBS Evening News to *Hard Copy, Larry King Live,* and *Geraldo,* it's more important than ever for journalists to sort out: What are unproven allegations and what are proven facts? Which facts are criminal and impeachable and which are merely embarrassing? And what information is coming from serious journalism and what is coming from entertainment programs that have some of the trappings of journalism but few of the standards?

All life is *Rashomon,*★ as was seen in the early reports on the testimony of [Clinton's personal secretary] Betty Currie, in which two of the nation's very best newspapers produced two very different stories from pretty much the same bits of information. The *New York Times* gave something very much like a prosecutor's view of the incident (i.e., Clinton was coaching her to lie) while the *Washington Post* gave something very much like a defense lawyer's view (i.e., Clinton was just trying to refresh his memory about his meetings with Monica Lewinsky). Sorting this out can be both difficult and time-consuming and no one should expect the press even at its best to come up with quick and conclusive answers.

Reporters need to keep reminding themselves that just because sources say they've obtained information doesn't mean that they've obtained all of it, or that it's fully corroborated, or that it means precisely what they suggest it means.

• **James O'Shea,** deputy managing editor, news, *Chicago Tribune*

We're in a new world in terms of the way information flows to the nation. The days when you can decide not to print a story because it's not well enough sourced are long gone. When a story gets into the public realm, as it did with *The Drudge Report,* then you have to characterize it, you have to tell your readers, "This is out there, you've probably been hearing about it on TV and the Internet. We have been unable to substantiate it independently." And then give them enough information to judge the validity of it.

Not reporting it at all is the worst thing you can do because you create a vacuum in which people begin thinking a story is true and you're not reporting it because you're a backer of the president. One of the most popular things we did was run a big chart in our Sunday paper that told what's been reported, what is known, and what is not known. We delineated, trying to separate fact from fiction and readers responded very well. The trouble with not reporting anything at all until it's substantiated is that you're not distinguishing between fact and fiction, and then fiction wins.

★*Rashomon* refers to the claim that life is seen from different perspectives. The term is taken from Kurosawa's 1951 film *Rashomon.* (Eds.).

16

The Public Defender:
A Journalism Professor's Crusade
to Bring the Community
into the Classroom

Scott Sherman

During the 1996 elections, fifteen North Carolina newspapers and TV stations collaborated on an unusual experiment known as "Your Voice, Your Vote." The local media asked two thousand residents to list the issues they were most concerned about: taxes and spending, crime and drugs, education and financial security. With this information in hand, the coalition then interviewed each candidate—except Senator Jesse Helms, who refused to participate—and produced a series of articles comparing their responses. Almost immediately, the *Washington Post,* the *Boston Globe,* the *Financial Times,* and other leading newspapers excoriated the endeavor, arguing that its reliance on polls to direct the coverage amounted to pandering and led to the exclusion of key issues —such as race—that didn't show up in the surveys. The campaign manager for Helms's rival, Harvey Gantt, complained that the apparently high-minded project ended up being unfair to his candidate by short-circuiting an open discussion of racial issues. (Gantt lost.) Jonathan Yardley of the *Washington Post* blasted the experiment as an attempt by the press to "control the political agenda," and Michael Kelly of *The New Yorker* slammed the project as "anti-democratic" and "dishonest." In response, *Charlotte Observer* editor Jennie Buckner retorted, in a *Washington Post* Op-Ed, that some big-city critics had not even bothered to

This article originally appeared in *Lingua Franca,* April 1998. Reprinted by permission from *Lingua Franca: The Review of Academic Life,* published in New York. E-mail: www.linguafranca.com

read the actual coverage, and she claimed to be "particularly astonished by the number of journalists who seem offended by the suggestion that they might learn something valuable by listening to citizens."

The North Carolina project is the most conspicuous example so far of "public" or "civic" journalism—a communitarian-flavored movement whose intellectual architect, leading theoretician, and chief provocateur is a tireless (some would say relentless) New York University journalism professor named Jay Rosen. Rooted in small- and medium-sized newspapers, public journalism calls on the press, in Rosen's words, to jettison the role of "detached observer" and "help revive civic life and improve public dialogue."

Jeremiads about the decline of public life are routinely issued in academic and political circles, but Rosen has been unusually energetic in his response to them, having spent the last eight years promoting what media scholar Michael Schudson calls 'the best-organized journalistic social movement in the history of the American press." The movement has inspired hundreds of news organizations—among them print, radio, and TV outlets—to experiment with the idea, and it has taken Rosen from Greenwich Village, where he lives and works, into scores of newsrooms from coast to coast. Reporters and editors, typically wary of academic language and ideas, were not always eager to listen to someone with a doctorate in media studies, but Rosen's persistence has paid off. Since 1990 he has addressed more than three thousand journalists, been interviewed by news organizations from Japan to South Africa, and garnered $1.3 million worth of foundation grants to pursue and develop the idea. Rosen also played a significant role in shaping James Fallows's influential book, *Breaking the News* (Pantheon, 1996).

The actual experiments carried out under the rubric of public journalism vary widely in style and breadth. But they all start from the premise that American public life is in lousy shape and the press has a responsibility to do something to help. Public journalists have used a wide range of techniques: town meetings, focus groups, polling, even pizza parties. In Huntington, West Virginia, the *Herald Dispatch* helped to organize task forces whose efforts eventually raised $3 million in federal funds for a ramshackle, deindustrialized region; in Norfolk, Virginia, the *Virginian-Pilot* asked political candidates to supply a "public application form," along with a résumé and letters of recommendation; in San Francisco, the *Chronicle* inserted postage-paid voter registration forms, which led to large numbers of new voters; in Spokane, Washington, the *Spokesman-Review* abolished the position of editorial-page editor and installed two "interactive" editors to help readers craft

Op-Ed pieces on topics ranging from the recollections of an impas-
sioned twenty-year-old woman on public assistance to an eighty-five-
year-old man's account of life inside a nursing home.

Few of these folksier projects have proven as controversial as the Charlotte experiment. Yet the mere mention of public journalism draws a
fierce response from some members of the media elite, who argue that
the movement amounts to little more than errant boosterism and that
it threatens the press's reputation as an independent watchdog.
"Reporters, editors, and publishers have their hands full learning to tell
it right," Max Frankel wrote in the *New York Times Magazine*. "They
should leave reforms to reformers." *Washington Post* columnist Richard
Harwood cautioned that "The press already has credibility problems
based on the public perception that it is an arrogant, self-serving institution that more often aggravates than cures the social illnesses that
afflict us. To anoint ourselves now as leaders of a new American Reformation may be a little more than the market will bear." And in *The New
Yorker*, David Remnick inquired, "Why abandon the entire enterprise
of informed, aggressive skepticism—even in its current state—in the
hope of pleasing an imagined public? When journalists begin acting like
waiters and taking orders from the public and pollsters, the results are
not pretty."

Although public journalism has made only modest headway in
journalism schools, some critics blame academia for the renegade ideas
swirling through smalltown newspapers. For Remnick, public journalism is "especially popular among ink-free journalism professors."
More pointedly, *Washington Post* editor Leonard Downie—whom
Rosen publicly debated in 1995—says it is a movement fueled by "academics who are risking the terrible prostitution of our profession."

Rosen, forty-one, was born and raised in Buffalo's middle-class
suburbs. His mother was a teacher who kept *Time* and *Saturday Review*
on the coffee table; his father was absent from the start. At SUNY Buffalo he began his undergraduate career as a management major. "My
aspirations were quite low at that time," Rosen says from his spotless
office just off Washington Square Park. Tall, lanky, and filled with ner-
vous energy, he recalls that he was "drifting into suburban life as a
member of the middle-managerial class. Then one day I got angry."

His sociology instructor had distributed a Socialist Workers party
propaganda leaflet to the class. Outraged that the professor had over-
stepped his boundaries and violated the canons of objectivity, the young
Rosen burst into the office of the school newspaper and demanded that

the editors write a story about it. In the time-honored tradition of college journalism, they replied: "Why don't you do it?" That article led to a staff job and eventually to the editorship; a summer position as a reporter at the Buffalo *Courier-Express* followed.

Rosen wanted to make a career of it. But an expected job at the *Courier-Express* did not materialize, and he went in another direction: press criticism. Eventually, he decided to enroll in graduate school, joining NYU's Department of Media Ecology. After writing a dissertation on John Dewey, Walter Lippmann, and the relationship between the press and the public, he was hired by NYU's Department of Journalism in 1986. Around this time, he began turning out press criticism for *Tikkun*, the *Listener*, and other small publications. According to Rosen, he was soon striving to connect with the world outside Greenwich Village: "Before I started doing public journalism, I was an imitation of a hip, downtown intellectual. In other words, I thought I was cool. Why? Because I had learned how to sneer at popular culture. It's just a pose you learn as a graduate student studying the media. You learn how to be witty and ironic . . . in your various put-downs of Vanna White and *USA Today*."

But Rosen would soon shuck this persona for something considerably more earnest. In 1990 he met the man who would set him on his future course: Davis "Buzz" Merritt of the *Wichita Eagle*, "the original public journalist."

Merritt was appointed editor of the *Eagle* in 1975. He had worked on newspapers in Charlotte and in Boca Raton, Florida, but his new assignment was a mixed blessing: In 1959 *Time* magazine had dubbed Wichita's papers the "bottom of the barrel." Merritt resuscitated the *Eagle*, garnering awards for writing, layout, and photography. But despite the laurels, readership and circulation were declining, and, worse, community problems seemed intractable. Moreover, the 1988 presidential campaign—with its charges and countercharges, contrived imagery, and endless mudslinging—convinced Merritt that he was witnessing nothing less than "a death spiral of democracy." In response, he conceived of an ambitious, perhaps even messianic, agenda for journalists: "It was . . . clear to me that the public couldn't change on its own, being merely a victim of the incestuous partnership of politics and the political press. Which left only us, the press, to change, to try to halt the devastating spiral."

Two years later, with the Kansas gubernatorial race approaching, Merritt had a chance to reclaim the election from consultants and spin doctors. Supported by polling data, the paper focused its coverage on ten concerns, such as education, economic development, agriculture, and social services, giving each a long background piece in the paper. The *Eagle* also introduced a weekly feature that summarized the candidates' positions on core issues and then noted what they had said about each one that week. If a candidate was silent, the box simply said: "This Week: Did not talk about it." In 1992 the *Eagle* formally launched the "People's Project" in the belief that journalism could "empower people to take back control of their lives." The paper interviewed Wichita residents about their problems and concerns, which led to a series of public forums, community events, and feature articles that included phone numbers of groups working on social problems. The result? Merritt claims that volunteerism in the Wichita school system soared 37 percent.

When Rosen was introduced to Merritt in 1991, he knew at once that he had located an ally and an accomplice: Merritt, entirely on his own, had put into practice some of the very ideas about the press and the creation of the public sphere contained in Rosen's dissertation. "Merritt understood that his challenge as an editor was to help *form* as well as inform the public," Rosen has said. So the two men joined forces. From the beginning there was a clear division of labor: Rosen supplied the vocabulary, intellectual framework, and rhetorical zest, while Merritt's forty-one years in the newspaper business, in addition to his Midwestern populist demeanor, furnished legitimacy.

In 1993 the duo invented the term "public journalism," and the concept began to attract the support of influential figures in the newspaper industry, especially James K. Batten, the late chairman of the Knight-Ridder newspaper chain, who in 1993 helped Rosen obtain the first of two $528,000 grants from the Miami-based Knight Foundation. Other foundations—primarily the Pew Charitable Trusts and Kettering —entered the fray, as did the American Press Institute and the Poynter Institute for Media Studies. Together they provided high-profile institutional backing for public journalism.

One reason that press barons and foundations were attracted to public journalism was the feeling of discontent that swept the newspaper industry in the 1980s and 1990s. Remnick has captured the prevailing mood: "Every good journalist is at least vaguely aware that his trade may one day go the way of phrenology—and, what's more, the population will hardly protest the extinction." In laying the groundwork for a novel approach to journalism, Rosen uses a barrage of statistics to illustrate the precarious state of the newspaper and the diminishing public confidence in the press. One 1995 survey showed that 45 percent of Americans had read a daily newspaper the previous day—a number down from 71 percent in 1965. A Yankelovich poll indicated that in 1988, 50 percent of respondents had high confidence in news from newspapers, but by 1993 only 20 percent felt that way. Some polls suggest outright hostility: 71 percent of Americans, according to 1994 *Times-Mirror* data, believe that the press "gets in the way of society solving its problems."

Add to that the stunning proliferation of "infotainment," cynicism at all levels of the news business, and the apparent erosion of journalistic credibility and you have some sense of the gloom that dominates industry gatherings. Though newspapers are generally a profitable business, publishers are understandably anxious about their future. Underneath it all is a pervasive fear that the newspaper itself may soon be a casualty of the computer age, as Neil Hickey argued in the November/December 1997 issue of *Columbia Journalism Review.* In "Will [Bill] Gates Crush Newspapers?" Hickey predicted that by 2001 newspapers will have lost nearly $5 billion in advertising to on-line services, a development that would cripple the industry.

For Rosen, public journalism offers a last chance to guarantee the profession's future. In order for such a rescue operation to succeed, however, he believes that journalists must forsake two of their most cherished principles: objectivity and adversarialism.

According to Rosen, adversarialism (or "the reporter-as-crap-detector," in his parlance) has been adopted as the identity of choice for many journalists—especially the young, the upwardly mobile, and those weaned on the *Washington Post*'s Watergate coverage. In his 1996 book, *Getting the Connections Right* (Twentieth-Century Fund), Rosen argues that adversarial reporting has engendered a peculiar form of journalistic nihilism, "a snarling and relentless cynicism—a categorical mistrust of all public figures." Beneath the "hardened realism" of the cynical reporter lies the illusion that a public "eager to see the veil stripped from politics will magically reappear each day to provide the journalist with an attentive audience." But the more likely result, Rosen insists, "is that people will ignore the news as they come to conclude that no honest leaders exist, no genuine debate can be had, no one cares much whether problems are solved, and therefore politics and journalism are a waste of time." Rosen doesn't deny that superb journalism has resulted from what he calls the "cult of toughness," nor does he believe that political coverage should be sycophantic, but he does object to reporters' masquerading as "zealous prosecutors." (As an example, he cites Tim Russert's efforts to blindside his guests on *Meet the Press.*)

Quite simply, journalists must see themselves as "political actors" who have "some stake in the health of the political system."

The notion of objectivity, what he calls the "epistemology of American journalists," is another favorite target. Rosen takes pains to argue that objectivity contains much that is useful for the press—the disinterested pursuit of truth, the attempt to restrain biases, and so on. But he also laments the feelings of insularity and superiority that he believes typically accompany its invocation. "Everybody who comes at the press with a dissatisfaction, with a complaint, or even with an idea is seen by journalists as subjective," he told the *New York Times*. "One of the most insidious effects of objectivity is that it creates a world in which journalists can live without criticism, because they're the only judges of what's objective."

Starting in the 1970s, objectivity was scrutinized by communication scholars but to little effect: After all, *Journalism Quarterly* doesn't exactly circulate in newsrooms. But by arguing his case in hundreds of face-to-face conversations with working journalists, Rosen forced the media establishment to take notice. In appraising the objectivity debate, he floats what he calls a disruptive question: "Since the press is already a player in public life, what should it be playing *for*?"

In fact, when Rosen asks that question, he is careful to avoid endorsing the openly partisan journalism one might find in European newspapers (which are often directly affiliated with political parties) or in American opinion magazines, such as the *Nation* and the *National Review*. As Merritt puts it, the public journalist has "left the press box and gotten down on the field, not as a contestant but as a fair-minded participant with an open and expressed interest in the process going well." Rosen, too, prefers to talk about process, not politics. Like many other left-leaning advocates of "deliberative democracy," he insists his goal is not to advance any particular political agenda but rather to promote greater public deliberation.

Rosen's brand of deliberative democracy stems largely from the communications theorist and Columbia Journalism School professor James Carey. During his long career as dean of the College of Communication at the University of Illinois, Carey played a major role in introducing the "interpretative" theories of thinkers like John Dewey, Max Weber, Lewis Mumford, Clifford Geertz, and Raymond Williams to communication, a field traditionally dominated by quantitative effects-based research. Yet Carey's work is little known outside the discipline, in part because he is an essayist (he hasn't produced a single monograph) and in part because his articles are buried in obscure academic journals. (Minnesota's recent publication of *James Carey: A Critical Reader* should add to his reputation; it is a stimulating compendium of essays by and about him.)

At its core, Carey's writing offers an overview of what he sees as the rise and fall of American journalism—a history that he closely links to the rise and fall of public life. For instance, in "The Press, Public Opinion and Public Discourse" (1995), he describes his vision of a robust American public sphere as it existed in the taverns of Colonial New England, where newspapers and pamphlets triggered heated debate among denizens and travelers. Of course, it was a world restricted by race and gender and class, but in Carey's view it was something special nevertheless:

> The public, in this phase, was not a fiction or an abstraction—a group of people sitting at home watching television or privately and invisibly reading a newspaper or numbers collected in a public opinion poll. The public was a specified social formation: a group of people, often strangers, gathered in public houses to talk, to read the news together, to dispute the meaning of events, to join political impulses to political actions.

Carey then documents the erosion of that milieu, beginning with the growth of Progressive-era journalistic professionalization, followed by the rise of expert knowledge, and finally, the consolidation of the survey research and polling industries. Modern journalism was the result, and Carey concedes that it has been "a bulwark of liberty in our time" and that "no one has come up with a better arrangement." Still, it is plagued by a near-fatal defect: It is a journalism that "justifies itself in the public's name but in which the public plays no role, except as an audience." He adds: "Journalism only makes sense in relation to the public and public life. Therefore, the fundamental problem in journalism is to reconstitute the public, to bring it back into existence."

In his search for a way out of this impasse, Carey looks to the work of John Dewey, in particular his celebrated debate with Walter Lippmann during the 1920s. Lippmann had insisted that the idea of an informed citizenry was a delusion: "They arrive in the middle of the third act and leave before the last curtain, staying just long enough to decide who is the hero and who is the villain." In response, Dewey agreed that democratic theory had erred in positing the omnicompetent citizen, but he defended the popular capacity for decision making. The problem, for Dewey, was how to create the kind of direct public interaction that could fulfill the promise of participatory democracy. But what happens when a town or a city grows to a size where face-to-face dialogue is impossible? Carey argues that it then falls to the press to foster that dialogue. In his interpretation of Dewey, "public opinion . . . is formed only in discussion," and, hence, "the purpose of the news is not to represent and inform but to signal, tell a story and activate inquiry." He warns: "The press, by seeing its role as that of informing the public, abandons its role as an agency for carrying on the conversation in our culture."

Like Rosen, the historian and social critic Christopher Lasch was convinced by Carey's argument. In a 1990 essay, "Journalism, Publicity, and the Lost Art of Argument," he put forth his own summary of Dewey's riposte to Lippmann: "Instead of dismissing direct democracy as irrelevant to modern conditions, we need to recreate it on a large scale. And from this point of view, the press serves as the equivalent of a town meeting."

A leading scholar who dissents from the Dewey-Carey-Lasch-Rosen line is University of California–San Diego's Michael Schudson, author of *Discovering the News* (Basic, 1978), the definitive account of the triumph of journalistic objectivity.

Schudson is uneasy about some of the more grandiose statements he has heard from Rosen and Carey. "I don't think the press has ever *constituted* the public," he says, adding that today's public life may not be as utterly passive and disengaged as critics say. Moreover, he is skeptical of Dewey's emphasis on face-to-face conversation. In an essay entitled "Why Conversation Is Not the Soul of Democracy," which appeared in the December 1997 issue of *Critical Studies in Mass Communication*, Schudson insists that the current "romance" with conversation, which is visible all over the academic landscape, is deeply problematic. Drawing from Jane Mansbridge's research on Vermont town meetings, Schudson points out that they can not only lead to stress, social discomfort, and the reinforcement of local hierarchies, but that conversation itself is hardly egalitarian or effortless. (Other critics of the conversation model have added that public dialogue may create discord just as easily as consensus and promote hypocrisy rather than sincerity.)

In a lucid essay forthcoming in *The Politics of News* (Congressional Quarterly Press), Schudson wonders if the goals of public journalism are really compatible with one another: "What is it that public journalism is supposed to be advancing? Is it 'community'? Or is it a healthy public discourse? Or is it a well-endowed public domain? What makes public journalists believe that these things are consistent rather than at war?" And he concludes that public journalism is, in fact, a conservative reform movement with a narrow political agenda—one that is too compatible with market-oriented journalism:

> It does not propose new media accountability systems. It does not offer a citizen media review board or a National News Council. It does not recommend publicly elected publishers or editors. It does not suggest that the press be formally, or even informally answerable to a governmental or community body. It does not borrow from Sweden the proposition that government should subsidize news organizations that would enlarge the diversity of viewpoints available to the reading public. It does not propose nonprofit news institutions (like PBS) or news institutions without advertising (like the reformulated *Ms.* magazine).

Still, Schudson applauds public journalism's vigorous challenge to standard media assumptions and practices—"What democratic process," he tartly asks, "led newspapers to follow local football teams with greater constancy and a richer sense of history than they follow local politics?"—and insists that it is "the most serious and most intelligent development in journalism in decades."

In newsrooms, meanwhile, the controversy continues. Current public journalism projects, funded by Pew, target economic reconstruction: In Aberdeen, Washington, a coalition of media outlets is examining the decline of the local fishing and logging industries and will attempt to come up with remedies; in Long Beach, California, the *Press-Telegram* is doing something similar in a community ravaged by defense cutbacks.

But the current wave of experiments also provides plenty of ammunition for critics: At the *Asbury Park Press* in New Jersey, for example, "grassroots community activists and leaders have been meeting at the *Press* monthly," according to a recently published account by the newspaper's staffers. This raises questions: If the local newspaper doesn't keep a critical eye on community leaders, who will? And what segment of a given community is most likely to benefit from public journalism in the first place?

An upbeat 1996 Pew study of four public journalism projects—in Charlotte, Madison, San Francisco, and Binghamton—found that considerable numbers of citizens knew about and approved of the projects, but those who were likely to be moved to participate in them were already part of "the active civic core." "What remains unknown," the study concluded, "is whether civic journalism *causes* community action or being active leads people to pay attention to public journalism."

What's more, Rosen must sometimes feel that he has helped to create a monster. In a 1995 advertisement that appeared on the front page of *Editor and Publisher,* the trade magazine of the newspaper industry, the Gannett Company blared: "We believe in 'public journalism'—and have done it for years." The ad, which Rosen calls a "heated exercise in hype," hailed the efforts of various Gannett papers— one of which, the *Gazette* in Elmira, New York, had "spearheaded the drive that raised $200,000 to bring a city-owned baseball stadium up to the standard to keep the [local minor league] baseball franchise in the city." "My heart sank when I saw it," Rosen recalls. "Stadium fixing was not the idea we had floated in any form I could recognize."

Rosen himself admits to having made plenty of mistakes, and he recounts them in the conclusion to his book *What Are Journalists For?* (Yale): "Turning people off by coming on too strongly, alienating potential supporters with inflammatory rhetoric, getting defensive in the face of criticism—or sounding clueless to three-quarters of [an audience]." One can add the following: his desire to have it both ways on the objectivity question; his readiness to demonize journalists (he writes in the *Carey Reader* that reporters indifferent to "democracy as a way of life" are "dangers to themselves and to the rest of us"); and his alarmist rhetoric about the "deepening ordeal" of American politics: In *Getting the Connections Right,* Rosen points to "militia members and black nationalists" who "read the papers with a savage mistrust." Nowhere in Rosen's writings does he address the issue of whether it's the duty of the press to sponsor public discussion, boost civic activity, and, as he often intones, "make public life go well"—or if that's a task better left to political parties, religious organizations, and trade unions. Meanwhile, critics point out that public journalism has thus far not been a profitable venture. Newspapers that pioneered the idea—the *Wichita Eagle,* among them—are still grappling with problems of dwindling circulation and public apathy.

But Rosen has many defenders. "Newspapers in Wichita, Charlotte, and many other cities are different now," says David Rubin, Dean of Syracuse University's S.I. Newhouse School of Public Communications. "One reason they are different is because of Jay Rosen." "In the end, we're going to find that Jay Rosen is one of the architects of the journalism we'll be seeing for decades to come," says Steve Smith of the *Colorado Springs Gazette.* "That's no mean feat for a nasally voiced academic from NYU."

In spite of his missteps, Rosen has fueled a vigorous discussion. Does the press have a responsibility that transcends objective journalism? What are journalists for? And now he is beginning to raise a related, and perhaps equally urgent, question: What are professors for?

Last year, Rosen participated in a conference on "public scholarship" sponsored by the Kettering Foundation. And in an interview published in Kettering's *Higher Education Exchange*, Rosen recently called for a new generation of "public scholars," who are to be differentiated from "public intellectuals." Public intellectuals, for Rosen, are basically mandarins, members of the avant-garde who step forward at urgent moments to enlighten the public. Public scholars, on the other hand, begin with the "realization that they don't know something, and the something can only be known in one way: through a process of inquiry conducted with others in public." For Rosen, public scholarship encourages academics to treat the subjects of their research as active, autonomous beings—and not just as bundles of data to be dissected and analyzed. But Rosen hasn't placed any firm limits on the idea, and that might well make some academics tremble: Must a graduate student in medieval studies hold a town meeting before choosing her dissertation topic?

In a scathing response to Rosen in the *Chronicle of Higher Education*, Kettering conference participant Alan Wolfe argued that many aspects of public scholarship are admirable but ultimately it's a "flawed concept" that conceals a political agenda. Taking issue with Rosen's Deweyan aspiration to revive the public, Wolfe noted, "There is an American public already in place, quite comfortable about making its views known via talk radio, letters to the editor, and electoral activity. Asking scholars to 'enlarge public understanding'—Rosen's words—is a way of saying that scholars do not like the understandings the public already has." Let's not be surprised, Wolfe adds, if the public, or at least the conservative wing of it, remains suspicious of professors who claim to seek cooperation "in deciding what we ought to value." Most significantly, Wolfe worried that the duty to engage in public scholarship might compromise a scholar's work: "As a scholar," Wolfe concludes, "I have only one principal obligation: to my quest for understanding."

In his response, Wolfe noted that "Dewey preferred a public that did not yet exist to the one whose influence could be felt everywhere around him." The same might be said of Rosen and Carey when they speak of "forming" and "reconstituting" the public. As Wolfe suggests, such language conjures up social engineering, and is at odds with the spirit of the movement they helped establish—a movement that, at its best, points the way toward a less distant and more equitable relationship between the press and the public. It's a point Rosen must bear in mind, for the fate of public journalism will ultimately rest on how effectively its disciples can conquer the hearts and minds of an actually existing public, not an imagined one.

17

Public Journalism: Balancing the Scales

Carl Sessions Stepp

From the first page of his treatise on public journalism, veteran editor Buzz Merritt preaches revolution.

"This book is about change," he announces. "It is not about journalists doing a few things differently. . . . It is fundamental, the adoption of a role beyond telling the news."

A soft-spoken son of the South who now edits a paper snug inside Middle America, the *Wichita Eagle*'s Merritt might seem an unlikely insurrectionist. But these are fighting words.

And the fight is on.

Not since "advocacy journalism" has a new direction in news aroused such furor. Public journalism's call for "a broader mission of helping public life go well" has reformers drooling and traditionalists seething. . . .

When James Fallows threw a compliment to public journalists ("they are more right than wrong") in his recent book *Breaking the News,* a fiery attack roared back from the very nerve center of mainstream journalism, the *New York Times* editorial page. There its editor, Howell Raines, branded Fallows "a fount of dangerous nonsense."

Reviewing a book by the divinely named Arthur Charity for *Editor & Publisher,* Hiley Ward compared public journalism to cults and religions, summoning all the trappings of guilt, confession, conversion, baptism, and salvation.

This article originally appeared in *American Journalism Review,* September 1994. Reprinted by permission of *American Journalism Review.*

So a holy war seems at hand, and the fireworks are irresistible. But public journalism is a serious, timely, well-intentioned effort to rejuvenate journalism and democracy. It deserves a more contemplative inspection.

In that spirit, this essay attempts to steer the debate toward a demilitarized zone and probe the underpinnings of this revolution-in-the-making.

"Public journalism does not apologize for having an agenda," writes Jay Rosen, the New York University professor who is the movement's intellectual architect.

"Public journalism calls on the press to help revive civic life and improve public dialogue—and to fashion a coherent response to the deepening troubles in our civic climate, most of which implicate journalists. . . . Its primary claim is that the press can do more . . . to engage people as citizens, to improve public discussion, to help communities solve problems, and to aid in the country's search for a workable public life."

Why do this? Merritt makes the case starkly: "If people are not interested in public life, they have no need for journalists or journalism."

While recognizing that such initiatives "ought perhaps to rest with politicians or private citizens rather than the news media," Charity concludes: "The facts are that the politicians and private citizens are doing an inadequate job of it, and that newspapers, as one of the few American institutions that still address people from all demographic groups . . . are well positioned to do better."

What strategies does public journalism embrace? Merritt lists them as follows:

- "It moves beyond the limited mission of 'telling the news' to a broader mission of helping public life go well. . . .

- "It moves from detachment to being a fair-minded participant in public life. . . .

- "It moves beyond only describing what is 'going wrong' to also imagining what 'going right' would be like. . . .

- "It moves from seeing people as consumers . . . to seeing them as a public, as potential actors in arriving at democratic solutions to public problems."

While Rosen and Merritt concentrate on the philosophic, Charity's book, *Doing Public Journalism,* collects public journalism methods and examples from dozens of papers.

Common techniques include " 'public listening,' the art of keeping the newspaper grounded in the concerns of ordinary people"; sponsoring "deliberative forums" where agendas can be shaped; developing "well-defined, value-based" recommendations and crusading to keep them on the agenda; and pushing for results, by "prodding both citizens and government officials to act on the public's judgment, without stepping 'over the line' " into "bias, advocacy and subjectivity."

Among his examples: The *Charlotte Observer* focused attention on a high-crime neighborhood, drawing help and suggestions from across the city, and helping coordinate efforts to "bring the neighborhood back." The *Cape Cod Times* used a citizens panel to help set priorities for covering elections. The *Wisconsin State Journal* convened citizen "grand juries" to deliberate a property tax plan. The *Bremerton Sun* in Washington held forty-seven town meetings and developed "a plan of action" for preserving open space.

In summary, Charity writes, "public journalism . . . inevitably comes to center on two tests of news value: Does this piece of writing or reporting help build civic capital? And does it help move the public toward meaningful judgment and action?"

To begin assessing public journalism, let's start with some reservations.

Public journalism hinges on several articles of faith. First, that journalism and public life depend on each other. Second, that both are faring poorly. Third, that in the absence of any other curative force, the press must take the initiative for restoring both to health.

These articles are all energetically asserted but not fully debated or carefully proven.

To the point that journalism depends on a healthy public sphere, for example, you could counterargue that the human appetite for news is primal and eternal, beyond dependency on a particular kind of public life. Especially as we enter the Information Age, the demise of the news media seems unimaginable.

Although Rosen and Merritt offer a variety of surveys and social science assessments suggesting public life and journalism are in trouble, their evidence seems substantial but selective. The turbulent history of this country and its news business—from the Civil War to Vietnam, from the partisan press to yellow journalism—suggests that tension, contention, and public agitation are anything but newcomers to our society.

Do they pose greater threats today than in the sixties (whether the 1760s, 1860s, or 1960s)? Maybe. But the public journalists haven't demonstrated it.

Also troublesome is what sometimes comes across as a distorted view of journalists' belief in objectivity or impartiality.

Merritt writes, for example, that traditional journalists feel they "must maintain a pristine distance, a contrived indifference to outcomes, else the news product be contaminated." They "insist that they cannot care what happens, or at least must not be caught caring." How then, he reasons, "can people who profess to not care what happens be trusted to inform us?"

I see his point, but it strikes me as unfair. "Pristine" and "contrived" seem snide. The logic leaps too quickly to equate "distance" (whose heritage suggests a professional effort at fairness) with the sinister "indifference." They aren't the same. There's nothing inherently untrustworthy in caring passionately as people but trying to act dispassionately as professionals (like, say, judges or teachers).

In some ways, public journalism creates a caricature of the traditional press, attacks it as corrupt, promotes itself as a reform "movement," and dismisses critics as reactionaries. There is a whiff of self-righteousness here, and it alienates some potential allies.

These are serious reservations. But they must be weighed against public journalism's contributions and possibilities.

Clearly, public journalism is a thoughtful effort to jump-start a tired industry and to reassert social responsibility in increasingly mercenary times. It offers not just complaints but a positive program for change.

It's impossible to read Merritt's book without being moved by his earnest, almost anguished, disappointment at the failings of his profession. (Readers should know that I have known Merritt for over twenty years and worked for him for about a year during the 1970s.) His disenchantment with the aloofness, smugness, and cynicism he sees in journalism is shared by many, including myself. Even public journalism's critics must worry about the media's quick-trigger willingness to humble anyone who ventures onto the public stage.

Rosen offers a brilliant critique of the media in a chapter called "American Journalism Is in Trouble." He cites several "alarm bells that are ringing simultaneously":

• "Economic: It is not clear what journalism produces that has enough economic value to sustain serious practice. . . .

• "Technological: Journalism holds an uncertain place in a reconfigured world where information will be everywhere. . . .

• "Political: Public support is badly eroded because the press is implicated in a political system that doesn't work. . . .

• "Occupational: Newsrooms need to become exciting and innovative places that are more democratic and more diverse. . . .

• "Spiritual: We don't know what journalists are willing to be 'for,' so familiar are they with what they're 'against.'"

These conditions require action, the public journalists conclude, in particular an effort to demolish journalists' "devastating illusion of themselves as bystanders."

Public journalism, according to Merritt, "does not mean trying to determine outcomes, but it does mean accepting the obligation to help the process of public life determine the outcomes." As Charity puts it, "Journalism should advocate democracy without advocating particular solutions."

Both Rosen and Merritt carefully point out that, like any tool or philosophy, public journalism can be misapplied and abused. Market-minded managers can use it as an excuse for pandering; fluff and boosterism can squeeze out the controversial and unsettling.

But they assert, convincingly, that savvy journalists can sidestep these hazards.

"If journalists are smart enough and professional enough to define some razor-thin line of objectivity and adhere to it," Merritt writes, "we are also smart enough and professional enough to define a slightly different line without tumbling all the way into the abyss of inappropriate involvement."

Where, then, does the scale balance on public journalism?

What concerns me most is not its intended consequences (bettering democracy without surrendering the watchdog role), but a potential unintended consequence that goes largely unexamined. What are the implications of relinquishing the outsider status the press has had for two centuries?

At its core, public journalism assumes that government is broken and the press must fix it. But to do so will inevitably link press and government as collaborators in both the public arena and the public mind. At some point, press independence could be compromised.

Outsider status, once worn proudly, may seem uncomfortable and even inappropriate these days. It risks alienating journalists from their sources and communities. It makes them seem indifferent and compassionless. Yet the press's outsider role—serving as a beyond-the-government check in our fragile but magical system of checks and balances— may well be uniquely necessary to democracy.

Journalism may have contributed to public alienation from government, as Merritt and Rosen contend, but we cannot overlook the cumulative corrosive impact of the last thirty years of government duplicity and scandal.

Messy as it sometimes is, an outsider press may contribute something irreplaceable by providing an escape valve for citizens to vent their disenchantment. This role is nettlesome, obnoxious—and quite possibly essential to our way of life. Advocates of public journalism owe us a more studied view of whether their revolution will sacrifice it.

To the degree it seeks to fix journalism, public journalism is a blessing. It offers many specific antidotes to what might be considered today's nonpublic journalism: involving citizens in the news agenda; divorcing coverage from officialdom and grounding it in people's lives; clearing away some of the snideness and smugness that have infiltrated the media. Surely we can achieve consensus that these are welcome reforms.

To the degree that public journalism seeks to fix government through journalism or, more grandly, to substitute journalism for government, I remain skeptical. That seems like public nonjournalism, and many other institutions are better suited to it. No other institution can inform, monitor, and critique. There is no alternative outside check. The press shouldn't try to be another branch of government; it must be the trunk of an entirely different tree.

Finally, this needn't be a holy war. Why make public journalism a take-it-or-leave-it package?

In many ways, public journalism's hardest work has been done; it has broken down barriers to change. It has energized the news community and mustered momentum that shouldn't go to waste.

I don't know that public journalism will triumph as a "movement." Its supporters would do well to frame it less as the Reformation and more as lower-case reform, a set of interesting experiments.

But critics should respond with more than complacency or contempt. Public journalism arrives at a ripe moment, when the market mentality seems on the verge of stifling public service ideals. Its gathering momentum heartens all supporters of change. A powerful lever is within reach, for who knows what brief period, and journalists everywhere should be leaping to grab it.

18

Missing the Point

Davis "Buzz" Merritt

The reporter on the phone wanted to talk about public journalism.

"Sure, happy to," I said.

"Okay, now public journalism is where you write a story and show it to readers to see if it's all right to print, right?"

"Uh, I think we need a longer conversation."

I'm not making this up. The anecdote is an admittedly abberational but approximate indicator of why no useful discussion of public journalism *as an idea or philosophy* has occurred within our profession. Instead, controversy—often rancorous—over experimental techniques has been at the forefront. To be informed about a controversy is not the same as engaging an idea.

It's time that engagement took place, for there is much within the philosophy of public journalism that warrants close, critical, and creative examination by the best minds in our business. I am confident that the core ideas, once considered, will withstand such scrutiny, but as no such examination and engagement have yet occurred, no one really knows if that is so.

Bear in mind that my use of such phrases as "public journalism says . . ." is a writing convenience and should be preceded by "in Merritt's view" in all cases. There is no Church of Public Journalism and no catechism, to employ the regrettable and seemingly unshakable evange-

This article originally appeared in *American Journalism Review,* July/August 1996. Reprinted by permission of *American Journalism Review.*

listic metaphor applied in *American Journalism Review* in the very first national piece on public journalism ("The Gospel of Public Journalism," September 1994). Those of us thinking and writing about this idea are hardly monolithic; we differ on many points. Nor do we claim either the ability or the aspiration to "fix" things—except insofar as citizens can be empowered to fix things themselves. But we do share at least three characteristics:

• Seriousness of purpose.

• Conviction that journalism has an obligation to public life beyond merely telling the news.

• Frustration that the discussion we are trying to induce is drowned out by the *Sturm und Drang* of debate and angry dismissiveness based not on what we are saying but on what some journalists say we are saying.

A notable if only recent exception was Carl Sessions Stepp's thoughtful book review and essay . . . "Public Journalism: Balancing the Scales."* That piece, Stepp wrote, "attempts to steer the debate toward a demilitarized zone and probe the underpinnings of this revolution-in-the-making."

What follows is part response to Stepp and part invitation to other thoughtful journalists. It's time for the profession to suspend the tag-team wrestling match over early public journalism experiments—some of which, in my view, have been clearly misguided and have gone too far—and replace it with critical examination of public journalism's intellectual roots. Only in that context can a truly useful and needed debate occur.

A review of public journalism's brief history is instructive in understanding why—despite dozens of panel discussions, many simmering tavern debates and a couple hundred articles and papers in the last two years—the fundamental ideas of public journalism remain largely unexplored by the profession at large.

Start with the fact that journalists, by nature and necessity, are pragmatic, results-driven people. For the most part we say, "Don't bother me with philosophy. Tell me how to do it; I've got a paper to get out." Or, as often, "Just give me a two-graf definition, and I'll decide if I like it or not."

Public journalism isn't that easy; if it were, it wouldn't be potentially important or particularly interesting; it would be merely a different, if controversial, technique. But public journalism is much more than technique. It requires a philosophical journey because it is a fundamental change in how we conceive of our role in public life.

---

*Chapter 17 in this volume. (Eds.)

The yearning for a facile definition and the fact that public journalism was first expressed in large projects invited journalists to regard it as a set of practices rather than as a philosophy. Public journalism became "focus groups" and "polling" and "holding forums" and "setting agendas" and "getting involved in the news" and "asking readers." A parallel definitional trap would be to define investigative journalism as "going to the courthouse to look up records." The tools have become identified as the thing itself.

The diversion is understandable given the pragmatic and often mimicking nature of journalists; but as a result, the debate thus far has been limited to techniques and focused on experiments undertaken by some well-intentioned practitioners who hadn't themselves taken the philosophical journey.

The first two steps on the journey are:

• Acceptance of the fact that—whether or not we like it or are comfortable with it—in the media age journalism is an integral part of the system of public life, an active, even if unwilling, participant in it.

Public life is the arena in which democracy is expressed and experienced, including but not limited to formal politics. How we do our journalism has direct and lasting impact on how public life goes, intended or not. In a word, journalists are unavoidably "players"—even though their proper role is not to be partisan or political in the traditional sense.

• Recognition that journalism's integral role in public life imposes an obligation on us.

The obligation is to do our journalism in ways that are calculated to help public life go well *by reengaging people in it.* Public life "going well" means, most simply put, that democracy succeeds in answering its core question: What shall we do? The answer, in a democracy, should be found by informed and engaged citizens. (Another way to express this is building "civic capital," a residue of knowledge and experience in the art of democracy.) Public journalism does not attempt to forge *its own* answer to the question. Rather, it actively seeks to help citizens arrive at *their* answer.

I believe the first point is inarguable, for to deny it is to deny that journalism is of any consequence whatsoever, which in turn would raise, unavoidably, the question of "Why do it?"

The second point is one of departure, for it requires taking a step away from traditional journalistic detachment. It calls for purposefulness and declared intent as we go about our work.

And it is precisely at this point that much concern and some confusion arises. Most journalists hear the critique of detachment and take not a step but a mental leap: If we're not talking about detachment, they say, then we must be talking about attachment; and if we're talking about attachment, then we must be talking about abandoning such indisputably important and useful roles as watchdog, outsider from government, independent observer, uninvolved-and-thus-credible source of information.

Some recent experiments under the name of public journalism, unfortunately and avoidably, have left themselves open to criticism because they have abandoned one or more of those ideals. But that need not be the case.

Public journalism and those traditional ideals are neither in conflict nor mutually exclusive. Public journalism adds to those ideals an additional imperative: concern for whether citizens become engaged in public life. For if people are not engaged, democracy fails. And—a lesser but important point for us—if people are not engaged in public life they have no need for journalists or journalism.

Public journalism is not aimed at solving problems; it is aimed at reengaging citizens in solving problems. It does not seek to join with or substitute itself for government (in either case an outrageous and impossible aspiration); it seeks to keep citizens in effective contact with the governing process. Its goal is not to better connect journalists with their communities, but to better connect the people in communities with one another. So public journalism is as much or more about public life than it is about journalism, a fact universally overlooked in the wild thrust and parry over technique and sacred, uncrossable lines.

In this respect, it's regrettable that public journalism was first expressed in large-scale projects (starting with the 1990 Voter Project and 1992 People Project at my newspaper, the *Wichita Eagle*). Those early projects gained some considerable attention, which led to wrong questions being asked. The question from ever-pragmatic journalists was always "*How* did you do it?" rather than "*Why* did you do it?"

The "how" answers focused the attention on technique, leading to mimicking of the "how" without regard for the critically important "why." For better or worse, "doing public journalism" became the objective and, in some precincts, a mandate, despite no grasp of underlying purpose. Let's be clear about this: It's silly—and dangerous—to set out to "do public journalism" simply because that's what some people are doing, or that's what the boss said, or that's one of our newsroom goals this year. If you don't "get it" philosophically, you won't get it right.

The project-oriented beginning, while perhaps unavoidable (and, at any rate, a fact), masked the underlying principles and delayed the idea's maturation. The useful future of public journalism is not in major projects, media combines, public forums, or the simplistic airing of the views of underinformed citizens. Its useful future lies in our learning to do daily and weekly journalism in ways that reengage people with public life. The way we now do "routine" reporting systematically discourages people about public life, including politics. "Learning" is an important word here, because no one really knows how to do that yet; it's an unfulfilled intellectual and occupational challenge.

This much is clear: Doing public journalism on a daily and weekly basis requires us to reexamine and modify some of our reflexes. We developed the reflexes to enable us to perform, under pressure, our daily and hourly reporting miracles. But they no longer serve us—or public life—well.

Those reflexes include:

- The overvaluation of conflict as a primary narrative device. (No, refining this reflex doesn't mean ignoring conflict, for conflict is the lifeblood of democracy.)

- Framing issues at the extremes, which not only has the disadvantages of inaccuracy, but which also relentlessly discourages the ambivalent majority of people from thinking usefully about those issues. (No, this doesn't mandate dull ambiguity; it permits more people to see themselves as included in the discussion.)

- Indulging in and clearly communicating a snarly adversarialism toward every person and institution instead of maintaining proper and useful journalistic skepticism. (No, this doesn't drug the watchdog; it keeps him from consuming his owner.)

- Imagining readers as our audience or as spectators at an event that we are reporting on rather than imagining them as potential participants. (No, adjusting this reflex doesn't mean exhorting people to "get involved," it means allowing them to see ways to do so.)

- Insisting that our credibility arises from our detachment, despite strong arguments to the contrary. This leads us into the trap of publicly claiming to be value-neutral when every person alive knows better. (No, this doesn't mean espousing personal values in print; it means declaring the core value that we have a stake in public life going well.)

These and related reflexes are deeply ingrained and not comfortably challenged. But public journalism is cultural, generational change, and neither its practice nor a useful discussion of it can be centered on shortcuts, gimmicks, and superficial understanding of its principles. It's past time for a useful discussion. Let's begin with the question democracy always comes to: What shall we do?

19

A Statement of Concern

Committee of Concerned Journalists

The Committee of Concerned Journalists is a consortium of reporters, editors, producers, publishers, owners, and academics worried about the future of the profession.

The group believes this is a critical moment in American journalism. Revolutionary changes in technology, in economic equations, in our relationship with the public, threaten the core principles that define journalism's role in democratic society.

Faced with splintering audiences and information overload, companies at once diversifying and merging and confronted by unimaginable complexity, we have begun to doubt ourselves and the meaning of our profession.

To secure journalism's future, the group believes that journalists from all media, geography, rank, and generation must be clear about what sets our profession apart from other endeavors. To accomplish this, the group wants to create a national conversation among journalists about principles.

The conversation has three goals: To clarify and renew journalists' faith in the core principles and function of journalism. To create a better understanding of those principles by the public. To engage and inform ownership and management of these principles and their financial as well as social value.

First, the group issued a statement of concern, articulating the need for such a process for self-examination, and creating a network of concerned professionals nationwide.

Then it set out to initiate a discussion about principles through many means. These include nearly a dozen public forums nationwide that examine key questions of principles, how and why we may not always be living up to those principles, and looking at which traditions of journalism may no longer be relevant to contemporary society.

The conversation will also include in-depth interviews with journalism leaders, a Website and discussion group about principles and ethics, a major survey of journalists about core values, a variety of empirical studies about press performance, teaching videos, and more. Committee members have come forward with ideas for various papers to present at the forums and a documentary. The group will listen carefully for common ground, and then prepare a written report that identifies shared principles.

The effort was convened by the Nieman Foundation and the Project for Excellence in Journalism* in June 1997 in Boston. The committee is a diverse group, from David Halberstam, the New York author, to Mark Trahant, the Navajo newspaper editor from Idaho; from Lucy Himstedt Riley, a news director in Montgomery, Alabama, to Vanessa Williams of the *Washington Post* and the president of the National Association of Black Journalists.

The group has no hidden or pre-set agenda. It is not interested in placing owners at odds with reporters, journalism with business, print with TV or the Internet. Its members are simply united in the belief that journalism is a unique form of communication. It is a mission, a service. We must clarify what that means—and remind ourselves why we were called to it in the first place—or it will cease to mean anything.

---

*See the following article. (Eds.)

20

Local TV News Project

The Project for Excellence in Journalism

In an initiative to clarify the definition of quality in local television news, PEJ [Project for Excellence in Journalism] will bring the practice of benchmarking—identifying models of quality in an industry—to local TV news. The backbone of the project will be a landmark attempt by a design team of local news professionals to create a basic model of quality that is grounded in reality, market success, and tenets of sound journalism.

HOW IT WILL WORK

This project involves three steps.

First, it will gather the leading local TV news professionals together to develop and create an empirical model of quality for local news based on their experience and expertise. This group, comprised of industry leaders, will meet in September [1997] to start the process.

Next, a team of top scholars, working under the design team, will measure the stations in twenty to twenty-five markets against this practitioners' model of quality.

The results will be then published annually in the *Columbia Journalism Review*. This project is funded initially for three years.

THE GOALS

The project is not grounded in any assumptions about quality; that is up to the local TV news professionals to decide. The idea, rather, is simply to bring the best minds in local TV together to develop standards, measure stations against that model and publish the results. The goal is to produce something as useful as possible to the industry. In that spirit, the two guidelines are that the project would come from local news professionals and would emphasize rewarding good work rather than merely criticizing bad.

This project will also be a major effort to test the relationship between content and ratings.

MORE ABOUT PEJ

The Project for Excellence in Journalism is an initiative by journalists to clarify and raise the standards of American journalism. This is a critical moment for the American press. While in many ways journalism is better than ever—consider the tools and talent in the profession—as journalism's means have grown, its ends have become less clear.

Revolutionary changes in technology, in the economics of news and the relationship with the public have left many news organizations uncertain about the future. In response, journalists are too often losing confidence in their professionalism and purpose.

Increasingly, the mission of journalism is seemingly overwhelmed by the sheer size of the media, by hidebound habits, by the values of entertainment, by the quest for sensation and gossip, by the imperatives of the stock market, or by a pursuit of ever-fragmenting audiences that lead us ever farther from home.

It is uncertain whether the essential mission of journalism—to be a public service for democracy—always remains clearly in mind. The crisis in journalism is a crisis of conviction.

We should not lose faith. The surest way for journalism to survive is by emphasizing what makes it unique—its basic purpose and core standards. Even in a new era, journalism has one responsibility other forms of communication and entertainment do not: to provide citizens with the information they need to navigate the society. That does not preclude being entertaining or profitable—or publishing something merely because it's interesting. That does not mean journalism should not abandon failed habits in the way we present news.

But it does imply a commitment to comprehensiveness, to offering certain information about democratic institutions, and to ordering information in some relationship to its significance so that people can use it as a map to travel through the culture.

The project pursues the aim of clarifying standards by bringing journalists together to decide for themselves what their purpose and aims are. It will do this first by sponsoring with the Nieman Foundation at Harvard the Committee of Concerned Journalists, which will call journalists to a period of national reflection through a series of nationwide public forums and a landmark report on the purpose of journalism. It will then engage in a series of follow-up projects to monitor the press's performance, including an extraordinary series on the state of the American newspaper edited by Gene Roberts, by a major study of local television news, and by a series of smaller projects examining discrete issues facing the profession.

Because our principal audience is working journalists, our projects will produce something useful and widely understood. To be relevant to our owners, even those who may have no historic stake in journalism, the project's work must be grounded in market reality. Since journalism's thriving depends on the public having some understanding of what distinguishes it from other forms of media, the project must involve the public.

Our aim, moreover, is not primarily on diagnosing the press' problems. It is on creating initiatives that can clarify what journalism's essential role is and identify examples of good journalism around the country that personify that.

The project is part of the Columbia University Graduate School of Journalism. It is underwritten by the Pew Charitable Trusts. It has initial funding for three years.

21

Should the Coverage Fit the Crime?
A Texas TV Station Tries to Resist
the Allure of Mayhem

Joe Holley

It's ten o'clock and news viewers across the country know where they'll be for the next few minutes: at the scene of the crime.

Crime and violence—what the Denver-based Rocky Mountain Media Watch calls "mayhem"—are as ubiquitous on local news shows as the winsome male-female anchor team and the happy chat between bite-sized bits of coverage. Critics argue that this mayhem not only crowds out more legitimate news but skews reality, that local TV newscasts must share responsibility for the fact that, at a time when crime rates across the country are going down, public anxiety about crime continues to rise.

What if a TV news operation refused to cover crime in the same old way? Would crime still make the same noise in the community? Would the station?

Since the beginning of [1996], Austin's ABC affiliate, KVUE-TV. a Gannett station, has been trying to find out. KVUE's experiment not only has given Austin[, Texas,] viewers something of a choice, but it has forced the station's staff to reassess long-held assumptions about how to cover crime, or even whether to cover it. It has forced reporters, editors, and news directors to ask that more basic question: What is news?

Partly because violent crime is relatively rare in the city, Austin TV has never been terribly crime-obsessed. But after a complicated net-

Reprinted from *Columbia Journalism Review,* May/June 1996. © 1996 by *Columbia Journalism Review.*

work-affiliation swap [in 1995], the local CBS station, renamed K-EYE, hit the market with a bagful of gimmicks, razzle-dazzle graphics, and hyperbole, focusing attention on the way crime gets covered. K-EYE's yen for mayhem may be only slightly more knee-jerk than its competitors', but its approach underscored the public's impression that local TV news thrives on violence and disaster. Although K-EYE's ratings remain in single digits nearly a year after the affiliation shuffle, the station has stayed with its format.

It was KVUE, meanwhile, the longtime ratings pacesetter, that decided to try to break its Pavlovian response to the squawking police scanner and the melodramatic visuals.

Now, before a crime story makes it on the air on KVUE, it must meet one or more of five criteria:

1) Does action need to be taken?
2) Is there an immediate threat to safety?
3) Is there a threat to children?
4) Does the crime have significant community impact?
5) Does the story lend itself to a crime-prevention effort?

No sooner were these guidelines installed on January 21[, 1996,] than they were tested by a trio of murder stories. In early February, in the small town of Elgin, thirty miles east of Austin and in the KVUE viewing area, three men shot and killed each other during a Saturday-night brawl. The triple murder failed to make the KVUE newscast.

The station's three competitors aired the story. "When somebody's killed, that's news," says Jeff Godlis, K-EYE's news director. But to Mike George, KVUE's news manager, the incident was unfortunate, but it wasn't news. George points out that a KVUE reporter drove to Elgin twice to investigate. She found that the men, all Mexican nationals, were not permanent Elgin residents, and that the dispute that prompted the shootings was an isolated incident fueled by drugs and alcohol.

"There was no immediate threat to public safety, no threat to children, and there was really no action that you would take, other than to say, 'I don't want to go to that part of Elgin,' " says Cathy McFeaters, KVUE's executive producer. "It really wasn't a crime-prevention story, so then the question becomes significant community impact, and the reaction that we got by just asking people about it was that they weren't too concerned." Staff members worried that some might think the reason this story did not air had to do with the nationality of the killers and victims. "We talked about whether it would make a difference if these guys were from Lubbock or New York or wherever," McFeaters says. "It didn't."

The second story, during the third week of the experiment, involved a man who stabbed his wife in the front yard of their home and then barricaded himself inside the house. Some of KVUE's competitors reported live from the scene.

KVUE's reporter on the scene found that the man inside the house was eighty-two years old, could barely walk, and was nearly blind. He had no criminal record and seemed to present no threat to neighbors or to the police. Again, the incident didn't meet the guidelines, and KVUE did not air the story.

The third story took place in a Wal-Mart parking lot, where a twenty-one-year-old man, after an argument inside the store with two teenagers, was shot and killed when he walked outside. Because the perpetrators were at large at the time of the newscast, thus meeting the threat-to-public-safety guideline, and because the shooting happened in a busy Wal-Mart parking lot, the story easily met KVUE's guidelines.

"Austin police need your help today," KVUE anchor Walt Maciborski began. "They are looking for suspects in a murder at a Wal-Mart store. The shooting happened in the parking lot of the store in Northeast Austin last night. . . . Police arrested a sixteen-year-old at his home this morning and charged him with murder. They are looking at store surveillance tape to find other suspects." A seventeen-year-old was later arrested and charged.

McFeaters, KVUE's thirty-one-year-old executive producer, is the catalyst for the crime-coverage experiment. An associate producer at KVUE during and after her college years at the University of Texas at Austin, she then went to the Gannett station in Jacksonville, Florida, and took a job in 1991 as a producer at ABC's WSOC in Charlotte, North Carolina. That ABC affiliate bears the dubious distinction of being the ninth-worst station for excessive "mayhem" out of a hundred that the Rocky Mountain Media Watch group examined last fall. (The top three stations on the "mayhem index" are WLKY-TV, Louisville, Kentucky; KNBC-TV, Los Angeles; and KFOR-TV, Oklahoma City.)

"That was the first time I had worked for a metered market, where you live or die by the daily ratings," McFeaters recalls. "You lead with crime. I always understood the thing about ratings, because I'm a very competitive person, and I love to be first. But being number one revolved around the lowest common denominator, and I got disgusted with it. But how could I argue, because we were doing really well?"

The solution, McFeaters thought, was to leave the business. She reached the nadir, she says, with a story about bestiality; she'd rather not recall the details. But in plotting her escape from WSOC, she discovered by accident that KVUE had an opening. Her boss there would be Carole Kneeland, a respected broadcast veteran who happened to share McFeaters's concerns about crime coverage.

Kneeland, who is forty-seven, was the capital bureau chief for nearly eleven years for Dallas's WFAA-TV before becoming KVUE's news director in 1989. Like McFeaters, she has long been concerned about what she calls local TV's overcoverage of crime and disaster. For her, a story that KVUE ran [in the] fall [of 1995] seemed to crystallize the issue. A pickup truck swerved off the highway and into the playground of a day care center, killing a child. It was a poignant story, but it happened in California. The story ran in Austin and elsewhere for one reason: the heartbreaking video of the little body lying on the playground.

Not long after that, Kneeland and McFeaters began putting together their crime-coverage concept. The station had been convening monthly community meetings for the previous year, and from those meetings they already knew that the coverage of crime and violence was a persistent viewer complaint.

"We wouldn't even have to ask about it specifically," Kneeland says. "We'd say, 'What do you think about local news coverage?' The first thing they'd always react with was, 'It's too violent. It's too sensational.' Or, 'There's too much crime coverage with no significance.' "

"I remember talking to Carole, and I said, just jokingly, 'I just wonder what would happen if no one covered crime?' " McFeaters recalls. "It wasn't like a mission of mine or anything; it was almost out of spite for Charlotte."

It was also a marketing strategy, she admits. "That is not why we are doing it, but that's certainly a part of it. I felt sure that people would appreciate this and would watch us because of it."

The two women encouraged the news staff to begin analyzing how —and why—the station was covering crime stories. "The reasons [reporters] gave about why something ought to he covered—'Somebody ought to do something about that!' or 'It affects the community'—gradually became the categories," Kneeland recalls. Informal criteria evolved over a period of three or four months.

The station's general manager, Ardyth Diercks at the time, signed off on the experiment in early December. Kneeland and McFeaters laid the final guidelines out for the staff on January 10[, 1996]. With a promotion barrage and explanatory spots during the newscasts, the station put the plan into practice a week and a half later.

A number of viewers complain that they got tired of *hearing* about the new approach. Indeed, until March, the explanation and promotion of the new guidelines were woven right into the newscast. A crime story typically concluded with a graphic of the new guidelines, with big red check marks on which guidelines the story was deemed to have met. There were oral explanations as well. "Today's marijuana bust is an example of a crimefighting or crime-prevention effort, one of the guidelines we're using now to change the way we cover crime," anchor Judy Maggio told her viewers in February. "The project is KVUE Listens To You On Crime. We're still going to cover crime, but we're doing it in a less violent and sensational way. We would like to hear your feedback." She went on to say that she and "Bob"—coanchor Bob Karstens—would host a discussion about the station's new crime-coverage philosophy on America Online that evening.

The response to the experiment itself has been overwhelmingly positive. "A big congratulations to KVUE for the efforts to keep unimportant violence off television . . ." reads a typical fax. "We are not interested in gory details about who got smeared on the interstate, who got murdered, etc.," reads another.

Austin Police Chief Elizabeth Watson, an outspoken advocate of community policing in this rapidly growing city of more than half a million people, also endorses KVUE's new approach, while she is critical of K-EYE's razzle-dazzle. "I think that it is commendable for a major TV news station to really take a look at responsible reporting, commendable from a community service standpoint." she says. "Sensationalized reporting fuels fear. It makes people feel powerless."

But when does "responsible reporting," to use Chief Watson's term, become a kind of cheerleading for local law enforcement or a device for self-censorship? In the first few weeks of the experiment, the station seemed to be blurring the distinction between straight reporting and being "a responsible member of the community." Its incessant efforts to tease out crime-prevention tips in every story often sounded more like police public-service announcements than news stories.

"We've got these neat little guidelines," reporter Kim Barnes says, "which means we've got to give a solution, so let's give some tips. My concern is that so much of our focus and concern is on getting the sidebar [the crime-prevention tips] that we're not getting the who, what, when, and where—which is our primary job."

Some viewers consider the KVUE experiment an effort to avoid reality. "Grow up," one viewer urged in another fax. "The world is violent. Your ignorance of it doesn't make it less violent. It only makes it more palatable to you when you stick your heads in the sand."

A similar objection came from Joe Phelps, pastor of an American Baptist church in an Austin suburb. "Frankly," the minister wrote in an op-ed piece that ran in the *Austin American-Statesman,* "hearing about violence is the least we can do to remain connected with our fellow citizens, our kin, who experience such tragedy. The reporting should not be sensationalized. Pictures may not always be appropriate. But the reality that people kill and are killed on a regular basis is newsworthy. We need to hear it."

Competitor K-EYE, meanwhile, is trying to make a little ratings hay with that no-crime perception of KVUE. "Is your newscast giving you all the news?" K-EYE's latest promo asks, a not-so-subtle dig at KVUE's highly publicized crime diet.

For Kneeland, McFeaters, and others at KVUE, the perception that the station no longer covers crime has been frustrating. When critics call, Mike George takes pains to explain the distinction the station makes between covering a crime story and airing it. His reporters listen to the police scanner just as they always have, he explains, and they still investigate crime and violence. But after they've asked the questions and nosed around the crime scene, they now have to decide whether the story is worth putting on the air. And if it's worth putting on the air, is it worth "packaging," giving it the full story-and-pictures approach? "This policy makes us think about the way we cover crime," George says. "It's just like any other story: we ask the question 'Why is this important?' "

"What we're trying to get away from is an automatic response to the way we cover crime," McFeaters says. "We're not trying to deny the ugliness in the world; that's not what this is about. However, we have a responsibility not to give that ugliness more play than it deserves."

McFeaters draws a sharp distinction between what KVUE is doing and the "family-sensitive" approach, pioneered by WCCO-TV in Minneapolis, one of a handful of stations around the country that are spurning violent, manipulative, and emotion-laden newscasts. The Minneapolis station pledges that its 5 P.M. newscast will never contain material that a family with children watching would find offensive. To McFeaters, such a pledge is a gimmick, in effect a kind of self-censorship. The Minneapolis station, she says, allowed the perception to develop that it had, in effect, "gone soft" on crime. She doesn't want that to happen to KVUE, and the station's promotional efforts are aimed at heading off that notion.

It is a Monday night toward the end of February, and McFeaters and Kneeland have called a meeting of the newsroom staff to assess their experiment. Minutes after anchors Bob Karstens and Judy Maggio wrap up the 6 P.M. newscast with a bit of happy chat with weatherman Mark Murray, the staff gathers around a white oval table in the corner of the large, airy newsroom. Behind them, floor-to-ceiling inverted-V windows in a stark white wall offer views of suburban Austin at dusk.

Maggio and Karstens sit side by side at one end of the table, just as they do on the set. Reporters, editors, producers, directors, news managers, engineers, and photographers, a couple of dozen in all, slouch in chairs and on desks or lean against the wall around the table. Several of their colleagues scurry about the newsroom getting ready for the 10 P.M. newscast. It's a youthful-looking group; the average age is probably under thirty.

Three video cameras record the gathering as McFeaters opens the meeting with a videotape of another gathering—a viewer focus group that had met several times over a two-month period. The seven members of this group—young and old; black, white, and brown; male and female—are thoughtful and articulate and uniformly supportive of the station's crime-coverage experiment. "I have to be perfectly honest," says Ora Houston, a grandmotherly African-American woman. "I have not missed the crime or the mayhem or the stabbings. It's like my life is much more settled, it's calmer. We know crime's going on. In our neighborhood, we're trying to be proactive about it, but we don't need to see it every day."

The tape ends. Standing in the shadows away from the table, McFeaters says, "Let's start with some of your frustrations."

A reporter replies: "Sometimes it's difficult when there's something you're not covering, and you know the other stations are covering it, and you wonder whether you're doing your job." Another says she worries about digging for the deeper angle and slighting the "who, what, when, where, why. Are we fulfilling our core responsibility?" Someone else, expanding on the thought, suggests a billboard-type graphic that would display such information, without pictures. Somebody else comments that "People are saying, 'Oh, y'all are the station that doesn't cover crime anymore.' "

"One of the frustrations is that we've made the decision that this particular life is more important than another one," reporter and weekend anchor Wendy Erikson says. "A family is out there saying, 'My family deserved at least a fifteen-second notice.' "

"Of course, we make those decisions all the time," McFeaters replies, "when we don't report the death of someone with AIDS or cancer or a baby that's died of SIDS." She adds that the only strong complaint she's heard about the experiment is about the promotion. "They're saying, 'All right, already! Quit telling us what you're going to do and just do it!' "

The group discusses ratings and how long the experiment might last if ratings slip. "Hypothetically, what if it costs us number one?" asks reporter Greg Groogan, surveying the faces of his colleagues. "Do we stand on principle, or do we backtrack?" Groogan urges taking a stand.

"I think we do have a more intelligent group of people here in Austin than in other cities," Carole Kneeland says, "so if it can work anywhere, I think it will work here."

Everyone around the table on Monday night was keenly aware that the experiment had undergone its most severe test just a day earlier, February 25. Groogan, who usually covers politics and investigative projects, had been doing weekend duty as part of a skeleton staff. He had arrived at work on Sunday thinking that he had made it through more than a month of the experiment without having to make a critical news judgment. A few minutes later he and photographer Chris Davis were rushing to the scene of a shooting at an apartment complex for married students at the University of Texas.

"We confirmed that there were three dead on the scene," he recalls, "and the thought process began right then. 'Is this going to meet the guidelines? If this was murder, was the murderer still at large? Was there an issue of public safety?' "

It seemed that a graduate student in engineering had shot his wife and four-year-old daughter and then turned the gun on himself. "We had a hook," Groogan says. "It was the first murder on UT properties since the Charles Whitman shootings from the UT tower in 1966. That wasn't a bad hook, but that wasn't going to cut it under our new guidelines."

Meanwhile, University of Texas police had found a weapon and told Groogan they had a 911 tape of the woman calling for help. Campus police were slow to provide much more, and the 5:30 newscast was looming. "We still weren't there," Groogan recalls, "at least for the early show."

If not for the guidelines, Groogan would already have been back at the station with a story in the can. Viewers might not have seen body bags, as they did on K-EYE that evening, but they might have heard the 911 tape and gotten the details about three violent deaths. Now, however, Groogan couldn't find a justification for airing the story: there was no immediate threat to the community, the crime itself was solved, and there was really nothing to say about prevention. There seemed to be no significant community impact; the family was new to the apartment complex, and the neighbors barely knew them. The guideline about children? In this case, the child was dead.

Back at the station, Sunday anchor Wendy Erikson had another killing on her hands, and another decision about the guidelines—an apparent drive-by shooting on Austin's predominantly black and Hispanic east side that had taken place late Saturday night. The suspect was in custody, there was no threat to children, no threat to the community.

"We were between a rock and a hard place," Groogan says. "With our limited weekend staff, we could follow both stories and still not get them on the air. We called Carole at home."

Erikson, thirty, is from suburban Chicago, where, she says, "I grew up watching death and destruction" on TV. She would have aired both Sunday stories without a second thought—before the experiment. Now she found herself in something of an ironic situation. Kneeland wanted to run the drive-by shooting story, but Erikson didn't believe it met the criteria Kneeland herself had developed. "Our credibility is on the line," Erikson told her boss.

"Carole told us to start digging on both, looking for larger issues," Groogan recalls. "She said, 'We cannot drop these stories. If we don't go on the air, that's the price we pay, but we cannot use these guidelines as an excuse not to cover them. Our job is to gather facts and then decide whether to air. The guidelines are not an excuse for not doing the nuts-and-bolts job of reporting.' "

Groogan and other reporters dug. Although neither story made the 5:30 newscast (except for a brief mention of the East Austin murder), Erikson fully aired them both at ten.

The story of the apparent murder/suicide at the university apartment complex focused on the immediate community's response to the tragedy. The residents of the apartment complex gathered at sunset on a playground and talked over what had happened, among themselves and with Groogan. Groogan also listened as counselors talked to the residents about signs of domestic abuse, which was an issue in the investigation, and what they could do to help prevent it.

Groogan believes that the guidelines forced him to stay with the story, and that this extra effort paid off in context and perspective. "In this place," Groogan reported at ten that night, "where small children are constantly at play, there is a new fear—a fear of guns. They're supposed to be illegal on all university property. Residents wonder if other neighbors have ignored the ban." The visuals were subdued—the apartment complex, children playing there, and, from a distance, the residents in discussion.

KVUE also determined that the other shooting, in East Austin, had significant community impact as well, and in ways KVUE might have missed had it covered the incident simply as a drive-by shooting. Groogan and reporter Robbie Owens—who was pulled off another story to explore the community's response—discovered a predominantly black neighborhood eager to let the rest of Austin know that this was not just another stereotypical incident. "Although this is a terrible time for Bobby Reed's family and friends, they want Austin to know that this was not a gang shooting or a crack deal gone bad," Robbie Owens explained on the air. "It was a family gathered—laughing, talking, and eating enchiladas. Then, witnesses say a white man pulled up, exchanged some words—including a racial slur aimed at the black family gathering. They say he then fired a shotgun, hitting two people, one of them Bobby Reed, who died. But tonight some family and friends say their concern right now is not about hatred, but about loss."

"We had a family pleading for peace, and the community impacted was more than just that block where he lived," Cathy McFeaters says. "It was all of East Austin, all of black Austin."

"I believe that Sunday night newscast was a litmus test," Groogan says. "To Wendy's credit and to our producers' credit, they didn't want to be hypocrites. To Carole's credit, she sensed that by digging a little deeper and looking a little wider, we could still cover those stories without breaking our commitment."

Wendy Erikson still feels a little unsettled by that Sunday experience, however. On the earlier newscasts, "all other stations aired both stories," she recalls, "and I was literally anchoring and feeling that we weren't covering crime. We had four people dead on a quiet Sunday, and we weren't covering it. I've been taught to present the facts, and now I'm in this position where I'm having to decide whether this particular story is something I feel viewers should see.

"I'm in transition," she adds. "I'm uncomfortable with the guidelines right now, but part of me does feel very good thinking I may somehow be contributing to a change in our society."

Is changing society a journalistic concern? Can new journalistic guidelines also be promotional vehicles? And can thoughtful coverage of important local issues, crime included, compete with gripping images of maimed victims and distraught relatives? "Crime is punctuation," anchor Bob Karstens says. "It grips people. It's hard-edged. The challenge for us is to find stories with the same hard edge that aren't crime stories." McFeaters, who takes pride in the flashy Florida TV tricks she picked up in Jacksonville, believes KVUE can offer good journalism *and* good TV.

She acknowledges that ratings will ultimately determine the fate of KVUE's experiment, but she hopes the station doesn't rush to judgment. "They usually give news directors and anchors two or three years, football coaches two or three seasons before they off 'em," she says. "I don't think you draw any conclusions by one book." If ratings slip, McFeaters says she'll blame the presentation, not the concept, and she'll press to keep trying.

"We characterize it as an experiment, because it is," she says, but adds, "It's not an experiment in the sense that there's an end to this, it's not a one-shot deal. There's no way that at the end of the month Carole or I can walk out into the newsroom and announce, 'Okay, now we can start covering crime the way we were.' This newsroom is forever changed. Everyone is going to look at how they cover crime differently from now on."

The February ratings came out in mid-March. They were KVUE's best ever. The station increased its already-solid ratings lead for every newscast, reaching its highest numbers in a decade for its 10 P.M. show. The crime-coverage experiment continues.

Part II

ENTERTAINMENT MEDIA AND ETHICS

Chapter Four

Entertainment Media
and Ethics:
The Terrain

22

Morally Offensive Content: Freedom and Responsibility

Louis A. Day

... The practice of journalism resides at the core of First Amendment values, but reporters are often confronted with an ethical quandary when it comes to including material that might offend the moral sensibilities of the audience. Should a videotape of nudity, for example, be included in a TV news report if such visuals contribute to the public's understanding of the story? Should public figures be subjected to a different standard from ordinary citizens when deciding whether to include quotes containing "colorful" and indecent language? Should offensive language be deleted from a quote or cleaned up to avoid embarrassment to the interviewee and offense to the readers or viewers?

Of course, altering a quote raises an ethical question within itself from the standpoint of truth and accuracy. Some publications employ what they believe to be a reasonable compromise by printing the first letter of the questionable word followed by a series of dashes. TV stations often "bleep" offensive language uttered by newsworthy subjects, which again raises questions of journalistic accuracy. The size and nature of the market often determine how liberal media practitioners can be toward reproducing scatological language, but most are still reluctant to challenge the public's tolerance for such material.

When public figures are concerned, and that includes professional athletes, the question of whether to report profane language becomes a

Originally published in Louis A. Day, *Ethics in Media Communications: Cases and Controversies* (Belmont, Calif.: Wadsworth Publishing Company, 1991). Reprinted by permission.

matter of ethical gamesmanship. Some editors take the position that if the questionable comments are essential to the story, they should be left in. Others are more comfortable with the use of euphemisms and indirect quotes in which the offensive remarks are sanitized. This is often a close call and may depend on the news figure's status and the context in which the remarks are made. It may also depend on the specific expressions used. The English language contains many words that are offensive to society's linguistic norms, but some are considered more indecent than others. Certain references to specific sexual acts and other bodily functions are usually taboo in the mainstream media, whereas some words that were once forbidden, such as *bastard,* are now commonplace. In fact, until recently even the word *condom* was shunned by the networks' program decision makers.

Sports figures are particularly troublesome, because their interviews are often peppered with colorful expletives. Sports editors usually sanitize these remarks before publication, although some use the "bleep" technique as a substitute for offensive language. Such editing can be justified, according to the rule stated above, because the rough language found in most interviews with sports figures is seldom essential to an understanding of the story. Nevertheless, there are times when an athlete's reaction to a situation is so revealing that an exact quote is justified.

This decision may depend, of course, on the readership of the publication. *Sports Illustrated,* which appeals to fans, might feel more comfortable with including offensive quotes from athletes than would magazines with a more diverse audience. In 1989, for example, the magazine published an article featuring the newly hired coach of the Chicago Blackhawks hockey team, Mike Keenan. In response to a question concerning his reputation as a tough-minded coach, Keenan said: "I've matured as a coach. My public persona is still the hard ass, the son of a bitch, but that's not accurate."[1] It is unlikely that many of the readers of the magazine would have been offended by this remark. But in addition, one might argue that this language was no more offensive than that offered up in prime time by the commercial networks. Cultural norms do change, and language that was unacceptable just ten years ago is now common in the mass media.

It is safe to say that most newsroom policies are fairly conservative on the matter of offensive and indecent language. A 1985 survey of twenty-five editors of daily newspapers in New England, for example, revealed a "family-newspaper" philosophy in the publication of such material. The *Portland Press-Herald,* in Maine, acknowledged that it skirted the problem with "euphemisms, indirect quotation or blank spaces." The *Providence*

Journal reported a written policy that listed taboo words. One newspaper in Connecticut avoided any vulgar language at all.[2]

The use of indecent language in broadcasting raises another host of moral problems because of the intrusion of radio and TV into the privacy of the home and the presence of children in the audience. Ever since the Federal Communications Commission first fined a Pennsylvania radio station for broadcasting an interview with the rock musician Jerry Garcia, of the Grateful Dead, that contained several indecent phrases, the commission has been concerned about the use of offensive language on the nation's airwaves. This concern was graphically reflected in the famous "seven-dirty-words" case, in which the FCC upheld a complaint against a New York radio station owned by the Pacifica Foundation. The complaint involved the broadcast of a satirical recording by the humorist George Carlin in which he repeated several words that one would never hear on the public's airwaves. In its order, the FCC described the language as "patently offensive as measured by contemporary standards for the broadcast medium."[3] The fact that children are in the audience at certain times of the day was also cited as justification for channeling indecent content into certain time periods. The commission's decision was upheld by the Supreme Court in 1978, thus putting licensees on notice that they were forbidden to broadcast indecent language for shock value.[4]

At first, few broadcasters saw this decision as a problem, but things have changed dramatically in the broadcast industry since 1978. Cable television and videocassettes have siphoned off the audience for over-the-air television. And because cable is not governed by the same rules as broadcast stations, there is a choice of explicit material not found in conventional broadcasting.[5] Competition in radio has also heated up, and some stations have resorted to talk shows that, to say the least, challenge the limits of moral propriety.[6]

The FCC has responded to this upsurge of explicit broadcast chatter by targeting the worst offenders. In 1987, for example, it moved against three stations for airing indecent programming. A Philadelphia station was cited for comments made by a drive-time "shock jockey," and a student-run station was cited for playing a song containing indecent lyrics. A Pacifica station in Los Angeles was even sanctioned for broadcasting a serious drama concerning AIDS in the gay community.[7] However, the issue of government regulation of indecency over the public's airwaves is far from settled. The battle has been joined between those who believe that government has a role in preventing the dissemination of morally offensive material and those who feel that such choices should be left to the marketplace. But regardless of the legal resolution of the use of indecent language in the electronic media, the ethical concerns will remain at the vortex of the social debate on this matter.

A MATTER OF TASTE: SHOCKING AND DISTURBING VISUALS

Offensive content does not always involve indecent or obscene material. Some photographs and TV news footage are so graphic as to shock the sensibilities of the average reader or viewer. Suppose for example, that a state official who has just been convicted of a felony calls a news conference to announce his resignation. But instead of the expected resignation announcement, he pulls a gun and, with cameras rolling, places the barrel in his mouth and pulls the trigger. Would you air this graphic footage? That was the question confronting TV news directors in Pennsylvania in January 1987, when R. Budd Dwyer, the state treasurer, convened a news conference in his office the day before his scheduled sentencing on counts of mail fraud, racketeering, and perjury. Following a brief, rambling statement critical of the justice system, the press, and the outgoing governor, he shot himself. As he slumped to the floor with blood gushing from his nose and mouth, the cameras followed him.[8]

This tape was quickly fed by satellite to stations across the state. Most news directors chose not to show this public suicide, but a few made the contrary decision. The most common reason cited by those who decided not to show the moment of death was the graphic nature of the footage. They felt it would be in bad taste and would shock the audience. Closely related to these concerns was the observation that showing the suicide itself was not necessary to the reporting of the story.[9] The three stations that chose to run the footage during the noon hour defended their decision on the values of newsworthiness and immediacy. They also argued that the footage they had shown was not particularly graphic.[10]

Most of the newspapers in and around the state capital of Harrisburg also refused to publish graphic photos of the suicide. Many editors gave the same reason: readers do not want to see such sensational photos. This comment from Ronald Millard, editor of the morning *Patriot and Evening News* in Harrisburg, was fairly representative: "It was a simple call. We did not want to offend the sensibilities of our readers. We were concerned about Dwyer's children, his wife, his relatives and friends."[11] Only two papers in the region published some of the photos. James Dible, publisher of the *Lewistown Sentinel,* said he had no second thoughts about using the "gun-in-the-mouth" shot and that reaction from the readers had been minimal. "A curious thing," he said, "is that much of the adverse reaction was linked to what people saw on television. The moving pictures were more startling."[12]

Such forays beyond what some believe to be the limits of aesthetic and dramatic propriety usually subject journalists to charges ranging all the way from poor taste to voyeurism. In deciding whether to use potentially offensive and shocking pictures, media practitioners must weigh newsworthiness against other values. Unfortunately, many editors appear to be oblivious [of] the impact of photos. They view them as supplements to news stories, ignoring the fact that the impact of a story is often determined by the accompanying photograph.[13]

Television news directors may be more sensitive to visual effects because of the fact that pictures are an inherent part of any TV report. News video does not always explain the meaning of a story, but it can create powerful images.[14] For example, the nightly visual coverage of the gruesome battlefield casualties in Vietnam has been credited with influencing the public opinion about the continued U.S. commitment to that conflict. Powerful news pictures also hastened the demise of the Ferdinand Marcos government in the Philippines.[15] And the Israeli government was so sensitive about world public opinion that it tried to restrict TV coverage of the Palestinian uprising in the occupied territories.

Given the inevitable psychological impact of visual images, it is little wonder that graphic photos of human tragedies evoke such strong reactions from the audience and even the professional community. In the Dwyer case, for example, the popular press was uniformly critical of the airing of his suicide. At one station some advertisers even withdrew their support in protest of the coverage.[16]

Newspaper readers were similarly outraged by an editorial judgment in 1980 when the Carter administration approved a mission to rescue American hostages held captive in Iran. The mission was aborted when a helicopter and cargo plane collided and exploded in the desert. Several papers published wire service photos of the charred bodies of U.S. servicemen killed in that accident. Under such circumstances some editors might justify their decision on the basis of newsworthiness or historical significance. But one could argue just as convincingly that such photos violate the norms of human decency and are in poor taste while contributing little to the essential truth of the story.

Photographs of the casualties of war are always disturbing and often gruesome. Who can forget the televised scenes of the mass victims of the Iraq-Iran war? Many Americans also remember the picture of a naked Vietnamese girl running down a road to escape a bombing attack. And then there was the photographic coverage of the summary execution of a Viet Cong soldier, who was shot with a pistol at close range by a South Vietnamese officer. These kinds of visual images remain etched in the memories of readers and viewers, a permanent reminder of the darker side of the human experience.

Of course, examples such as the Dwyer case, the hostage-rescue mission, and the casualties of combat are subjected to more public and professional scrutiny than most photographic coverage. Despite the alleged newsworthiness of such visuals, media practitioners have a moral obligation at least to consider the sensibilities of family, friends, and relatives of the victims. Nevertheless, pictures of tragedies are a staple of photojournalism, and some editors feel that because they are so compelling and so memorable, such graphic representations must be used, even at the risk of distressing readers and family members. Many scenes of auto accidents, shootings, drownings, and suicides are prizewinners in annual news photography competitions.[17]

Media gatekeepers are confronted with another decision involving taste when news coverage includes nudity. Pictures of the human body often offend the moral sensibilities of the audience, prompting charges of sensationalism. Once again, editors and news directors must balance the news value of such pictures against other considerations. Assume, for example, that a TV news crew accompanies police officers on a raid of a topless bar. Should the evening news, presented during the dinner hour, graphically depict the arrest of the naked dancers? Because television is a visual medium, these shots are arguably at the heart of the news story. Nevertheless, many audiences are offended by such journalistic candor, and some stations sanitize this kind of material by electronically blocking out the bare breasts.

Many editors refuse to run nude photographs of even those involved in newsworthy events or matters of public interest. Despite the prevalence of sexually explicit material in our society, they apparently do not believe that the public will accept nudity in their hometown newspapers. When one considers that the audience is an important ingredient in the moral-reasoning process, it is difficult to fault such caution.

In deciding whether to include nude photographs in news coverage, we should keep one guideline clearly in mind: such visuals should not be used just for shock value or to increase circulation or ratings.

These pictures should be justified according to the same rules of good journalism as any other editorial matter. They should, first of all, be newsworthy. Once the news value of such photos has been ascertained, a determination should be made whether they are essential to the story. Do the nude visuals, for example, provide significant information or understanding that would otherwise be lacking in the story? These factors should then be weighed against other competing values, such as good taste and a respect for human decency.

THE LINGERING LEGACY OF BLASPHEMY

Although blasphemy statutes remain on the books in fifteen states, the crime of blasphemy is today of little more than historical interest.[18] The question of teaching religious doctrine that conflicts with majority community opinion has seldom been a significant legal issue it since the adoption of the Bill of Rights.[19] But irreverence, usually in the form of messages perceived as mocking the deity or the basic beliefs of the Christian religion, was sometimes prosecuted as blasphemy well into the early part of this century.

In 1811 a Mr. Ruggles was convicted in New York of having made blasphemous remarks about Jesus and Mary. A few years later the courts of Boston convicted Abner Kneeland for circulating irreligious remarks in a newspaper. In 1928 a warrant was issued but never served for the arrest of a well-known editor for suggesting that Socrates and Jesus had been anarchists. In the same year an atheist was convicted in Arkansas of the "crime" of ridiculing the Christian religion.[20] And as late as 1937 a Connecticut man was convicted of violating that state's blasphemy statute.[21]

Despite the legal problems prompted by such irreverence, the Supreme Court has never directly considered the issue of state blasphemy statutes. However, the Court did examine the question indirectly in a New York film-censorship case in 1952. The controversy arose when the state revoked the license to distribute an Italian film, *The Miracle*, following a public outcry that it was sacrilegious. The film concerned a simple-minded woman who had given birth to a baby in a church after being impregnated by a bearded stranger whom she believed to be St. Joseph.[22] Although the Supreme Court did not overturn the state's practice of censorship, it struck down the application of prior restraint to this film. "It is not the business of government," wrote

Justice Tom Clark, "to suppress real or imagined attacks upon a particular religious doctrine."[23] Thus, there is serious doubt whether any statute leading to a conviction for blasphemy would be upheld by the high tribunal.

But despite the fading of blasphemy from the legal arena, the ethical dimensions of the debate remain problematical. . . . [T]he controversy surrounding *Life of Brian* [some two decades] ago demonstrates the continued vigilance of religious conservatives over what they consider to be blasphemy and irreverence in the mass media. And more recently, protests were lodged against a movie company and local theaters for the distribution of *The Last Temptation of Christ,* a skillfully produced film dealing with the more human qualities of Jesus, a view that religious critics were unwilling to tolerate. Once again, cries of "blasphemy" resounded in the public furor over the film.[24]

These examples notwithstanding, charges of blasphemy against media practitioners are relatively rare today. Nevertheless, blasphemy is considered by some to be among the most offensive forms of content, because it challenges the fundamental principles of religious doctrine.

The controversy over morally offensive content, perhaps more than any other media ethics issue, touches on the kind of society we want to be. Our libertarian heritage propels us in the direction of freedom. But even in an open society there are limits, and much of the ethical debate has focused on them. The ferocity of this moral dialogue would challenge even the wisdom of Socrates in forging an accommodation of competing values in the intellectual marketplace.

On the one hand, a system of ethics based on moral prudishness would lead to such austere media content that it would probably be rejected by a majority of the audience. On the other hand, absolute freedom leads to moral chaos and destruction of cultural continuity. Practically speaking, neither extreme is workable. Thus, in a diverse society the strategy should be to reach some middle ground, an accommodation between the excesses of moral prudishness and moral chaos.

THE CASE FOR MORAL LIMITS

A search for an ethical meeting of the minds on the issue of morally offensive content must begin with an understanding of the arguments for and against societal controls. One way of approaching the matter of moral limits is to note the grounds that might be advanced to justify those limits.

Four liberty-limiting principles are relevant to this inquiry: (1) the *harm* principle, (2) the principle of *paternalism*, (3) the principle of *moralism*, and (4) the *offense* principle. Although these grounds have most often been cited to justify the legal regulation of obscenity, they are equally applicable to the control of other forms of morally offensive content.[25]

The Harm Principle

Under the first concept, based in part on the ideas of John Stuart Mill in *On Liberty*, individual liberty may be reasonably restricted to prevent *harm to others*. For example, some allege that exposure to pornography is directly related to sex crimes such as rape. Even in a libertarian society few would disagree with the harm principle as a general notion. But there is little evidence that morally offensive content causes physical or psychological harm to others. Thus, the supporters of this principle have turned their attention to the detrimental impact on cultural values and the exploitation of certain segments of society. This view is reflected in an observation from Professor Franklyn S. Haiman in *Speech and Law in a Free Society*:

> If communication is so vital to the functioning of a free society as to warrant the extraordinary protection afforded to it by the First Amendment, it must have the power—we are often reminded—for harm as well as good. If speech can enlighten, it can also exploit. If literature can enrich our values, it can also debase them. If pictures can enhance our sensitivities, they can also dull them.[26]

The harm principle does attract an interesting cast of supporters, on both the right and the left of the political spectrum. In 1986, for example, a feminist, Andrea Dworkin, testified before the Meese Commission in favor of the regulation of pornography.* Invoking images of women being brutalized and even killed for the profit of pornographers, Dworkin explained: "The issue is simple, not complex. Either you're on the side of women or on the side of pornographers."[27] Such a view shows that the cause of censorship is not the exclusive preserve of conservatives or liberals.

---

*Appointed by President Ronald Reagan in 1985, the Attorney General's Commission on Pornography (known as the Meese Commission for Attorney General Edwin Meese) investigated the impact of pornography on society. (Eds.)

The Principle of Paternalism

Under the second principle, morally offensive content should be controlled to prevent *harm to self.* In other words, exposure to obscene and other sexually explicit matter is harmful because it dehumanizes individuals and even corrupts their value system. In common parlance, we need to be protected from ourselves. If nutritionists believe that we are what we eat, then proponents of paternalism believe that we are what we read (or view).

Some accuse the media of emphasizing freedom at the expense of responsibility. A recent study, for example, found that there had been an increase in the depiction of sexual behavior on television but little portrayal of the possible consequences, such as pregnancy and venereal diseases.[28]

The paternalistic view is captured in an unequivocal comment attributed to Larry Parish, who once prosecuted the porno star Harry Reems in Memphis, Tennessee.[29] Parish, who apparently viewed the elimination of obscenity as a divine mission, told a reporter, "I'd rather see dope on the streets than these movies," because drugs could be cleansed from the body, but pornography's damage was permanent.[30]

The Principle of Moralism

According to the third view, morally offensive content should be controlled by society in order to prevent *immoral behavior* or the *violation of societal norms.* This principle raises the question of the kinds and degrees of regulation that should be tolerated in a pluralistic society. Some believe that ready access to pornographic material, for example, encourages promiscuous sexual behavior. But even if there is no demonstrable harm from exposure to content such as pornography and blasphemy, some support societal controls merely because this material offends community standards. This is an extreme position, because it could lead to social ostracism of even those who choose to consume controversial content within the privacy of their homes.

The Offense Principle

Some argue that society is justified in restricting individual liberty to prevent offense to others. In this context, offensive behavior is understood as behavior that "causes shame, embarrassment, discomfort, etc., to be experienced by onlookers" in public.[31] This principle is usually employed to justify the protection of nonconsenting adults from public displays of offensive material. Likewise, objections to the publication of gruesome or disturbing photographs are usually made on the basis of taste and the desire to avoid offending the moral sensibilities of the audience. When newspapers agree to accept only listings for adult theaters but no promotional ads, or when bookstores conceal adult magazines behind the counter for sales by request only, these decisions are grounded primarily on the offense principle.

THE CASE AGAINST MORAL LIMITS

The arguments against societal censorship are based primarily on the notion of individual autonomy and a rejection of the liberty-limiting principles just described.[32] Proponents of this view have little trouble, for example, dispensing with the harm principle as a viable foundation for regulation. There is no evidence, they say, that morally offensive material harms others (for example, by causing an increase in sex-related crimes), and the so-called societal harm is so speculative as to pose no immediate threat to the cultural order.

Likewise, libertarians feel paternalists are wrong when they argue that pornographic and blasphemous material harms the individual. But even if such harm did occur, according to those who oppose restrictions, paternalism is an unacceptable liberty-limiting principle.

The principle of moralism is also rejected, because the alleged consensus on what constitutes community standards does not exist. But even if it did, moralism would be unacceptable, because standards vary tremendously from community to community. Undoubtedly, the liberal cultural environment of New York City would be anathema in the Bible Belt. In addition, reliance on such fluid and often elusive criteria imposes the majority's will without respecting individual autonomy and minority interests.

The anticensorship position is rather persuasive from a legal standpoint, especially in view of the Constitution's expansive protection of speech and press rights. But it remains for the ethicist—and each of us should participate in this process—to search for that balance between individual autonomy and the need for moral standards.

THE SEARCH FOR STANDARDS

The notion of morally offensive content poses a problem for deontologists. These duty-based theorists would not desire that such material become common within society. The production and distribution of offensive material just for the sake of commercial exploitation cannot be justified, because (1) the purpose of artists in producing such content does not flow from any universal moral obligation and (2) exploitation does not show the proper respect for persons as ends unto themselves.

On the other hand, deontologists also acknowledge the right to free expression.[33] Under the duty-based approach to ethical decision making, the value of actions lies in motives rather than in consequences. Artistic freedom by itself does not justify such material, but works of art that in some way contribute to cultural enrichment should be protected. Thus, the deontologist would examine the purpose and motive of the author in producing the allegedly morally offensive work, regardless of the ultimate consequences of the material. The problem with this approach is that it requires an exploration of the vast recesses of the author's mind, a perilous and uncertain journey. Sometimes the author's motives are evident, but at other times they are concealed.

Consequentialists (teleologists), as always, would look to the probable effects of the content. So far there does not appear to be any demonstrable physical or psychological harm resulting from the consumption of some forms of morally offensive material, such as obscenity. Nevertheless, a teleologist must still consider the more fundamental effects on societal values and attitudes. For example, does the viewing of sexually violent pornography result in the degradation and subordination of women in society's collective consciousness?

If there is no demonstrable harm to others or to society, perhaps censorship is unwarranted. Of course, teleologists rest more comfortably on this position than deontologists, because they are not really concerned with the motives of the author but only the consequences. And some believe that even hardcore pornography, regardless of whether it is produced for the purposes of commercial exploitation, can have beneficial effects. For example, G. L. Simons, an Englishman who has written extensively on various aspects of human sexuality, believes that exposure to pornography can aid normal sexual development and that it can invigorate sexual relationships.[34] But even if one were to reject Simons's observations, a teleologist might conclude that the consequences of censorship are fraught with dangers in that some material possessing social value might be swept aside with that containing no demonstrable literary or cultural utility.

Aristotle's golden mean, on the other hand, seeks the middle ground between the excesses of moral prudishness and moral chaos. An ethicist, applying the golden mean, would examine the content, the medium of distribution, and the audience to which it is directed. The real centerpiece of the golden mean is "information and reasonable control." Distributors of potentially offensive content have a moral obligation to provide consumers with adequate information and warnings so that they can make rational choices about their reading or viewing. The film ratings system and the disclaimers included at the beginning of controversial network programs are two well-known examples.

The principle of reasonable control ensures the availability of material for consenting adults while protecting the sensibilities of nonconsenting adults and children. Zoning laws, bans on public promotions for offensive material, and the placement of adult magazines behind the counters at retail outlets would appear to be a reasonable middle ground between the excesses of prudishness and affronts to public morality.

The various media deserve different levels of control, depending on audience accessibility. Radio and TV, for example, are still predominantly family media and are almost ubiquitous. Movies and books, on the other hand, require consumers to make more active and conscious decisions.

Where children and nonconsenting adults are concerned, greater controls would also be justified. This is the principle on which the FCC has built its programming standards regarding indecent content. . . .

NOTES

1. Austin Murphy, "Toothsome Sacrifice," *Sports Illustrated*, May 8, 1989, p. 26.

2. Linda Lotridge Levin, "Dirty Words and Blushing Editors," *The Quill*, September 1986, p. 25.

3. See *FCC* v. *Pacifica Foundation*, 3 Med.L.Rptr. 2553, 2554 (1978).

4. Ibid.

5. For a discussion of this issue see Howard M. Kleiman, "Indecent Programming on Cable Television: Legal and Social Dimensions," *Journal of Broadcasting and Electronic Media* 30 (Summer 1986): 275–94.

6. See Don R. Pember, *Mass Media Law*, 5th ed. (Dubuque, Iowa: William C. Brown, 1990), p. 541.

7. Ibid.

8. See Patrick R. Parsons and William E. Smith, "Budd Dwyer: A Case Study in Newsroom Decision Making," *Journal of Mass Media Ethics* 3 (1988): 84–85.

9. Ibid.

10. Ibid., pp. 89–90.

11. "News Photo of Public Suicide Placed Many Editors in Quandary," *ASNE Bulletin,* February 1987, p. 4.

12. Ibid., p. 5.

13. William L. Rivers and Cleve Mathews, *Ethics for the Media* (Englewood Cliffs, N.J.: Prentice-Hall, 1988), pp. 137–38.

14. See Conrad Smith and Tom Hubbard, "Professionalism and Awards in News Photography," *Journalism Quarterly* 64 (Summer-Autumn 1987): 352.

15. See Thomas Griffith, "The Visuals Did Marcos In," *Time*, March 17, 1986, p. 72.

16. Parsons and Smith, "Budd Dwyer," p. 92.

17. See John L. Hulteng, *The Messenger's Motives: Ethical Problems of the News Media,* 2d ed. (Englewood Cliffs, N.J.: Prentice-Hall, 1985), pp. 148–49.

18. Harold L. Nelson, Dwight L. Teeter Jr., and Don R. Le Duc, *Law of Mass Communications,* 6th ed. (Westburg, N.Y.: Foundation Press, 1989), p. 379.

19. Thomas L. Tedford, *Freedom of Speech in the United States* (New York: Random House, 1985), p. 152.

20. Ibid.

21. Nelson, Teeter, and Le Duc, *Law of Mass Communications,* p. 380, citing the *New York Times,* October 14, 1937, p. 29.

22. Ibid., p. 153.

23. *Burstyn* v. *Wilson,* 1 Med.L.Rptr. 1357, 1361 (1952).

24. For an examination of the controversy surrounding this film see "Wrestling with 'Temptation,' " *Newsweek,* August 15, 1988, pp. 56–57.

25. These categories are based on those described by Joel Feinberg in *Social Philosophy* (Englewood Cliffs, N.J.: Prentice-Hall, 1973), chaps. 2–3. However, they are also dealt with in some detail in Thomas A. Mappes and Jane S. Zembaty, *Social Ethics: Morality and Social Policy,* 3d ed. (New York: McGraw-Hill, 1987), pp. 284–87; and Tom L. Beauchamp, *Philosophical Ethics: An Introduction to Moral Philosophy* (New York: McGraw-Hill, 1982), pp. 270–97.

26. Franklyn S. Haiman, *Speech and Law in a Free Society* (Chicago: University of Chicago Press, 1977), p. 164.

27. Described in Alan M. Dershowitz, *Taking Liberties: A Decade of Hard Cases, Bad Laws, and Bum Raps* (Chicago: Contemporary Books, 1988), pp. 179–80. The commission issued its report and conclusions in 1986. See U.S. Attorney General's Committee on Pornography, *Final Report*, 2 vols. (Washington, D.C.: U.S. Government Printing Office, 1986).

28. Dennis T. Lowry and David E. Towles, "Prime Time TV Portrayals of Sex, Contraception and Venereal Diseases," *Journalism Quarterly* 66 (Summer 1989): 347–52.

29. Reems's real name was Herbert Streicker.

30. Quoted in Alan M. Dershowitz, *The Best Defense* (New York: Random House, 1982), p. 158.

31. Mappes and Zembaty, *Social Ethics*, p. 285.

32. For a discussion of the pros and cons of these liberty-limiting principles see ibid., pp. 285-87.

33. For a discussion of the public's right to pornography see Ronald Dworkin, *A Matter of Principle* (Cambridge, Mass.: Harvard University Press, 1985), pp. 335–72.

34. G. L. Simons, "Is Pornography Beneficial?" in Mappes and Zembaty, *Social Ethics*, pp. 301–306.

23

Stalking the Wild Viewer

Ien Ang

In the first half of this century, cartoonist Harold T. Webster became famous for his sharp depictions of the affective hang-ups of the average American. He drew cartoon series under telling titles such as "The Timid Soul" and "The Thrill That Comes Once in a Lifetime," and he had no mercy for the TV audience. He never owned a TV set himself and was thus no regular practitioner of the art of TV viewing—an art that, when he died in 1952, was rapidly becoming a general domestic activity in the United States. Nevertheless, he felt sufficiently qualified to visualize what he believed happens when people watch TV. In a once-a-week cartoon series for the New York *Herald Tribune,* he presented taunting portraits of the TV and radio audience. In a relentlessly mocking manner characteristic of cartoons, Webster pictured the broadcasting audience "at its moments of greatest strain: clubbed senseless by commercials, drowned in the soap opera flood, lacerated by thrillers, held slack-jawed and limp before the endless, banal assault on ear and eye and mind," according to *Time* magazine.[1]

Television's entrance into the fabric of everyday life was accompanied with great ambivalence in postwar America. The medium was not simply promoted as a new technological and cultural blessing to the public at large; instead, it provoked deeply contradictory expressions of hopes and fears, excitement and anxiety.[2] Webster, considered by *Time*

This article originally appeared in *Continuum: The Australian Journal of Media and Culture,* Volume 4, Number 2 (1991). Reprinted by permission of the author.

to be "one of the nation's best and best-known critics of radio and television,"[3] was undoubtedly only one of many cultural critics who contributed to this mood of distrust and caution. What makes his series of cartoons particularly interesting, however, is that he explicitly made the medium's unknown relationship with its audience the central object of concern. In other words, the cartoonist's critical discourse established itself by pictorially fixing the medium's presumably distressing effects on its ordinary consumers. And he was not alone in this. Indeed, as Lynn Spigel has shown, the popular press at that time was full of articles which expressed worry about the problems that might arise with the spread of TV as a mass consumer item: there was widespread concern about TV's possible disturbance of family harmony and children's education, about the medium's power to distract the housewife from her daily domestic tasks, about the problems the TV set would pose for home decorating and architecture, about TV's damaging influence on people's health (eye strain!), and so on.[4] Such worries indicate that the anxiety around TV primarily found expression in a sense of suspense about the impact of the medium in the private sphere. Because TV was set up as a domestic medium, it was hard to assess and control the process and context of its consumption. It is not for nothing that Webster called his cartoon series "The Unseen Audience." This title suggests that the TV audience is an invisible mass, hidden behind the closed doors of private homes, virtually inaccessible to the outsider.

What Webster did then was to take up the outsider's perspective, from which he drew scenes and events that depicted the strainful confrontations of people with TV in their homes. In this process, he did not implicate himself: his own position was that of the knowing subject who stands at a comfortable distance from what he visualized. Thus, through his cartoons, he established a *symbolic relationship* with the TV audience: a relationship characterized by distance, noninvolvement, skepticism. Rather than empathizing with those whose activities and experiences in front of the TV set he strived to represent, he constructed images of them as strange and alien human beings with whom no one would like to identify.

Webster's pictures of the TV audience still feel surprisingly familiar today because we recognize in them the stereotypical typecasting of TV viewers as not-so-smart, naive, and pitiful cultural dupes. The popular (self-)derogatory term "couch potatoes" to designate people who watch (too much) TV in America is only one illustration of the persistent cognitive power of the way in which critics continue to imagine the TV audience.

It is important to emphasize that this image of the TV audience is not just stereotypical because of the negative typifications that emanate from it (stereotypes can also contain positive idealizations), nor simply because it produces extremely partial fantasies of how people watch TV—fantasies that, in their exaggerations and exclusions and their emotionally charged value judgments, are a combination of distortion and validity. Decisive for the stereotypical quality of this image is the rhetorical tone of certainty by which its crude simplifications are presented, and by extension, its short-circuiting effect: not a trace of doubt that it tells an essential truth about a group of others.[5]

In her article "Rethinking Stereotypes," Tessa Perkins has remarked that "[a] stereotype will probably develop about a group because it has, or is presenting, a problem."[6] The core of the "problem" of the TV audience, I suggest, lies precisely in its invisibility: it is an evasive, intangible reality that is hard to define. We generally refer to the TV audience as if it were a self-evident category, but as with all common sense, its meaning seems utterly obvious until we have to define exactly what we mean by it. Exactly who or what is the TV audience? The difficulty of finding an unambiguous and final answer to this question is a problem for those who want such an answer. In such a context, stereotypes are useful because they reduce the uncertainty, ease the anxiety for the unknown. As Sander Gilman has noted, "the stereotype is a momentary coping mechanism, one that can be used and then discarded once anxiety is overcome."[7] The production of stereotypical representations, then, can be seen as a discursive strategy to come to terms with the invisibility of the TV audience.

The invisibility of the TV audience is closely related to the already mentioned domestic context of TV consumption. And precisely the fact that people generally watch TV at home, is felt as problematic and threatening because it renders the TV audience *out of control*—in a double sense: both chaotic and beyond control. Consider, for example, the following quote from a horrified cultural commentator, written up in 1958 in the *New York Times*:

> The scene in front of the living-room TV screen is apt to be much different [from that of the public space of the cinema]. Casualness of dress is apparent, for one thing, and the master of the house may be unshaven and the mistress of the house in curlers or facial cream. Food snacks and liquid refreshments are often on hand. When the commercial appears, the husband may rise to put another log on the fire and the wife to attend to something in the kitchen that needs

attending to. During the performance itself silence is not at all rigorously observed. Remarks of displeasure at a hammy line or gesture come forth uninhibitedly from those gathered in front of the TV set.[8]

This fantasy displays an acute awareness of the lack of order and discipline that characterizes the everyday setting in which people watch TV. From this commentator's perspective, watching TV is a "wild" practice, as it were: the living room is imagined as a barbaric space, full of "wild," uncivilized viewers.

It must be noted, however, that this problem of the "wild viewer" is not just a cultural question, the focus of moral concern over the presumably debasing effect of TV. More fundamentally, it poses a very material, practical problem for the TV-producing institutions. This is because, in the words of John Hartley, TV institutions "are obliged not only to speak *about* an audience but—crucially, for them—to talk *to* one as well: they need not only to represent audiences but to enter into *relations* with them."[9] To put it simply, the "wild viewer" is a problem for the TV industry because the TV must "catch" viewers and have an audience in order to survive.

In his article "The Imaginary Signifier," film theorist Christian Metz has identified a similar problem for the film industry. Here is how he has characterized the problem:

> In a social system in which the spectator is not forced physically to go to the cinema but in which it is still important that he [*sic*] should go so that the money he pays for his admission makes it possible to shoot other films and thus ensures the auto-reproduction of the institution—and it is the specific characteristic of every true institution that it takes charge of the mechanisms of its own perpetuation—there is no other solution than to set up arrangements whose aim and effect is to give the spectator the "spontaneous" desire to visit the cinema and pay for his ticket.[10]

Conjured up here is the problem of institutional reproduction. The cinema can only continue to exist if and when enough people are willing and prepared to be regular members of the film audience, but the film industry does not have the means to provide itself with a guarantee that people will not stop going to the movies. The problem seems to be a rather far-fetched one, because since the turn of the century, when the cinema first entered our cultural life, the world has obviously turned into a place full of filmgoing women, men and children. However, the principle of the problem is undeniable, and that it is not entirely hypothetical, is easily exemplified by the sharp and steady decline in cinema-going since the fifties, when TV made its entrance in people's homes.[11] At stake, then, is the institution's control—or better, lack of control—over the conditions of its own reproduction.

Broadcast TV faces the same institutional problem: it, too, cannot take its audience for granted. Contrary to other social institutions such as the school or the family, TV (as well as all other mass media) does not have the means to coerce people into becoming members of its audience. Television audience membership is not a matter of compulsion or necessity, but is principally voluntary and optional. Therefore, the TV institution is ultimately dependent upon people's unforced appetite to continue watching day after day. Again, the problem seems far-fetched given TV's manifest success in securing huge audiences for its transmissions, but this still does not mean that success comes naturally and effortlessly. On the contrary, numerous institutionally orchestrated activities such as the publication of TV guides, advertisements, and press interviews with TV personalities, as well as previews of forthcoming programs during an evening's flow, the use of teasing jingles, logos, and so on, testify to the enormous amount of money and energy being spent to reinforce and update people's desire to watch TV.[12] The very fact that these strategic institutional activities are of a continuous, never-ending character indicates that TV networks and broadcasting organizations know that they must continually find ways to attract the attention of potential audience members, because they cannot *control* them in any direct manner.

The audience, *sine qua non* for both TV's economic viability and cultural legitimacy, forms its ultimate insecurity factor because in principle there is no way to know in advance whether the audience will tune in and stay tuned. Audiences must constantly be seduced, attracted, lured. How to get an audience is, willy-nilly, the TV industry's key predicament, even though this is not always acknowledged as such.

The seriousness of this predicament is deeply ingrained in the domestic content of TV consumption. Television's dominant institutional arrangement is embodied within the framework of broadcasting, a framework whose basic configuration has been extended, without any radical changes, to cable and satellite TV. According to Raymond Williams, the broadcasting framework is characterized by a "deep contradiction between centralized transmission and privatized reception."[13] This "deep contradiction" refers to the circumstance that while TV is generally seen as a form of "mass communication," no true communication—in the "ritual" sense of that word: an exchange of meanings which is both intentional and interactive[14]—between the TV institution and the TV audience generally takes place. Broadcast TV transmission is both adamantly intentional and resolutely noninteractive: the diffuse and dispersed TV audience, locked in its condition of privatized reception, is an invisible and mysterious interlocutor.[15]

Over the years, a range of risk-reducing techniques and strategies of regulating TV programming such as serial production, usage of fixed formats and genres, spinoffs, horizontal scheduling, and so on, have been developed. These strategies do not only serve as a way to facilitate the organization and coordination of the industry's production practices, but are also aimed at the codification, routinization, and synchronization of the audience's viewing practices, so as to make them less capricious and more predictable. In this sense, the iron repetitiveness of TV programming, especially in the most commercialized systems, can be seen as an instance of orchestrating and disciplining the people's leisure time —the time people are supposed to be "free."[16] But all these strategies can only help to manage, not remove the basic uncertainty with which the TV institution has to live. There are no guarantees that actual viewers will comply to the codes, routines, and synchronicities of viewing behavior as designed by the institutions. Ultimately, then, the problem of (lack of) control amounts to one thing: the impossibility of knowing the audience—in the sense of knowing ahead of time exactly how to "get" it, and tame the "wild viewer."

This does not mean that no knowledge about the audience is produced in the multilayered organizational process of TV broadcasting. On the contrary, both formal and informal knowledge about the audience is constantly operative in the complex decision-making procedures which determine the shape and content of TV's daily output of programs. "Know the audience" is the first basic principle every handbook for commercial broadcasting teaches the would-be TV programmer. And in this respect, one type of knowledge about the audience has over the years gained uncontested prestige and truth value in industry circles: the knowledge emanating from audience measurement.

Consider, for example, the language used by network executive Brandon Tartikoff, president of NBC Entertainment and responsible for airing much-acclaimed series such as *Hill Street Blues, Cheers,* and *Miami Vice.* But this does not stop him from setting his standards within a discourse which problematizes—and, as a result, stereotypes—"the audience" as object of concern and control. He asserts:

I probably have more esoteric tastes than the average television viewer. I'll go to see *Amadeus* and pay my five dollars and fifty cents,

but when the salesman from Orion [a production company] comes
and asks me to buy it for the networks, I'll say no, because it's going
to get a twenty-two share,

which is, he implies, not enough because "as a programmer I had to ask
myself if it was something that would get a thirty share or better."[17]

Thus separating personal taste and market judgment (and consequently creating an antagonism between "us" [the industry] and "them"
[the audience]), Tartikoff self-evidently adheres to the principle of
"audience maximization," which reigns supreme in the operations of
American commercial TV. The language in which he articulates this
principle is the quantitative one of "shares" and "ratings"—a language
that is only made possible by audience measurement.

As a form of systematic research in which empirical information is
gathered through scientific methods, audience measurement supplies a
technical, formal, and seemingly objective and factual kind of knowledge. The conventional assumption is that ratings figures indicate the
popularity of TV programs, pure and simple. Apparently, this is a
straightforward and unambiguous fact. Can we say then that audience
measurement is the perfect solution for the TV industry to deal with the
invisibility of the audience? And does the quantitative discourse of ratings escape the stereotyping process we have discussed earlier?

A look at the recent history of how ratings are produced tells us that
this is not the case. It is a fascinating history—a history about the contradictory intertwinings of knowledge, technology, and subjectivity—
which makes clear that no matter how successful TV is in attracting
viewers, it will never be able to completely domesticate the wild viewer.
It is this history to which I will now, necessarily in an abridged way, turn.

Let us begin with a short exposition of how ratings data are produced. Historically, two major methods have been used: the diary and
the setmeter. In the diary method, a sample of households is selected
whose members are requested to keep a (generally, weekly) diary of
their viewing behavior. At the end of the week the diaries must be
mailed to the ratings firm. In the second case, an electronic meter is
attached to the TV sets of sample households. The meter gives a
minute-by-minute automatic registration of the times that the TV set is
on or off, and on which channel it is turned on. The data are transmitted to a home storage unit, where they are stored until they are
accessed by the central office computer during the night.

The data so provided offer more than just factual information about
who's watching what. They bring about a more general *sense* of

knowing, and the reassuring feeling of certainly that goes with it. Consequently, their function is not merely instrumental, but ritualistic: one of the most important achievements of ratings is that they help establish a relationship between the industry and the audience, a relationship, however, that is not "real" but symbolic. Through the discourse of ratings the "TV audience" is represented as a unified totality, a thing that can be known in terms of size, profile, and demographic composition. An object the industry can define its relationship to by cutting it into segments or using it as a target, a commodity that can be bought and sold. It is thanks to ratings that TV companies can "deliver audiences to advertisers," as the slogan goes.[18]

But this audience object/commodity is a fictive entity. This does not mean, of course, that ratings dream the audience into existence. They are based on actual information on what real people do. The knowledge produced by ratings is therefore neither "false" nor "untrue." On the contrary, ratings are so powerful precisely because of their ability to define a certain field of empirical truth. That regime of truth is fictive, however, in the sense that its very terms to describe TV viewers inevitably foreground very specific conceptualizations of the audience. For one thing, it is already a rather peculiar move to perceive the audience as something that can be measured—an assumption originating in the general idea of "measurability of markets" quintessential for the parameters of marketing thought as it began to be developed in the United States in the early twenties.[19]

However, "TV audience" as represented by audience measurement is not a static, stone-like object whose characteristics can be described once and for all. It is a continually changing, dynamic object that always seems to elude definitive descriptions. This slipperiness is already obvious enough in the fact that the production of ratings is an ongoing practice, repeated day after day. Ratings are very fleeting products: they become obsolete almost instantly.

A crucial factor in the dynamism of the construction of the "TV audience" is induced by the subjective nature of TV viewing as such. However, inclusion of the singular concreteness of the heterogeneous practices and experiences of TV viewing would make the production of ratings utterly unmanageable. Therefore, audience measurement, as is the general rule in quantifying social science, is designed to abstract from the detailed singularities in experience and practice. In other words, in order to construct an objective "TV audience," it has to squeeze the "wild viewer" into a manageable and measurable mold.

The technical instruments used for audience measurement testify to this reductionist tendency. Nielsen's setmeter, for example, can only register whether the TV set is on or off. Here, then, "audience behavior" is implicitly defined as a simple, one-dimensional, and purely mechanical act. As Todd Gitlin has rightly remarked, "The numbers only sample sets tuned in, not necessarily shows watched, let alone grasped, remembered, loved, learned from, deeply anticipated, or mildly tolerated."[20] In other words, what the discourse of ratings erases from its field of discernment is any specific consideration of "the lived reality behind the ratings." TV viewers here are thus merely relevant for their bodies: strictly speaking, they appear in the logic of ratings discourse only in so far as they are agents of the physical act of tuning in.

In short, what the discursive strategies of audience measurement succeed in constructing is a *streamlined* image of the TV audience. This imagined streamlined audience is stereotyped as a "disciplined" audience. It is constructed by ratings discourse through a smoothing out of problematic subjectivity and translating it into ordered and regular instances of viewing behavior. In the streamlined audience, each viewer will ideally find her or his exact place in a comprehensive table of knowledge, formed by the central components of size and composition. After all, the quantifying perspective of audience measurement inevitably leads to emphasizing averages, regularities, and generalizable patterns rather than idiosyncrasies and surprising exceptions. What all this amounts to is the construction of a kind of map of the "TV audience," on which individual viewers are readable in terms of their resemblance to a "typical" audience member whose "viewing behavior" can be objectively and unambiguously classified. In other words, in foregrounding the stable over the erratic, the likely over the fickle, and the consistent over the inconsistent, ratings discourse symbolically turns "wild viewers" into well-organized, serialized viewers, displaying dependable viewing habits and routines.

Imagining viewers in this way is very handy for the industry; indeed, it supplies both networks and advertisers with neatly arranged and easily manageable information, a form of knowledge which provides not only a vision of predictability, but also controllability, of the audience. Empirically found variations within the streamlined audience are conveniently contained and fixed in a limited number of "types" and "patterns," developments over time are straightened out in terms of convenient "trends."

But TV viewers are by definition more than just "typical" audience members. When people watch TV they are of course inevitably positioned as members of the audience, but they also always simultaneously inhabit a myriad of other subject positions such as parent, critic, fan, democrat, Southerner, or whatever—subject positions which elude the symbolic world of audience measurement. As a consequence, the map of the streamlined audience as provided by audience measurement inevitably stands in a strained relationship with what actual audiences are up to. The map never quite fits, as it were.

But this epistemological gap does not necessarily constitute a problem for the industry. So long as the map works, the industry will not bother to look for more "realistic" knowledge. The gap will only be problematized when the streamlining process tends to slacken; that is, when it seems no longer possible to establish fixed viewing habits, behavioral categories, and so on, by which viewers can be unproblematically typified and classified. At such moments, consensus over the map of the "streamlined audience" provided by ratings discourse breaks down, and audience measurement is thrown into crisis. In fact, the late eighties are witness to such a crisis, and it is to this that I will now turn.

The rise of the so-called new technologies has provided people with new options and choices, especially the VCR and cable. An entirely different TV landscape unfolds before the viewer's eyes these days, one characterized by abundance rather than scarcity. And viewers seem to have responded by eagerly multiplying their viewing behaviors: they zip through ads when playing back their taped shows, they zap through channels with their remote controls, they time-shift—in short, they have become less and less "loyal" to the carefully composed schedules of the mighty networks. "After years of submitting passively to the tyranny of [network] television programmers, viewers are taking charge," comments Bedell Smith.[21]

Indeed, from the industry's perspective, some sort of "revolt of the viewer" seems to have erupted: they feel that they are losing their grip on the audience. And in this chaotic situation, audience measurement is a central focus of concern, the site on which the uncertainties and worries are expressed and articulated. What we witness here then is the industry's anxiety and uneasiness about the growing unpredictability of audience behavior, or viewing habits, as a consequence of the fragmentation of the electronic media landscape. In short, what is at stake is a disruption of the streamlined "TV audience." Consequently, diverse branches of the industry began to call for more finely tuned knowledge of the audience, to be acquired through better measurement.

This call for better measurement was articulated by criticizing the prevailing techniques and methods of measuring the TV audience: the diary and the setmeter. For example, the proliferation of channels through cable has acutely dramatized the problems inherent to the diary technique. All of a sudden, the built-in subjective (and thus "unreliable") element of the diary technique was perceived as an unacceptable deficiency. Thus, officials of the pop music channel MTV complained that their target audience, young people between twelve and twenty-four, consistently comes off badly in the demographic data produced through diaries, because "younger viewers . . . tend not to be as diligent in filling out diaries as older household members."[22]

The videocassette recorder has also played a major destabilizing role in the measurability of the TV audience. "Time-shifting" and "zipping" (fast-forwarding commercials when playing back a taped program) effectively deregulate the carefully composed TV schedules of the networks. This phenomenon has come to be called "schedule cannibalization" in industry circles,[23] a voracious metaphor that furtively indicates the apprehension, if not implicit regret, felt in network circles about the new freedom viewers have acquired through the VCR. Through the VCR, the wild viewer clearly manifests her/himself!

Wiped out, then, are the good old days when TV was a relatively neat and simply structured business, with a limited number of channels and viewing styles for viewers to choose from, and in which the diverse branches of the industry could complacently believe in and rely on the premise of a streamlined "TV audience." That premise can no longer be taken for granted. Consequently, the one-dimensional assumptions about TV viewers that have been the traditional basis for audience measurement can no longer be held. Thus, behind the controversy over the diary methodology lurks a great suspicion of the capriciousness of the new viewing behaviors brought about by the emergence of the new TV landscape. Viewers just can no longer be trusted to report their viewing accurately: they lack perfect memory, they may be too careless. In short, they behave in too subjective a manner! In this situation, the sentiment thrives that there should come a better method to obtain ratings data. And better means more "objective," that is, less dependent on the fallibilities of viewers in the sample. A method that erases all traces of wild subjectivity.

It is in this situation that the ratings business has now come up with the *people meter,* a new audience measurement instrument that was introduced in the United States in 1987, and that has already been in use in several European countries and in Australia as well.[24] The people meter is supposed to combine the virtues of the traditional setmeter and the paper-and-pencil diary: it is an electronic monitoring device that can record individual viewing rather than just sets tuned in, as the traditional setmeter does. It works like this: When a viewer begins to watch a pro-gram, she must press a numbered button on a portable keypad, which looks like the well-known remote control device. When the viewer stops watching, the button must be pressed again. A monitor attached to the TV set lights up regularly to remind the viewer to the button-pushing task. Every member of a sample family has her or his own individual button, while there are also some extra buttons for guests.

Linked to the home by telephone lines, the system's central com-puter correlates each viewer's number with demographic data about them stored in its memory, such as age, gender, income, ethnicity, and education.

The intricate measurement technique is attractive for the industry because it holds the promise of providing more detailed and accurate data on exactly who is watching what. The people meter boosts the hope for better measurement of the wider spectrum of cable and VCR viewing (including zipping). Smaller audience segments may now be detected and described, allowing advertisers and broadcasters to create more precise target groups. New sorts of information are made avail-able, hitherto hidden and unknown minutiae of "audience behavior" are now becoming visible. The people meter, then, opens up the poten-tial of drawing a new, more detailed map of the audience. In line with the cartographic metaphor, it could be said that the old map was no longer adequate as a guide in the rocky terrain of the TV business, because more traffic is now on the road, making careful driving more necessary. With the people meter, the industry sees the promise of a new map that should enable finding the correct signposts and avoiding the danger zones more efficiently.

Still, the existing versions of the people meter are by no means con-sidered a perfect measurement instrument, as they still involve too much subjectivity; after all, they require viewer cooperation in the form of pushing buttons. A professional observer wonders: "Will the families in the sample really take the trouble? Will they always press the buttons as they begin watching? Will they always remember to press their buttons when they leave the room—as when the telephone rings, or the baby cries?"[25] It should come as no surprise, then, that furious attempts are being undertaken to develop what is called a *passive* people meter—one with no buttons at all—that senses automatically who and how many viewers are in front of the screen. For example, Nielsen has recently dis-closed a plan for a rather sophisticated passive people meter system, con-sisting of an image-recognition technique capable of identifying the faces of those in the room. The system then decides first if it is a face it recognizes, and then if that face is directed toward the set (unfamiliar faces and even possibly the dog in the house will be recorded as "visitors"). If tested successfully, Neilsen executives expect this system could replace the imperfect, push-button people meter by the mid-nineties.[26]*

These developments illustrate the attractiveness of the idea of a "perfect" people meter in industry circles: so pressing is the need felt for knowing exactly who is watching what and how. But they also reveal the more general "political" issue involved in the audience measurement project as such. At stake in the turmoil around people meters is more than just a methodological "improvement" of measuring the TV audience: the significance of the people meter is not just a technical matter, but a matter of control.

Now that the industry as a whole is confronted with multiplying ways of practicing the act of watching TV, a loss of manageability of the audience—a streamlined audience, one that can be objectified and acted upon—threatens to take place. The solution, of which the people meter is a historical embodiment, is sought in more and faster information, allowing for more microscopic differentiations and characterizations. A more detailed categorization of the peculiarities of audience behavior, so the implicit philosophy goes, will supply the industry with new symbolic means to sharpen its power to define the audience, and to specify its relation to it in more concrete ways. The people meter, as an idea, symbolizes the wish for provision of a continuous stream of precise data on who's watching what, every day, all year long. Its projected task is to put the streamline back in the profile of the "TV audience."

In trying to make sense of these developments in audience measurement, I am, in fact, reminded of Michel Foucault's considerations of "panopticism."[27] The principles of panoptic discipline are central to the technological operation of audience measurement; its core mechanism, and ultimate ambition, is control through visibility. Audience measurement is a form of hierarchical examination: its aim is to put TV viewers under constant scrutiny, to describe their behavior so as to turn them into suitable objects in and for industry practices, to judge their viewing habits in terms of their "productivity" for advertisers and networks alike.

But, unlike prisoners or schoolchildren, TV viewers cannot be subjected to officially sanctioned disciplinary control. In the school or the prison, disciplinary techniques are aimed at transforming people's behavior through punishment, through training and correction. The

---

*This system has not yet become a regular part of Nielsen's data-gathering methods. (Eds.)

living room, however, is emphatically not a classroom or a prison cell, nor is TV a carceral institution. Therefore, the commercial TV industry does not have the power to impose the conversion of viewers into what Foucault has termed "docile bodies"—that is, to *force* them to adopt the "ideal" viewing habits (for example, watch all the commercials attentively)—to stop being "wild viewers."

This "problem"—that is, the "problem" that viewers are not prisoners but "free" consumers—accounts for the limits of audience measurement as a technology of power. It is also against this background that the importance of methodological accuracy and objectivity may be understood: emphasizing that audience measurement is a matter of research increases its credibility and legitimacy and reduces distrust against it. All this amounts to the fact that audience measurement can only be an *indirect* means of disciplining TV audiences; it is through discursive, and not literal, objectification and subjection that audience measurement performs its controlling function. It does not effect the *actual* discipline of TV viewers, it only conjures it up in its imagination. This leads to a fundamental contradiction in the very motif of audience measurement. Just as the disciplinary technologies described by Foucault, it puts viewers under constant examination, but contrary to what happens, for example, in the prison, the visibility of the audience achieved is not linked up with the organization of direct behavioral control; the observation of bodies and their regulation do not go together here. This does not mean that there is no power and control involved in the setup of audience measurement (that power is articulated, for example, in what audiences get to see on TV); it does mean, however, that the production of ever more refined knowledge as such becomes a rather autonomous pursuit: audience measurement is carried out in the belief that the production of knowledge per se must somehow automatically lead to actual control over the audience. We will see, however, that the project has quite contradictory effects, not at all uniformly leading to the desired increased control.

No matter how sophisticated the measurement technology, there will always be aspects of the activity of watching TV that will elude the "gaze" of audience measurement. The subjective moment can never be completely "domesticated" in ratings discourse, because TV viewing is, despite its habitual character, dynamic rather than static, experiential rather than merely behavioral; it is a complex cultural practice that is more than just an activity that can be broken down into simple and objectively describable "habits." In other words, watching TV is an activity replete with significance; in its everyday uses it can take on a myriad of specific and changing meanings, which the sensors of audience measurement technology cannot possibly register fully.

It is true that audience measurement does not need to include all those heterogeneous uses and meanings of watching TV in its discourse. But as we have seen, it is exactly the disruption of the "streamlined audience" by VCR and cable-related viewer practices that has impelled the development of more sophisticated techniques to put viewers through more meticulous rituals of examination. In other words, the recognition that watching TV is done by people of flesh and blood, and that "TV audience" is not so easily streamlinable by ratings discourse as had been assumed, has resulted in an attempt to incorporate an ever widening range of components of TV viewing activity in the measurement endeavor.

But paradoxically, the increasingly microscopic technological "gaze" of audience measurement only seems to lead to an ever greater elusiveness of the invisible audience it is presumed to measure. The more it sees, the less it can get to grips with what it sees, as it were. The more visible the audience is made, the less certain it comes to define exactly what takes place in people's homes when they watch TV. No longer can it be conveniently assumed—as traditional ratings discourse does—that having the TV set on equals watching, that watching means paying attention to the screen, that watching a program implies watching the commercials inserted in it, that watching the commercials leads to actually buying the products being advertised.

Thus, the activity of watching TV loses its imagined one-dimensionality: measuring "it" can never be the same anymore. The calculable audience member tends to dissipate before the ever more sensitive microscope of audience measurement, and increasingly regains his or her status of active subject—of "wild viewer." Audience measurement, in short, is an example of how the practice of panoptic examination, when severed from the attendant power of regulating behavior, turns out to have a contradictory outcome: rather than facilitating control, it makes it more difficult!

This whole turn of events, and the crisis of audience measurement it has generated, coincides, as we have seen, with the emergence of the new, postmodern TV landscape. The perceived "return of the wild viewer" is not some sort of romantic eruption of viewers, rebellion on the basis of their "authentic" needs and desires, but is brought to the surface by the very technological changes introduced by the TV business itself. Perhaps a permanent disruption of the streamlined audience is bound to take place; perhaps the proliferating range of activities people perform with and around TV will increasingly resist being straitjacketed in a streamlined discursive construct, a fixed stereotype—in the literal sense of that word—of the "TV audience."

Brandon Tartikoff, NBC's President of Entertainment, testifies fully to the sense of change within the industry:

> Lucille Ball said that TV changed with the invention of the remote control device. As soon as a guy doesn't have to get up from his chair to switch the channel, TV becomes a new ball game. Viewer inertia, which supported many an uninspired show, has given way to viewer impatience.[28]

Of course, viewer inertia has never been "real" in the first place. It was just the fictional stereotype of the streamlined audience member complacently and arrogantly indulged in by the industry. As for viewer impatience, it may be the new stereotype by which the TV industry seeks to combat its uncertainty about the TV audience—a fiction which, if anything, betrays a declining sense of confidence over the power of the medium. It is, in fact, an acknowledgement of the industry's plight always to be stalking the "wild viewer."

NOTES

Large parts of this article are extracted from my book *Desperately Seeking the Audience: How Television Viewership is Known* (London: Routledge, 1991).

1. See *Time*, October 22, 1951, p. 83.
2. Lynn Spigel, "Installing the Television Set: The Social Construction of Television's Place in the American Home, 1948–1955," unpublished Ph.D. diss., UCLA (Los Angeles, 1988).
3. Spigel, "Installing the Television Set"; *Time*, (see note 1).
4. Spigel, "Installing the Television Set."
5. Of course, this is an essential rhetorical strategy by which cartoons in general drum up their message. In this sense, cartoons can be seen as a genre that relies upon, and contributes to, the construction of stereotypes.
6. Tessa Perkins, "Rethinking Stereotypes," in Michele Barrett, Philip Corrigan, Annette Kuhn, and Janet Wolff, eds., *Ideology and Cultural Productions* (London: Croom Helm, 1979), pp. 139–59.
7. Sander L. Gilman, *Difference and Pathology* (Ithaca and London: Cornell University Press, 1985), p. 18. According to Gilman, only pathological personalities hold on to rigid stereotypes about a group they fear on a consistently permanent basis.

8. *New York Times,* February 11, 1958.

9. John Hartley, "Invisible Fictions: Television Audiences, Paedocracy, Pleasure," *Textual Practice* 1, no. 2 (1987): 127.

10. Christian Metz, "The Imaginary Signifier," *Screen* 16, no. 2 (1975): 19.

11. See Douglas Gomery, "The Coming of Television and the 'Lost' Motion Picture Audience," *Journal of Film and Video* 37, no. 3 (1985): 5–11; David Docherty, David Morrison, and Michael Tracey, *The Last Picture Show?* (London: BFI, 1987). Docherty et al. criticize the technological determinism implied in the popular explanation of the decline of the cinema audience as being directly caused by the rise of TV as the most important mass visual medium. The authors claim that both developments can be explained, in Britain at least, by the same sociological factors, most importantly, the expansion of home-based consumer culture after World War II. Gomer discusses the American context of the same phenomenon.

12. See John Ellis, *Visible Fictions* (London: Routledge and Kegan Paul, 1982).

13. Raymond Williams, *Television: Technology and Cultural Form* (London: Fontana, 1974), p. 30.

14. On the "ritual" view of communication, see James Carey, *Communications as Culture* (Boston: Unwin Hyman, 1989).

15. It is worth noting here that TV was not naturally destined to be a medium for private, domestic consumption. Early experiments with TV technology were set up with several alternative uses in mind. Television's initial entertainment setting was that of public showings on large-screen TV in theaters, while it was also envisioned as a monitoring device for factory production and as a surveillance device in military settings. Furthermore, the possibilities of two-way TV as a replacement for the two-way telephone were explored by AT&T in the twenties, while radio amateurs were also enthusiastic about the interactive potential of TV communication. However, these alternative uses were finally marginalized in favor of a development of TV analogous to that of radio broadcasting. See Jeanne Allen, "The Social Matrix of Television: Invention in the United States," in E. Ann Kaplan, ed., *Regarding Television* (Frederick, Md.: University Publications of America, 1983), pp. 109–19.

16. Cf. Chris Rojek, *Capitalism and Leisure Theory* (London and New York: Tavistock, 1985).

17. Quoted in Richard Levinson and William Link, *Off Camera* (New York: Plume/New American Library, 1986), pp. 256–57.

18. See, for some critical accounts of the functions of ratings in the operations of the (commercial) TV industry, Donald Hurwitz, "Broadcast Ratings: The Missing Dimension," *Critical Studies in Mass Communication* 1, no. 2 (1984): 205–15; and Eileen Meehan, "Ratings and the Institutional Approach: A Third Answer to the Commodity Question," in *Critical Studies in Mass Communication* 1, no. 2 (1984): 216–25.

19. James Beniger, *The Control Revolution* (Cambridge, Mass.: Harvard University Press, 1986).

20. Todd Gitlin, *Inside Prime Time* (New York: Pantheon, 1983).

21. Sally Bedell Smith, "Who's Watching TV? It's Getting Hard to Tell," *New York Times*, January 6, 1985, p. E21.

22. Quoted in Victor Livingston, "Statistical Skirmish: Nielsen Cable Stats Vex Cable Net Execs," *Television/Radio Age*, March 17, 1986, p. 130.

23. See Edmond M. Rosenthal, "VCRs Having More Impact on Network Viewing, Negotiation," *Television/Radio Age*, May 25, 1987.

24. I extensively discuss the introduction of the people meter in the American TV industry in Part Two of Ien Ang, *Desperately Seeking the Audience* (New York: Routledge, 1991).

25. William F. Baker, "Viewpoints," *Television/Radio Age*, November 10, 1986, p. 95.

26. "New 'People Meter' Device Spies on TV Ratings Families," *San Francisco Chronicle*, June 1, 1989.

27. Michel Foucault, *Discipline and Punish* (Harmondsworth: Penguin, 1974).

28. Quoted in Levinson and Link, *Off Camera*, p. 263.

Chapter Five

The Controversy
over Content

24

Media Mongols at the Gates

Akbar S. Ahmed

A political cartographer with a bold eye for simplification would reject the clumsy apparatus of global classification that has prevailed so far—First, Second, Third World, North-South, East-West, and so on. He would divide the world map in the 1990s into two major categories: the civilizations that are exploding—reaching out, expanding, bubbling with scientific ideas, economic plans, political ambitions, cultural expression—and those that are imploding, collapsing in on themselves with economic, political, and social crises which prevent any serious attempt at major initiatives. The former are, above all, exploding with optimism, with sights firmly fixed on the future; the latter are weighted down by their history, traditions, "certainties," their ethnic and religious hatreds.

Western, or global civilization—in essence the G-7—is exploding; much of the rest of the world is imploding.

This exploding-imploding world is so shrunk by the ubiquitous media that define our postmodern era, so interlinked and so claustrophobic, that elbowroom on this planet is ever more scarce. We have all been shoved face to face with each other. As the exploding West continues through its domination of the media to expand its cultural boundaries to encompass the world, traditional civilizations will resist in some areas, accommodate to change in others.

Originally published as "Media Mongols at the Gates of Baghdad," in *At Century's End: Great Minds Reflect on Our Times,* ed. Nathan P. Gardels (La Jolla, Calif.: ALTI Publishing, 1995). Reprinted by permission.

In the main, only one civilization, Islam, will stand firm in its path. Only the Muslim world, poised both to implode and explode, offers a global perspective with a potential alternative role on the world stage. Islam, therefore, appears to be set on a collision course with the West. More than a clash of cultures, more than a confrontation of races, the collision between the global civilization emanating from the West and Islam is a straight-out fight between two approaches to the world, two opposed philosophies. Under the layers of history and the mosaic of cultures, we can simplify in order to discover the major positions. One is based in secular materialism, the other in faith; one has rejected belief altogether, the other has placed it at the center of its worldview.

While conflict has long brewed between the traditional religious precepts of Islam and the materialism and scientific reason of modernity, the challenge postmodernism presents is more decisive for the ultimate fate of Islam.

While Muslims appreciate the spirit of tolerance, optimism, and the drive for self-knowledge in postmodernism, they also recognize the threat it poses to them with its cynicism and irony. This is a challenge to the faith and piety that lie at the core of their worldview.

Pious Muslims know that the problem with the G-7 civilization is the hole where the heart should be—the vacuum inside, the absence of a moral philosophy. What gives the West its dynamic energy is individualism, the desire to dominate, the sheer drive to acquire material items through a philosophy of consumerism at all costs, to hoard. Such frenetic energy keeps society moving.

Patience, pace, and equilibrium, by contrast, are emphasized in Islam. Haste is the devil's work, the Prophet warned. But the postmodern age is based on speed. In particular, the media thrive on and are intoxicated by speed, change, news. The unceasing noise, dazzling color, and restlessly shifting images of the MTV culture beckon and harass. Silence, withdrawal, and meditation—advocated by all the great religions—are simply not encouraged by the media.

The African and South Asian are dazzled with images of *Dallas*- and *Dynasty*-like plenty, of a cornucopia. But they have no access to such a reality. These tantalizing images are thus no more than dangerous illusions for the majority of the people on the planet. They cannot solve anything; but they can, through the envy and desire they spread, spoil a great deal of contentment, patience, and balance—the virtues of traditional societies, which no longer have the power to soothe or mollify.

Nothing in history has threatened Muslims like the Western media; neither gunpowder in the Middle Ages, which Muslims like Babar used with skill on the fields of Panipat, thus winning India for his Mughal dynasty; not trains and the telephone, which helped colonize them in the last century; nor even planes, which they mastered for their national airlines earlier this century. The Western media are ever present and ubiquitous, never resting and never allowing respite. They probe and attack ceaselessly, showing no mercy for weakness and frailty.

The powerful media offensive is compounded for Muslims: they appear not to have the capacity to defend themselves. Worse, they appear unable even to comprehend the nature and objectives of the onslaught. The empty bluster of the leaders and the narrow-minded whining of the scholars make them appear pitiful, like pygmies arguing among themselves while the powerful giant of an enemy is at the gate.

It is the ordinary Muslim who senses the immensity of the danger. He is conscious of the potential scale of the battle and the forces arrayed against him; his tension is made worse because he has so little faith in his own leaders.

It must have been something like this in 1258 when the Mongols were gathering outside Baghdad to shatter forever the greatest Arab empire in history. But while the Abbasids remained in ruins, other, equally significant structures with glorious edifices were created: the Fatimids in Egypt, the Umayyads in Spain, and later, the Saffavids in Iran, the Mughals in India.

This time the decision will be final. If Islam is conquered, there will be no coming back.

THE MEDIA IS POWER

It is the American mass media that have achieved what American political might could not: the attainment for America of world domination. Hollywood has succeeded where the Pentagon failed. The link between the two is established in the fact that films and defense equipment are the two largest export earners in the U.S. economy. J. R. Ewing has triumphed in a way John Foster Dulles could not even dream. The world watches with hypnotic fascination the rerun episodes of American soaps: Across the world people ask "Who shot J. R.?" in *Dallas* or "Who killed Laura Palmer?" in *Twin Peaks*. The American dream is seen as irresistible.

The demise of communism and the collapse of its monolithic state structures are widely considered as the Western media's greatest victory.

With their incessant propaganda, their capacity to satirize and ridicule, the Western media made deep inroads into the communist world, dooming it years before Gorbachev and his successors arrived.

Muslims ask: now that the Western media have helped conquer communism, who will be their next opponent? It is not difficult to guess: Islam. We have here a thesis in need of investigation: the more traditional a religious culture in our age of the media, the greater the pressures upon it to yield.

All traditional religions, whether Buddhist, Hindu, Muslim, or Christian, encourage piety, contemplation, and mysticism. In contrast, as I indicated earlier, the full-scale onslaught of the media is an obscene cry for noise, materialism, for consumerism and *blague*. The seductive ads, the glamorous stars, all drown thoughts of piety and austerity. Then it robs human beings of that most delicate of crowns, dignity. In the knockabout irreverence and turbulence of the postmodern wit there is no dignity allowed anyone.

The purity of the past can no longer be guaranteed under such relentless assault. It is thus understandable why Muslims reject post-modernism as nihilism and anarchy.

For the Western media, civilizations "out there" tend to be shown in stereotypes. Islam continues to be marginalized and degraded. In a hundred hours of CNN or other television coverage, Islam might get ten minutes of projection, which will be Muslims burning books or expressing rage in a threatening mob. Hinduism and Buddhism are shown to be holy priests, half-naked and meditating, to be dismissed in the popular media as exotic relics of the past.

What I wish to emphasize here is the concept of media as power, as assertion of cultural superiority, as extension of political arguments, indeed, as the main player. Through the media the opposing position can not only be triumphed over but also, by denying it access, it can cease to exist altogether. The media is thus one of the most important weapons in the arsenal of any country. This is the paramount lesson of our times.

While triumphant on the world stage, the basic unit of human organization, the family, is in grave danger in Western civilization. One of the main quarrels Muslims have with contemporary Western culture concerns the disintegration of the Western family, whose authoritative function in the moral formation of the person has been eroded by the invasion of the media in the home.

In the Islamic family, integrity, unity, and stability are the ideal. Muslims thus see the pressures of the consumerist culture of the West—

the promiscuity, the drugs, the high expectations—as taking their toll on Western marriages, with about half of them falling apart. They fear that these pressures are now being brought to bear on Muslim homes. They fear *din* (religion) is in danger of being totally submerged under *dunya* (the world). This would be catastrophic to the Muslim concept of a just and balanced order.

Muslim parents blanch at the modern Western media because of the universality, power, and pervasiveness of their subversive images, and because of their malignity and hostility toward Islam.

The images on television that come nonstop at the viewer are of couples performing sex, men inflicting terrible pain, limbs and guts dismembered, *disjecta membra* everywhere. The videocassettes that accompany pop songs produce ever more bizarre images, from Madonna masturbating to Michael Jackson's transmogrification into a panther.

They blot out other images, whether the *gravitas* of the serious documentaries or the false conviviality of the chat shows. The VCR is a trapdoor to the darkest, most depraved images humans can possibly conjure up. Anything and everything is available. Even a Marquis de Sade would be satisfied at what he could find here.

These intrusions corrode the innermost structure of balance and authority in that crucible of all civilization, the family, adding to the crumbling authority structures of the West that have been under attack now for the last two generations.

Take the case of Britain. The father at home, the bobby [police officer] in the street, the teacher at the school, and the monarchy and politicians in public life are all the subjects of constant media ridicule. In particular, men are singled out. To be a male in authority is to be suspect.

People in authority were the special target of the brainless Marxist intellectual brigade of the last generation. The media took over after them. In the West, stories of political corruption in public life, incest at home, ritual satanic abuse in the schools, and so on, have finally ended whatever little respect remained for authority. In the place of the old structures is a vacuum.

If the power of the Western media dictated the 1980s social agenda —feminism, homosexuality, AIDS—we are, in the 1990s, already discussing post-feminism, post-homosexuality, and post-AIDS.

Many of the issues that Islam never conceded, such as the abuse of alcohol and drugs, are now being widely reaccepted in the West. Many in the West are also now reevaluating divorce, the challenge to parental authority, the marginalization of the elderly, the regular relocation of the home because of work and related issues. All are devastating to the family. The legitimate questions being raised by Muslims are the following: Why should they be dragged along the path of social experimentation which they know diverges from their own vision of society? Why should they disrupt their domestic situation for temporary values, however overpowering in their immediate and glamorous appeal?

Why is a religion advocating goodness, cleanliness, tolerance, learning, and piety so misunderstood and reviled? Many of the currently accepted social positions in the West—the undesirability of cigarettes, drugs, and alcoholism, and the promotion of family life—have always been advocated by Islam. *Jihad* has become a dirty word in the media, representing the physical threat of a barbaric civilization. Yet the concept is noble and powerful. It is the desire to improve oneself, to attempt betterment, and to struggle for the good cause. It is Tennysonian in its scope: to strive, to seek, and not to yield.

BUSTING MUSLIM STEREOTYPES

I wish to avoid what I see as sterile sexist and religious polemics about Muslim women. But I feel it necessary to point out in passing the wholly incorrect, negative media stereotype of women as inanimate objects, submissively attending to the needs of their lord and master, locked away in darkened homes. I believe this is a stereotype partly reflected from the poor opinion, bordering on misogyny, that Western society (inspired by the ancient Greeks) holds of women.

The potential of women in Islam is far superior to anything offered by Confucius in China or Aristotle in Greece, or to what Hindu or Christian civilizations offered. Muslim women are central to family affairs, from domestic decision making to rituals. Where their lot is miserable and they have virtually no rights, as in certain tribal areas, it is to be attributed to Muslim male tyranny, not Islamic advice, and is in need of urgent redress.

We know that the modern political life of many Muslim nations has been enriched by the contributions of women. Miss Fatimah Jinnah, the sister of the founder of Pakistan, mounted the most severe political challenge to the military dictatorship of Ayub Khan in the 1960s. Two decades later, Benazir Bhutto followed the same pattern, challenging General Zia and succeeding in becoming the first female Muslim prime minister, one of just a handful of women premiers in the world until that time. Begum Khalida Zia in 1991 continued the trend by becoming the first female prime minister of Bangladesh.

Muslims also face dilemmas in education. Away from the educated scholars, in the villages of Asia, Islamic scholarship faces serious problems. In lengthy and intimate discussions with orthodox religious scholars this was made plain to me. To them the outside world simply does not exist. The works of Marx or Weber are unknown. Faith and fervor are sufficient to carry all before them. This blocking-out provides Muslims with their supreme confidence but also poses the most formidable threat to them. And the threat is felt most sharply at the moment of realization that there are other, outside systems. It was first heard in the plaintive complaint of Aurangzeb, the Mughal emperor, to his tutor. The emperor chided his tutor for filling his head with the most exaggerated notions of the Mughal empire, and for dismissing the European kings as petty *rajas*. The same questioning is heard today among the more honest and intelligent *ulema,* the religious scholars.

These dilemmas provoke passionate responses. There is an interesting parallel in recent history that illustrates the principle prompting Muslim action against Salman Rushdie. A century ago, advancing European imperialism met Muslim resistance determined to defend the traditional way of life, from Sudan in Africa to Swat in Asia. The picture that symbolizes the clash is that of illiterate tribesmen crying "Allah-u-Akbar" (God is most great), waving swords blessed by holy men, charging at the formations of European infantrymen firing the latest most deadly guns. The slaughter did little to dim Muslim commitment.

In our times, the one picture that perhaps best symbolizes a similar clash between the West and Islam is that of the burning of Rushdie's book; it is the contemporary equivalent of the nineteenth-century charge. This time Muslims, once again convinced that they were protesting against an attack on their beliefs, shouted "Allah-u-Akbar," brandished matches endorsed by elders, and marched toward the waiting media. Once again the most advanced Western technology met Muslim faith; once again it was a massacre, this time of the Muslim image in the West. We witness again two mutually uncomprehending systems collide: monumental contempt and arrogance on one side, blind faith and fury on the other.

MUSLIM ANGUISH

It is the nature of this complex historical encounter, exacerbated by each incident, that feeds into the Muslim incapacity to respond coolly and meaningfully. Muslims being killed on the West Bank or in Kashmir, their mosques being threatened with demolition in Jerusalem or in Ayodhya, India, are seen throughout the Muslim world on television and cause instant dismay and anger. The threat to the mosques has deep resonances in Muslim history. The one in Jerusalem is named after Umar, one of the greatest Muslims and rulers after the Prophet, and the one in India after Babar, the founder of the Mughal dynasty. One is over a millennium in age, the other almost half a millennium.

It is a milieu of distrust and violence within which Muslims see their lives enmeshed. The recent killings of Muslims by Muslims across the world—a vice chancellor in Kashmir, an Imam in Belgium, an aged writer in Turkey—is one response. It demonstrates the attempt to force greater commitment on the community, to push people off the fence, to obliterate the moderate and reasonable position; it also demonstrates desperation.

Muslims throughout the world cite examples of gross injustice, particularly where they live as a minority in non-Muslim countries. This group forms a large percentage of the total number of Muslims in the world today. Their problems in non-Muslim countries stem as much from their powerlessness as from the shortsightedness of those dealing with them. Repeated shootings and killings have led to desperation among Muslims. The state appears to have few answers besides the bullet and the baton. Lord Acton would have sneered; repression tends to corrupt, and absolute repression corrupts absolutely.

However, Muslims themselves are not blameless. Muslim leaders are failing in the need to feed and clothe the poor. The greatest emphasis in Islam is given to the less privileged. This, alas, remains a neglected area of attention as leaders prefer to fulminate against their opponents.

Muslim leaders are also failing in another crucial area. Those Muslims living in the West and complaining about racism would do well to turn their gaze on their own societies. Pakistanis have been killing Pakistanis on the basis of race, in the most brutal manner possible, for years in Sind province; political messages are carved into the buttocks of ethnic opponents. Kurds have been gassed and bombed in Iraq by fellow Muslims for decades. The sordid and all but forgotten matter of the future of almost half a million Biharis living in the most wretched camps in the Dhaka remains unresolved. The Biharis, demoted to the status of alien creatures, maintain they are legitimate citizens of Pakistan. Their sin was the belief in an Islamic, united Pakistan. After 1971, in Bangladesh, they were seen as a fifth column. Islamic Pakistan is reluctant to allow residence to these Muslims—its legitimate citizens—

and Islamic Bangladesh is equally reluctant to own them, so their lives remain suspended in the squalor and filth of the refugee camps. The concept of *ummah* (the Muslim brotherhood) is an excellent one; but it remains inchoate and needs to be pursued with more vigor than that presently exhibited by Muslims.

In this period, many Muslim leaders and heads of government across the Muslim world have met a violent end by shooting (Sadat, Faisal, Mujib, and, starting with Daud, too many to name in Afghanistan). They have been hanged (Bhutto), or even blown up in the air (Zia). What Muslims have done to their leaders is more than matched by what the leaders did to their Muslim followers. Nightmare images are seared in the mind. State power—the army and police—has been responsible for the massacre of innocent country-folk, and even entire towns in Syria, in East Pakistan (now Bangladesh), in Iraq, and in Iran.

Furthermore, large proportions of the unprecedented wealth from oil revenues have been squandered on an unprecedented scale, in an unprecedented style. Call girls in London and casinos in the south of France, ranches in the United States and chalets in Switzerland diverted money that could have gone into health-care provision, education, and the closing of the vast gaps between the rich and poor. In Islamic countries, oil money created an arrogance among some Muslims who cherished a sense of special destiny around their family or clan. These antics provided legitimate ammunition for the Western satirists wishing to lampoon Muslims; they became the caricature of a civilization. Ordinary Muslims, therefore, have good cause to complain.

Also in need of pursuit is the notion of a just and stable state. Contemplating the prospects for the twenty-first century, some Middle East experts conclude that the lack of "a civil society" is the great bane of the Muslims. Repression and stagnation—in spite of a certain record of durability in some states—mark their society. Lawyers and journalists are unable to work freely, and businessmen operate in an economy that may be labeled "socialist" or "capitalist" but, in either case, is controlled by the state. Nevertheless, the picture is not entirely pessimistic. As has been noted by British scholars, Egypt has developed and maintained elements of a civil society and separation of powers within the state in spite of its long tradition of authoritarianism—from the Pharaohs, through Muhammad Ali and Cromer, to Nasser and Sadat.

THE MUSLIM RESPONSE

The main Muslim responses appear to be chauvinism and withdrawal; this is both dangerous and doomed. The self-imposed isolation, the deliberate retreat, is culturally determined. It is not Islamic in spirit or content. Muslims who are isolated and self-centered sense triumph in their aggressive assertion of faith. They imagine that passionate faith is exclusive to them. Yet a similar religious wave exists also in Christianity, Hinduism, and Buddhism. Preferring to ignore this, Muslims will point out that the Western world is intimidated by them, and fears their zeal. That Rushdie was driven underground is cited as one proof of this. It seems that Muslim spokesmen are in danger of being intoxicated by the exuberance of their own verbosity.

Because orthodox Muslims claim that Islam is an all-pervasive, all-embracing system, this affects the way in which Muslim writers and academics think. The increasing stridency in their tone is thus linked to the larger Muslim sense of anger and powerlessness. They advocate confrontation and violence, an eye for an eye, a tooth for a tooth; this attitude confirms the stereotypes of Muslims in the West. They argue that moderation has failed and that extremism will draw attention to their problems. Perhaps in the atmosphere of violence and blind hatred, of injustice and inequality, they have a certain logic in their position. At least they will be heard. They will force Muslim problems onto the agenda where more sober voices have failed, and because we live in an interconnected world, no country can isolate itself from or immunize itself against Muslim wrath. Nevertheless, violence and cruelty are not in the spirit of the Qur'an, nor are they found in the life of the Prophet, nor in the lives of saintly Muslims.

LOCATING THE ESSENCE OF ISLAM

The Muslim voices of learning and balance—whether in politics or among academics—are being drowned by those advocating violence and hatred. Two vital questions arise with wide-ranging, short- and long-term implications: In the short term, has one of the world's greatest civilizations lost its ability to deal with problems except through violent force? In the long term, would Muslims replace the central Qur'anic concepts of *adl* and *ahsan* (balance and compassion), of *ilm* (knowledge) and *sabr* (patience), with the bullet and the bomb?

Islam is a religion of equilibrium and tolerance, suggesting an encouraging breadth of vision, global positions, and the fulfillment of human destiny in the universe. Balance is essential to Islam, and never more so than in society, and the crucial balance is between *din* (religion) and *dunya* (world); it is a balance, not a separation, between the two. The Muslim lives in the now, in the real world, but within the frame of his religion, with a mind to the future afterlife. So, whether he is a businessman, an academic, or a politician, he must not forget the moral laws of Islam. In the postmodern world, *dunya* is upsetting the balance, invading and appropriating *din*.

Yet the non-Muslim media, by their consistently hammerheaded onslaught, have succeeded in portraying a negative image of it. They may even succeed in changing Muslim character. Muslims, because of their gut response to the attack—both vehement and vitriolic—are failing to maintain the essential features of Islam. Muslim leaders have pushed themselves into a hole dug by themselves in viewing the present upsurge simplistically as a confrontation with the West. They are in danger of rejecting features central to Islam—such as love of knowledge, egalitarianism, tolerance—because they are visibly associated with the West. In locating anti-Islamic animosity firmly in the West, they also implicitly reject the universalism of human nature.

But Allah is everywhere. The universal nature of humanity is the main topos in the Qur'an. God's purview and compassion take in everyone, "all creatures." The world is not divided into an East and a West: "To Allah belong the East and West: whithersoever Ye turn, there is Allah's countenance" (Surah 2:115). Again and again God points to the wonders of creation, the diversity of races and languages in the world. Such a God cannot be parochial or xenophobic. Neither can a religion that acknowledges the wisdom and piety of over 124,000 "prophets" in its folklore be isolationist or intolerant. With its references to the "heavens" above, the Qur'an encourages us to lift up our heads and look beyond our planet, to the stars.

The divine presence is all around; it can be glimpsed in the eyes of a mother beholding her infant, the rising of the sun, a bird in flight, the first flowers of spring. The wonders and mystery of creation cannot be the monopoly of any one people. The Sufis—like Iqbal—see God everywhere, even among the godless, not only in the mosque. In their desire for knowledge, compassion, and cleanliness, many non-Muslims possess ideal Muslim virtues. We note goodness and humanity in people like Mother Teresa, [Nelson] Mandela, and [Vaclav] Havel. Islam has always shown the capacity to emerge in unexpected places and at unexpected times. The true understanding of Islam will therefore be critical in the coming years—and not only for Muslims.

WHAT CAN ISLAM GIVE TO THE GLOBAL CIVILIZATION?

On the threshold of the twenty-first century, what can Islamic civilization contribute to the world? The answer is a great deal. Its notion of a balance between *din* and *dunya,* is a worthy one. It can provide a corrective and a check to the materialism that characterizes much of contemporary civilization, offering instead compassion, piety, and a sense of humility. The philoprogenitivity of Muslims is a social fact. The qualities mentioned above underline the moral content of human existence; they suggest security and stability in family life, in marriage, and in care for the aged. Recent signs in Western societies indicate that perhaps the time is ripe to readmit care and compassion into human relations; here, too, postmodernist sensibilities can help.

In its abjuration of materialism, Sufism provides a balance to the dominant values of Western civilization, although many see the impact of Sufism as limited in our world. Especially in the Sufistic message of *sulh-i-kul* (peace with all), Islam has a positive message of peace and brotherhood to preach. This message is irrespective of color or creed, and has stood the test of time. Not surprisingly, Sufistic Islam has made significant inroads in the West, especially among European converts.

Islam places knowledge at the highest level of human endeavor. Repeatedly the Qur'an and the sayings of the Prophet urge the acquisition of knowledge. Indeed, the word knowledge (*ilm*) is the most used after the name of God in the Qur'an. The Prophet urged his followers to "seek knowledge, even unto China." Human beings are asked in the Qur'an to think of and marvel at the variety confronting them: "And among His signs is the creation of the heavens and the earth, and the variations in your languages and your colors" (Surah 30:22).

Change and reinterpretation are embedded in Islamic history and text. The following discourse between the Prophet and Muadh ibn Jabal, a judge, on his way to the Yemen clearly indicates the principle:

Prophet: How will you decide a problem?

Muadh: According to the Qur'an.

Prophet: If it is not in it?

Muadh: According to the *sunna* [Islamic custom].

Prophet: If it is not in that either?

Muadh: Then I will use my own reasoning.

The Islamic principles that encourage flexibility and rational choice are reflected in the exchange: *ijtihad* (independent judgment), *shura* (consultation), and *ijma* (consensus). Clearly, rationality and man's own judgment play a part in arriving at decisions.

YOU CAN'T FLEE CNN

The Muslim response to postmodernism, unfortunately, is the same as it was a century ago: retreat accompanied by passionate expressions of faith and anger. From the Sanusi in North Africa to the Mahdi in Sudan to the Akhund in Swat, Muslims appeared to challenge the European imperialist and, under fire, disappeared back into the vastness of their deserts and mountains. In the mountains and deserts was escape from the colonial European; there lay the strength of tradition, the integrity of custom, and the promise of renewal. For the European, the Muslim, in the vastness of his mountains and deserts, had secured a place out of his reach, free from his rules and administrators; the Muslim reverted to the past as if the present did not exist.

But there is one significant difference today. Whereas a century ago Muslims could retreat so as to maintain the integrity of their lives, their areas are now penetrated, and technological advances have made escape impossible: the satellite in the sky can follow any camel across any Arabian desert, the laser-guided missile can land in any home in any remote Afghan mountain valley, and the VCR is available in the desert tent as well as the mountain village.

The Muslim tribesman has always possessed a shrewd eye for strategy—more so than his compatriot in the city. He was quick to identify the media as a source of potential disruption to traditional life. Consequently, until a few years ago, a radio, as a symbol of modernity, was ritually shot to pieces in Tirah, deep in the inaccessible tribal areas of Pakistan. The rejection was a clear message for the young with ideas of change in their minds.

Today, however, the media cannot be stopped; they can penetrate the most remote home, and no place could be more remote than Makran, in the Baluchistan Province of Pakistan. Makran is one of the most isolated and inaccessible parts of the Muslim world. It is a vast, sparsely populated area and still without electricity, and therefore, television. No highways or railways connect it to the rest of the country. There are only a few miles of blacktop road in the main town. The rest are dirt tracks that shift with the sands. Little has changed in Makran since Alexander, returning from his Indus adventure, got lost there.

Even Islam is twisted according to local tradition and clouded in ignorance: the Zikris, an autochthonic sect, possess their own Makkah, Arafat, *haj*, Kaaba, and prophet. Their physical isolation allows them to escape the wrath of the orthodox in Pakistan. Yet the latest foreign films are freely available through the miracle of diesel-powered generators and the VCR, which are among the first possessions of those who can afford them; these were commonly owned in the most distant villages, which I visited as Commissioner of Makran in 1985. What impact contemporary values are making on these societies that are centuries old has not yet been studied. We are left with conjecture, with stories of tension and clash in society. In Makran, traditional values are coeval with the most up-to-date ones; Alexander's age runs parallel to the post-McLuhan era.

Similarly penetrated is the secure, comfortable, and timeless Muslim middle-class urban life as depicted so well by Naguib Mahfouz, for instance, in his 1990 novel, *Palace Walk*. His story is set in Cairo, but it could be Marrakesh in the extreme west of the Muslim world, or Kuala Lumpur in the extreme east. The frequent references in conversation to the Qur'an, the underlying class and color prejudices, the simmering sexual and political tensions, are authentic. But this cocooned, privileged timelessness is now shattered; it is irretrievably lost with the invasion of the Western media. By the late 1980s, CNN and the BBC, the Western media's stormtroopers, were preparing to broadcast directly, via satellite, to the Muslim world. Neither Cairo nor Marrakesh nor Kuala Lumpur is inviolate.

The age of the media in Muslim society has dawned. Muslims need to face up to the fact that there is no escape now, no retreat, no hiding place, from the demon.

The postmodernist age in the 1990s hammers at the doors of Muslim *ijtihad*, or reasoned innovation within the faith. Muslims ignore the din at their peril. Before they creak open the doors, however, they must know the power and nature of the age, and for that they must understand those who represent it. These include figures they do not admire, like the singer Madonna and the writer Salman Rushdie. More important, Muslims must understand why these figures represent the age. The onslaught comes when Muslims are at their weakest; corrupt rulers, incompetent administrators, and feeble thinkers mark their societies. For all the rhetoric and symbolic form, the spirit of Islam is often palpably missing from their endeavors, while, more than ever, *ijtihad* is urgently needed where women, education, and politics are involved. The old methods and the old certainties will not hold the forces swirling and eddying around Muslim societies; there can be no evolution of Muslim society without a comprehension of the non-Muslim age we live in.

Another Muslim ponders on *ijtihad*. The fate of the Muslims in Spain makes the Aga Khan thoughtful. He talks of the loss of vigor, the drying up of initiative, the emphasis on empty dogma as causes of the Muslim downfall. The Aga Khan sees parallels in our times:

> Those who wish to introduce the concept that you can only practice your faith as it was practiced hundreds of years ago are introducing a time dimension which is not a practice of our faith. Therefore, what we have to be doing, I think, is to be asking as Muslims how do we apply the ethics of our faith today? This is a matter for Muslims to think about and it is a very delicate issue whether it is in science, in medicine, in economics.

In our postmodern age, rigid boundaries are no longer easy to maintain. A person can, and does, possess overlapping identities. He can be both a devout Muslim and a loyal citizen of Britain. Multiple identities mean eclecticism, which requires tolerance of others. In such a world, the confrontation between Islam and the West poses terrible dilemmas for both.

The test for Muslims is how to preserve the essence of the Qur'anic message, of *adl* and *ahsan*, *ilm* and *sabr*, without it being reduced to an ancient and empty chant in our times, and how to participate in the global civilization without their identities being obliterated.

It is an apocalyptic test: the most severe examination. Muslims stand at the crossroads. If they take one route they can harness their vitality and commitment in order to fulfill their destiny on the world stage. If they take the other they can dissipate their energy through internecine strife and petty bickering. The choice is between harmony and hope versus disunity and disorder.

The challenge for those in the West is how to expand the Western idealistic notions of justice, equality, freedom, and liberty beyond their borders to all humanity without appearing like nineteenth-century imperialists, to reach out to those not of their civilization in friendship and sincerity.

The logic of this argument demands that the West use its great power—which includes the media—to assist in solving some of the long-festering problems, most urgently of the Palestinians and the Kashmiris, that plague Muslim society. There is the need to push unwilling rulers who subsist on Western arms and aid toward conceding democracy and a fairer distribution of wealth, and of ensuring the rights and dignity of women and children, the less privileged, and those in the minority. The problems are interwoven, binding Muslims and non-Muslims together. There can be no viable world order if these wrongs are not redressed.

Into the predicament postmodernism has plunged us all, there is also promise. Such a conclusion might appear illogically optimistic, but it is understandable in the context of the Islamic vision, which is rooted firmly in history and belief. That vision has much to offer a world saturated with disintegration, cynicism, and loss of faith.

However, regaining integrity and overcoming cynicism will only be possible if there is a universal tolerance of others among Muslims and non-Muslims alike placed at the top of the agenda in preparation for the next millennium, embraced both as personal philosophy and national foreign policy. This, too, is the largesse of postmodernism.

25

Television—The Phantom Reality

David Chagall

. . . TV's War against Traditional Values

Losing our sense of history sense is just part of the TV quagmire. While early TV programs served to reinforce traditional family life and values, today's television subverts or openly repudiates those same principles. In their book *Prime Time*, sociologists [Robert] Richter, [Linda] Richter, and [Stanley] Rothman aptly define our present dilemma. "Television," they write, "once served as an agent of social control. But it has now become an agent of social change. It now fosters suspicions of traditional mores and institutions . . . and is apt to cast a jaundiced eye on the very standards the medium embraced so enthusiastically a mere generation ago."

How does this play out in everyday life? Let us look first at the much-discussed issue of "sexual harassment." Researchers at the University of Dayton studied sexual behavior on [recent] prime-time comedy programs broadcast by the four networks—ABC, NBC, CBS, and Fox—and found that two of every five encounters involved sexual harassment. While 40 percent of the accosted women did not welcome the approach, 36 percent did, and 24 percent displayed no visible reaction. Popular shows like *Roseanne, Murphy Brown,* and *Married . . . With*

Originally published in David Chagall, *Surviving the Media Jungle* (Nashville: Broadman & Holman Publishers, 1996). Reprinted with permission.

Children constantly portray sexual remarks, leers, and gestures, along with invasive touching and grabbing, as nothing more than harmless humor, thereby establishing it as acceptable behavior. So the basic message telecast is clear: "Boys will be boys, and most girls really *like* it!"

The second shoe drops with another study on sexual harassment in public schools. Conducted by Louis Harris and Associates among 1,600 students in eighth through eleventh grades, the investigators found that *four of every five* pupils report being sexually harassed during the school day. "America's schools are filled with hostile hallways where students are daily targets of sexual harassment," a study spokesperson concludes. "Our children learn at a very early age that sexual harassment is just an everyday part of life."

Tie that assertion to recent news items. In New York City, twenty boys ages twelve to seventeen years old link arms around a lone girl at a public swimming pool. Playing a "game" called "Whirlpool," they chanted "Oops, there it is!" while pushing her under, ripping off her swimsuit, and grabbing her chest and private parts. In Fort Worth, Texas, six boys ages twelve to fourteen held down a thirteen-year-old girl while another boy sexually assaulted her on a crowded school bus as other students laughed and cheered him on. In Lakewood, California, nine suburban high-school students molested and raped girls in a competition to accumulate "points" for sexual conquests.

A survey of New York youngsters by the *New York Times* underscored the coarse, vulgar world inhabited by today's teenagers. Romance has disappeared, replaced by casual sex and filthy language. From vulgarity to sexual harassment and fornication—willing or forced—today's adults and youth alike receive much of their inspiration from the never-never land of television's ratings-driven "morality." From morning gabfests to afternoon soap operas to prime-time sitcoms and dramas, sex runs like a glossy glue that attracts viewers and binds it all together.

PRIME-TIME FILTH

A brief survey of today's soap-opera heroines illustrates the trend. Ashley claims an abortion drove her insane; Maria thinks she miscarried while horseback riding; Vivian filched another woman's eggs to have her lover's baby; Adam has three children by three different mothers with another on the way by wife number four; and Michelle keeps a jar of condoms on her coffee table for everyday use.

Where ten years ago one had to pay for premium cable channels to receive "Blue TV," today's airwaves are filled with freely distributed network raunch, available to anyone with a TV set and a rooftop aerial. Any time of the day or night, channel surfers of any age can encounter grappling, groping human bodies or some talk-show panel featuring sexual athletes, freaks, or "experts." The trick these days is to find a drama or discussion show that does not degrade and exploit our procreative impulse.

Morning talkfests like *Rolanda, Jerry Springer, Richard Bey,* and *Leeza* give way to the noontime soap operas. The afternoon talk shows like *Donahue, Geraldo,* and *Oprah* segue into drive-time news shows followed by evening prime-time sitcoms and dramas. Throughout the day Americans everywhere are deluged by a flood of programming depicting recreational adultery, perversion, teenage sex, child molesters, gender-change freaks, and degenerate exposés veiled by a overlay of hypocritical "objectivity" to lend this filth an aura of respectability.

THE RATINGS GAME

It is virtually impossible to really understand why networks and television producers so eagerly embrace this garbage until we look at the ratings game that rules the industry. Since advertising pays all the bills on television, advertisers who buy time on any TV show naturally want to know how many people—prospective customers—will be exposed to their commercials. The more people, the more products they will sell. So the entire industry has anointed one judge to count viewers' noses—the A. C. Nielsen Co. headquartered in Northbrook, Illinois.

Ratings act as judge and jury for all network and local-station shows, deciding which ones stay on the air and which are canceled. Ratings are typically based on a secret sample of approximately 1,500 homes, chosen from "random locations" from a Census Bureau list. Nielsen field reps then drive to the designated neighborhoods and try to persuade families to join their ratings panel. To help convince them, they offer prospects $50 to sign a contract, $50 for each of the five years they stay on the panel, and half of all TV-set repair costs during that period.

Once a family says yes, the hardware moves in. The house gets an audiometer wired from a closet or basement to every TV set in the house. The meter records when the sets are on or off and which channels are being viewed. Special telephone lines feed the meter to

Nielsen's Florida center, where all TV watching is tabulated twice a day by company computers. The family gets regularly mailed literature, chatty newsletters, and periodic calls from the field rep. The home has become a "Nielsen family."

During any biweekly rating period, not all Nielsen families are counted. Some have agreed to allow the hardware into their homes but have not yet been visited by a rep and wired up. Others are lost because of malfunctions in the telephone lines or the meters. So, on any typical day, the Nielsen ratings report viewing information from about 1,200 homes. A ratings number is the percentage of those 1,200 homes tuned to the same show.

For example, if a top-rated show like *Roseanne* scores a "13 rating" for the week, that means that 13 percent of the sample homes had tuned in *Roseanne* for at least six minutes—about 156 sets throughout the entire U.S.A.! Nielsen then assumes the same proportion of all American TV households—some 93 million—are watching *Roseanne* and so reports in its rating books that an estimated 12 million homes are tuned in. Nielsen sells its ratings service to TV networks, program producers, ad agencies, and advertisers. All of them pay fees based on a portion of their total business. A top-ten ad agency may pay $500,000 a year for the Nielsen service. Networks pay more; other users less. In return for their money, subscribers get a series of reports filled with rows of numbers—Nielsen estimates of TV-show popularity.

The public sees the tip of the ratings iceberg in newspaper stories explaining how ABC is beating NBC and CBS 20.1 to 19.6 to 18.3, or through banner headlines in the entertainment section exclaiming "Seinfeld Tops Again!" Behind the scenes where the money changes hands, the game of who pays how much for what is based strictly on the Nielsen numbers. Networks and local stations base their charges for commercial time on the ratings. A commercial minute on a top-rated show like *Seinfeld,* for instance, costs an advertiser $500,000 compared to a charge of $60,000 or less for shows scoring low in the ratings.

That is why new shows die so quickly—often within six weeks— and old shows with respectable numbers hang on so long. Observes a media buyer from a top-ten ad agency, "Agencies are forced to live and die with the Nielsen numbers. There is no appeals court." Former NBC-TV president Grant Tinker summed up the feelings of many insiders when he said, "I've spent forty years of my life in television. And all those years I've been vitally affected by the Nielsen ratings. Quality shows go down the tube because Nielsen says nobody is watching. I hate to think I've been living a lie all these years."

The sad truth is that Tinker and the others have been "living a lie" when it comes to the ratings. Let's start with what statisticians call "sampling error." Whenever you set up a panel of 1,200 homes to represent 93 million, sampling error says that a ratings of 13 points could actually be 2.5 points *higher* or 2.5 points lower. That means that *Roseanne* might really score as low as 10.5, which would drop the show from sixth place down to fifteenth place. The even more serious problem with the Nielsen ratings, however, is the question of which kinds of homes get wired for viewing.

About half of all families asked say no. Two classes of Americans are much more prone to be suspicious of anyone putting recording machines in their homes, namely higher- and lower-income families. Another factor is liberalism versus conservatism, where liberals tend to be more agreeable to experiments of this kind while conservatives are not. Those who do sign on are mostly the more susceptible middle-class families. When the field reps interview prospective families, they will bypass homes where TV viewing time is minimal. So what the ratings really reflect is a highly selective panel of television addicts, mostly responding to shows that appeal to the emotions—in short, sex, fear, and bawdy humor. And so, an axiom of the industry is that if you want to attract high ratings, you need to inject sensationalism, gossip, blood, and money into your programs.

OUR CHILDREN ARE WATCHING

For the rare reader who has somehow avoided running into this circus of television carnality, a brief survey of soap-opera storylines will show how the formula works. To quote excerpts from newspaper summaries covering the major soaps for a typical week, consider the following:

- *All My Children*: "Julia, fearful she will get pregnant or contract AIDS, is terrified when Louie insists on unprotected sex. Noah learns of an impending drug bust and rushes to tell Louie. Noah arrives in time to stop Louie from forcing himself on Julia. When Julia tells Noah she can't be a hooker, he says she doesn't have to work the streets and can stay with him as long as she wants."

- *Another World*: "Ian tells Josie he supports her plan to be a model. Josie stops Ian just as they are about to make love, revealing she has tested positive for a sexually transmitted disease and must wait for her latest

test results. Donna is thrilled when she learns that what she thought was early menopause is actually a hormone imbalance."

- *As the World Turns*: "Tom is furious when he learns that Barbara told Margo he and Dawn had an affair."

- *The Bold and the Beautiful*: "Karen told Macy she is in love. While Karen waited for Connor, he was making love to Brooke, who said she wanted a relationship with him. The next morning, Karen was crushed when she went to Brooke's pad and saw Connor, who had just stepped out of the shower."

- *Days of Our Lives*: "Billie planned to seduce Bo. After Alan threatened Alice, she lied on the witness stand that he was a gentleman after their one date. The judge threw out Sami's rape charges against Alan after his lawyer forced Carrie to testify Sami has a history of telling lies."

- *Guiding Light*: "Matt later accused Vanessa of being ashamed of their Summit Lake romance. Alan heard Vanessa ask Matt to return her key chain. As the contractor, Dylan assigned Matt to a remodeling job at Vanessa's home. After looking at Cutler's mug books, Tangie and Alan-Michael learned Harry attacked her on the beach."

Even though prime-time sex-drenched sitcoms like *Married . . . With Children* [are] scheduled at 9:00 P.M. [or later] in most markets, reruns air during "kid-prime" hours in the mid or late afternoons. So it should come as no surprise to learn that young children tune in these shows by the millions every weekday. The A. C. Nielsen Co. reports that not only are *Married . . . With Children* Children reruns the most popular afternoon/evening show among kids ages twelve to seventeen, but it also ranks tenth among toddlers and youngsters ages two to eleven.

LONG-LASTING HARM

Should any reader be naive enough to suppose that viewing such raunch has no long-lasting harmful effects, the U.S. Center for Disease Control discloses that better than one out of *every five* Americans is currently infected with a sexually transmitted disease. The center estimates *56 million* people are afflicted with such pestilences as hepatitis B, chlamydia, HIV, and gonorrhea. Some 31 million Americans—one in eight—carry the genital herpes virus, an incurable infection that can break out at any time. It keeps getting worse. Currently about 12 million new infections occur every year, and two-thirds of the victims are *under* twenty-five years of age and *one-fourth* are *teenagers.*

A quick look at a few charts will complete this mini-tour of television sexuality—

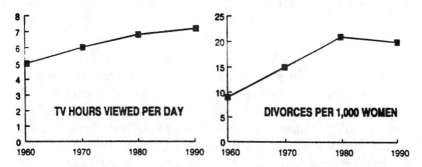

No cause-and-effect relationship can be *absolutely* proven between the 40 percent increase in TV watching, the proliferation of dramatized sexual promiscuity on television, and the 265 percent jump in the divorce rate over the past thirty-five years. Still, it takes an ostrich with head buried in sand not to see a connection between TV's relentless "liberalization" of sexual content from 1970 onward and today's popular acceptance of casual sex, "swinging," and adultery in American society.

Finally, two other end-of-century trends confirm our thesis. First, the U.S. Census Bureau indicates that 1993's median age for first marriages hit its oldest level ever at 24.5 years for women and 26.5 years for men. "More and more couples are choosing to live together first," says marriage therapist Thomas Seibt, in explaining this drift to later marriages. Second, another government report reveals that half a million U.S. teenagers have babies each year, the highest adolescent birth rate in the *entire developed world.* Is television solely and exclusively to blame? The answer must be no. But if the question is changed to "Does TV play a role in the carnal decay afflicting America?" the answer is clearly yes.

Researchers from Children Now, a national advocacy group, interviewed 750 youngsters ages ten to sixteen and asked them how, if at all, television influenced the way they lived. The results were surprising. More than two out of three admit they are strongly affected by what they see on television. Though 77 percent complained there was too much sex before marriage portrayed, two out of three admitted that TV and movies influence "their peers" to have sex too young. Another two out of three said TV encouraged youngsters to disrespect their parents.

A separate independent study at the University of Illinois found that television molded a child's character more than any other societal influence—including their own families!

THE CASE FOR VIOLENCE

While apologists for the television establishment may deny its influence on *sexual* behavior, when it comes to television *violence*, the facts are not even arguable. A study by the American Psychological Association estimates that before he or she ever leaves elementary school, the typical child will have viewed 8,000 TV murders and 100,000 violent acts. By the time he or she graduates high school, that number has more than doubled.

Television spokesman George Vradenberg, vice-president of Fox Inc., offers the chicken-or-the-egg argument. "We aren't really certain whether some people who see violence tend to become violent, or whether violent people just like to watch programs with violence," he says. Hogwash, counters Leonard Erons, one of three authors of the A.P.A. research. "The scientific debate is over."

Eron has researched TV violence for more than thirty-five years, tracking a study group of the same 875 males and females from age eight to thirty. His analysis clearly established that those boys and girls who watched more violent television as children were much more likely to commit serious crimes and to use violence when disciplining their own children. "What one learns about life from the television screen will be transmitted to the next generation, as well," Eron concludes.

The Center for Media and Public Affairs recently monitored a typical June day's worth of programs to check for violent acts. The stations monitored included network fare on ABC, CBS, NBC, and Fox; PBS offerings; independent station WDCA in Washington, D.C.; and cable stations WTBS, USA, HBO, and MTV. After eliminating all acts of unintended or accidental savagery, violent sports encounters, or brutality by animals on nature shows, over an eighteen-hour period the center counted 2,000 intentional, scripted, and real-life violent acts. Even more alarming, the majority of this mayhem appeared during children's programs, with cartoons registering twenty-five violent acts per hour.

Underscoring the international aspects of this phenomenon, another study published in the *Journal of the American Medical Association* concluded that the introduction of television into the United States, Canada, and South Africa almost exactly paralleled the increased murder rate in all three nations. From 1945 to 1970, the murder rates rose 92 percent and 93 percent respectively in the United States and Canada. In both countries, ownership of TV sets increased at almost the exact same proportions as the homicide rate.

To factor out the volatile racial climate in South Africa, the study focused strictly on the murder rate for whites. The analysis found a gradual decline in the murder rate from 1945 to 1970, which stabilized until 1975, the year television was first introduced into that nation. Thereafter the murder rate exploded, rising 130 percent by 1983. In an incendiary footnote, the editors of the *Journal of the American Medical Association* estimated that up to half of all homicides are inspired or influenced by television. Underlining that point, a French mother sued Télévision Française because her son was killed by a homemade bomb he made after a recipe aired on the American TV series *MacGyver.*

BLOOD ON THE STREETS

On the street, youthful carnage is epidemic. In California, homicide is the second leading cause of death for youngsters thirteen to nineteen years old. Nationwide, the Centers for Disease Control report that the homicide rate for teenage boys ages fifteen to nineteen almost *tripled* between 1985 and 1991. Arrests for crimes of violence by children under eighteen has almost doubled between 1970 and 1992.

Youths are arrested for violent crimes at earlier ages. In 1982, 390 youths ages thirteen to fifteen were arrested for murder. By 1992, this figure had jumped to 740. Teenagers are 2.5 times more likely to be victims of violence than those over age twenty. Three million thefts and acts of violence now take place at our nation's schools each year. One in five students carry weapons to school, while metal detectors and body searches are as common as fire drills and recesses. In a nationwide survey of 65,000 teenage schoolkids, two out of five say they "do not feel safe in their school."

CARNAGE BECOMES CASUAL

The almost casual way youngsters use violence today to settle disputes or take someone else's possessions is frightening. In Los Angeles, a teenager shot a cheerleader for her portable radio. In Oakland, a teenage boy stabbed another boy when he refused to pay back a twenty-five-cent debt. In Monrovia, a twelve-year-old boy killed a store owner over a bicycle. A fourteen-year-old Venice boy pushed an elderly woman out of the moving car he was trying to steal. A thirteen-year-old student at a parochial school in Riverside shot the principal and then himself.

In Harlem, Georgia, a ninth-grader killed one boy and wounded another in the school corridor. At an Atlanta high school, a fifteen-year-old was shot to death in the lunchroom by a boy with whom he had differences. In Dallas, another fifteen-year-old was fatally shot in the hallway by a fellow student. In Dartsmouth, Massachusetts, a ninth-grade boy was stabbed to death in his classroom by three other boys who laughed and traded high-fives after the attack. In Portsmouth, New Hampshire, a six-teen-year-old boy was convicted for raping and repeatedly stabbing a twenty-eight-year-old woman who miraculously survived the attack.

And it's not just the children of the poor who commit mayhem. At a prep school in New Hampshire, two students, ages fourteen and fif-teen, bashed a sixteen-year-old acquaintance over the head with an aluminum baseball bat, severely injuring him. "We're seeing an epidemic of youth violence," observes Sergeant Paul Famulari of the Portsmouth Police Department. "Kids now deal with any dispute by using weapons."

THE TELEVISION INDUSTRY AGREES—ALMOST

Even people in the television industry itself now concede—albeit grudgingly—that there is a causal relationship between TV violence and the acting out of aggressive feelings by children. A survey of television executives, writers, actors, and directors by *U.S. News & World Report* found that three in five—63 percent—of the Hollywood elite say the industry glorifies violence. The majority even admit they have avoided watching a program because of its violent content. But when it comes to cutting down on the savagery, Hollywood's ideas on how to improve things amount to pasting a bandage on an arterial wound.

While the four networks have established onscreen "parental advisory warnings," industry spokesmen admit that only one prime-time program—ABC's *NYPD Blue*—had been judged violent enough to merit such a warning notice.* No cartoons or sports shows were so

---

*Since the ratings system's latest revision, more prime-time shows (such as *Millennium*) have carried a violence warning. (Eds.)

labeled, and cable networks and independent stations are totally outside the coverage. In actual practice, these voluntary "violence warnings" now apply almost exclusively to TV movies and miniseries.

Venerable Hollywood producer Aaron Spelling, commenting "There's too much of this going on in society," offered a sop in the form of a *Beverly Hills 90210* episode that had one character buy a gun with near-fatal results. Naturally, he made the pistol the villain rather than violence per se. Another producer, Arnold Shapiro, produced a CBS *Schoolbreak Special* called *Kids Killing Kids* that featured four unconnected short dramas all ending in violence. But once the congressional hearings ended, media concern abated and with the pressure eased, it was back to showbiz as usual.

Other efforts to quell television savagery have been well intended but ultimately useless. For example, researchers from Harvard University launched an anti-violence campaign named "Squash It," featuring lead television characters who say "Squash it!" while walking away from potentially violent confrontations. Another Harvard-led commission recommended school programs to teach students how to manage anger, negotiate conflicts, and adopt another child's perspective as an antidote to television incitements. Mainline church groups have launched a Christian Peacemaker Corps, challenging recruits with the motto "Are you willing to lay down your life for peace?" Sending "peace foot soldiers" to inner-city streets, they are trained to "treat every human being like they are a child of God." Sounds noble, but after six years of operation, the corps has proven highly ineffective—not to say dangerous— against long knives, semi-automatic weapons, and the contemptuous barbarians who carry them.

Even as American society feels helpless against terror on the streets, the people see through the subterfuge and directly connect the carnage to the profusion of violence on television. According to a *Los Angeles Times* poll, four out of five Americans are convinced that television entertainment programs directly affect the level of violence in society. That same majority supports government intervention in the form of guidelines to restrict the mayhem on TV.

Overseas, violence on television is far more restricted than in the United States. Great Britain, Germany, Sweden, and Australia openly banish violent programming during key parts of the day, use strict rating systems to warn viewers, and impose tough penalties on those who violate government standards. While foreign rating boards are composed of social scientists and child development experts, the American board— the MPAA—only requires its board members be parents. In fact, the

MPAA panel consists of people connected to the television industry, a case of the fox guarding the hen house.

TV's ASSAULT AGAINST CHRISTIAN VALUES AND TRUTH

But as harmful as television's embrace of carnality and carnage may be, the deeper philosophical level from which it operates explains why it has been so destructive to modern society. It is television's *life values*—the ideas the medium chooses to emphasize and extol at the expense of Judeo-Christian principles—that have spearheaded the decline of western culture.

Peggy Wehmeyer, an evangelical Christian who works for ABC Television, reported, "The elite in this country—the courts, education, media, the arts—tend to view people who take their faith very seriously . . . with a smug, arrogant attitude." Harvard law professor Alan Dershowitz told a National Public Radio audience that Harvard Law School would never hire an evangelical Christian, since they would fail to pass the "acceptable ideology" test applied to all applicants.

Irving Kristol, prominent Jewish writer and conservative chronicler of the "culture wars" between leftist secularists and Judeo-Christian traditionalists, has emphatically declared victory for the left. "Those wars are over," he observes. "The Left has won. The Left today completely dominates the educational establishment, the entertainment industry, the universities, and the media. There is no point in trying to inject 'family values' into these institutions. They will debase and corrupt the very ideal while pretending to celebrate it."

Do those views paint a true picture of today's moral landscape? Sadly enough, they do. Three of four Americans today do not believe in absolute truth. More shockingly, nearly two of three professing born-again Christians reject the idea of absolute truth. To understand how this happened, we must consider the most basic battleground of all—the traditional family. For thousands of years the western world has held the biblical model as its highest ideal—a man and woman leave their parents, join together as "one flesh," honor their parents, raise children according to dictates of Scripture, reject divorce except in cases of adultery, and hold fast to the moral absolutes defined by the revealed Word of God.

Then, with the advent of television came a gradual erosion of historical perspectives and Bible-based morality. By 1962, the erosion began to show itself at all levels of society. The next year the Supreme Court, ruling on a suit brought by atheist Madalyn Murray O'Hair, effectively banned moral instructions and all activities based on religious teachings from public schools and by extension from all public institutions.

From that time on, the decline was dramatic. On the premise that ten pictures are worth 10,000 words, the following series of graphs speak for themselves and vividly illustrate the way the media jungle has impacted the decline and fall of the United States.

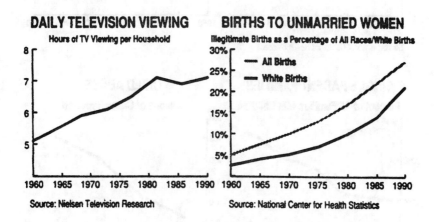

DAILY TELEVISION VIEWING
Hours of TV Viewing per Household
Source: Nielsen Television Research

BIRTHS TO UNMARRIED WOMEN
Illegitimate Births as a Percentage of All Races/White Births
All Births
White Births
Source: National Center for Health Statistics

LYING AND LOVE AS A LIFESTYLE

A recent survey by the Josephson Institute of Ethics found that lying, cheating, and stealing are now "an acceptable norm among high school and college students." Three out of five high schoolers and a third of all college students admit they cheated on an exam the past year, a third of the preppers and 16 percent of the collegians report stealing something during that same period, while 16 percent of the high school kids and 32 percent of the college students confessed to lying on a résumé or job application.

People have always lied, but in the era of the electronic village, young and old alike see and hear the rich and famous lie in full TV color. From George ("read my lips") Bush to Richard ("I'm not a crook") Nixon, the Menendez brothers ("someone's killed our parents!"), and Susan Smith ("a man stole my children"), the nation has

MARRIAGE AND DIVORCE RATES

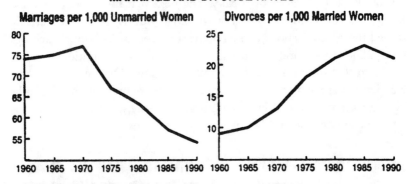

Marriages per 1,000 Unmarried Women   Divorces per 1,000 Married Women

Source: National Center for Health Statistics

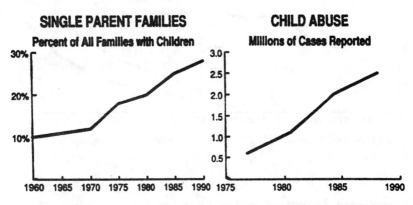

SINGLE PARENT FAMILIES

Percent of All Families with Children

Source: US Bureau of the Census

CHILD ABUSE

Millions of Cases Reported

Source American Humane Association; National
Committee for the Prevention of Child Abuse

NUMBER OF CRIMES COMMITTED

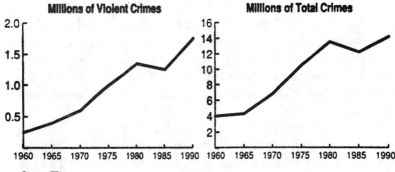

Millions of Violent Crimes   Millions of Total Crimes

Source: FBI

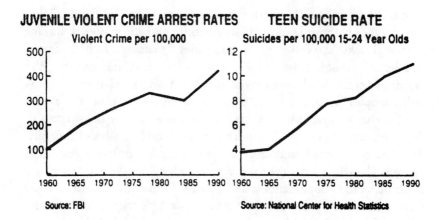

JUVENILE VIOLENT CRIME ARREST RATES

Violent Crime per 100,000

Source: FBI

TEEN SUICIDE RATE

Suicides per 100,000 15-24 Year Olds

Source: National Center for Health Statistics

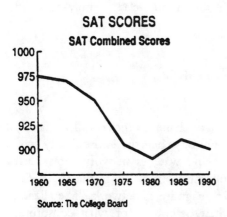

SAT SCORES

SAT Combined Scores

Source: The College Board

seen lying elevated to a tactical communications tool. Jack Benny remained a perpetual thirty-nine-year-old, actor David Leisure as "Joe Isuzu" made the line "he's lying" a potent sales tool for Isuzu cars, *Saturday Night Live* featured a pathological liar named Tommy Flanagan, and Olympic skater Tonya Harding's tearful denial of her plot to cripple arch competitor Nancy Kerrigan is a vivid memory.

Whether treated as comedy, drama, or political tragedy—and even when their lies were exposed—only one of these widely publicized liars went to jail (Susan Smith) and one (Tonya Harding) was rewarded with fame and accompanying wealth as she went on public appearance tours. The unstated social message is that lying pays off.

Numerous studies of the Hollywood elite reveal that they share a predominant worldview—one that evolved out of the 1960s "love generation." This mindset favors "alternative" lifestyles and advocates recreational drug use, sexual experimentation, nontraditional "families" that live together without legal or social sanction, and affirmative action for women, blacks, and other ethnic minorities. It champions homosexual and lesbian causes, bends over backwards for anything carrying the "environmental" label, and grows misty-eyed over third-world and socialist peoples "victimized" by "western imperialism" around the world.

On the negative side, most television movers and shakers detest all things military, America's European heritage, and Bible-based morality. They bear particular animosity for evangelical Christians and their "narrow" beliefs. Under the protective mantle of *entertainment,* they use dramatic, comic, documentary, and musical formats to popularize their ideas, values, and philosophy. As a result, today's television programming offers a relentlessly "politically correct" vision of America—a view that constantly tears down the middle-class, family-centered motifs of earlier generations.

THE DEATH OF FAMILY VIEWING

The best example of this revolutionary change is the so-called "family viewing hour," the 8:00–9:00 P.M. period when the entire family supposedly gathers before the TV set and watches network shows that reflect idealism, innocence, and uplifting themes. But in the 1990s, the eight o'clock hour has turned into a quagmire, as networks "liberalized" their guidelines and broadened their definitions of what constitutes "appropriate" early-evening fare.

"There is no 'family hour' anymore," laments Joan Ganz Cooney, founder of Children's Television Workshop. "The standards have fallen. I suspect it has to do with what has happened to the family in general. Family life has simply disintegrated along with the proliferation of media, and the lowest common denominator is finally prevailing."

Once upon a time, mom, dad, grandma, and the kids would circle the TV set after dinner and the network shows spoke to them. *The Waltons, The Brady Bunch, The Flying Nun, The Partridge Family, The Odd Couple, Happy Days, That Girl,* and *Little House on the Prairie* spun wholesome, clean-funny, uplifting yarns that primed the children for a sweet night's sleep. Even into the 1980s, the family hour was characterized by such comparatively noncontroversial programs as *Webster, The Facts of Life, The Cosby Show, Highway to Heaven, Full House,* and *Murder, She Wrote.* Then came the revolution.

THE NEW "FAMILY HOURS"

Parents sitting down with their kids to watch today's 8:00–9:00 P.M. shows find themselves hit by a bucket of sludge. CBS's *The Nanny,* for example, features a character who often makes racy sexual jokes. Fox's *Get Smart* episodes on Sunday evening features its lead characters doing slapstick stunts about copulation. The same network follows up on Mondays with *Melrose Place,* a soap opera about young men and women perpetually lusting after one another. On Thursdays, they run *Martin,* where the title character is constantly enmeshed in some kind of sexually provocative situation.

"All bets are off," notes Grant Tinker, former head of NBC. "The networks can do pretty much what they want. And that is even more true of cable. They seem to care very little about what kind of material is seen by the family."

The industry unashamedly confirms Tinker's view. Peter Jacobson, producer of CBS's *The Nanny,* insists that a show needs to be "hip and sexy" these days or it will fail. "You've got to be able to compete with the New Order or get left in the dust," he points out. "There's always room elsewhere for children's programming. It's up to the parents to judge what's appropriate. I believe it's okay to run anything on television any time. Freedom of choice is what made this country, and if you don't like it, you can change the channel."

Ed Hynes, director of the nonprofit group Morality In Media, feels we've reached the end of the road. "The death of family viewing on television is inevitable in a medium so dedicated to gratuitous sex, nudity, and foul language," he says. "Kids are being bombarded with smut, and not only in the evening. You see people grabbing their crotches and mooning one another during the daytime shows, too."

TELEVISION AND CHRISTIANITY

When it comes to religion generally—and the Christian faith particularly—television is, in the words of former FCC chairman Newton Minnow, a "veritable wasteland." At a time when four of five Americans profess belief in Jesus Christ and 100 million claim a "born-again" experience, and Bible churches experience dramatic growth, the world of television largely ignores or belittles the Christian faith.

A recent study conducted by researchers from Duke University Medical School, Northwestern University Medical Center, and the University of Dayton examined a random sample of one hundred network TV episodes. Out of 1,462 characters, only 82—or 5.6 percent— had an identifiable religious affiliation. Five of those eighty-two were members of religious cults while none were identified as being observant Jews. If few characters were notably religious, almost none were shown praying, attending church, or enjoying a group Bible study or other religious experience. The research report concludes, "The exploration of religion and spirituality in the lives of fictional characters is nearly invisible on network television."

A 1994 Media Research analysis studied 1,700 hours of prime-time programming and found religion alluded to only 253 times. That works out to only one mention of faith for every seven hours of prime-time programming. And when religion is referenced, it is usually demeaned, as when characters in NBC's *Cafe Americain* joked about having sex in a confessional booth or when an actor portraying a Protestant minister on CBS's *Picket Fences* quipped that the Vatican opposes contraception because a population explosion will enable Rome to dominate the world. Thomas Johnson, the study's co-author, observes, "We have a cultural disconnect between mainstream America and the creed of the Hollywood community."

The networks do occasionally throw a bone to Christian America —as in a Fox movie about the role of faith in former New York Jets linebacker Dennis Byrd's recovery from paralysis, or the later miniseries *Christy*. But William Fore, author of *Television and Religion,* thinks the small increase in shows showing faith as part of life is more an attempt to mollify the outrage of viewers and possible government regulators than an idealistic desire to fairly portray the role of religion in society.

26

The Pursuit of Sensation

Leo Bogart

Endlessly chasing the audience numbers, advertising media gravitate toward established formulas of entertainment, toward the lowest common denominator of taste. Commercial culture as a whole is laced with infantilism and insipidity. It thrives on fictional clichés that are guaranteed to produce satisfaction every time. It favors the vulgar, the mean, and the hackneyed, and shies away from experiment and variety. . . .

INNOCENT—AND NOT-SO-INNOCENT—PLEASURES

The media system is permeated by a sensationalism that seems to become progressively more blatant as national mores change: in turn, it has had profound effects on the national mores. There is nothing novel about the exploitation of prurient and sadistic instincts. What is disturbing is the scale on which this can now be done and the cynicism applied to the task. The outrageous coexists with the most dismal banality. Great works of art, literature, or drama are apt to arouse anxiety, irritation, or grief; commercial culture thrives on the happy ending. The innocent but idiotic refrain of dubbed laughter on the comedy sound track exemplifies a studied inanity that even staunch defenders of commercial culture find it hard to justify.

Headlines of supermarket tabloids:

"Dead Mom Gives Birth in Coffin"
"Princess Di Raped by Skinheads from Mars"
"A Space Alien Made Me Pregnant"
"Cat Eats Parrot—Now It Talks"
"Son Kills Father and Eats Him"[1]

Press release from Fox Broadcasting, synopsizing a new television show:

Marcy loses her wedding ring down the pants of Zorro the Great, a male exotic dancer.[2]

Newspaper headlines:

"2 Teen-Age Children are Held as Plotters of Father's Murder"
"Madman Sears 2 with Acid in Subway"
"Says Hotel Forced Her to be Sex Spy"
"Kinky Hubby's Into Bondage"
"Arizona Bishop Jailed Over Shootout"

Record titles:

Screaming for Vengeance
Children of the Grave
Bad to the Bone
Maneater
Paranoid

Names of rock groups appearing on MTV:

The Dead Kennedys
3 Teens Kill 4
Sadist Faction
Rash of Stabbings[3]

Television programs:

An Eye for an Eye
Destroyer
Shark Bait
Juggernaut

The Howling
Peeping Tom[4]

Such colorful specimens are hardly representative of the nation's mass media output, but they occur often enough to arouse revulsion and signal deliberate exploitation. A vice-president of Twentieth Century Fox Film, describing the possibilities in a new syndicated program, *Famous Jury Trials,* says: "There's a tremendous reaction to rape or murder. Everybody wants to look over everybody else's shoulder. It has great women's appeal."

This forthright pronouncement encapsulates the principal objection that can be made to commercial culture on moral and aesthetic grounds: It represents deliberate pandering to the worst instincts of the crowd. Disdain for the habits, manners, and tastes of the masses is in a long line that stretches back to Plato and Aristotle. To the old argument that the common is also commonplace and coarse, a new dimension has been added by a media system in which popular culture is manufactured for profit, and by rules that have little to do with the instincts or principles of creative expression. . . .

CHANGING STANDARDS

Prevailing notions of good taste have undergone constant change throughout history, and indeed vary widely among different societies. Our media system is unique in its tendency—and its capacity—to manipulate social standards in the pursuit of its commercial interest. The attempt to capture larger audiences has impelled media to press farther and farther against currently acceptable boundaries of propriety, and thus to move back the boundary posts themselves.[5]

Media standards are set not so much by censors as by those who produce content and have their own sense of the limits that cannot be transgressed. Newspapers and most magazines have resisted the temptation to intrude four-letter words or explicit sex into their columns (though they have become increasingly willing to be tolerant in straight news reporting). When they self-consciously refer to their responsibilities as "family" publications, they are expressing not only the conservative proclivities of their managements, but also a perception of their civic mission.

Pressures on the government-franchised and -regulated broadcast media have always been more potent than those on print or film. Program producers gear their content to what they believe will arouse the greatest public response. Says Rosalyn Weinman, NBC's head of broadcast standards and practices: "We view our job as trying to help the producers. . . . We're really trying to help them do what everyone wants to do: attract the most, offend the least."[6]

The program acceptability standards set by the networks in part reflect changes in popular mores; in part they are set arbitrarily. (The CBS program practices department rejected an episode of *Maude* [produced by Norman Lear] that involved spouse-swapping when it was produced for the 1974–75 season, but let it run in 1976.[7] In 1993, NBC cut a masturbation scene from *Saturday Night Live* but permitted a skit in which Britain's Prince Charles had his head transferred to a tampon to "get closer to" his girlfriend.)[8]

Enforcement of the acceptability rules was sharply curtailed at the close of the 1980s by budget cuts. Those standards were of declining significance as the networks lost audiences, and as every conceivable form of vice, in depiction and language, could be encountered on cable channels.

In 1991, ABC's highest-rated "movie of the week" was a violent and sadistic film called *The Tracey Thurman Story*, which advertisers avoided. ABC's Bob Iger said,

> We're programming to what we perceive to be the tastes and desires of the American public. If that means stories about AIDS, homosexuality or abortion, so be it. That's our pursuit and our right. There seems to be a great reluctance from advertisers. We lose millions a year over this.[9]

This seems doubtful, given the ample opportunity for advertising on other types of programs, even on ABC.

Networks are quite capable of making courageous decisions when the issue at stake is not entertainment but public information, where different conventions and rules apply. In 1978, ABC's Helen Whitney produced a documentary, "Youth Terror—The View From Behind the Gun," which interviewed a young man who repeated the word "motherfucker" over and over. The network's top brass assembled to judge the suitability of this interview, the climax of the film. Chairman Leonard Goldenson said, "I don't see how we can cut the language," and the film went on the air. Nineteen stations refused to carry it.[10] In this case, what was at stake was honesty in the portrayal of reality. Many changes in mass media mores cannot—even with great generosity—be put under that heading.

FILM IN THE AGE OF TELEVISION

The heightening of sensation in film and television content reflects the present interdependence of these media, even though one is supported by consumers and the other—until recently—by advertisers. Their mutual dependency reflects their intense competition as well as their common personalities and business interests. Radio was not a direct competitor of film as television was to become. Rather radio reinforced the movies' appeal, used their stars, their imagery, and their formulas. In contrast, television, which provided a cheaper, more readily accessible source of entertainment, changed America's movie experience. In 1946 the average American (including children) went to the movies twenty-nine times a year. By 1985, per capita movie attendance had declined to a rate of five times a year, and it has continued to drift downward slowly since then.[11] Movie experience changed again with the advent of cable television and the videocassette recorder.

Television occupied over twice as many hours of the day for the average person as radio did in its Golden Age, thus greatly enlarging the total amount of time spent with the media. The already well-established formulas rapidly became a major part of everyday experience in a way that had never existed in the past.

As film competed with television for audiences, production costs escalated, first in the process of vying for stars who could command their own price and a share of the gross, and then for scripts. At the start of the 1990s, Hollywood was veering away from films based on a name star and a simple plot to more complex plots that required a more literary origin. This increased the competition for options on new novels and escalated their prepublication prices, sometimes to the million-dollar level.

A generation earlier, the studios had moved to color productions as their standard, to emphasize the difference between films in the theater and the black and white images on the tiny tube. The theater screen became wider and larger. Multichannel sound (later stereo and Dolby) was introduced, and three-dimensional projection techniques were tried and abandoned. Casts became larger; locales, more exotic, and budgets, ever more extravagant.

Most important, Hollywood dramatically changed the content of the films themselves to differentiate them as much as possible from the blander programming material permitted by television network censors.

Violence became both more prevalent and more gory, sex progressively more explicit (especially after court rulings that restricted censorship), vulgar and obscene language more commonplace. Violence, sex, and obscenity often seemed to be introduced gratuitously, not as an essential component of the plot or character depiction, but to titillate the audience in ways that had once been forbidden by the office of the Motion Picture Association's director, Will Hays, and that the self-imposed codes of television still discouraged.

First general principle of the 1930 Motion Picture Association of America Code:

> No picture shall be produced which will lower the moral standards of those who see it.

The Hays Office's rigidly enforced production code was effective as long as the principal producing firms and the theater chains had common or closely associated ownerships. The code lost its teeth as a result of the forced divestiture of distribution facilities, competition from television and foreign films, the rise of independent producers, and the shifting of judicial standards of obscenity. In the 1960s, Supreme Court decisions on censorship raised the boom on the use of obscenity, nudity, and explicit sexual references in both print and motion pictures. Popular tolerance moved in parallel fashion.

When Hollywood lowered the barriers imposed by the old MPAA (Hays) Code, new problems were created for film promotion. Some newspapers set limits on suggestive copy and illustrations in advertisements for pornographic films; others refused to take them altogether—even mere listings of the title and cast. One prominent publisher rejected any advertising at all from a certain distributor who specialized in this kind of film. Would he extend this policy as a punitive measure if the distributor switched exclusively to films intended for general family audiences? He was troubled by this question but insisted that he had a perfect right to refuse even legitimate advertising from someone of whom he disapproved. A publisher's right to print only what he chooses to print is fundamental to the freedom of the press. But what of the theater owner's right to peddle his product, or the public's right to know about it? The argument that alternative means of communication exist, while true as a legal abstraction, has no bearing on the market realities of information flow in a one-paper town. There are far more serious issues involved here than the promotion of dirty movies or the censorship of one medium by another.

As more marginal films appeared, and "frank" or "adult" scenes and foul language became more commonplace, the fear of a renewed popular reaction led in 1968 to the creation of a new film-classification system designed to restrict juvenile attendance, rather than to modify content directly. The film ratings system was set up to protect children rather than the public at large, but it puts the burden of enforcement on parents, who must take their own steps to comply with the restrictions.

Of the films rated in 1968–69, 6 percent were given an X for their sexual content. In 1985, only one film was rated X. Erotic films were still being made, but they simply bypassed the ratings system altogether and slipped into their own channels of distribution. In 1968–69, 32 percent of the films rated received G ratings, which meant they were approved for a general audience of children as well as adults. A dozen years earlier, every film released by Hollywood might have qualified for such a rating. By 1985, only 4 percent of the films were rated G. It was widely believed in the industry that this rating discouraged attendance. (In spite of the prevailing assumption that a restricted rating is good box office, the handful of G-rated movies do better.)[12]

In 1990, the film industry went to a different rating system that somewhat blurred the former categories. Of the 621 films rated in 1992, only 3 percent were rated G, and another 14 percent PG (recommending parental "guidance" to ward off the obscenities or nudity shown); 18 percent were rated PG-13; 63 percent were R; and the remaining 1 percent were euphemistically labeled NC (not for children). The availability of pornographic videocassettes sharply reduced attendance at movie theaters specializing in X-rated movies, forcing substantial numbers of them to close down.

When MPAA president Jack Valenti invited him to chair the film ratings board, Richard Hefner's reaction was, "My mother didn't raise me to count nipples." After nineteen years as chairman, he said,

> We are in deep trouble. . . . I am saddened by what we do to ourselves in the media today. . . . The ratings system is designed purely to protect the asses of the motion picture industry against censorship. . . . I am appalled by most of what I see when I look at films. I wish the roof would open up and swallow the people who make the films and distribute them. . . . It is counterproductive, the way we create anti-social attitudes in the form of the garbage we spew forth in the media.[13]

To meet the competition of television, feature films became increasingly venturesome, testing the limits of what the audience would find acceptable, and defying conventional wisdom and morality. The changes in film content facilitated and legitimated the changes that took place during the same period in standards of language use and sexual mores.

Film and television content mirrored the transformation in values, but through a distorting lens. As always, the media also provided new role models and guidance for behavior. The changes in sexual attitudes and practices were facilitated by the universal exposure, through films and television, to subjects and scenes that had long been accessible only in secret, or with difficulty.

Television network programming practices also changed in direct response to the examples set by theatrical filmmaking. In spite of recurrent government protests and investigations, violence remained an important element of primetime TV drama. After one congressional inquiry, the television networks restricted its depiction, but as the scenes of mayhem moved off-camera, they were replaced by even more frightening images of terrorized or screaming victims.[14]

Behavior and speech that had been adopted by the film industry as a defense against television became staple fare on television itself. The effect was to drive motion picture content farther and farther beyond its former limits. Hollywood's current output wallows in gore, in contrast to the bygone epoch of the Hays Code, when it showed what the critic Stephen Farber calls "bloodless and painless" murder. He suggests that "this kind of 'tasteful,' antiseptic violence is in the long run more dangerous than the graphic brand of violence on movie screens today."[15] The anxiety created in the audience by suspense is probably far more damaging than the horror evoked by the actual sight of bodies mangled with all the art of studio makeup. . . .

Even more disturbing than the mayhem that fills screens large and small is the indifference to established codes of morality. To do what television could not do, Hollywood abandoned a fundamental theatrical convention that long antedated the movies themselves: punishment or retribution to wrongdoers. For the first time in the history of fiction, antisocial actions were glorified in those films whose heroes were criminals and whose villains were the forces of justice, depicted as incompetent, mean-spirited, and vindictive.

First film and then television fiction made criminal activity seem commonplace and its perpetrators sympathetic.[16] Wrongdoers inhabit splendid domiciles and move through glamorous surroundings. More and more typically, they successfully avoid the traditional painful consequences of their actions and instead survive to live more happily ever after.[17] Feature films show characters smoking marijuana or sniffing cocaine and enjoying it or joking about it. Civility and obedience to the law are commonly portrayed as antiquated and ridiculous. . . .

THE FICTIONAL WORLD OF TELEVISION

The fictional world of television, to which the American public dedicates a substantial part of its waking time, is one that differs markedly from that in which the same public spends its workaday life. It is inhabited by very different kinds of people and ruled by very different values. In this respect it is not distinguished from the imaginary worlds of other media. What really matters is the sheer pervasiveness of this fictional experience.

Dramatic programming in broadcasting has used a familiar assortment of genres, some providing unique situations and characters, as in feature-length films (including those made for TV), most of them using off-the-shelf themes, backgrounds, and personalities that maintain continuity—and therefore, a stable audience—from episode to episode: the serial drama, action series (with police, spy, mystery, or Western themes), and situation comedies. There is an extraordinary similarity of subject matter across different program types.[18]

What is the world of TV fiction like? It is an unusually violent place, but the violence is blissfully unattended by pain and suffering. Television's people drink alcohol fifteen times as often as water (which is not, after all, a social drink), but they smoke only in old movies. In daytime serials, they are preoccupied with health problems, though their ailments are exotic rather than commonplace; in the evening they turn remarkably healthy and trim. Virtually all of them either have perfect vision or wear permanent contact lenses. They bed down with prostitutes more often than with their spouses; in fact, their sex lives consist largely of extramarital affairs, with considerable dollops of violence and rape.

Fictional characters interest us precisely because they are different from us in certain critical respects, though not so different as to make us lose our capacity for identification and empathy. All forms of fiction, from the earliest legends to the present day, deal with atypical characters and scenes. The figures of the stage, of novels, films, and television dramas have never depicted a true cross-section of society.[19] Nearly three-fourths of television prime-time characters are male (typically in their late thirties to early forties), and men account for nearly nine out of ten of the college graduates and professionals. Television's elderly often tend to be senile or sinister, its blacks are comics; its workingmen, buffoons. Its women still often tend to pretelevision stereotypes; nearly three-fifths of them are shown simply in terms of their private lives. The world of work shown on television is glamorous; routine service and factory jobs are in the background or invisible. Lawyers outnumber plumbers, forty-four to one. Businessmen are commonly shown as criminals.[20]

Constant exposure to television's imaginary characters, settings, and situations molds the public's expectations of the surrounding reality.[21] The fantasy distortions of TV fiction are transferred into everyday life, and conduct depicted by television is easily taken to be acceptable conduct, even when it includes the antisocial.

Although televised fiction teaches no significant moral lessons in the tradition of the Greek theater, it does teach a large number of minor ones—often in contradiction to the standards of conduct to which society pays lip service—simply by virtue of its constant reiteration of the same formulaic characterizations and dilemmas. And by constantly diverting us from unpleasant reminders of the human condition, it restrains us from dealing with them too closely at the same time that it protects us from feeling their full force.

If the world of the mass media—especially that of television, the most pervasive medium of all—is permeated with unreality, does this not inevitably affect the public's judgment, its ability to see and cope with things as they are? It is easy to fall prey to the notion that what is out there is out there, that the reports of reality can be blotted out by a change of channel, just like the entertainment on the television set.

THE APPEAL OF VIOLENCE

Violence and sex—the two aspects of American commercial culture that generate the greatest popular and legislative concern—are significant ingredients in the recipe for success in building audiences. On the stage, the essence of dramatic conflict is in the clash of personalities and values, but in film and television, psychological confrontations are outnumbered by graphic portrayals of physical conflict. Corporal punishment, or the threat of it, takes a prominent part. Even the video footage of a tennis match is more exciting and enjoyable to viewers when accompanied by an audio commentary that describes the players as bitter enemies than when it describes them as friends or ignores the relationship altogether.[22]

"Violence is as American as apple pie," said the sixties black militant H. Rap Brown. It has surely been part of the scene since Columbus landed in the Caribbean, and it has been reenforced by centuries of armed combat. America's high rate of violence reflects both its past history and its present urban problems, but the content of mass media has also helped to shape our violent national character, through a process that starts early in life. And the violence in American mass media arises from the impersonal forces of the market as well as from the human appetite for sensation.

Newspapers and television news programs daily confront us with reports and images of a perilous world, beset by wars, catastrophes, and crime—a world incongruous with the one most Americans know firsthand. When people are asked what they remember in the news, murders and murderers are mentioned far more than foreign wars.[23] In fact, homicidal maniacs were seven times as memorable, at the time, as the bloody war between Iran and Iraq. Disturbing news reports and images are strongly reenforced by their fictional counterparts, which make horror seem commonplace and thus acceptable. (Televised imagery described as real arouses more attention and produces more aggressive feelings than when the identical scene is described as fictional.[24]) . . .

The U.S. murder rate (one every 22 minutes, doubled since 1960) is eleven times higher than Japan's and four times higher than Europe's.[25] Even so, the rate in prime-time network television is one thousand times higher than in real life.[26] Commercials for theatrical movies and promos for television programs are especially violent. TV murders do not result from quarrels—as they overwhelmingly do in the real world—but in the course of another crime.[27] Property crimes are underplayed, since burglary does not usually make for high drama. Although in reality only 5 percent of all arrests are for violent crimes, over half of all illegal acts shown on television involve violence.[28]

Antisocial content pervades television programming of all types.[29] Violence directed at innocent bystanders is also now a stock feature of comic films, in which mass annihilation, torture, and mutilation are presented as legitimate causes for amusement. . . .

Violence and sex were deliberately injected into NBC's programs on orders of Robert Kintner, the network's president in 1959. A former head of programming, David Levy, says, "There was nothing casual or accidental about the policy," and notes that the secretary of the program board was told to delete the directive from the minutes. "We don't want that kind of stuff in our records."[30] It would be hard to find a media executive who publicly espouses the use of violence for its own bloody

sake, but it is often defended as a part of everyday life and as a necessary device to maintain audience interest. According to CBS's 1985
program standards,

> a CBS television program is a guest in the home. It is expected to
> entertain and enlighten but not to offend or advocate. CBS enter-
> tainment programs are expected to conform to generally accepted
> boundaries of public taste and decorum. . . . As a component of
> human experience, the dramatic depiction of violence is permitted.
> . . . It should not be gratuitous, excessive, or glamorized. Violence
> should not be used exploitively to entice or shock an audience.

Speaking in less unctuous tones, Frederick S. Pierce, then president
of ABC Television, told the House Subcommittee on Communications[31] that programs

> that contain incidents of violence . . . have a legitimate place in a
> diverse program schedule. The best-made programs of this type have
> very large audiences, and the mail we receive commenting on these
> programs is both heavy and overwhelmingly positive. Throughout
> history, the essence of some drama has been conflict, and in such
> works violence has always been one means to resolve conflict. . . . We
> require that where programs contain conflict as a natural and dramatic
> consequence of plot development, it be responsibly portrayed and its
> consequences depicted. Gratuitous violence serves no useful purpose.

The CEO of one media conglomerate, who describes himself as
"very comfortable with what I get," was asked about violence in the
media. He answered,

> violence—that's greed. That's capitalism. If that's what the public
> wants, just give it to them. The New York Times and the Washington Post
> have the editor give the reader what the editor wants to see. I don't see
> that. I want to give the public what the public wants to see.[32]

A question may even be raised as to whether viewers identify the
aggressive acts that they see on television or in the movies as violence.[33]
People's reactions on the subject are characterized by an ambiguity that
suggests a conflict between the id and the superego. Only a third of the
public identify programs employing violence, sex, gross language, or
bad taste with poor quality. Less than a fourth dislike or avoid specific
programs because of such features, and of these only one in five claims
to take any specific action, like switching from an advertised brand.[34]

While half of the public acknowledge[35] that "I personally enjoy watching some entertainment programs featuring violence," three out of four agree that "violence on TV entertainment programs stimulates dangerous behavior in some adults." Two people in three think there is a relationship between violence on television and "the rising crime rate."[36] Three out of four say that graphic violence is shown "just to attract viewers" rather than to make a point.[37]

Is the public correct in its view that televised violence carries real-life consequences? To answer, we must confront the larger question of media effects. Before we come to those, however, we should consider another aspect of the sensationalism that media cultivate in their quest for audiences.

MEDIA EXPERIENCE AND MEDIA SUBSTANCE

What do mass media do to people? Objections to them on aesthetic, moral, or political grounds are surely less compelling than charges of specific damage to public safety or well-being. The rest of this [essay] considers how they have shaped the American scene and the American character, including its less admirable features. We must consider both the effects of their content and the effects of the activity—or lack of activity—they entail.

Media certainly occupy a great many hours. In particular, television, the supreme embodiment of commercial culture, eats up a substantial amount of the public's disposable time, though the amount has not changed appreciably since set ownership became almost universal. (Though daily set use in the average TV home grew from five hours in 1960 to over seven hours in 1993,[38] increase was offset by a decline in the number of viewers per set.) It should be noted that overall viewing levels (and ratings) are always inflated by those households in which the set is almost never turned off, and that the time spent in the presence of television is not necessarily a valid indication of its impact.

Viewers follow the path of least effort, watching those programs that make the fewest intellectual demands, that provide easy relaxation. Within these limits, however, they seek a range of content to avoid boredom. For this reason, every network and station program department—including even those of specialized cable networks—seeks a balance of different program types, including some of above average intellectual level or aesthetic merit. Television is bland and lacks real variety, but programs of quality may well be overrepresented in their share of broadcast time, relative to their actual appeal to the public.

As the medium that commands by far the greatest investment of the public's time, television has come in for an exceptional amount of criticism, partly because of regret that it has not lived up to its great potential for enlightenment. Edward R. Murrow remarked once, "If TV can merely 'entertain, amuse and insulate,' it's nothing but wires and lights in a box." He confessed to his sponsor "I wish we could uninvent television." . . .

Looking back thirty years after a memorable speech he delivered as chairman of the Federal Communications Commission, Newton Minow (who later became a director of CBS) said television was still (as he had earlier described it) a "vast wasteland," though it had improved in its range of choice, in its educational broadcasts, and in its news programming. "Prime-time entertainment shows still tend to underestimate the intelligence of the viewer."[39]

George Gerbner, a communications scholar who believes that American tastes and preferences are today cultivated mostly by television, argues that

> the more viewers watch . . . the fewer basic content choices they have. . . . Many of the most typical content patterns of life on television—action structure, casting, social typing, and fate—are common to most types of programming and news. They are inescapable. . . . The more viewers watch television, the more they share common conceptions of reality.[40]

Gerbner's last statement is no mere assertion; it is amply supported by research evidence. The "common conceptions of reality" to which he refers are imposed by media managements in their constant quest for larger audiences.

One recurrent criticism of all media is that, because they consume so much time and attention, they overload the senses and strain mental functions, creating a passive outlook toward life. They may just as easily be criticized for reducing the stimulation people get from direct human contacts.

What are the consequences of the sheer time expenditure on television? There is some indication that the prolonged passive inactivity of viewing inhibits reflection[41] and leaves its traces on personality, just as the tube's dominance over conversation has its subtle effects on the intimacy of family relationships. . . . The fragmented, disjointed nature of communication that is subjected to constant commercial interruption may have altered patterns of perception and learning. It is not altogether true that the medium is the message, though the medium is undoubtedly one of the messages and maybe one of the most important. But Marshall McLuhan was correct in calling attention to the psychological effort required to assemble meanings out of the flow of electronically driven light impulses bombarding the cathode ray tube, and in speculating on how these mental processes differ from the act of reading.

Incoherence may be innate in the special vocabulary of video, regardless of how it is programmed. Editing and camera techniques—cuts, pans, zooms, closeups, and flashbacks—are taken for granted by an experienced viewer. Children now master them as a normal part of the process of cognitive development, much as the infant at an early stage penetrates the mystery of peek-a-boo, but television's rapid pace and frequent cuts and shifts seem to stymie their learning. Psychologists Fred and Merrelyn Emery assail television's "inability to instruct as distinct from its ability to inform,"[42] and conclude that it

> not only impairs the ability of the viewer to attend, it also, by taking over a complex of direct and indirect neural pathways, decreases vigilance—the general state of arousal which prepares the organism for action should its attention be drawn to a specific stimulus.

After a thirteen-year study in which people recorded their moods throughout the day in response to electronic beepers, Robert Kubey and Mihaly Csikszentmihalyi found that

> people report feeling more passive and less able to concentrate after they view television. The passivity spills over into how they feel after viewing. A kind of inertia develops, and it becomes more and more difficult to get up and do something active. In other words, viewing leads to more viewing.[43]

Paradoxically, the more people watch, the less they enjoy it. Activities that engage other people are enjoyed more than television viewing, which generates the same level of emotional affect as work and doing chores. Next to resting, it is the least active of all "activities," most resembling "idling" and daydreaming. After watching TV, viewers find it more difficult to concentrate, are less activated, and don't feel as relaxed or as well.

The mere activity—or rather, nonactivity—of viewing appears to have physiological side effects. People who watch television a lot are in worse physical shape than light viewers.[44] During the past twenty years, obesity has increased considerably among children—especially boys, who are more responsive than girls to TV ads for candy and soft drinks.[45] Thus the physical and psychological effects of television content interact with those produced by excessive viewing.

IQ scores are substantially lower among children who spend more time viewing. So, by a smaller but consistent margin, are their school achievement levels.[46] Television does not affect homework,[47] but it seems to slow down the acquisition of reading skills, displaces reading practice for at least some children, and has a negative effect on creativity and the imagination.[48]

Most significantly, the character of the particular programs viewed has no bearing on the findings, for children or for adults. Perhaps the mainstream content of television has an increasingly homogeneous character that seems to blur the distinction between program types. In short, while media content and character are hard to separate, the substance is far less important than the viewing experience itself. . . .[49]

Audio or video, media dependency reflects the direct impact of technology on human behavior and not the sins attributable to commercial culture. Addiction to television, stereo headsets, comic books, or other media anodynes, like addiction to substances, has causes that go deep. Yet media's power over people is inseparable from the motives that lead those who own them to strive for the largest audiences they can get. Commercial culture can hardly be altogether absolved of blame for the consequences of media exposure.

MEDIA AS CHANGE AGENTS

If mere exposure to the media has effects, what of their messages? Consider the *Communist Manifesto* or *Mein Kampf. Uncle Tom's Cabin* did not bring on the Civil War, but it had a profound influence on attitudes toward slavery.

Numerous studies of newspapers and of certain types of magazines, books, and radio programs have illuminated their positive, life-enhancing, and socially adaptive functions. Television has also prompted some research of this style into what has been called its "pro-social" influence (for example, how it broadens intellectual horizons and teaches children cognitive skills). But far more money and effort have been devoted to investigation of the harm it can do.

Some scholars hold to a theory of "powerful effects," and others maintain that media merely reinforce the workings of primary social institutions: family, school, church, workplace. The "minimal effects" theory is exemplified by former FCC chairman Mark Fowler's flip characterization of TV as "a toaster with pictures." (He is actually not that far off the mark, at least for a substantial minority of viewers, who say they use TV as a "background.") But only a fraction of the exposure to media is on this incidental level.

Debates have raged for years regarding the specific effects of media violence on children's behavior and of pornography on sexual mores. In such public confrontations, media advocates have generally argued that their effects are minor: that the public does not imitate what it sees or reads about, that antisocial aggressiveness is caused by family and environmental conditions, and that the added impact of the media is negligible. The television industry's contention that its social effects are small is in marked contrast to its eagerness to assert its sales power for advertisers, of which there is abundant evidence. . . .

No one has ever seriously argued that media content is a more significant influence on children than family upbringing or peer group pressure. The media are now so firmly woven into the fabric of American culture that their effects are almost impossible to disentangle from all the other influences on patterns of conduct and thought. The values they promulgate have already been incorporated to differing degrees and in different ways in the subcultures of various parts of the population.

Consider the changes in sexual mores. They were induced by a variety of complex forces: the new technology of contraception; the massive entry of women into the work force, with the consequent alteration of sex roles, household composition, and living patterns; the coming of age of the postwar baby-boom generation, whose sheer size put pressure on existing institutions and whose rebelliousness was spurred by the strains of the Vietnam War. The proportion of fifteen-year-old girls who had had sexual intercourse nearly doubled between 1971 and 1986.[50] It is impossible to say in what measure the media were cause, in what measure effect. . . .

The years of television have coincided with a vast increase in social pathology in the United States. Crime, delinquency, illegitimacy, divorce, drug and alcohol abuse, mental illness, and suicide arise from the stresses of a society that has undergone remarkable and rapid change. These ailments particularly afflict the economically disadvantaged, as do milder manifestations like interpersonal aggressiveness, mistrust, family tension, and inferior school performance. But it is the disadvantaged who have been most drawn to television entertainment both as an inexpensive pastime and as an easy form of fantasy-fulfillment. (Blacks watch half again as much television as other Americans.)

Any attempt to establish the effects of television must control for the fact that wealthy, well-educated, self-confident people spend less time viewing than poor people whose lives are stressful and empty. Social class relates closely to psychological traits that are associated with, and perhaps reinforced by, viewing: anxiety, loneliness, and a lack of purpose.[51] (Heavy smokers are likely to be TV addicts, too.) Poor, less-educated, and divorced or separated people are especially inclined to use television to avoid dark moods that come from being alone and having time on their hands. These patterns heighten the complexity of tracing connections between television viewing and the indicators of social disintegration.

There is no conclusive way to compare adult behavior and beliefs before and after television. Even if there were accurate benchmarks, we could never be sure that television in and of itself was the cause of the change. After all, the attributes of American television that are most criticized—its commercialism, violence, vulgarity, and stereotyping of character and population groups—were firmly established in American mass media long before it arrived on the scene. Television has merely intensified public exposure to the dismal aspects of commercial culture.

In short, the impact of television, or of the mass media in general, is hard to record with scientific precision. It might be compared to that of water dripping on a stone. Any individual drop might not leave a detectable trace, but over time a long succession of drops would wear away an impression. Though the obstacles to measurement are formidable, and perhaps insurmountable, the effects of mass media have generated a very large amount of empirical research—disproportionate, in fact, to the appropriate rank of this important subject amidst the panoply of social issues deserving study. The evidence has been hard to translate into social policy.

MEASURING TV'S EFFECTS

Says Mark Fowler:

> If I am asked, "Do broadcasters have a responsibility when it comes to the special child audience upon which their license renewal will depend?" the answer, I think, should be no.[52]

The greatest public and legislative concern over the impact of the mass media has always centered on children, impressionable creatures who lack the judgment required to distinguish the merits or validity of what they are exposed to. Attention has at various times focused on the harmful influences of the movies, of comic books, and of the lyrics in popular musical recordings. The criticism has a number of facets, related to learning ability, the distortion of reality, and the specific subjects of violence and sex. As usual, television has been at the center of the criticism, comment, and study. There is good reason for this, as Cedric Cullingford points out:

> When children talk about their interests, without any soliciting about television, it is firstly clear that television is a most important part of their lives. It is, by far, the most mentioned commodity. But it is nearly always part of a larger pattern of play, of domestic details, of the texture of family life. Other activities are not excluded, or replaced.[53]

Not excluded or replaced, I would agree, but inevitably diminished. Children spend an enormous part of their time in front of the tube, an average of about four hours a day, by some estimates.[54] In an era of working mothers, when television is widely used as a substitute for parental supervision, childhood viewing habits have inevitably reflected those of adults. The more television the parents watch, the more their children watch. Children differ from adults not only in what they view, but in how they view it. Adults are bored by repetitive content; children enjoy it. Adults see programs as wholes, with beginnings, middles, and ends; children do not.[55]

Children's programming on television is intended as diversion rather than instruction, with a few notable exceptions in public broadcasting. Fiction represents 80 to 90 percent of all children's series. The Saturday morning cartoons are violence-filled, crudely rendered, and heavily loaded with commercials.

The character of children's programs may not be altogether to the point. By the age of nine or ten, most of the television a child sees is adult programming. (Conversely, many adults also watch children's programming, with or without children present.) With the deregulation of broadcasting in the Reagan years, the networks could disregard the presence of the vast juvenile audience after 8 P.M. According to NBC's chief programmer at the time, Brandon Tartikoff, "heavy adventure with acts of violence, jeopardy, and threatening action" were now allowed.

Television addresses children directly with a substantial flow of commercials for toys, sweets, cereals, and soft drinks. But children watching adult programs are exposed to a much greater volume of advertising that is not intended for them, and that becomes a powerful formative influence. They are also exposed to a kind·of violence different from the knockabout zapping of cartoons.

I have just pointed out that the households where children and adults spend most time watching are those where learning is least valued, family tensions are greatest, and aggressive behavior is more common. If we compare heavy and light *adult* viewers of dramatic programming (with its heavy component of violence), we anticipate that the heavy viewers will be more aggressive—and they are. We may suspect that a consistent and heavy dosage of television violence boosts their existing aggressive propensities. If we took pains to factor out the attributes initially associated with heavy viewing, could we establish the effects of several years of *additional* viewing in raising the level of aggression to an even higher point? Such a demonstration would require an extraordinarily complicated and costly experiment and exceed the practical capacities of applied social research. The same questions might well apply to the juvenile audience.

In one expensive and elaborate effort, a group of NBC researchers tried to investigate what additional television viewing, at different levels, did to the behavior of school-aged children who at the outset already had widely varying degrees of preschool television exposure.[56] With the best of intentions, the samples were not large enough to prove the case that the additional television made a difference, since the heavy-viewing children were already more aggressive to start. NBC touted the conclusion that this conformed to the "null hypothesis" that additional TV watching did not make a difference. What was really shown were the limitations of the survey budget.

The sheer amount of television children watch might be expected to have consequences for their learning abilities and behavior, as I have already shown they do. But what of the actual content of the television programs they look at? How do children interpret the world they see on television and reconcile its features with what they see at home and in the everyday life around them? The eminent child psychologist Jean Piaget observes that children before the age of seven are egocentric and thus unable to understand reality. The images in fairy tales seem real for them because they accord with their fantasies.[57]

Whether children interpret the television violence they see as "fantasies" or "real" is very much influenced by the context and by whether the violence shown is justified by some rationale.[58] They imitate powerful and successful figures more than weak and unsuccessful ones. Children who are most aggressive in their attitudes (particularly the most avid viewers, from disadvantaged backgrounds) are most likely to regard what they see on the tube as similar to real life. The imaginary world of television has the power to overwhelm the world the child observes directly.[59] The evidence generally confirms that television is an influence on the way children behave, and violent television makes them behave badly. Most of this violence is embedded in the adult programming that youngsters freely watch.

A substantial body of social research supports the commonsense conclusion that antisocial media content encourages and channels antisocial behavior, both in children and in adults.[60] The media bring aberrant forms of behavior into general awareness. They provide models of behavior for disturbed individuals, whether these get their ideas from books, like *Don Quixote,* or from films, like juvenile delinquents whose lawyers try to blame producers for their clients' crimes. After the assassinations of President John F. Kennedy, his brother Robert, and Martin Luther King Jr.,[61] the number of threats a year against the lives of prominent government figures jumped more than fivefold. The number of homicides increases significantly after publicized prizefights "in which violence is rewarded" and drops significantly after publicized murder trials, death sentences, life sentences, and executions "in which violence is punished." Suicides increased after Marilyn Monroe's death.[62]

The response to violence depends on its context; it varies for individuals with different capacities for fantasy. Barrie Gunter, a researcher for British commercial television, suggests that "the practiced day-dreamer can turn to fantasy activity to work out or resolve anger-arousing problem situations, whereas the inexperienced daydreamer is more limited to the direct behavioral expression of aggression."[63] But the qualifying effects of individual personality, like those of the interpretation or context for violence, should not obscure the central point, which is the link between media content and violent actions.

Laboratory experiments show that exposure to media violence produces aggressive feelings or actions; it also increases tolerance for violence committed by others. A comprehensive review of the voluminous literature on the relationship between aggressive behavior and viewing television violence demonstrates what the distinguished authors call "a bidirectional causal relation"—that is to say, a two-way connection.[64] What can be convincingly seen in the psychological laboratory is hard to replicate in the infinitely more complex conditions of real life—but the connection is there, all the same.

Social scientists seek to understand the subtle relationships between different kinds of media experience and subsequent behavior. Government commissions look for "proof," using the metaphors of jurisprudence. Why is it so difficult to extract causal proof from social field experiments? Given the absence of a smoking gun, broadcast industry researchers have continued to insist that "there is no consensus among researchers regarding the relationship between television and aggression, and a spirited debate continues within the scientific community."[65] The senior scientific advisers to the National Institute for Mental Health [NIMH]—which had squarely affirmed the relationship—called this statement

> a shallow attempt, ostensibly for public consumption, to focus on only one portion of the NIMH review, rehash industry attacks on independent research of the past ten years, ignore or distort both the evidence presented in the NIMH report and the consensus of the field, and present conclusions that obscure the issue and deceive the readers.[66]

Reinforcing this strong position, the Council of the American Psychological Association in 1985 passed a resolution stating that "the conclusion drawn on the basis of twenty-five years of research and a sizable number of experimental and field investigations is that viewing televised violence may lead to increases in aggressive attitudes, values and behavior, particularly in children" and urged the television industry to reduce "direct imitable violence."[67]

Social science is a dynamic body of knowledge and theory that represents current understanding of human beings and their relationships. It must constantly confront new evidence that appears inconsistent with what is already known or believed, and assimilate that new evidence by refining its theories or improving its methods. By contrast, applied social research is always conducted with pragmatic ends in view; it is intended to guide the policymaker. In social science, no statements can ever be accepted as final; in policymaking they must be, as a basis for taking action.

In 1993, the networks yielded to congressional pressure and introduced, as a two-year experiment, a "parental advisory" label preceding programs that, in *their* own judgments, were unsuitable for young children to watch.[69] But this accommodation was accepted with great indignation, as a strictly pragmatic act. At the press conference announcing the new system, Howard Stringer, president of the CBS Broadcast Group, noted that *Julius Caesar* had violence and that "tragedy ends in death." MPAA's Jack Valenti, who also participated, placed the burden of responsibility upon parents,[69] thereby evading the main point—that violent shows are most often viewed in the very households where television is used as a babysitter and where parental control is least likely to be exercised.

Under pressure from Attorney General Janet Reno,[70] the networks also appeared to be accepting the idea of an independent evaluation of the violence levels in their programming. Meanwhile, the cable industry prepared a plan to rate programming violence, shift violent shows to late evening hours, and introduce an electronic control system that would allow parents to block unacceptable programs.

As the experience of the motion picture industry has shown, labeling violence tends to enhance, not lessen, its presence. Production and programming practices have not changed, notwithstanding the best scholarly evidence and judgment, simply because it is widely believed that the ratings depend on the existing prescription. But the evidence does not support the contention that violence and sex are essential to capture the audience's interest.[71] Action and sound are sufficient to mobilize attention; literary history confirms that there are an infinite number of ways to arouse an audience; shifts in programming formulas do not affect viewing levels in the aggregate. Violence prevails because it pays off and is therefore in style, not because it satisfies intense innate human cravings.

Does the quality or character of what the media disseminate really matter at all, as I have been arguing . . . ? There is little scientific proof to back up the broad-gauge criticisms of commercial culture's preoccupation with material possessions, or of its standards of intelligence and taste. Those criticisms may resonate at a gut level, but their truth cannot be demonstrated. By contrast, the evidence quite conclusively shows that media sex and violence influence social behavior, although they do so in a way that interacts with more direct and powerful interpersonal forces. In recent years the spotlight has focused on television, but no medium of communication can be blamed for the way it is controlled and used. Sensationalism is a salient feature of commercial culture. . . .

NOTES

1. One should not have the illusion that these tabloids operate on a shoestring. The *National Enquirer's* newsroom budget was $16 million at one point.

2. *New York Times,* December 8, 1987.

3. Compiled by National Coalition on Television Violence.

4. Cited in *The New Yorker,* December 6, 1982.

5. Most of the public agrees that television "presents a permissive and immoral set of values which are bad for the country." (*Time,* June 1, 1981.)

6. *New York Times,* March 23, 1993.

7. Robert Sklar, *Prime Time America: Life On and Behind the Television Screen* (New York: Oxford, 1980), p. 7.

8. *Inside Media,* February 17, 1993.

9. *Inside Media,* February 18, 1991.

10. Richard Richter, "The Network Documentary—Never More," paper presented at the Wilson Center Conference on the Future of News, 1989.

11. Admissions totaled 964 million in 1992, compared to 1.2 billion in 1984. (Motion Picture Association of America).

12. Study by Robert Cain of over one thousand films, cited by Michael Medved, *Hollywood vs. America: Popular Culture and the War on Traditional Values* (New York: HarperCollins, 1992), p. 287.

13. Address to the Dutch Treat Club, February 22, 1993.

14. Edward K. Palmer, *Children in the Cradle of Television* (Lexington, Mass.: Lexington Books, 1987), p. 35.

15. Stephen Farber, "The Bloody Movies: Why Film Violence Sells," *New York,* November 29, 1976, pp. 39–45.

16. As Robert and Linda Lichter and Stanley Rothman put it, "television manages to enforce the law without glorifying the law-enforcement establishment. . . . More and more often on prime time, the insiders break the law and the outsiders enforce it." S. Robert Lichter, Linda S. Lichter, and Stanley Rothman, *Watching America* (New York: Simon and Schuster, 1991), p. 230.

17. As Thomas Morgan describes it, "dealers and pushers are often depicted as enjoying the good life. They generally live in luxurious mansions, hold extravagant parties aboard yachts or on sprawling well-groomed lawns; they wear the finest designer clothes and drive the most expensive sports cars." (*New York Times,* September 3, 1986).

18. Nancy Signorielli, after an extensive content analysis, observes that "references to program themes (for example, the mention of nature, science, education, politics, drugs, etc.) health and illnesses, sexual behavior, eating and drinking, and the time-place-setting of a story tend to occur with the same frequency and with the same degree of emphasis no matter what type of program is seen. . . . Life is portrayed across genres in a remarkably similar way. . . . Whether characters are good or bad, are successful or fail, use drugs, are physically or mentally ill, or drink alcoholic beverages does not differ much from program type to program type. Moreover, characters tend to exhibit similar personality traits: they are attractive, fair, sociable, smart, etc." Nancy Signorielli, "Selective Television Viewing: A Limited Possibility," *Journal of Communication* 36, no. 3 (Summer 1986): 64–76.

19. "Television characters and their doings may be more exciting than people in their everyday lives, but in another respect televised fantasy is tamer than the real world. While reality can be uneven and full of surprises, our nightly entertainment is highly regular and patterned." Jib Fowles, *Television Viewers vs. Media Snobs: What TV Does for People* (New York: Stein and Day, 1982), p. 45.

20. They account for 12 percent of the characters in identifiable jobs, but for 32 percent of all the crimes (generally motivated by naked greed) and 40 percent of the murders. Their portrayal, more positive in television's earlier period, became sharply negative in the Vietnam War era. Moreover, programs that raised the theme of business ethics presented a progressively worse picture of corruption over the three decades analyzed. By contrast, professionals are overwhelmingly portrayed in a positive light, and their preoccupations have increasingly moved to broader social concerns. Ibid., pp. 132, 179. Nine out of ten private detectives are heroes, but only a little over half of the police officers. Linda and Robert Lichter, "Prime Time Crime: Who and Why," *Wall Street Journal,* January 6, 1984.

21. George Gerbner posits the notion of a "cultivation effect": Viewers perceive the real world in terms of what they see on TV and acquire feelings related to these perceptions. To illustrate this point, heavy viewers among blacks are more likely to believe that racial integration is prevalent, that blacks and whites are similar, and that most blacks belong to the middle class. Paula W. Matabane, "Television and the Black Audience: Cultivating Moderate Perspectives of Racial Integration," *Journal of Communication* 38, no. 4 (Autumn 1988): 21–31.

22. Jennings Bryant and Dolf Zillmann, "Pornography, Sexual Callousness, and the Trivialization of Rape," *Journal of Communication* 82, no. 4 (Autumn 1982): 10–21.

23. Survey by the Radio and Television News Directors Association.

24. Charles Atkin, "Effects of Realistic TV Violence vs. Fictional Violence on Aggression," *Journalism Quarterly* 60, no. 4 (Winter 1983): 615–21.

25. Violent crimes grew 355 percent between 1960 and 1990. Murder rates doubled, and reported rapes increased fourfold. The death rate for persons fifteen to twenty-four was 19 percent higher in 1973–74 than in 1960–61, because of the increase in violent deaths. (These figures are assembled by the Federal Bureau of Investigation from local statistics; as Christopher Jencks points out, surveys of victimization show a far less alarming rate of change.)

26. Lichter, Lichter, and Rothman, *Watching America,* p. 185. In 180 hours of prime-time programming on April 2,1992, there were 1,846 acts of violence, of which 175 resulted in death. (MTV videos were just as violent as the networks. Cf. study conducted by the Center for Media and Public Affairs and reported in *TV Guide,* August 22, 1992.)

27. Violent crimes shown on television have actually decreased somewhat in recent years, but the overall depicted crime rate is up. In a reappraisal of

television, Newton Minow called "the most troubling change . . . the rise in the quantity and quality of violence." By the time a child reaches the age of eighteen, Minow estimated, he had seen 25,000 televised murders. Newton N. Minow, "How Vast the Wasteland Now," address to the Gannett Foundation Media Center, March 9, 1991.

28. Lichter, Lichter, and Rothman, *Watching America*, p. 204.

29. Deadly weapons appeared nine times in each hour of prime-time action programs in 1977 (though 84 percent of the shots they fired were misses). Maria Wilson and Patricia Beaulieu Higgins, "Television's Action Arsenal: Weapon Use in Prime Time," U.S. Conference of Mayors, 1977.

30. David Levy, "Guns, Sex and Network Secrets," *Washington Post*, August 1, 1993.

31. *Washington Post*, March 2, 1977.

32. Personal interview.

33. Cf. Cedric Cullingford, *Children and Television* (New York: St. Martin's Press, 1984).

34. Opinion Research Corporation survey reported in *Marketing News*, September 2, 1983.

35. In a 1977 Trendex survey.

36. 1982 Gallup poll.

37. Times-Mirror survey, 1993.

38. These figures are reported by A. C. Nielsen. Other estimates of viewing time, based on academic studies, run well below the figures projected by the commercial ratings services, which indicate that there is, on average, about one viewer for every set turned on. In a pioneer use of the "people meter," a device that measures individual viewing, AGB found that the proportion of people viewing was 56 percent of the household rating.

39. Newton N. Minow, "TV's Still a Vast Wasteland—But Improving," *TV Guide*, March 17, 1986, pp. 2–3.

40. George Gerbner, "Miracles of Communication Technology: Powerful Audience, Diverse Choices and Other Fairy Tales," in Janet Wasko, ed., *Illuminating the Blind Spots* (New York: Ablex, 1993).

41. "It is possible," write Dorothy and Jerome Singer, "that the immediacy of television precludes our more active integration of images and words. We need time to replay mentally material just witnessed and also to link pictures and sounds to word labels that make for the most efficient kind of storage and retrieval. So rapidly does television material come at us that it defies the capacities of our brain to store much of it unless we actively turn our attention from the set and engage in some kind of mental rehearsal." Dorothy G. Singer and Jerome L. Singer, "Is Human Imagination Going Down the Tube?" *Chronicle of Higher Education*, April 23, 1979, p. 56.

42. Fred Emery and Merrelyn Emery, *A Choice of Futures* (Leiden: Martinus Neihoff, 1976), pp. 38, 67.

43. Robert Kubey and Mihaly Csikszentmihalyi, *Television and the Quality*

of Life: How Viewing Shapes Everyday Experience (Hillsdale, N.J.: Lawrence Erlbaum Associates, 1990).

44. Men who watch television for three or more hours a day are twice as likely to be obese as those who watch for less than an hour. Study by Larry Tucker, in *Adolescence* 21 (1987): 797–806, reported in *Psychology Today,* September 1989, p. 8. High-school boys who watch more than four hours of television a day do significantly less well on tests of physical exertion than infrequent viewers.

45. Analysis by William Deitz of data from the National Center for Health Statistics. *Psychology Today,* November 1988, p. 12.

46. Heavy viewing correlates with low school achievement. Cf. Gary D. Gaddy, "Television's Impact on High School Achievement," *Public Opinion Quarterly* 50, no. 3 (Fall 1986): 340–59. The students most adversely affected are both those who watch television most attentively and those who are most studious. Socially advantaged children are most harmed academically by heavy television watching.

47. A report prepared by Daniel Anderson and Patricia Collins for the Department of Education reviewed more than two hundred studies and did not find significant proof that television viewing affected homework performance. *APA Monitor,* March 1989. Jerome L. Singer points out, however, that this conclusion merely reflects the need for more research.

48. The National Assessment of Educational Progress studied thirteen-year-old children in Ireland, Korea, Spain, the United Kingdom, and four Canadian provinces. In every country, the more time a child spent with TV, the lower the performance in math and science. When sixth- and seventh-grade children were asked to provide ideas for solving social problems presented in video, audiotape, or print form, those exposed to video consistently gave fewer and less original solutions, and also more hackneyed ones. Caroline W. Meline, "Does the Medium Matter?" *Journal of Communication* 26, no. 3 (Summer 1976): 81–89. Television increases aggressive behavior both for children who are highly aggressive to begin with and for those who initially exhibit low aggressiveness. (Tannis MacBeth Williams, ed., *The Impact of Television: A Natural Experiment in Three Communities* (Orlando, Fla.: Academic, 1986.)

49. The substance still affects the common currency of known personalities and symbols. When there were fewer choices on TV, a single program could be familiar to proportionately far more viewers than today. *I Love Lucy* had a 46 rating in 1956. In 1992, the top show, *Roseanne,* had a 20.

50. Planned Parenthood Federation of America.

51. Robert W. Kubey, "Television Use in Everyday Life: Coping with Unstructured Time," *Journal of Communication* 36, no. 3 (Summer 1986): 108–23.

52. Cited by John Weisman, "Public Interest and Private Greed," *Columbia Journalism Review,* May/June 1990, p. 47.

53. Cedric Cullingford, *Children and Television* (New York: St. Martin's, 1984), pp. 136–37.

54. Nielsen reports they watch TV twenty-nine hours a week; those between two and a half and five and a half are said to watch over thirty-five hours, and those six to eleven average twenty-seven hours a week.

55. Marianne P. Winick and Charles Winick, *The Television Experience: What Children See* (Beverly Hills, Calif.: Sage), 1979.

56. J. Ronald Milavsky, Horst H. Stipp, Ronald C. Kessler, and William S. Rubens, *Television and Aggression: A Panel Study* (New York: Academic, 1983).

57. Jean Piaget, *The Child's Conception of the World* (New York: Harcourt Brace, 1929), p. 140.

58. Children aged nine to eleven were less frightened by a scene from *The Wizard of Oz* when told to remember it wasn't real than when asked to imagine themselves in the heroine's place. But with three- to five-year-olds, there was no difference in the reaction. Cf. Joanne Cantor, "Fright Responses to Mass Media Production," in Jennings Bryant and Dolf Zillmann, eds., *Responding to Television* (Hillsdale, N.J.: Lawrence Erlbaum Associates, 1991).

59. Cf. Timothy P. Meyer, "Children's Perceptions of Justified/Unjustified and Fictional/Real Film Violence," *Journal of Broadcasting* 17, no. 3 (Summer 1973): 321–32. Cf. also Jonathan L. Freedman, "Effect of Television Violence on Aggressiveness," *Psychological Bulletin* 96, no. 2 (September 1984): 227–46. Children's antisocial behavior diminishes and their prosocial behavior increases when they perceive television programs to be realistic. (Byron Reeves, "Children's Perceived Reality of Television and the Effects of Pro- and Anti-Social TV Content on Social Behavior," paper delivered to the Association for Education in Journalism, 1977.) Personal experience with the subject matter of TV programming does not appear to change the child's perceptions of whether or not it is real.

60. The most influential analyses of this subject, directed by George Gerbner, have classified violence in cartoons (characters beating or otherwise assailing each other) just like violence in other forms. A former CBS public relations executive, Gene Mater, scoffed, "Do you look upon that as violence? I sure in hell don't." *Wall Street Journal,* October 19, 1976. Another observer, in the same vein, comments: "Much of what children see on television passes them by. The more they see, the less likely it is that they will pay attention." Cullingford, *Children and Television,* p. 32. But the more they see, the more profound the effects may be. Indeed, children who watch a lot of television are less aroused (as measured by their skin conductance and blood volume pulse amplitude) by a violent film than light viewers, suggesting a "definite and measurable desensitization," comparable to what has been found among adults. Victor B. Cline, Robert G. Croft, and Steven Courrier, "Desensitization of Children to Television Violence," *Journal of Personality and Social Psychology* 27, no. 3 (September 1973): 360–65. Affirmation of the damage done by television violence is found in: The Committee on Social Issues, Group for the Advancement of Psychiatry, *The Child and Television Drama: The Psychosocial Impact of Cumulative Viewing* (New York: Mental Health Materials Center, 1982).

61. The question of media responsibility for individual acts of violence has been intensely debated for many years. It was a major focus of attention by the Presidential Commission on the Causes and Prevention of Violence. Cf. R. K. Baker and S. J. Ball, eds., *Violence and the Media* (Washington, D.C.: GPO, 1969). For a major series of studies on the effects of televised violence on children, cf. *Television and Growing Up: The Impact of Televised Violence.* Report to the Surgeon General from the Scientific Advisory Committee on Television and Social Behavior (Washington, D.C.: GPO, 1972).

62. David P. Phillips and John E. Hensley, "When Violence Is Rewarded or Punished: The Impact of Mass Media Stories on Homicide," *Journal of Communication* 34, no. 3 (Summer 1984): 101–16. An attack on the statistical validity of the findings was met by a convincing rejoinder: James N. Baron and Peter C. Reiss, "Same Time, Next Year: Aggregate Analyses of the Mass Media and Violent Behavior," *American Sociological Review* 50, no. 3 (June 1985): 347–63. David P. Phillips and Kenneth A. Bollen, "Same Time, Last Year: Selective Data Dredging for Negative Findings," ibid., pp. 364–71. Cf. also David P. Phillips, "The Influence of Suggestion on Suicide: Substantive and Theoretical Implications of the Werther Effect," *American Sociological Review* 39, no. 3 (June 1974): 340. This kind of epidemiological evidence has not been replicated in the psychological laboratory.

63. Barrie Gunter, "The Cathartic Potential of Television Drama." *Bulletin of the British Psychological Society* 33, no. 48 (1980): 448–50.

64. A more cautious look at the same body of research found "a consistent small positive correlation between viewing television violence and aggressiveness" but "little convincing evidence that in natural settings viewing television violence causes people to be more aggressive." Lynette Friedrich-Cofer and Aletha C. Huston, "Television Violence and Aggression: The Debate Continues," *Psychological Bulletin* 100, no. 3 (April 1983): 364–71. Jonathan L. Freedman, "Television Violence and Aggression: A Rejoinder," ibid., pp. 372–38.

65. Alan Wurtzel and Guy Lometi, "Researching Television Violence," in Arthur Asa Berger, ed., *Television in Society* (New Brunswick, N.J.: Transaction Books, 1987), pp. 117–32.

66. Steven H. Chaffee, George Gerbner, Beatrix A. Hamburg, Chester M. Pierce, Eli A. Rubinstein, Alberta E. Siegel, and Jerome L. Singer, "Defending the Indefensible," in Arthur Asa Berger, ed., ibid., pp. 133–42.

67. The association reaffirmed this position in 1992 through its Task Force on Television and Society. Leonard Eron, a task force member, reported to a congressional hearing on two hundred studies of television violence conducted between 1970 and 1990 and reckoned that an elementary school graduate had seen 8,000 televised murders and over 100,000 other violent acts. The task force report is: Aletha C. Huston et al., *Big World, Small Screen: The Role of Television in American Society* (Lincoln: University of Nebraska Press, 1992).

68. Congressman Edward Markey of Massachusetts suggested a blocking

device that parents could use to cut automatically a child's access to appropriately labeled shows.

69. *New York Times,* July 7, 1993.

70. Cf. Dolf Zillmann, "Anatomy of Suspense," in Percy H. Tannenbaum, ed., *The Entertainment Functions of Television* (Hillsdale, N.J.: Lawrence Erlbaum Associates, 1980).

71. Footnote not included in original source. (Eds.)

Chapter Six

Entertainment Media
and Ethics:
Toward Solutions

27

Changing the Way We Think

Newton N. Minow and Craig L. LaMay

Train up a child in the way he should go: and when he is old, he will
not depart from it.

—Proverbs, 22:6

The prospects for change in a world of wired "information highways"
are full of promise. As traditional communications regulations are made
obsolete by the development of new technologies, a sound and effective children's telecommunications policy can and should be strengthened by First Amendment principles. The single most important thing
Americans should do is think less about the technology that makes the
next communications revolution possible and more about what direction we want the revolution to take. This means acknowledging that we
can shape the future that is at hand. How should we do so? . . . [We
argue] that the guiding principle should be the public interest—and that
we all know what the public interest is: it is the best interests of our
children. In its Madisonian sense, to care about the public interest
means to address issues of civic responsibility. And nothing is more central to that responsibility than protecting and educating children.

Thus the foremost principle for realizing the public interest is to put
children first. They are our future; before long, they will be our gover-

nors. At the minimum, therefore, public policy should focus on three goals:

- It should meet the child's need to be prepared for life as a productive citizen. Television, the nation's most powerful teacher, should be a conduit for the generational transmission of democratic values and the values of simple decency.

- It should meet the child's need to be protected from harm that comes from continuous exposure to violence whose primary purpose is to serve as a conveyance for commercial matter.

- It must give every advantage to parents, helping them not only to control the passage of strangers in and out of their home but also to be better parents; it should place a premium on parent education and support, including parent-to-parent support.

Though . . . we have focused primarily on broadcast television, these principles are equally applicable to SuperTube.* For the present, and for the foreseeable future, broadcasting channels command far larger audiences of children than cable channels do, but the habits of mind and practice that dominated children's broadcast television for so long will almost certainly find their way into television's next generation if they are left unchallenged and unchanged today. It will not do to put off for the future what must be done now, before another generation of children is abandoned for sale in the marketplace. The evidence for such urgency is in the words and deeds of the men and women now running the television and interactive communications industries, and in the many years we have listened to them insist that any children's television—even bad children's programming—isn't worth the trouble unless the children who are watching can be delivered to advertisers as marketable products. The principles above, therefore, and the recommendations that follow from them concern the present, what Robert Pepper calls television's second and third stages. Our recommendations focus on broadcasting, but have implications for cable and for the world of SuperTube. Our principles, on the other hand, have *nothing* to do with television per se, and *everything* to do with the well-being of American children. As a nation we cannot ignore what Sissela Bok describes as the "call for all concerned—parents, educators,

---

*Newton and LaMay define Supertube as "a computer-driven video server . . . that will expand exponentially the power of individual viewers to manipulate information." (Eds.)

industry officials and . . . government, to come to grips" with the television environment which our children grow up in, where they learn
so much, so young, about the values of the adult world.[1] If we cannot
honor these simple principles—worse, if we cannot agree on their
importance—then we are not worthy of calling the United States the
world's standard-bearer for democracy.

There is a little-noted episode in American broadcast history that
suggests how deeply all of us already know this, and can act on what we
know. Of the preeminent children's television systems in the world, one
is Japan's, another Germany's. Both countries make extraordinary use of
television in their national educational systems. Both put a premium on
parent involvement and on education. But Japan's system was not created by the Japanese, nor Germany's by the Germans. The foundation
for each was laid after World War II by others who knew all too well the
dangers of leaving the public interest exclusively to the whims of private
power in the marketplace—by the occupying Americans. Now it is time
for Americans to rebuild our own television system. Translating the
public interest into a commitment to our children will take time and
public debate. We challenge the American people to demand that debate
and participate in it, for in the long run it will take a combination of
broad education, wise parenting, corporate responsibility, and smart and
forceful lawmaking to improve children's telecommunications.

We propose these recommendations:

**1. Congress should fulfill the promise of the 1990 Children's
Television Act. It should explicitly define the Communications
Act's "public interest" standard in terms of broadcasters' service to children, then give broadcasters two alternatives: either
make an enforceable commitment to meet a specified standard
of programming service for children on each of however many
channels they operate, or forgo public service to children and
pay for their use of the spectrum.**

With the first alternative, Congress needs to make the "educational
and informational" requirements of the Children's Television Act explicit
and require broadcasters to make public the record of their compliance.
Without clear requirements in the law, the alternative will be a failure—
for the simple reason that the FCC has never successfully enforced any
public-interest requirements over a long period of time, instead changing
its interpretation of the law with each new presidential administration
and congressional hearing. Explicit requirements for service to children
need to be clear, so as to be enforceable; farsighted, recognizing that

broadcasters will soon be using additional channels in the spectrum for purposes other than traditional programming; broad, to permit experimentation; and narrow, to prevent their being ignored or circumvented, regardless of who is in the White House or controls Congress.

Since 1993, the FCC under Chairman Reed Hundt has somewhat clarified the meaning of the Children's Television Act's "educational and informational" requirement. In June 1994, the commission took testimony from children's advocates, industry representatives, parents, and other concerned citizens. In April 1995, it issued several proposals for public comment, including one that would allow broadcasters within each market to pay other broadcasters to meet their children's programming obligations for them. At a minimum, said children's advocates, that obligation should be one hour a day of quality programming during times when children might actually be watching.

The proposal is a good start. But if history is any guide, even this mild recommendation will pass with the political winds. It will work only if two conditions are met. The first is that Congress grant broadcasters an antitrust exemption so that they may cooperate in the production and scheduling of quality children's programming. Requiring broadcasters to meet such a minimal public service is reasonable, but asking them to take financial lumps in the name of public service is counterproductive—and, more important, competition in this area will not benefit children. Far better that a network such as Fox, which has already had success with its preschool series *Cubhouse*, continue to program for younger viewers, while CBS serves six- to ten-year-olds and NBC, perhaps, young teens. Broadcasters might also differentiate their programs by subject matter. CBS, for example, airs the wonderfully wacky science show *Beakman's World* for older children and young teens; ABC might offer a science show for younger viewers, or perhaps a reading or news program. If broadcasters could discuss scheduling and avoid concurrent airtimes, children would also be able to watch all the quality programs made just for them, providing children themselves a brighter palette of weekly programming (and avoiding the kind of ghettoization that occurs when children's programs are all bunched into the same time period) and giving broadcasters a realistic opportunity to build a loyal viewership for their programs. Finally, says David Kleeman, director of the American Center for Children's Television,

> If kids knew that every day, at a consistent time, there would be a full hour of television just for them, broadcasters wouldn't need to be tied to the convention of half-hour and hour programs. The sixty minutes

could include any number of shorter pieces, each a length that suited its content. A ten-minute drama, a five-minute documentary, a twelve-minute game show—these just fit the attention span of young viewers, and writers, excited by the prospect of designing programming that broke all the rules, would love the challenge of creating shorter, tighter stories. . . . The children's hours could become the most innovative on television.[2]

The need for an antitrust exemption in this area is obvious: a diverse and quality children's programming service cannot be summoned out of thin air; broadcasters should be allowed to cooperate if an hour-a-day requirement is to benefit children.

No such initiative will work without a critical second step: that the hour of required programming be clearly labeled as the broadcaster's compliance with the law. The label should work just as the signs do that millions of Americans post prominently in the windows of their homes and businesses, letting children know that these places are safe refuges. The programming label indicates that the program's primary purpose is to educate, not to sell toys or junk food, and that it is safe, that there is a friend in the house instead of a stranger. In October 1994, ABC began experimenting with something very much like what we propose when it announced that it would use a special on-air logo to designate programs that are "particularly enjoyable for family viewing," according to ABC entertainment president Ted Harbert. The new "Family Viewing Logo" is to appear in the lower right-hand corner of the screen at the beginning of family programs and for several seconds after each commercial break. The label is a marketing device, not an advisory, says ABC's Chris Hikawa. But a similar label on educational programs would help parents or children who are searching for something to watch to find it easily. A label of this kind is friendly to viewers, to broadcasters, *and* to the First Amendment: it notifies parents that a program has special value, thus drawing attention to it and increasing its chances for success; it gives the public clear notice not only that the law's requirements are being met but how they are being met; and it protects broadcasters from constant government inquiries into programming practices and policies that do offend the First Amendment.

If broadcasters choose the second alternative, they will effectively be relieved of their public-interest obligations to children under the 1934 Communications Act; but, in return, they will have to pay a percentage of their annual revenues—between 1 and 3 percent—for spectrum leases. The money from those leases should, in turn, be required by statute to go to the production of children's programming on public broadcasting.

This second alternative has not been seriously considered since Congressman Van Deerlin's attempt to rewrite the Communications Act in the late 1970s. Its most ardent advocate today is Henry Geller, former FCC general counsel and head of the National Telecommunications and Information Administration—and also principal proponent of the 1990 Children's Television Act. Geller argues that sixty years of the Communications Act's public-interest standard have been a failure, and a particularly dismal failure where children are concerned. No amount of coaxing, cajoling, or threatening has produced an adequate or sustainable amount or quality of children's programming, nor is it ever likely to, he believes. Minimal requirements, such as an hour a day, are still woefully insufficient, Geller argues, and broadcasters will heed them with as little imagination, effort, and cost as possible. Far better, he says, to charge broadcasters a fee for the publicly owned spectrum they now use for free, and put that money toward funding noncommercial, not-for-profit children's programming.

In July 1994, Congress and the administration discovered just how valuable the spectrum could be when, for the first time ever, the FCC auctioned off a "narrowband" portion of the radio spectrum, soliciting bids for ten nationwide licenses for use with electronic pagers. The auction was expected to earn the government approximately $20 million; instead, after days of furious bidding, it earned nearly *thirty times that much*, almost $600 million. "My little socks are knocked off," said FCC commissioner Rachelle Chong. In the fall of 1994, a second narrowband auction earned more than $489 million. Finally, the FCC began an auction of "broadband" spectrum for wireless telephone service in December 1994, which, when it finally ends sometime in 1995, is expected to earn about $10 billion★; in its first week it earned more than $800 million. Such a windfall, says Geller, should wake Americans up to "what six megahertz of valuable spectrum is worth." Six megahertz is the valuable chunk of spectrum used by each commercial broadcaster, and Geller believes that Congress and the administration will inevitably ask broadcasters to pay for its use.

The important question is: where does the money go once the federal government gets it? Currently it disappears into the $1.5 trillion federal budget. The enormous lost opportunity that money represents is illustrated by the case of Austrian immigrant Stanley S. Newberg,

---

★While the auction is continuing, the present earnings are $7.7 billion. (Eds.)

who came to the United States in 1906, succeeded in manufacturing and real estate, and, when he died in 1986, bequeathed his fortune of $5.6 million to the United States government "in deep gratitude for the privilege of residing and living in this kind of government—notwithstanding many of its inequities." After Newberg's will was finally settled in 1994, the money went directly to the U.S. Bureau of Public Debt, where it lasted about ninety seconds.[3] And then it was gone, spent in the service of who knows what.

Coming as they do from publicly owned telecommunications resources, the revenues from the auctions ought to be invested in improving telecommunications for children. The idea of taking the money earned from the administration of a valuable public resource and investing it in another is not unprecedented. In 1965, Congress created the Land and Water Conservation Fund to provide federal financing for the acquisition of parks and other public lands by using money from offshore oil and gas leases. Later, in 1978, the Urban Parks and Recreation Recovery Program included similar financing provisions. The principle in both cases is the same: use the revenues from one irreplaceable resource to protect another.

Why should the revenues raised from spectrum auctions be used any differently, without some sort of real payback to the public? The money generated by a spectrum fee on broadcasters, for example, could go a long way. Edward Palmer, a noted observer of children's television practices throughout the world, has calculated that the cost of creating four years' worth of first-rate children's programs—an hour of original programming each weekday for each of three different age groups (two to five, six to nine, and ten to thirteen)—is about $63 million a year (or $1.50 per child per year).[4] Markle Foundation president Lloyd Morrisett, who has chronicled the meanderings of telecommunications policy for a quarter century, estimates that the cost is higher, between $200 million and $300 million. Either way the point is the same: even the most modest spectrum fee could easily turn children's television from a wasteland into a garden of delights. Today, annual gross television broadcasting revenues in the United States are conservatively estimated at about $25 billion, radio at $9 billion; *by itself, a bare minimum of 1 percent of broadcast television revenues would pay annually for $250 million of children's programming;* 3 percent would provide $750 million, a sum with which Americans could transform not only children's television, but childhood itself, and bring to fruition some of the extraordinary advances in education, health care, and family support that futurists predict for SuperTube. Currently, the Children's Television Endowment, created by the Children's Television Act in 1990 to support high-quality, educational programming, is pitifully underfunded. In 1994 it asked for $24 million to do its job, but Congress appropriated $1 million; for 1995, it appropriated $2.5 million. A similarly underfinanced effort to improve the lot of America's children is the Ready-to-Learn programming and satellite service, a virtual blueprint for dedicated, educational children's television. Congress created the service in 1993 but appropriated less than $7 million—after authorizing $30 million—with which to start it.*

Why not take some of the money from the administration or auction of telecommunications resources and put it toward children's services? Is there a better investment in our children's future? We should learn from past mistakes, such as the misuse of cable franchise fees, which cable companies must pay to make use of public streets, telephone poles, and other rights-of-way. Those fees yield about $800 million annually, but there is no stipulation that the money be used to support public-service programming, as was originally intended. Cities can spend the money any way they choose. Based on 5 percent of revenues, cable fees provide a city like Chicago more than $7.6 million a year. In most places this money simply disappears, as Geller says, into "pensions and potholes."

In every instance where the auction or administration of telecommunications resources yields revenues—whether from broadcast, cable, or even SuperTube—Congress should require by statute that at least a portion of the money be earmarked for children. The larger the tax base, the lower the percentage rate needed in any one medium; and the rate required to serve our children well is very small to begin with. Of the $10 billion minimum the federal government expects to earn from its spectrum auctions, for example, 2 to 3 percent would meet the annual programming costs that Morissett has calculated. A larger portion of the windfall could be given to connecting America's primary and secondary schools to the information highway, to testing new electronic educational services, and to training teachers to use them.

If instead the federal government does with that $10 billion what it did with Stanley Newberg's bequest—spend it—the money will last about forty-four hours. And then it, too, will be gone. By even the most conservative cost-benefit analysis, a much superior alternative would be to make that money last a lifetime—many millions of them. Invest public telecommunications revenues in our children.

---

*In 1995 Congress was considering rescinding the Ready-to-Learn budget even further.

2. Parents should monitor their children's television viewing and, whenever possible, watch television with them. This recommendation seems obvious, but remarkably few parents actually do it. Political and philosophical opposites—such as Charles Murray and Roger Wilkins—agree that if there is one thing that might make a genuine difference in the lives of America's children, it is parents who are effective and nurturing.* "No job is more important to our nation's future than that of a parent," the Carnegie Corporation has recently reported, "and no job is more challenging."[5] Certainly one place to begin is in front of the family television set.

Experts on children's television agree that the importance of the role of parents in making television better for children cannot be overestimated, and they begin and end their advice with one imperative: Sit down and watch with them.[6] Peggy Charren, former president of Action for Children's Television, has argued for years that if parents actually knew and cared about what their children watched, her job would be a lot easier. Research supports her view. The psychologist Patricia Marks Greenfield writes that an adult presence encourages a child to be an active, critical viewer:

> A pervasive finding in television research is that the effects of television programs on knowledge are stronger if an adult interacts with the child during the viewing process. The adult can encourage the children to pay attention, can make interpretations, and can explain things the child finds incomprehensible. Watching with the child is not enough; it is crucial to talk about the show being watched.[7]

What do you talk about? Experts recommend many different questions, comments, and activities, depending on the age of the children. Some can focus on teaching children to differentiate between TV and reality ("How come Theo on *The Cosby Show* seldom studies? Do you think he has as much homework as you?"). Some can get kids interested in the basics of television production ("Does the music make the story more exciting?" or "Have you noticed that the music always seems less happy whenever the bad guy comes on?"). Some can spur creative thinking ("How would you have preferred to see the story end?"), while others may point out racial or sexual stereotyping or educate chil-

---

*Charles Murray, co-author of *The Bell Curve*, is a conservative social scientist and commentator. Roger Williams, currently a professor of history at George Mason University, is a liberal who served in the Johnson administration's Justice Department.

dren about TV commercials ("They're trying to make you think that all that sand and ocean and sun come with Barbie. Did you fall for it?"). Many activities suggested by experts to complement TV viewing are didactic. For example, one resource suggests, "Teach your youngster the habit of writing down words he or she doesn't understand while watching television. Help your child to look those words up in the dictionary."[8] Of course, every time a child watches television the experience does not need to become a lesson in critical viewing. Like adults, children often want only to be entertained. One parent found that "it works well to intersperse several comments in one show, then leave the subject alone for several shows or days afterwards."[9]

Perhaps the most important reason parents should watch television with their children is that people like Dick Wolf, the producer of such programs as *Miami Vice* and *Law & Order*, dismiss the idea that the industry has any responsibility whatsoever toward parents or children. His own children, Wolf said, have "never seen any of the shows I've ever produced. They shouldn't be watching them."[10] Wolf may well be a fine parent, but the problem remains that millions of children *do* watch his programs. If their parents watched with them, they would have a chance to offset the messages they disagree with (such as gender or racial stereotyping) or find confusing or frightening (such as portrayals of sex and/or violence).

To mitigate the effects of televised violence, the American Psychological Association suggests that parents discuss why the violence happened and how painful it is; ask the child how the conflict might have been solved without violence; and explain how violence in entertainment is "faked" and not real. Parents should encourage children to watch programs with characters that cooperate with, help, and care for one another, and they should watch at least one episode of a program their children watch regularly to judge for themselves the program's suitability for their children.[11]

Parents who watch television with their children know that programs aren't the only thing to worry about. On commercial channels, children are bombarded with advertisements, many of them intended for adults. In a country where 85 percent of households own a VCR, one way to solve this problem is to establish a family video library, since parent-approved "family library" tapes need no future screening for replays. The television critic David Bianculli writes that he vigilantly screens what his children watch. "When they were younger," he says, "the only 'live' TV shows my children watched were *Mister Rogers' Neighborhood*, *Sesame Street*, and old *Looney Tunes* cartoon showcases. Otherwise, their TV came pretaped and prescreened."[12]

Parents who don't have the time to screen individual shows and episodes often wish they had the power to screen out entire channels. What they often do not know is that by law cable companies must offer parents some type of device that allows them to block out channels. Some technologically advanced cable companies offer sophisticated electronic equipment that allows one to program channels one would like to receive (CNN and C-SPAN are perennial parent favorites) and block out those not wanted (usually MTV or movie channels). In Evanston, Illinois, for example, such a device is available for an extra $1.95 per month.

Of course, many parents are dismayed less by what their children watch than by how much time they spend watching it. Their concern is not unfounded. Research shows that children who watch excessive amounts of television are less likely to do well in school, and that they are more likely to develop the kinds of health problems associated with a sedentary lifestyle and a diet high in junk food.[13] Parents who simply want to reduce their children's viewing time might consider purchasing a "mechanical disciplinarian" such as TV Allowance. In order to turn on a set equipped with TV Allowance, a child punches in his or her individual code; the machine then deducts each minute the television is on from a total number of minutes allotted by a parent. According to Randal Levenson, its creator, TV Allowance "allows children to budget their time, to learn to make choices, and to control their viewing."[14] Some strong advocates of TV rationing, such as the pediatrician and writer T. Berry Brazelton, recommend that children watch no more than an hour of television on school days and two hours a day on weekends. Brazelton, however, admits to a certain ambivalence about devices like TV Allowance. "Parents," he says, "ought to have the guts to do it themselves and not do it by a machine."[15]

In either case, the larger point is the same: parents must, in some way, take primary responsibility for what their children see on television. Very often the source of the problem is parents themselves, who on average watch between five and ten *more* hours of television a week than their children do.[16] Parents cannot control their children's viewing unless they also control their own, and when they do that they discover something else—the power of a good example.

3. Help parents protect their children from television violence and other programming they find objectionable. As Congress thinks about television's adaptation to the world of information highways, it should keep in mind that on real highways the law requires infant seats and seat belts to ensure children's safety. Children should travel the information highway with at least as much protection. Therefore Congress should, as Massachusetts congressman Edward Markey has proposed, empower parents to the fullest extent possible with the technological means of blocking unwanted strangers from their home, including those whom they consider violent, crude, and harmful. One such technological means is the v-chip, and it should be a required component of all television sets.*

Parents need to be aware of its availability, however; more important, there should be multiple sources of judgment about which programs are violent or otherwise unsuitable for children, since parents will differ in their views on this. While Congress should call on broadcast networks, independent television stations, and cable and satellite programmers to place parental advisories on material they may consider unsuitable for children, the government should not itself get into the business of rating programs. The best source of parental information must be parents themselves, using their own personal taste and discretion. Community groups—schools, PTAs, churches—can also rate programs, and other organizations may find a way to make such rating schemes profitable. The most ambitious and inventive such effort to date is OKTV Inc., which uses an independent advisory board of experts in children's issues to rate programs as either "OK" or "NOT OK" for each of two age groups (one to six, and seven to twelve), matches those ratings to local television viewing schedules, and then uses chip technology in TV set-top units to display either general programming (whatever happens to be on television) or children's programs that have been judged "OK." Significantly, OKTV works with cable and broadcast-only television service, and it does more than merely block out programs unsuitable for children—it can also lock in those that are good for them. Says OKTV creator Richard Leghorn:

> With OKTV service parents retain complete control of the system and can conveniently override it for whatever reason whenever they like. They can override OKTV ratings based on their own assessment of what is suitable or not suitable for their children based on press critiques, word-of-mouth opinion, or ratings and monitoring reports of others such as the motion picture classifications of MPAA or the violence warning labels planned by the cable and broadcast industries.

---

*The 1996 Telecommunications Act mandated the installation of the v-chip. By July of 1999, fifty percent of all sets sold with screens larger than thirteen inches must have the v-chip.

But OKTV service, which will be biased in favor of protection rather than permissiveness, will always be there to handle most, and for many parents all, of the tremendous burden parents now have in trying to protect their children from harmful programs and guide their viewing toward beneficial programs.[17]

Undoubtedly many parents will not take advantage of choice technology, and others will not consult either a ratings scheme or their own judgment. But so long as Congress sees to it that they have every opportunity to block programs they do not want their children to see, and does not itself engage in making content decisions, the First Amendment will be satisfied. Parents will have a realistic way of keeping unwelcome strangers out of their homes, and the range of programming available to adults on television will expand.

4. End Television's Commercial Exploitation of Children. Of all the research findings about children and television, the one on which there is virtually no disagreement is that small children do not understand the difference between programs and commercials. The FCC and the FTC have implicitly recognized in the past that commercials aimed at the very young are inherently deceptive. Congress should reconsider the commercial time constraints in the Children's Television Act, and forbid commercials in programming directed primarily at preschool children, those younger than six.

Objections to this recommendation will be of two kinds. The first, from broadcasters, will be that a commercial ban is economically irrational, that in the absence of commercials to support good programming for the very young, such programs will not exist. This is another way of saying that although they have received a valuable economic privilege for free in return for serving the public interest, broadcasters must now violate that interest in order to maximize profit levels. Is the idea of "sustaining time" first proposed by David Sarnoff and William Paley now a crime against nature? Were Adam Smith available for consultation on the matter, he would say that the burden of irrationality in this matter lies with broadcasters.

A second objection will be that a prohibition like this is unworkable. Those who believe so need only look to Canada for proof that it can work. The Canadian Association of Broadcasters, in cooperation with the Canadian Advertising Foundation (a private industry organization), voluntarily created a broadcast code for advertising to children twelve and under. Written in 1971 and revised in 1993, the code was created to

> serve as a guide to advertisers and agencies in preparing commercial messages which adequately recognize the special characteristics of the children's audience. Children, especially the very young, live in a world that is part imaginary, part real and sometimes do not distinguish clearly between the two. Children's advertising should respect and not abuse the power of the child's imagination.

The code, neither vague nor toothless, is an eleven-page document with specific restrictions regarding the "factual presentation" of products; the use of "undue pressure"; the scheduling of ads; the discussion of price and purchase terms; endorsements by program characters and celebrities; the promotion of "values inconsistent with the moral, ethical or legal standards of contemporary Canadian society"; the portrayal of unsafe toys or toy use; and comparison claims with other products. The Canadian Advertising Foundation can require an advertiser to substantiate any claim it makes for a children's product, and has the authority to administer the code anywhere in Canada—except Quebec, which bans broadcast advertising to children altogether. Broadcasters who air commercials for children that do not meet the CAF's standards can have their licenses revoked.

Do American children deserve any less protection than Canadian children do? It should no longer be acceptable for the programmers to claim, as the Fox Children's Network does in its trade advertisements, "We deliver more young viewers than anyone." Children are human beings, not commercial opportunities.

5. Congress should exempt broadcasters and other programmers from the antitrust laws for the purpose of developing a code of professional standards. The earlier code of the National Association of Broadcasters was abandoned in 1982 after an overeager, shortsighted, and ideologically driven Justice Department succeeded in destroying it. The Justice Department's action made effective self-regulation virtually impossible in the industry, and left the government in the position of being the only judge of programming practices, a situation clearly unfavorable to the First Amendment.

Congress should not only permit the creation of a code of practice but require membership of all licensed broadcasters. A code of professional standards for broadcasters would be analogous to similar codes in other industries, from real estate to manufacturing, that prohibit deceptive, discriminatory, or abusive practices. The code of the National Association of Securities Dealers, for example, specifies what brokers may not say or do in their dealings with the public and with each other.

Other professionals—such as lawyers and doctors, engineers and teachers—have to meet minimum standards of professional practice. Journalists, of course, are not professionals in this sense of the term, but most broadcasters are not journalists; instead, they are licensed operators of a publicly owned spectrum. Are their character and performance any less important than that of other professionals? Broadcasters and cable operators should be held to a standard of practice that meets their own best professional judgments.

Business groups, particularly, have an important role to play here, since their advertising influences so much television programming. Sanford McDonnell, chairman emeritus of McDonnell Douglas, is a proponent of what he calls "character education" in schools, but worries that "television is creating a very strong headwind into which we character education proponents must fly." For that reason McDonnell has wisely urged his colleagues in the influential Business Roundtable to use their influence "to leverage the cable and television industries into establishing a self-policing mechanism," but so far has had no success.[18] If the members of the roundtable sat with their children and grandchildren and watched and discussed the programs sponsored by their companies—if all advertisers did—they would change their policies. Producers and advertising executives should similarly spend time with their children and grandchildren, watching the programs they have produced and funded. Are they proud of what they're doing?

Recently a number of business associations announced their commitments to "children's best interest," as one group, the New American Revolution, put it in a full-page *New York Times* advertisement in September 1994. The New American Revolution includes among its members top executives from several communications companies, including Time Warner CEO Gerald Levin and USA Network president Kay Koplovitz, both of whom, in different circumstances, have publicly denied their own companies' responsibility to children and parents. Inconsistencies like these raise questions about whether the revolution was launched in the boardroom or the marketing department. Now the real question is whether these executives and the companies they represent will make good on their promises.

6. The nonprofit community, especially foundations and universities, should become more active in the debate over children's television and its place in the new world of SuperTube. About seventy-five not-for-profit groups have been active in the Telecommunications Policy Roundtable, a consortium that lobbies to guarantee equal and affordable access to the information superhighway. Others have sponsored projects related either to SuperTube or to children's television. Laudable as these efforts are, they need to be brought together lest their debate—and their message—go unheard. In the years between 1927 and 1934, divisiveness among educators, labor unions, churches, and foundations was perhaps the single most important reason why the Wagner-Hatfield amendment was defeated and the success of commercial broadcasters assured in controlling virtually the entire radio spectrum. Today we are in danger of repeating the mistake. If Americans compound the error they made in 1934, it will be because the institutions that fought so resolutely in the 1930s are now sitting silently on the sidelines.

Our foundations and think tanks have offered few imaginative ideas about SuperTube except the standard homilies about competition and free speech. They have said virtually nothing about the place of children in television's next generation. Some members of the American Academy of Arts and Sciences, the organization that supported the writing of this book,* expressed doubts about the importance of television serving the public interest, and even asked whether the public interest can be defined except in economic terms. Would George Washington, Thomas Jefferson, and John Adams, three of the academy's founders, have spoken in the same way?

Perhaps the most remarkable absentees in the debate over Super-Tube—and least forgivable—are the nation's educators. The two failed information highway bills in the 103rd Congress, H.R. 3636 and S. 1822, both barely mentioned children except to consider linking schools to the National Information Infrastructure as cheaply as possible, an undertaking that few people familiar with the costs of such linkage think feasible.[19] Just how these linkages should be financed is a critical public-policy question, one that the nation's educational establishment has scarcely acknowledged.† Until it does, the billions of dollars that will come from spectrum auctions will simply disappear into federal spending, with no benefit whatsoever to children.

---

*I.e., *Abandoned in the Wasteland*. (Eds.)

†Among the educational organizations that have proposed funding mechanisms for wiring the nation's schools are the National Association of School Principals, the National School Boards Association, the American Library Association, the National Education Association, and the Council of Chief State School Officers. In 1994, these groups proposed that the FCC use the "consumer productivity dividend" derived from the access charges local phone companies collect from long-distance companies to wire the schools. The groups estimated the annual revenue from such charges to be about $300 million.

Finally, the nation's colleges and universities, which should be leading the fight on this issue, have been content to follow instead. "The universities are letting the business community set the agenda," says Jeffrey Chester of the Center for Media Education. "They have abdicated their responsibility. Where are the intellectuals, the innovative models, where are the studies—other than those that are funded by big business?"[20] An urgent question, and as yet unanswered.

7. The news media should distinguish legitimate concerns about free speech from equally legitimate concerns about the health and well-being of children. No one makes this point better than Sissela Bok, who writes that, in the debate over television violence particularly, journalists too easily accept a number of poorly thought-through rationalizations about the problem as reasons for doing nothing about it.[21] In doing so, Bok says, they fail to advance public understanding or debate, indeed become obstacles to debate.

It is true, for example, that America has a history of violence; that other factors besides television contribute to violence; that the link between televised violence and real violence, as with smoking and cancer, is not infallibly conclusive; that television violence is in some measure a reflection of violence in society; that "violence" is hard to define; that SuperTube may eventually create many hundreds more outlets for video violence; that parents have primary responsibility for what their children watch; and that public policy should not tread lightly on free expression. Yet none of these truths, Bok correctly argues, justifies ignoring the legitimate concern that television violence is inappropriate for, and possibly damaging to, children. It was rationalizations such as these, Bok notes, that once sustained such abhorrent practices as slavery and child labor. Similar rationalizations would not permit toy manufacturers to make dangerous toys, pharmaceutical companies to neglect childproof packaging, contractors to build homes with asbestos ceilings and lead-based paint, or stores to sell weapons or explosives to minors. When journalists allow the First Amendment to foreclose debate on the issue of children's television, Bok says, the free speech argument

> produces a chilling effect all its own. It will matter, therefore, for the press to scrutinize its own role in covering the debate over television, . . . to be on the lookout for rationales and rationalizations, . . . and to explore the obstacles that stand in the way of providing better coverage. On such a basis, it ought to be possible, when reporting on contributions to this debate by public interest groups, industry officials, officeholders and others, not only to convey more thoroughly

what is being said and done (something which would already represent a significant improvement) but to provide the type of analysis routinely offered with respect to other societal problems.[22]

8. A program for media education should be developed and supported in the nation's primary and secondary schools. In the end, the best people to judge the way television treats children are parents. Schools, universities, and foundations, therefore, must give much more attention and support to media education for parents as well as for children. Elizabeth Thoman, a former English teacher and the director of the Los Angeles-based Center for Media Literacy, says, "Today, you have to teach the underlying messages around the visuals. . . . Media literacy as an organizing discipline incorporates sociology, political science, literary criticism, economics and political analysis. It's an organizing umbrella for seeing problems in a different light and for seeing solutions, all of which are interrelated."[23]

Thoman is by no means alone. The state of New Mexico, at the urging of Governor Bruce King and state educational leaders, formally introduced media literacy programs to its K-through-12 curriculum in 1994. Harvard University has for several summers operated a Media Education Institute, a program for elementary- and secondary-school teachers that introduces them to the principles and methods of media education, and Yale began research on the uses of media for children in 1976.[24] In 1990, the American Academy of Pediatrics formally recommended that parents, teachers, and pediatricians place greater emphasis on "critical television-viewing skills," and the Harvard psychologist Ronald Slaby has for years urged Congress and parents to call upon a variety of institutions, from the television industry to the nation's schools, to help children develop those skills that can reduce the damaging effects of television violence.

At times, the television industry has responded thoughtfully to such encouragement. In 1993, for example, the television journalist Linda Ellerbee did a special program for Nickelodeon in which she interviewed children about their perceptions of televised violence. HBO, in cooperation with *Consumer Reports*, produced its award-winning *Buy Me That*, a film for children about the half-truths and deceptions hidden in advertising.

To be effective over the long term, media literacy programs need to become a basic part of the school curriculum, just as schools now include courses on the potential uses and abuses of the Internet. At a minimum, media education should introduce pupils to the classic techniques of persuasion and propaganda, and to the art classics of film and television. Wherever possible, media education should also familiarize children with the techniques of telling stories using the grammar and syntax of the moving image. Says Kubey,

> With the growing availability of video cameras and the extremely low cost of videotape, this can be done more readily than ever before. Even if cameras aren't available, students can also learn by "storyboarding" scenes and writing scripts. . . . One of the ways to increase students' interest in literature is to help them recognize that many of the same storytelling techniques used in the classics are also used in the popular programs and films with which they are already familiar.[25]

Many of the people who advocate media literacy programs have little or no connection to the people who write school curricula; and the media literacy movement as a whole has little understanding of the research on how children of different ages watch television and process its messages.[26] To solve these problems, the nation that creates more media product than any other cannot continue to neglect media education.

9. Congress should commit to a deadline for updating and amending the Children's Television Act, to serve the needs of children both now and in the age of SuperTube. Inevitably, congressional efforts to rewrite the 1934 Communications Act will focus largely on competition between the cable industry, the Baby Bells, long-distance companies like AT&T, broadcasters, and others.* In this morass of private interest and technical details, the needs of children will be minimized (as they were in 1994) or forgotten altogether. Congress should therefore refine and expand its finding in the Children's Television Act that the public interest requires special attention to young viewers. The new world of telecommunications is amenable to human choice in direction; the right direction to go is the one consistent with the public interest; and the public interest is the protection and development of children. Congress should therefore establish a deadline by which time it will report to the American people how it is meeting the national commitment to children in the new communications revolution.

Specifically, Congress should begin public discussion and debate on these topics: protecting children from the harm of violence; promoting parenting skills through television; promoting media education for parents and children; determining the obligations and professional stan-

---

*The 1996 Telecommunications Act did achieve this focus. (Eds.)

dards of broadcasters, narrowcasters, producers of video games, and other purveyors of new communications technologies; ending television's commercial exploitation of children; and engaging universities, foundations, and other nonprofit institutions in the active debate over the future. A new Children's Telecommunications Act, an overhaul of the 1990 act, should be passed into law within two years.

As we approach the age of SuperTube and its glowing promises, we would do well to remember the reservation expressed by the great journalist and broadcaster Edward R. Murrow as he looked at television's future in 1958. "This instrument can teach," he said, "it can illuminate; yes, it can even inspire. But it can do so only to the extent that humans are determined to use it to those ends. Otherwise it is merely lights and wires in a box."[27] The technology that delivers pictures and other information to our home has changed since Murrow's day to include coaxial cable, fiber-optic cable, cellular and other wireless systems, and direct broadcast satellites. But the box is still a box. What we use it for is still up to us. The telecommunications revolution already under way in America and around the world demands sustained attention, lest its promise go unfulfilled. If it does, the cost of our failure will be borne by our children.

When Douglass Cater looked ahead to the age of SuperTube, he called the new technology MOTHER out of his concern that it would become an instrument of control—by the government, perhaps, but more likely by private commercial interests—rather than an instrument of freedom and creativity. But it doesn't have to be that way. If we act wisely, SuperTube can bring the First Amendment fully into the digital age, empower real mothers and real fathers to decide what is best for their children, and establish children themselves—as the Communications Act did not—as the principal beneficiaries of our nation's communications policy. Though SuperTube may eventually dispense with many of the public-interest obligations that marked the age of broadcasting, our responsibility to protect and educate our children will never be among them. Even skeptics who believe the public interest is beyond definition know that it lies in the hearts and minds of children. If as a nation we cannot figure out what the public interest means with respect to those who are too young to vote, who are barely literate, who are financially and emotionally and even physically dependent on adults, then we will never figure out what it means anywhere else. Our children *are* the public interest, living and breathing, flesh and blood.

Or will we, once again, abandon our children to the wasteland?

NOTES

1. Sissela Bok, *TV Violence, Children, and the Press: Eight Rationales Inhibiting Public Policy Debates*, Joan Shorenstein Barone Center on Press, Politics and Public Policy, Harvard University, April 1994, p. 1.

2. Personal communication to the authors. See also David Kleeman, "The Children's Hour: A Future History," *Electronic Media*, July 19, 1994.

3. See "Grateful Man Leaves $5.6 Million to Federal Government," *The New York Times*, October 8, 1994.

4. Edward L. Palmer, *Television and America's Children: A Crisis of Neglect* (New York: Oxford University Press, 1988), pp. 122–26.

5. *Starting Points: Meeting the Needs of Our Youngest Children*, Report of the Carnegie Task Force on Meeting the Needs of Young Children, Carnegie Corporation of New York, April 1994, p. 36.

6. See Milton Chen, *The Smart Parent's Guide to Kids' TV* (San Francisco: KQED Books, 1994).

7. Patricia Marks Greenfield, *Mind and Media: The Effects of Television, Video Games, and Computers* (Cambridge, Mass.: Harvard University Press, 1984), p. 66.

8. Michael Kelley, *A Parent's Guide to Television* (New York: John Wiley & Sons, 1981), p. 65.

9. Jay F. Davis, "Five Important Ideas to Teach Your Kids About TV," *Media and Values*, Fall 1990/Winter 1991.

10. *Violence on Television: A Symposium and Study Sponsored by the Editors of TV Guide*, June 1992.

11. "What We Can Do," *TV Guide*, August 22, 1992.

12. David Bianculli, *Teleliteracy* (New York: Continuum, 1992), p. 165.

13. See Aimee Dorr, *Television and Children* (Beverly Hills: Sage Publications, 1986), p. 113; and Shari Roan, "Tuned In and At Risk," *Los Angeles Times*, March 10, 1993.

14. Randal Levenson, "Teaching Children to Say No to TV," *The New York Times*, March 24, 1993.

15. "Zap! The Smart Set," *The Washington Post*, August 29, 1992.

16. Larry McGill, "By the Numbers—What Kids Watch," *Media Studies Journal*, Fall 1994, pp. 95–97. According to Nielsen media research data from 1992 to 1993, men eighteen and older watch about twenty-nine hours of television a week; women in the same age category watch almost thirty-three hours.

17. Richard S. Leghorn, "The OKTV Program," memorandum of November 11, 1994.

18. Sanford McDonnell, letter to Newton N. Minow, September 15, 1994.

19. FCC commissioner Rachelle Chong has called the undertaking "staggering," not only in terms of cost but also in terms of planning. See *Telecommunications Reports*, October 17, 1994.

20. Quoted in *Academe*, September–October 1994.

21. Bok, *TV Violence, Children, and the Press*, p. 1.

22. Ibid., p. 15.

23. Quoted in Judy Mann, "Learning to Read TV," *The Washington Post*, September 3, 1993.

24. See Kate Moody, "Growing Media Smarts—The New Mexico Project"; and Renee Hobbs, "Teaching Media Literacy—Yo! Are You Hip to This?" *Media Studies Journal*, Fall 1994. See also Dorothy G. Singer, "Creating Critical Viewers," *Television Quarterly*, Winter 1994.

25. Robert Kubey, "The Case for Media Education," *Education Week*, March 6, 1991.

26. See Patricia Aufderheide, *Media Literacy: A Report of the National Leadership Conference on Media Literacy* (Washington, D.C.: The Aspen Institute, 1993), pp. 5–8.

27. Edward R. Murrow, address to the Radio and Television News Directors' Association Convention, October 15, 1958, reprinted in Harry J. Skornia, *Television and Society* (New York: McGraw-Hill, 1965), p. 237.

28

The Man Who Counts the Killings

Scott Stossel

In the unlikely event that a major Hollywood studio were to make a movie based on the life of George Gerbner, it might go something like this:

A passionate young Hungarian poet, dismayed by the rise of fascism in his country in the late 1930s, emigrates to America.

Cut to 1942. The ex-poet, motivated by his hatred of fascism, enlists in the U.S. Army. He volunteers for the Office of Strategic Services and ends up in a group of fifteen men trained, like William Holden and his comrades in *The Bridge on the River Kwai*, in the techniques of blowing up bridges and roads.

Cut to January 15, 1945—a sabotage mission gone awry. The young man and his OSS comrades, under heavy fire over Slovenia, parachute into enemy territory. They climb into the mountains and hide in farmhouses, subsisting on emergency rations until they encounter the partisan brigades, with whom they spend the remainder of the war fighting Germans who are in retreat from Greece.

The war takes a bloody toll on the young man's brigade; by V-E Day it has been reduced from four hundred men to seventy. But the Allies prevail. And the ex-poet, now a war hero, falls in love. Roll credits: the camera freezes on George and Ilona Gerbner embracing on the deck of their New York–bound ship.

In the more imaginable yet still unlikely event that an independent

Originally published in *The Atlantic Monthly,* Volume 279, Number 5 (1997). Reprinted by permission of the author.

production company were to make a film based on the life of George Gerbner, it might go something like this:

After the Second World War, in the course of which he has seen enough violence, suffering, and pain to harden even the softest sensibility, and during which he has personally identified and arrested the fascist Hungarian prime minister, who is subsequently executed, a brooding Hungarian poet travels with his wife to America. He earns a Ph.D. from the University of Southern California, in the process writing the first-ever master's thesis on the subject of education and television, and begins a long career in academia studying the effects of television on its viewers. In 1964 he becomes the dean of the newly founded Annenberg School of Communication, at the University of Pennsylvania, where he builds a curriculum and a faculty from scratch. In 1989, after twenty-five years as dean, George Gerbner retires.

This second film might concentrate on Gerbner's recent activities. Now seventy-seven years old, he is free to pursue more or less full-time what has been a longtime project of his: trying to awaken television viewers from their stupefaction. Television, Gerber believes, is modern-day religion. It presents a coherent vision of the world. And this vision of the world, he says, is violent, mean, repressive, dangerous—and inaccurate. Television programming is the toxic by-product of market forces run amok. Television has the capacity to be a culturally enriching force, but, Gerbner warns, today it breeds what fear and resentment mixed with economic frustration can lead to—the undermining of democracy.

Though in general respected within his field, Gerbner is misunderstood, misrepresented, and even mocked outside it. Network executives make what sound like commonsense dismissals of his Cassandra-esque claims. The central question of this film might be, What are we to make of this complex man and his provocative message?

Is Gerbner tilting at windmills? Is he just a mediaphobe with a quixotic message? Or is he a lonely voice of insight, telling us things that are hard to comprehend but that we need to hear if we are to remain free from repression? Right or wrong, is his crusade at bottom a futile one? Do we need to change television programming, and if so, how can we do it? After all, network executives say, viewers are simply getting what they want. The film might end with a shot of a gaunt George Gerbner quoting, as he often does, the toast of Russian dissidents under Soviet rule: "Now let us drink to the success of our hopeless endeavor." . . .

THE NEW RELIGION

"Whoever tells most of the stories to most of the people most of the time has effectively assumed the cultural role of parent and school," Gerbner says, ". . . teaching us most of what we know in common about life and society." In fact, by the time children reach school age, they will have spent more hours in front of the television than they will ever spend in college classrooms. Television, in short, has become a cultural force equaled in history only by organized religion. Only religion has had this power to transmit the same messages about reality to every social group, creating a common culture.

Most people do not have to wait for, plan for, go out to, or seek out television, for the TV is on more than seven hours a day in the average American home. It comes to you directly. It has become a member of the family, telling its stories patiently, compellingly, untiringly. We *choose* to read the *New York Times*, or Dickens, or an entomology text. We *choose* to listen to Bach or Bartók, or at least to a classical station or a rock station or a jazz station. But we just watch TV—turn it on, see what's on. And in Gerbner's view it is an upper-middle-class conceit to say "Just turn off the television"—in most homes there is nothing as compelling as television at any time of the day or night.

It is significant that this viewing is nonselective. It's why Gerbner believes that the Cultural Indicators project methodology—looking at television's overall patterns rather than at the effects of specific shows—is the best approach. It is long-range exposure to television, rather than a specific violent act on a specific episode of a specific show, that cultivates fixed conceptions about life in viewers.

Nor is the so-called hard news, even when held distinct from infotainment shows like *Hard Copy* and *A Current Affair*, exempt from the disproportionate violence and misrepresentations on television in general. The old news saw "If it bleeds, it leads" usually prevails. Watch your local newscast tonight: it is not unlikely that the majority of news stories will be about crime or disaster—and it may well be that all six stories will be from outside your state, especially if you live far from any major metropolis. Fires and shootings are much cheaper and easier to cover than politics or community events. Violent news also generates higher ratings, and since the standards for television news are set by market researchers, what we get is lots of conformity, lots of violence. As the actor and director Edward James Olmos has pointedly observed,

"For every half hour of TV news, you have twenty-three minutes of programming and seven minutes of commercials. And in that twenty-three minutes, if it weren't for the weather and the sports, you would not have any positive news. As for putting in even six minutes of hope, of pride, of dignity—it doesn't sell." The author and radio personality Garrison Keillor puts it even more pointedly: "It's as bloody as Shakespeare but without the intelligence and the poetry. If you watch television news you know less about the world than if you drank gin out of a bottle."

The strength of television's influence on our understanding of the world should not be underestimated. "Television's Impact on Ethnic and Racial Images," a study sponsored by the American Jewish Committee's Institute for American Pluralism and other groups, found that ethnic and racial images on television powerfully shape the way adolescents perceive ethnicity and race in the real world. "In dealing with socially relevant topics like racial and ethnic relations," the study said, "TV not only entertains, it conveys values and messages that people may absorb unwittingly—particularly young people." Among viewers watching more than four hours each day, 25 percent said that television showed "what life is really like" and 40 percent said they learned a lot from television. African Americans especially, the study showed, rely on television to learn about the world.

Television, in short, tells all the stories. Gerbner is fond of quoting the Scottish patriot Andrew Fletcher, who wrote to the Marquise of Montrose in 1704, "If I were permitted to write all the ballads I need not care who makes the laws of the nation." Fletcher identified the governing power of, in Gerbner's words, a "centralized system of ballads— the songs, legends, and stories that convey both information and what we call entertainment." Television has become this centralized system; it is the cultural arm of the state that established religion once was. "Television satisfies many previously felt religious needs for participating in a common ritual and for sharing beliefs about the meaning of life and the modes of right conduct," Gerbner has written. "It is, therefore, not an exaggeration to suggest that the licensing of television represents the modern functional equivalent of government establishment of religion." A scary collapsing, in other words, of church into state. . . .

MEDIA MONOPOLIES AND CENSORSHIP

Television violence, Gerbner has written, "is but the tip of the iceberg of a massive distortion in the way in which we make cultural policy in this country. [Cultural decision making] is drifting dangerously out of democratic reach." In his view, television violence is just one symptom of a serious underlying problem that threatens to stifle democracy: the very structure of the culture industry.

Most of the debate about acceptable television programming is cast, especially by those in the industry, in terms of censorship versus free speech. But Gerbner says this is misleading: although censorship is unquestionably a problem (there's altogether too much of it), it is not the usual culprit, government, that is doing the censoring. It is private corporations. Gerbner writes,

> The Founding Fathers did not foresee the rise of large conglomerates acting as private governments. Nor did they envision their cultural arms, the mass media . . . forming a virtual private Ministry of Culture and Established Church rolled into one, influencing the socialization of all Americans. In licensing broadcasters and then letting the marketplace take its course, Congress has made law respecting the establishment of the modern equivalent of religion and has given a few giant conglomerates the right to abridge freedom of speech.

The market, Gerbner says, is a plutocracy, not a democracy. And the largest market interests use the First Amendment as a shield while denying it to the disenfranchised. Censorship! Censorship! broadcasters cry when anyone suggests that their programming has deleterious social effects, that they might try distributing something different. Yet these interests exercise de facto censorship themselves: in co-opting all programming (as recently as 1986 ABC, CBS, and NBC controlled 70 percent of the television market) a media monopoly has consolidated the diversity of human experience into a few basic formulas. A concentrated marketplace puts distinct limits on the range of views represented. The people have no say in what gets broadcast. This, in Gerbner's view, is plainly undemocratic. But we have become so accustomed to the dominance of a market-driven, advertiser-sponsored media system that we don't realize it doesn't have to be this way.

Alternatives to the American system of broadcasting do exist. Britain, for example, requires all television owners to pay a yearly license fee, which goes into a fund to subsidize independent productions on the BBC. In France proceeds from a tax on entertainment fund private and public producers, ensuring that a range of perspectives gets represented. Whereas in the United States the federal commitment to public broadcasting is less than $1.50 per capita, other countries typically pay about $25 to $30 per capita. Aside from the establishment of the currently besieged Corporation for Public Broadcasting (which runs PBS) in the 1960s, the only serious attempts to legislate federal protection of the public interest in broadcasting were made in the 1930s. Herbert Hoover, who presided over the original Communications Act, for example, called for a two percent tax on radio-set sales to "pay for daily programs of the best skill and talent."

In most truly democratic countries television is subject to the electorate; the public interest is upheld. In the United States, however, the few laws requiring broadcasters to serve the public interest have never been enforced. This is in large part because federal policy for U.S. broadcasting, set in the 1930s, heavily stacked the deck in favor of a market-driven system. During the Depression policymakers hoped that a commercial broadcasting model would ensure sufficient programming diversity. But when the commercial model was codified in the Communications Act of 1934, its only—albeit important—concession to a broader civic responsibility was the stipulation that holders of broadcast licenses agree to serve the "public interest, convenience, and necessity."

The vaunted 1996 Telecommunications Act is the first significant update of the 1934 Communications Act. It has many elements, but one of its basic goals is to restore "competition" in the broadcasting market through further deregulation. Robert W. McChesney, a professor at the School of Journalism and Mass Communication at the University of Wisconsin at Madison, spoke in blunt Gerbnerian terms at the founding convention of Gerbner's Cultural Environment Movement, held in March of [1996] in St. Louis. "The 1996 Telecom Bill is truly one of the most corrupt pieces of legislation in American history," he said. "It has basically covertly handed over all communications to a few conglomerates. And it's all based on a big lie that Goebbels would have been impressed by: that the bill is meant to focus competition." By deregulating the industry, the Telecommunications Act has ensured that it will be consolidated still further. A rash of mergers has already taken place.

McChesney and Gerbner believe that it is structurally impossible for advertising-based television programming to represent the range and diversity of positions in our society. The problems, McChesney wrote in *Telecommunications, Mass Media, and Democracy: The Battle for the Control of*

U.S. Broadcasting, 1928–1935 (1993), are that "U.S. political culture does not permit any discussion of the fundamental weaknesses in capitalism" and "corporate media have encouraged the belief that even the consideration of alternatives was tantamount to a call for totalitarianism."

According to Gerbner, a 1974 House committee report on television, suppressed by the broadcasting lobby before it could reach the House floor, suggested that the very organization of the network industry led to violent programming. Gerbner has long believed this to be true. Look at lists of the ten top-rated shows each year, he urges. Most of them are not violent; they're more likely to be comedies or nonviolent dramas. Yet producers still make scores of bloody shows. If network executives are merely obeying free-market forces, how can it be that they're making lots of shows that aren't in the highest demand?

Because, Gerbner told me, "there is no free market in television." It is well known in the industry that few television programs will break even in the domestic market. According to Todd Gitlin's book *Inside Prime Time* (1983), it costs more to produce one minute of your own programming than to buy an hour's worth from the world market. A programmer in Copenhagen, for example, can lease an old episode of *Dallas* for under $5,000, less than the cost of producing one minute of original Danish drama. The high cost of production means that producers must sell their shows into syndication or abroad—from which more than half the receipts come—if they wish to make a profit. Selling shows abroad requires a proven story formula that, in distributor lingo, "travels well." The most common formulas are obvious: sex and violence. . . .

THE CULTURAL-PROTECTION MOVEMENT

After he retired from the deanship at Annenberg, George Gerbner became, as he puts it, "a part-time researcher, full-time agitator" and continued to lecture all over the world on television violence. At the end of his speeches people would ask, What can we do? He would answer, Write your politician or broadcaster. Teach your children about television formulas. But this, Gerbner came to realize, was "feeble and humiliating—why should we have to ask for something that ought to be a right?" In other countries people had a right and a voice equal to those of conglomerates and broadcasters. Why couldn't people in the United States? So in late December of 1990 Gerbner and some like-minded friends got together in a borrowed conference room in Washington, D.C., to launch the Cultural Environment Movement (CEM). A quarter century earlier Rachel Carson's *Silent Spring* awakened readers to the perils of pollution and stimulated a generation of environmentalists to action. Gerbner's Cultural Environment Movement would do the same for media culture.

The movement yielded its first significant fruit [in 1996], when it held its founding convention. Hundreds of delegates (left-leaning academics, progressive activists, former TV-industry people, and cultural policymakers from all over the world) assembled in a Holiday Inn on a bland commercial strip along Highway 366 in St. Louis. Their mission, as articulated in a draft of CEM's Viewer's Declaration of Independence, was to "dissolve the cultural bands which have tied human development to marketing strategies, and to assume an active role in making policy decisions about the cultural environment into which . . . children are born." A serious mandate, and an ambitious one.

Too ambitious? The convention, a three-day affair jam-packed with working groups, cultural events, and plenary sessions, throbbed with activity and optimism. It had much of the tone of a civil-rights rally, swollen with the revolutionary fervor and progressive rhetoric of the sixties. Sumi Sevilla Haru, a four-foot-ten-inch, ninety-pound Filipino labor leader full of compressed energy, spoke in the language of the labor union when she told the convention, "We have to do something about the media massacre. We don't want to agonize—we need to organize." When *Washington Post* columnist Dorothy Gilliam entreated delegates in an after-dinner speech to "think of your work as civil-rights work—CEM can be part of the civil-rights movement" (for which she got a standing ovation), she was making explicit the broader mission by which most of the delegates defined themselves. The general effect of the idealistic enthusiasm was inspiring. But there was in all this an element of Pollyannaism, of preaching to the converted. No one was there to disagree. As one sober-minded delegate, a former television writer and producer and now a retired professor of media studies, confided to me, "These people are zealots. They're naive. Notice that there are no network people here. Things would be different if there were."

The last night of the convention I asked Gerbner how he thought this sometimes radical progressivism would play in the mainstream cultural arena, which is in general fairly moderate, even conservative. He replied that CEM should perhaps be seen not as radical or leftist, or even as liberal, but as "liberating." Americans have been responding to the rhetoric of family-values conservatives who, Gerbner says, really are on to something. The specific example Dan Quayle chose to use—

Murphy Brown's getting pregnant out of wedlock—may have been unfortunate, but in Gerbner's opinion he made a good general point. "Fundamentalists have preempted the cultural issue," Gerbner says. "They're appealing to legitimate concerns of American families and organizations who resent dependence on media." This is precisely why CEM is so important: "The culture wars are heating up, and we need a liberating alternative to stop fundamentalists from expropriating the issue and taking it in a repressive direction."

CEM intends to fight for alternatives both to censorship and to the old-fashioned pieties of the cultural conservatives. But, I asked Gerbner, aren't we just talking about competing visions of cultural reality, of morality—one on the left, one on the right? Each side wants to impose its vision on the country, and therefore naturally favors whatever cultural products advance it. Gerbner replied, "We are not just providing a single alternative cosmology to, say, the religious right. We're advocating diversity." But "diversity" is weak tea, protest some of those who deplore today's violent television. Censorship is dangerous, Gerbner would be likely to reply. Conditioned by his dislike of fascism to distrust any kind of concentrated power (governmental, corporate, or otherwise), Gerbner cannot abide censorship, which can be both a means to and an end of such concentrations. Thus he can be very explicit about the sorts of programming we should and should not have—up to a point. We *should* have shows that depict minorities and women more favorably; we *should* have fewer mindlessly violent shows; but we *should not* use censorship to attain the programming we want.

The Cultural Environment Movement's basic mission, in other words, is to see that more stories by more different kinds of people are broadcast. Stories by people with something to tell, as Gerbner likes to say, rather than stories by people with something to sell. Think of a cafeteria, he says. When you enter a cafeteria, you feel that you have a right to choose what you will consume. But although some would argue that the choices in the cultural cafeteria are better now than they were for a parochial customer of the past, the choices remain limited: you have to choose from what's there. As a citizen, Gerbner believes, you have a responsibility to ask, What are the possibilities? How do we make this into a much richer and more nourishing and more diverse cafeteria? People don't realize that they have a say in what gets served here. CEM's mission is to make them aware of this fact, so that cultural choices get pushed into the political realm, where they belong.

"THE COMMONS IS NEEDED"

Of course, one problem with this mission is that when culture is sub-sumed under a political rubric, debates about artistic values become debates about political values. The notion of aesthetic taste gets pushed aside. Taste, to be sure, can be a dangerous concept, a smokescreen to obscure political designs: Keyan Tomaselli, a combative South African media theorist who spoke at the CEM convention, points out that "good taste" can be its own form of censorship. For years in South Africa it was considered in "poor taste" to bring up certain aspects of race relations in middle-class white society; standards of "decency" ensured that art depicting these issues would be rare and marginalized. Clearly, "decency" and "poor taste" were bourgeois prettifications con-jured to dress up (and thereby protect) outright racist attitudes. Never-theless, art in the Western tradition is generally founded in some sense on taste, maybe even on elitist taste. When CEM tries to make political values interchangeable with cultural ones, it risks junking the critical standards we do have, many of which can be and are used as arguments against the quality of Hollywood's standard violent schlock.

And then there are those, conservatives in particular, who will argue that what Gerbner is advocating when he speaks of diversity is really "identity politics," or quotas applied to culture. The implications of total diversity, these people will say, will be total fragmentation. True, in the ideal CEM imagining, shows would represent minorities more accu-rately and in truer proportions relative to the overall population. But taken to its logical extremes, that might mean accepting Pat Buchanan's *No Way José* show (exploring the lives and views of xenophobic white male economic protectionists) and the *Ralph Reed Family Values Show* (with nary a homosexual or nonbeliever in sight), not to mention *Madonna's S&M Hour* (for those who find their taste in sexuality inade-quately represented by current programming). The pursuit of diversity, if overzealous, leads to proliferating factions and subgroups. The result is tribalization, as each group retreats to its own set of stories.

A nation, almost by definition, must have some stories its citizens hold in common. From the 1950s to the 1970s the three television networks provided considerable common cultural ground for the United States. Everybody watched the same programs and televised events and was in some sense linked by this shared experience. But in the 1970s, with the spread of niche marketing and cable television, channels proliferated. The audience fragmented. America lost its common hearth.

"To recognize diversity," Todd Gitlin wrote in *The Twilight of Common Dreams: Why America Is Wracked by Culture Wars* (1996), "more than diversity is needed. The commons is needed." The danger inherent in CEM's using cultural diversity as a political tactic is that the idea of the commons gets lost. Of course, without this tactic we're in danger of being stuck with a limited set of master narratives favored either by conservative absolutists or by corporate conglomerates whose first concern is profit, not public interest, and for whom the universalist principle means appealing not to a common humanity but to the lowest common denominator. The trick for CEM will be to navigate between the Scylla of standardized, noninclusive, corporate-conglomerate-produced, market-strategy-conforming formulas that at least provide much of the nation with common cultural capital and the Charybdis of more inclusive, more diverse, less formulaic, community-produced stories and programming that isolate each subgroup behind its respective cultural bulkhead. Gerbner believes that the Cultural Environment Movement can develop a mosaic that will to some extent incorporate ideological differences while representing the cultural claims of a larger cross-section of society than existing mainstream culture represents. In fact, he says, CEM can be the forum for all those who want to regain some say in what culture gets produced, in what they and their children consume.

At the convention's invocation, a slightly weird, touchy-feely affair with Jewish, Muslim, Christian, and Navajo prayers and progressive exhortations, Gerbner said his standard piece about returning cultural decision making from the invisible Ministry of Culture to the people. To me, the most interesting words he spoke were these: "Our task now is to assemble a coalition like the anti-fascist coalition of the 1940s, with the partisan brigades."

FIGHTING FASCISM

Fascism is the specter that looms, tenebrous, over all of Gerbner's life and work. There are at least two ways to interpret the shadow it casts. The first is to grant his warnings about creeping fascism all the more authority for his having lived under fascism, and for his having risked his life to fight it during the Second World War. The second is to discount everything he says on the subject because his significant early experiences under fascism have unduly colored his worldview: since the war he has seen everything in terms of it.

My initial instinct was to incline toward the second interpretation. In my early conversations with Gerbner, I sometimes had to stifle the urge to say, Lighten up. My own cultural experience—watching violent cartoons when I was little, and violent action movies when older—has yet to produce any obvious violent or fascist impulses. And I am by no means alone in believing that, disproportionate quantities notwithstanding, violence in culture generally reflects the violence that is already present in real life. Family-court prosecutors scoff at the notion that television causes violent children; bad living conditions or bad genes do. Art since ancient times has depicted violence, and even tried to use it as catharsis. (Though Greek plays, Gerbner points out, never showed violence onstage: it was almost always reported by a messenger.) Moreover, although the studies that find the most dramatic correlations between television and violence get the most publicity, there are other respectable studies whose conclusions are more restrained. "Television in the Lives of Our Children," for instance, one of the first major undertakings in the field, was published in 1961 after people became concerned about violent new shows like *The Rifleman* and *The Untouchables*. Researchers examined ten North American communities from 1958 to 1960, scrutinizing in great detail many aspects of television's effects. Their conclusion was a model of common sense.

> For *some* children, under *some* conditions, *some* television is harmful. For *other* children, under the same conditions, or for the same children under *other* conditions, it may be beneficial. For *most* children, under *most* conditions, most television is probably neither harmful nor particularly beneficial.

Beyond this, CEM's criticisms of "the market" will not be popular. If the flip side of freedom, innovation, comparative material prosperity, and global leadership is some crass commercialism, philistinism, and formulaic television shows, wouldn't most people say, So be it? It is easy to imagine the bafflement of free-market conservatives—and of the viewing public in general—at the phenomenon of CEM: What's wrong with television? What's fascist about *I Dream of Jeannie?* What's bothering the leftist malcontents this time?

But CEM has at least as many relatives on the right as on the left. In fact, one of CEM's closest older cousins grew out of the Moral Majority. In the 1980s Jerry Falwell's Coalition for Better Television complained, as CEM does today, that the industry's commerce-at-all-costs ethos adversely affected programming. In advocating television that strictly reflected the cultural values of the Moral Majority, CFBT was more a predecessor of Dan Quayle than of CEM. But today people of all political persuasions are insecure. They worry about their safety and their future, and about the safety and the future of their children. This insecurity is aggravated, if not actually caused, by the cultural environment. Conservatives have recognized the insecurity and speak to it. Gerbner's view is that conservatives exploit it, and use it to push the country in a repressive direction. If this is true, then it may be that CEM does have a role to play as a guardian against fascism. Only it is less television per se that CEM is guarding against than the tendency of fundamentalists to favor absolutist measures in both the political and the cultural realm.

The Hollywood version of Gerbner's life would probably be a great movie. It tells a heroic story. And I don't think it would do most people any harm to watch it. But I do understand why Gerbner might say that the movie would contribute in a subtle way to neofascist impulses. In its simplicity, its glorification of violence as a means of resolving conflict, and its glossing lightly over the suffering and tragedy of violence, the movie would add to an aggregate that fosters the Mean World Syndrome and greater acceptance of martial measures. Maybe Gerbner could afford to lighten up a little anyway. But I can see why he might find the independent film version of his life (its less straightforwardly heroic portrayal of him notwithstanding) superior to the Hollywood version in a way that is more than just aesthetic.

Television, in Gerbner's view, is by no means inherently bad. It does much that is good. For many people who would otherwise be just plain bored, television represents an enrichment of cultural horizons. It has gone a long way toward diminishing isolation and parochialism and has given us cultural capital to hold in common. No modern state can govern without television; it is the social cement that religion once was, holding disparate groups and subgroups together. But, Gerbner firmly believes, so potent is television's power to inform and control, so strong is its power to teach us who gets away with what against whom, that a democratic people that cedes control of television to a nonelected few will not remain a democratic people for long. The more one contemplates the pervasiveness of stereotypical patterns in television, the more one perceives the inaccurate picture of reality it cultivates in viewers— and the more one inclines toward a charitable understanding of Gerbner's fears about fascism.

29

Why the Cultural Environment Movement?

George Gerbner

Most of what we know, or think we know, we have never personally experienced. We live in a world erected by the stories we hear and see and tell.

Unlocking incredible riches through imagery and words, conjuring up the unseen through art, creating towering works of imagination and fact through science, poetry, song, tales, reports and laws—that is the true magic of human life.

Through that magic we live in a world much wider than the threats and gratifications of the immediate physical environment, which is the world of other species. Stories socialize us into roles of gender, age, class, vocation, and lifestyle, and offer models of conformity or targets for rebellion. They weave the seamless web of the cultural environment that cultivates most of what we think, what we do, and how we conduct our affairs.

The stories that animate our cultural environment have three distinct but related functions. They are (1) revealing how things work; (2) describing what things are; and (3) telling us what to do about them.

Stories of the first kind, revealing how things work, illuminate the all-important but invisible relationships and hidden dynamics of life. They make perceivable the invisible and the hidden. Fairy tales, novels, plays, comics, cartoons, and other forms of creative imagination and

George Gerbner, "Why the Cultural Environmental Movement?" 1996, www.cemnet. org/cem@libertynet.org Reprinted by permission of George Gerbner, president and founder, CEM.

imagery are the basic building blocks of human understanding. They show complex causality by presenting imaginary action in total situations, coming to some conclusion that has a moral purpose and a social function. You don't have to believe the "facts" of *Little Red Riding Hood* to grasp the notion that big bad "wolves" victimize old women and trick little girls—a lesson in gender roles, fear, and power.

Stories of the first kind build, from infancy on, the fantasy we call reality. I do not suggest that the revelations are false, which they may or may not be, but that they are synthetic, selective, often mythical, and always socially constructed.

Stories of the second kind depict what things are. These are descriptions, depictions, expositions, reports abstracted from total situations and filling in with "facts" the gaps in the fantasies conjured up by stories of the first kind. They are the presumably factual accounts, the chronicles of the past and the news of today.

Stories of what things are usually confirm some conception of how things work. Their high "facticity" (i.e., correspondence to actual events presumed to exist independently of the story) gives them special status in political theory and often in law. They give emphasis and credibility to selected parts of each society's fantasies of reality, and can alert it to certain interests, threats, and opportunities and challenges.

Stories of the third kind tell us what to do. These are stories of value and choice. They present things, behaviors, or styles of life as desirable (or undesirable), propose ways to obtain (or avoid) them, and the price to be paid for attainment (or failure). They are the instructions, cautionary tales, commands, slogans, sermons, laws, and exhortations of the day. Today most of them are called commercials and other advertising messages and images we see and hear every day.

Stories of the third kind clinch the lessons of the first two and turn them into action. They typically present a valued objective or suggest a need or desire, and offer a product, service, candidate, institution, or action purported to help attain or gratify it. The lessons of fictitious Little Red Riding Hoods and their realistic sequels prominent in everyday news and entertainment not only teach lessons of vulnerability, mistrust, and dependence, but also help sell burglar alarms, more jails and executions promised to enhance security (which they rarely do), and other ways to adjust to a structure of power.

Ideally, the three kinds of stories check and balance each other. But in a commercially driven culture, stories of the third kind pay for most of the first two. That creates a coherent cultural environment whose overall function is to provide a hospitable and effective context for stories that sell. With the coming of the electronic age, that cultural environment is increasingly monopolized, homogenized, and globalized. We must then look at the historic course of our journey to see what this new age means for our children.

For the longest time in human history, stories were told only face to face. A community was defined by the rituals, mythologies, and imageries held in common. All useful knowledge is encapsulated in aphorisms and legends, proverbs and tales, incantations and ceremonies. Writing is rare and holy, forbidden for slaves. Laboriously inscribed manuscripts confer sacred power to their interpreters, the priests and ministers. As a sixteenth-century scribe put it:

> Those who observe the codices, those who recite them. Those who noisily turn the pages of illustrated manuscripts. Those who have possession of the black and red ink and that which is pictured; they lead us, they guide us, they tell us the way. State and church ruled the Middle Ages in a symbiotic relationship of mutual dependence and tension. State, composed of feudal nobles, was the economic and political order; church its cultural arm.

The industrial revolution changed all that. One of the first machines stamping out standardized artifacts was the printing press. Its product, the book, was a prerequisite for all the other upheavals to come.

The book could be given to all who could read, requiring education and creating a new literate class of people. Readers could now interpret the book (at first the Bible) for themselves, breaking the monopoly of priestly interpreters and ushering in the Reformation.

When the printing press was hooked up to the steam engine the industrialization of storytelling shifted into high gear. Rapid publication and mass transport created a new form of consciousness: modem mass publics. Publics are loose aggregations of people who share some common consciousness of how things work, what things are, and what ought to be done—but never meet face to face. That was never before possible.

Stories can now be sent—often smuggled—across hitherto impenetrable or closely guarded boundaries of time, space, and status. The book lifts people from their traditional moorings as the industrial revolution uproots them from their local communities and cultures. They can now get off the land and go to work in faraway ports, factories, and continents, and have with them a packet of common consciousness—the book or journal, and later the motion picture (silent at first)—wherever they go.

Publics, created by such publication, are necessary for the formation of individual and group identities in the new urban environment, as the different classes and regional, religious, and ethnic groups try to live together with some degree of cooperation and harmony.

Publics are the basic units of self-government, electing or selecting representatives to an assembly trying to reconcile diverse interests. The maintenance and integrity of multiple publics makes self-government feasible for large, complex, and diverse national communities. People engage in long and costly struggles—now at a critical stage—to be free to create and share stories that fit the reality of competing and often conflicting values and interests. Most of our assumptions about human development and political plurality and choice are rooted in the print era.

One of the most vital provisions of the print era was the creation of the only large-scale folk institution of industrial society, public education. Public education is the community institution where face-to-face learning and interpreting could, ideally, liberate the individual from both tribal and medieval dependencies and all cultural monopolies.

The second great transformation, the electronic revolution, ushers in the telecommunications era. Its mainstream, television, is superimposed upon and reorganizes print-based culture. Unlike the industrial revolution, the new upheaval does not uproot people from their homes but transports them in their homes. It retribalizes modern society and changes the role of education in the new culture.

For the first time in human history, children are born into homes where mass-mediated storytellers reach them on the average more than seven hours a day. Most waking hours, and often dreams, are filled with their stories. Giant industries discharge their messages into the mainstream of common consciousness. The historic nexus of church and state is replaced by television and state.

These changes may appear to be a broadening and enrichment of local horizons, but they also mean a homogenization of outlooks and limitation of alternatives. For media professionals, the changes mean fewer opportunities and greater compulsions to present life in saleable packages. Creative artists, scientists, humanists can still explore and enlighten and occasionally even challenge, but, increasingly, their stories must fit marketing strategies and priorities.

Despite being surrounded with sales messages, or perhaps because of it, a Consumer Federation of America survey concluded in 1990 that "Americans are not smart shoppers and their ignorance costs them billions, threatens their health and safety, and undermines the economy. . . ."

Broadcasting is the most concentrated, homogenized, and globalized medium. The top one hundred advertisers pay for two-thirds of all network television. Four networks, allied to giant transnational corporations—our private "Ministry of Culture"—control the bulk of production and distribution, and shape the cultural mainstream. Other interests, minority views, and the potential of any challenge to dominant perspectives lose ground with every merger.

The Cultural Environment Movement was launched in response to that challenge. Its Founding Convention was held in St. Louis, Missouri, March 15–17, 1996, in cooperation with Webster University. It was the most diverse representation of leaders and activists in the field of culture and communication that has ever met.

The concepts that motivated us developed after thirty years of media research. It became clear that research is not enough. The new globalized and centralized cultural environment demanded a new active approach. Working separately on individual issues, rallying to meet each individual crisis, was not sufficient. Treating symptoms instead of starting to prevent the wholesale manufacturing of the conditions that led to those symptoms was self-defeating. Dealing with systemic connections requires coordination and organization. Individual effort, local action, and national and international constituencies acting in concert can, together, help to begin that long, slow, and difficult task. It involves:

- **Building a new coalition** involving media councils in the United States and abroad; teachers, students, and parents; groups concerned with children, youth, and aging; women's groups; religious and minority organizations; educational, health, environmental, legal, and other professional associations; consumer groups and agencies; associations of creative workers in the media and in the arts and sciences; independent computer-network organizers and other organizations and individuals committed to broadening the freedom and diversity of communication.

- **Opposing domination and working to abolish existing concentration of ownership and censorship** (both of and by media), public or private. It involves extending rights, facilities, and influence to interests and perspectives other than the most powerful and profitable. It means including in cultural decision making the less affluent, more vulnerable groups who, in fact, are the majority of the population. These include the marginalized, neglected, abused, exploited, physically or mentally disabled, young and old, women, minorities, poor people, recent immigrants—all those most in need of a decent role and a voice in a freer cultural environment.

- **Seeking out and cooperating with cultural liberation forces** of other countries working for the integrity and independence of their own decision making and against cultural domination and invasion. Learning from countries that have already opened their media to the democratic process. Helping local movements, including in the most dependent and vulnerable countries of Latin America, Asia, and Africa (and also in Eastern Europe and the former Soviet Republics), to invest in their own cultural development; opposing aggressive foreign ownership and coercive trade policies that make such development more difficult.

- **Supporting journalists, artists, writers, actors, directors, and other creative workers** struggling for more freedom from having to present life as a commodity designed for a market of consumers. Working with guilds, caucuses, labor, and other groups for diversity in employment and in media content. Supporting media and cultural organizations addressing significant but neglected needs, sensibilities, and interests.

- **Promoting media literacy, media awareness, critical viewing and reading, and other media education efforts** as a fresh approach to the liberal arts and an essential educational objective on every level. Collecting, publicizing, and disseminating information, research, and evaluation about relevant programs, services, curricula, and teaching materials. Helping to organize educational and parents' groups demanding pre-service and in-service teacher training in media analysis, already required in the schools of Australia, Canada, and Great Britain.

- **Placing cultural policy issues on the social-political agenda.** Supporting and, if necessary, organizing local and national media councils, study groups, citizen groups, minority and professional groups, and other forums of public discussion, policy development, representation, and action. Not waiting for a blueprint but creating and experimenting with ways of community and citizen participation in local, national, and international media policy making. Sharing experiences, lessons, and recommendations and gradually moving toward a realistic democratic agenda.

The Founding Convention participants debated and approved a People's Communication Charter, the Viewer's Declaration of Independence, and an Agenda for Action. . . .

The Cultural Environment Movement (CEM) is a coalition of

independent organizations and supporters in every state of the United States and sixty-three other countries on six continents.. Its over 150 affiliated and supporting organizations and its individual supporters represent a wide range of social and cultural concerns, united in working for freedom, fairness, diversity, responsibility, respect for cultural integrity, the protection of children, and democratic decision making in the media mainstream. . . .

30

Viewer's Declaration of Independence

Cultural Environment Movement

This Declaration originated at the Founding Convention of the Cultural Environment Movement (CEM) in St. Louis, Missouri, on March 17, 1996. It was revised following suggestions by a committee elected at the convention.

We hold these truths to be self-evident:

- that all persons are endowed with the right to live in a cultural environment that is respectful of their humanity and supportive of their potential.
- that all children are endowed with the right to grow up in a cultural environment that fosters responsibility, trust, and community rather than force, fear, and violence.
- that when the cultural environment becomes destructive of these ends, it is necessary to alter it.

Such is the necessity that confronts us. Let the world hear the reasons that compel us to assert our rights and to take an active role in the shaping of our common cultural environment.

1. Humans live and learn by stories. Today they are no longer hand-crafted, homemade, community-inspired. They are no longer told by

Cultural Environmental Movement, "Viewer's Declaration of Independence," 1995, www.cemnet.org/cem@libertynet.org Reprinted by permission of George Gerbner, president and founder, CEM.

families, schools, or churches but are the products of a complex mass-production and marketing process. Scottish patriot Andrew Fletcher once said: "If one were permitted to make all the ballads, one need not care who should make the laws of a nation." Today most of our "ballads"—the myths and stories of our culture—are made by a small group of global conglomerates that have something to sell.

2. This radical transformation of our cultural environment has changed the roles we grow into, the way we employ creative talent, the way we raise our children, and the way we manage our affairs. Communication channels proliferate, but technologies converge and media merge. Consolidation of ownership denies entry to newcomers, drives independents out of the mainstream, and reduces diversity of content. Media blend into a seamless homogenized cultural environment that constrains life's choices as much as the degradation of the physical environment limits life's chances.

3. This change did not come about spontaneously or after thoughtful deliberation. It was imposed on an uniformed public and is enshrined in legislation rushed through Congress without any opportunity for public scrutiny or debate about its consequences and worldwide fallout. The airways, a global commons, have been given away to media empires responsible to no one but their stockholders.

4. In exchange for that giveaway, we are told, we get "free" entertainment and news. But in truth, we pay dearly, both as consumers and as citizens. The price of soap we buy includes a surcharge for the commercials that bring us the "soap opera." We pay when we wash, not when we watch. And we pay even if we do not watch or do not like the way of life it promotes. This is taxation without representation. Furthermore, the advertising expenditures that buy our media are a tax-deductible business expense. Money diverted from the public treasure pays for an invisible, unelected, unaccountable, private Ministry of Culture making, behind closed doors, decisions that shape public policy.

5. The human consequences are also far-reaching. They include cults of media violence that desensitize, terrorize, brutalize, and paralyze; the promotion of unhealthy practices that pollute, drug, hurt, poison, and kill thousands every day; portrayals that dehumanize, stereotype, marginalize, and stigmatize women, racial and ethnic groups, gays and lesbians, aging or disabled or physically or mentally ill persons, and others outside the cultural mainstream.

6. These distortions of the democratic process divert attention from the basic needs, problems, and aspirations of people. They conceal the drift toward ecological suicide; the silent crumbling of our vital infrastructure; the cruel neglect of children, poor people, and other vulnerable populations; the invasions of privacy at home and in the workplace; the growing inequalities of wealth and opportunity; the profits made from throwing millions of people on the scrapheap of the unemployed; the commercialization of the classroom; and the downgrading of education and the arts.

7. Global marketing formulas, imposed on media workers and foisted on the children of the world, colonize, monopolize, and homogenize cultures everywhere. Technocratic fantasies mask social realities that further widen the gaps between the information rich and the information poor.

8. Repeated protests and petitions have been ignored or dismissed as attempts at "censorship" by the media magnates who alone have the power to suppress and to censor. No constitutional protection or legislative prospect will help us to loosen the noose of market censorship or to counter the repressive direction the "culture wars" are taking us. We need a liberating alternative.

We, therefore, declare our independence from a system that has drifted out of democratic reach. Our CEM offers the liberating alternative: an independent citizen voice in cultural policy making, working for the creation of a free, fair, diverse, and responsible cultural environment for us and our children.

31

Fighting Back

David Chagall

GET INVOLVED

We can try to change the television industry's way of doing business. Christian organizations have launched a frontal assault on the television industry itself, sponsoring periodic letter-writing and petition campaigns aimed at television network executives and corporate sponsors of objectionable programs. One has even instituted a nationwide boycott of sponsors' products to pressure them to withdraw their advertising from programs "which attack our values, our children, and our families." If you feel this is an effective tactic and wish to get involved, you may contact them directly as follows:

American Family Association
107 Parkgate, P.O. Drawer 2440
Tupelo, Mississippi 38803

Phyllis Schlafly
Box 618
Alton, Illinois 62002

Originally published in David Chagall, *Surviving the Media Jungle* (Nashville: Broadman & Holman Publishers, 1996). Reprinted with permission.

RECOGNIZE THE ADDICTION

There is also the personal approach. Although we cannot guarantee what anyone else does, we can take full responsibility for what we ourselves choose to do. On that premise, then, we need to understand that television watching is an *addictive habit*. Reams of research conclusively show that TV viewing contains all the defining characteristics of any addiction, even including drug addiction. These include a mind-numbing effect that allows one to escape the stress of everyday realities, a powerful compulsion to repeat the experience, and telltale withdrawal symptoms encountered when one attempts to eliminate the addiction from one's life.

Biochemistry reveals just how we form our habits and addictions. Our nerve cells contain fibers for sending *out* messages (*axons*), and other fibers for receiving *incoming* messages (*dendrites*). When we use axons frequently, they form little bumps called "boutons." The more boutons a nerve cell has, the easier it is to send out messages. Habits are simply actions we repeat over and over again that build boutons on our nerve cells, which makes it easier and easier to repeat that same action. Even when they are no longer used, boutons do not disappear. Because the old pathways are still there, we always risk the chance of falling back into an undesirable habit, just like an alcoholic who "falls off the wagon."

FORM NEW HABITS

So how do we break free? We build new habits and responses that are stronger than the old ones. Before too long, more boutons will grow on the new pathway than the old one, and the "path" will grow deeper. Then it actually becomes easier to travel that new route and a new, more desirable habit is established.

Most people find it takes about three weeks to form one new habit. Applied to television, we can substitute other, more uplifting activities in place of just staring like dummies at the tube. For example, we can choose to lead a family devotional time. Or we can read classic stories to our younger children. Or we can all gather around the piano for singalongs, or play Pictograms. Or we can institute a family reading and study time after dinner so the kids can do their homework and we can start some of those fine books we've always meant to read but somehow have gathered dust on our bookshelves.

BANISH TV

Once we have weaned ourselves and the family from the habitual TV "fix," we can go one of two ways. The first is the more drastic decision to banish television from your house. Families that have taken this step recorded their family's reactions in daily logs. A common response was a feeling of aimlessness experienced most strongly the first week of the blackout. "We kind of hung around, not knowing what to do with ourselves. . . ." "Sometimes I'd just go and look at the [TV] set, even though it was off. . . ." During this initial withdrawal period, many reported feeling "disoriented" or "weird."

Then the substitute activities kicked in. The "no TV" families found themselves enjoying the following benefits:

- more interaction between children and adults;
- greater feeling of closeness as a family;
- children more eager to participate in household chores;
- more peaceful home atmosphere;
- more outdoor play and sports activities;
- children playing together more;
- longer meal times with more discussion;
- more reading by everyone;
- earlier bedtime and rising hours;
- improved relations between parents and other adults in family.

There were some negatives, too. Cold-turkey families report missing the fine, uplifting programs such as *Masterpiece Theater*, the Disney Channel, the Family Channel, or *The 700 Club*. Another minus was the fact that parents had lost one of their most effective disciplinary tools, namely, the threat to withhold television viewing as punishment for bad behavior. Over time, however, most families who "go black" eventually opt to turn the set back on again, though this time with much more awareness of their viewing choices and time spent before the tube.

USE GRACE CONTROL

Which brings us to a second alternative, what I would call "grace control." The overriding principle here is to use television instead of letting it use you. That is the standard we have set for our own home, and you may find it will work for you, too.

It requires that you set up new house rules and strictly observe them. From now on, you and you alone will be responsible for ensuring that your family will watch only those shows that are good, uplifting, useful, and appropriate for building up and upholding your family's Christian standards (see Phil. 4:8).

That necessitates that you take total charge and become your own programmers. It does take some work and planning, but the benefits far outweigh the efforts. Each family's preferences will be unique, so I won't presume to specify what you should include in your viewing schedule. But whatever your family's choices, they need to be *limited as to time* and *fully supervised.*

An adult should sit with the kids during their viewing times to help them understand any complicated ideas, show them how commercials use tricks to excite them to want things that may be of poor quality or not good for them, and teach them that hitting, punching, and kicking is a bad way to solve problems and only makes things worse.

If at times that's not feasible, the very least you should require is that the children report on what they have viewed. Ask them to tell you why they thought they learned something new, or how to be a better person or in some other way benefited from their TV experience.

As for prime-time viewing, it's best not to watch as a family until you feel secure that you won't be "surprised" during "family" shows by unexpected allusions to sex, drugs, or other undesirable subjects. You can get some help from a guide called *Parents' Guide to Prime Time* published by the Media Research Center in Virginia. The booklet reviews all major programs from the four networks (ABC, NBC, CBS, and Fox).

Part III

LOOKING
TO THE FUTURE

Chapter Seven

New Challenges
to the Media

32

The First Amendment
and Democracy:
The Challenge of New Technology

Adam S. Plotkin

New technology is forcing reevaluation of historic definitions, standards, and rules for press regulation. Early in this century the press functioned either through print or broadcast media. Thus, press regulation focused on the medium through which the press worked. Cable, computer networks, interactive technologies, and the like do not fit comfortably in the established mold. We need, therefore, a definition of press that looks beyond the medium to another, still undefined, framework for regulation.

This article is a search for a more satisfactory framework, recognizing the need to foster democratic dialogue as the primary social function of the press and exploring questions of regulatory policy in light of that primary need. Problems of press regulation, historical functions of the press, early philosophical foundations, the practical efforts of early Americans to harness press efforts to serve public needs, and a more modern search for adequate contemporary models are all explored, concluding with essential recommendations.

Beginning in 1943, the United States Supreme Court (*National Broadcasting Co.* v. *U.S.*, 1943) conferred upon the press a sliding scale of protection based on the scarcity theory of technology. The policy culminated in two decisions. In *Red Lion Broadcasting* v. *FCC* (1969), the Court upheld FCC Fairness Doctrine and personal attack rules,

Journal of Mass Media Ethics, Volume 11, Number 4, pp. 236-245. Copyright 1996 by Lawrence Erlbaum Associates, Inc.

mandating that radio stations guarantee right-of-reply to anyone wishing to rebut previously aired opinions. In contrast, five years later the Court (*Miami Herald Publishing Co.* v. *Tornillo,* 1974) overturned a Florida statute imposing right-of-reply on the print media. These two cases make a clear distinction between characteristics of print and "air" requiring differing regulation.

With new technologies requiring regulative adaptations by the courts, a 1984 case that never reached the Supreme Court provides the most concise example of the problem of new media convergence. District of Columbia Circuit Judge Robert Bork reluctantly required application of the *Red Lion* model of regulation to the teletext medium, which combines print and broadcast technologies to present words and pictures via television (*TRAC* v. *FCC, 1984*). Bork reasoned that teletext, "whatever its similarities to print media, used broadcast frequencies, and that [allowing content regulation of teletext], given *Red Lion,* would seem to be that" (p. 509). However, Bork explained:

> The basic difficulty in this entire area is that the line drawn between the print media and the broadcast media, resting as it does on the physical scarcity of the latter, is a distinction without a difference. Employing the scarcity concept as an analytic tool, particularly with respect to new and unforeseen technologies, inevitably leads to strained reasoning and artificial results. (p. 508)

The task, then, is to formulate a definition of press in the new technology era that will allow the courts to focus on messages disseminated rather than on the medium through which messages are delivered. Examination of traditional press roles and analysis of what have come to be accepted philosophical foundations upon which the press operates should clarify the role of the press and provide the courts with a model for applying press protection based on content rather than on medium.

Such a policy should recognize the potential inherent in new communication technology for community formation and expansion of the democratic dialogue, striving to counteract the potential isolation of citizens who withdraw from the public to "interact" via computer rather than face-to-face public fora.

CHANGING PRESS FUNCTIONS

Alexis de Tocqueville (1835/1988) observed that the American press carried much influence: "Freedom of the press is the principal and, so to say, the constitutive element in freedom" (p. 191). He saw newspapers, then the dominant mass medium, as thoroughly pervading American society, a catalyst in formation of community: "Without newspapers there would be hardly any common action at all . . . hardly any democratic association can carry on without a newspaper" (p. 518).

Today, however, participation in the marketplace of ideas differs markedly from postcolonial times, with the differences posing a serious test for democracy. Comparisons of de Tocqueville's press to today's institutional press suggests today's press falls short of the linking abilities of the early press. While serving as a watchdog, today's institutional press may have lost sight of the fact that it exists also for the purpose of forming community and fostering the dialogue de Tocqueville observed. Dialogue cannot exist unidirectionally. The institutional press cannot simply provide information to the public with the hope that dialogue will ensue. People must be encouraged to participate, and the institutional press may be failing to provide that encouragement. Perhaps overconcern with the essential watchdog function has produced media system that causes citizens to become mere receivers of informa tion rather than the aggressive information seekers of the early nine teenth century.

Prior to emergence and widespread use of new communicatio: technology, cost of access to America's press rose substantially, makin access nearly impossible for the average individual. Institutional medi have drifted from their colonial form of a participatory press tha engaged the citizenry and encouraged social communication.

Ease of entry provided by cable access and desktop publishing i effecting a return to the colonial model, aided by plummeting economic costs of engaging in the public dialogue and operating a booth in the marketplace of ideas.

Based on the capabilities of new technology to open up the marketplace of ideas, Garry (1994) concluded that the best way to merge new technology with current communications law is through a technology-blind approach: Focus on and emphasize the nature of a "participatory press" (p. 132). Such a press not only informs but involves the audience in debate and facilitates democratic dialogue.

The participatory press, Garry (1994) claimed, is the only hope for fulfilling three steps of political action: (a) informing the people, (b) facilitating a feeling of consultation leading to the formation of opinions (public and private), and (c) forming a commitment to action. Today's institutional press seems to encourage passivity instead of embracing and encouraging participation.

A technology-blind definition of First Amendment protection is also recommended by Smolla (1994), because media convergence will make technology-based regulations too confusing to maintain.

The Hutchins Commission of the 1940s found five social needs that may be useful in discussions justifying technology-blind definitions of a free press: (a) truthful, comprehensive, and intelligent accounts of the day's events; (b) a forum for exchanging comments and criticisms; (c) a means of projecting the opinions and attitudes of groups to others; (d) a method for presenting and clarifying societal goals and values; and (e) a way of reaching everyone through currents of information, thought, and feelings that the press supplied (Commission on Freedom of the Press, 1947, pp. 20–21).

Many people seem content with separation from the democratic dialogue, finding it easier to receive information than to gather and introduce it into the dialogue. This situation may be reversible through new technology that fosters cheap and easy participation in the marketplace of ideas.

PHILOSOPHICAL FOUNDATIONS

The Hutchins Commission built its philosophical foundations for outlining the press's function from Mill, Locke, and Milton.

Mill's (1859/1985) utilitarianism is results-based and participatory, classifying morality of actions according to resultant benefit or harm. Best actions result in the greatest good for the greatest number:

> The "people" who exercise the power are not always the same people as those over whom it is exercised; and the "self government" spoken of is not the government of each by himself, but of each by all the rest. The will of the people, moreover, practically means the will of the most numerous or the most active part of the people—the majority, or those who succeed in making themselves accepted as the majority. (p. 62)

Preventing evil from coming upon others represented a good act, and that was precisely what the press was supposed to do: "Make anyone answerable for doing evil to others . . ." (Mill, 1859/1985, p. 70). Mill staunchly supported freedom of expression and opposed silencing any opinion: "If all mankind minus one were of one opinion, mankind would be no more justified in silencing that one person than he, if he had the power, would be justified in silencing mankind" (p. 76). Mill is also credited with the introduction of the concept of *social responsibility*, which embraces the idea that the people possess insufficient means and motivation for providing themselves with necessary information and would rather become immersed in gossip. The press, in this view, has the responsibility for providing the public with necessary information, including editorial and commercial information and entertainment (Altschull, 1990).

John Milton developed in *Areopagitica* the self-righting principle of truth that, metaphorically speaking, occurs in the marketplace of ideas. The self-righting principle asserts that in conflicts between truth and falsehood, truth will win in the end. The marketplace metaphor equates the press with the marketplaces of ancient Greece in which citizens gathered, among other reasons, to discuss politics. Milton saw liberty of press as a "means to the end of truth" (Altschull, 1990, p. 40). Truth was to be achieved, or accepted, only after people were confronted with an array of opinions.

Merrill (1994), confirming Altschull's conclusions, said "American journalists consider Milton a foundational hero, a thinker who was the first to plant the idea of a free press firmly in the intellectual soil of England, [from] where it was later transferred to the American Colonies" (p. 41).

John Locke's contract theory and his assertion of the right of revolution provide, according to Altschull (1990), two strong foundations for American journalism. The contract theory holds that the government thrives under the consent of the governed, while the doctrine of the right of revolution holds that citizens have a duty to revolt against tyrannical leaders and "throw the rascals out" (p. 51), by force or violence if necessary.

Merrill (1994), however, focused on the Lockean view that all humans begin with empty minds that resemble a blank tablet, or *tabula rasa*, waiting to be filled by sense data. The good journalist, according to Locke, would be the one who throws himself into the uncovering, analysis, and presentation of information, following certain moral guides. By using reason, compiling experiences, and being ethical a journalist becomes good.

These foundations suggest that the media, as virtually the only channels pervasive enough to reach entire communities, have certain duties. Protected by law to provide an open forum for discussion, press units are obliged to devote themselves to disclosing and distributing truth, allowing citizens to make better decisions and more effectively govern themselves. Commitment to truth must spring from a sense of duty in which people are respected as ends rather than as means to ends. Exposure to opinions in the search for truth should lead to effective self-government.

PRACTICAL EFFORTS BY THE PRESS

Benjamin Franklin, William James, and John Dewey may have had the strongest philosophical impact on how journalists actually work. Franklin reinforced Milton's self-righting principle of truth as an editor who maintained the need to provide publication space for presenting all sides of the story (an effort to let truth and falsehood grapple). Altschull (1990) saw a duality in Franklin's influence on press practice:

> On the one hand there is the drive to operate in the interest of the public, to provide information for the good of mankind and a free society; on the other there is the drive for private profit in the commercial world of the free marketplace. (p. 107)

James influenced American journalism as a protagonist of pragmatism; an embrace of dialectical analysis and encouragement for use of scientific method in uncovering the truth, which science sees as an accretion of fact. A pluralist, James preferred the presence of many ideas to any single dictum. Pragmatism and pluralism thus combined make a journalist, contemporary or not, "comfortably at home with James" (Altschull, 1990, p. 227).

Dewey advocated an inherent *right to know* in response to Adolf Hitler's censorship practices. He thought that someone should fight for the people, especially in a democracy where information is essential to leadership and self-government, relying on Milton's self-righting principle and the belief that knowledge "provided the American citizen the raw substance he needed to carry out his constitutional role" (Altschull, 1990, p. 249).

MODERN SEARCH FOR BETTER MODELS

Outlining the Clinton administration's view of communication regulation, Vice President Gore (1993) talked of zeroing in

> not on the technology but on what we use technology for. Our goal is not to design the market of the future; it is to provide the principles that shape the market. And it is to provide the rules governing this transition to an open market of information.

Recognizing in the early 1980s the emerging problem, Pool (1983) declared that unless the regulatory scheme changes as electronic technology explodes, press freedom is unsure because historically less protection has been conferred on electronic technologies than on print media:

> As computers become the printing presses of the twenty-first century, ink marks on paper will continue to be read, and broadcasts to be watched, but other new media will evolve from what are now but the toys of computer hackers. Videodiscs, integrated memories, and data bases will serve functions that books and libraries now serve, while information retrieval systems will serve for what magazines and newspapers do now. Networks of satellites, optical fibers, and radio waves will serve the functions of the present-day postal system. *Speech will not be free if these are not also free.* [emphasis added]
>
> The danger is not of an electronic nightmare, but of human error. It is not computers but policy that threatens freedom. The censorship that followed the printing press was not entailed in Gutenberg's process; it was a reaction to it. The regulation of electronic communication is likewise not entailed in its technology, but is a reaction to it. Computers, telephones, radio, and satellites are technologies of freedom, as much as was the printing press. (p. 226)

Smolla (1992), in considering the First Amendment future, described a free speech model and outlined a content-based regulatory framework for deciding high-tech free speech issues. The model establishes a three-part procedure for regulating speech. Part one examines the content of speech in the general marketplace, the second describes the non-content regulatory scheme described in *United States* v. *O'Brien* (1968), with a procedure for evaluating special situations, while the final part explains a procedure for analyzing speech outside the general marketplace.

In turn, the content-based regulatory structure emphasizes six principles Smolla (1992) saw as forming "the core of the modern First Amendment" (p. 53), which structures for regulating speech content must embrace: neutrality, emotion, symbolism, harm, causation, and precision.

Neutrality asserts that opposition to the meaning of an idea is never enough to merit censoring distribution of the idea; the government must remain "viewpoint neutral" (Smolla, 1992, p. 46) and neutrality may be the only absolute rule associated with the First Amendment. Modern First Amendment cases establish a per se rule making the punishment of speech flatly unconstitutional "if the penalty is based on the offensiveness or the undesirability of the viewpoint expressed" (p. 46).

The Supreme Court has said:

> Under the First Amendment there is no such thing as a false idea. However pernicious an opinion may seem, we depend for its correction not on the conscience of judges and juries, but on the competition of other ideas. (*Gertz* v. *Robert Welch, Inc.*, 1974)

The *emotion* principle prohibits censorship because of the passion or vulgarity inherent in it. Not universally praised, the emotion principle is denounced by those seeking to force rough speech beyond the purview of the First Amendment. Symbolic speech acts (burning a flag, wearing a jacket embroidered with obscenities, etc.) might no longer survive scrutiny if we separate the intellectual and emotional components of speech, for without the emotion principle, "much of the First Amendment as we know it would unravel" (Smolla, 1992, p. 46).

Protecting expressive conduct, the *symbolism* principle holds that when the expression outweighs the conduct, or when the conduct is used merely as a symbol for a message,[1] the act is considered symbolic speech (Gillmor, Barron, Simon, and Terry, 1990). Since many demonstrations and protests rely heavily on symbolic acts, and since the messages conveyed through these acts greatly contribute to the democratic dialogue, the symbolism principle must be represented in any future free speech model.

The *harm* principle allows for penalizing an individual or group for damaging speech. This principle arises from the relation between the emotional and neutrality principles. Speech can cause or result in either physical, relational, or reactive harms. Physically, speech can incite to violence or result in violent opposition to a speaker for promoting certain views. Speech may interfere with relationships. For instance, information may be used to damage another's social status or position in business transactions. Reactive harms could result from certain intellectual or emotional responses to the content of speech.

The *causation* principle provides the foundation for the neutrality, emotion, and harm principles and is exemplified by the clear and present danger test. Asserting the need to scrutinize a connection between speech and the resultant harm implies a recognition of the inherent connection between speech and action that must be understood before steps may be taken to prevent or remedy the harm done (Smolla, 1992).

Precision allows for the overturning of speech regulation serving a compelling state interest if those regulations are substantively or definitionally imprecise; that is, not tailored to serve that state interest (Smolla, 1992).

O'Brien's conviction on a draft card burning offense was upheld, despite his argument he committed a symbolic speech act, because the statute under which he was convicted met four criteria necessary for non-content-based regulation:

> A government regulation is sufficiently justified if it is within the constitutional power of the government; if it furthers an important or substantial governmental interest; if the governmental interest is unrelated to the suppression of free expression; and if the incidental restriction is no greater than is essential to the furtherance of that interest. (*United States* v. *O'Brien,* 1968, p. 680)

Future models, at the moment, must include the O'Brien test for determining whether a regulation is non-content based (Smolla, 1992).

In other circumstances, speech occurs outside the marketplace when the government speaks, making necessary both content and non-content regulation of speech. In public schools, where the government teaches, obscenity is not permitted (*Bethel School District No. 403* v. *Fraser,* 1986). Even in these special conditions, rules must be "carefully crafted to permit the maximum possible exercise of free expression consistent with the mission and function of the setting" (Smolla, 1992, p. 64).

The goal for future theorists and regulators should be to provide an atmosphere that allows maximum access and availability of information. This can be accomplished best by abandoning the courts' traditional technology-based approach to regulating the marketplace of ideas and by focusing instead on the functions the press perform. If used, regulation such as the right-of-reply denied for print media in *Miami Herald Publishing Co.* v. *Tornillo* (1974) should be devoted to enabling maximum access to the cyberspace marketplace of ideas. Similarly, must-carry regulations for cable companies (*Turner Broadcasting System* v.

FCC, 1994) should promote dialogue and exposure to a wide variety of opinions, both of which are essential for self-government and indispensable for nurturing communities.

CONCLUSIONS

Media convergence renders inadequate the technological approach to establishing First Amendment protection. The Information Superhighway depends upon broadcast technology, but applying the broadcast model to as yet undeveloped media risks infringing the rights of more traditional press instruments such as newspapers and magazines taking advantage of the newer and cheaper technology. Also to be considered, of course, is the inherent injustice in regulating traditional broadcast technologies after the foundation for such regulations is rendered inapplicable.

Without a democratic dialogue, democracy would be impossible, so it is imperative that the courts protect under the press clause of the First Amendment the medium through which speech is disseminated while protecting under the speech clause all speech, whether disseminated through electronic or traditional means. After deciding on regulation, the task for the future is to tackle the problem of how to encourage participation in the democratic dialogue.

NOTE

1. See *Texas* v. *Johnson* (1989). Johnson was arrested for burning the American flag under a Texas statute forbidding the "desecration of a venerated object" (Gillmor et al., 1990, p. 915). The U.S. Supreme Court overturned his conviction on the ground that his conduct was predominantly expressive and therefore protected under the First Amendment.

REFERENCES

Altschull, H. 1990. *From Milton to McLuhan: The Ideas behind American Journalism.* New York: Longman.

Bethel School District No. 403 v. Fraser, 478 U.S. 675 (1986).

Commission on Freedom of the Press. 1947. *A Free and Responsible Press.* Chicago: University of Chicago Press.

De Tocqueville, A. 1988. *Democracy in America,* J. Mayer (ed.). New York: Harper. (Original work published in 1835)

Garry, P. 1994. *Scrambling for Protection: The New Media and the First Amendment.* Pittsburgh, Pa: University of Pittsburgh Press.

Gertz v. Robert Welch, Inc., 418 U.S. 323 (1974).

Gillmor, D., J. Barron, T. Simon, and H. Terry (eds.). 1990. *Mass Communication Law: Cases and Comment.* 5th ed. New York: West.

Gore, A. (Speaker). 1993. VP address given to the National Press Club. (Cassette Recording No. NA 1993-21-12). Alexandria, Va: Wave Communication.

Merrill, J. 1994. *Legacy of Wisdom: Great Thinkers and Journalism.* Ames: Iowa State University Press.

Miami Herald Publishing Company v. Tornillo, 418 U.S. 241 (1974).

Mill, J. 1859/1985. *On Liberty,* G. Himmelfarb (ed). London: Penguin.

National Broadcasting Co. v. U.S., 319 U.S. 190 (1943).

Pool, I. 1983. *Technologies of Freedom.* Cambridge, Mass: Belknap.

Red Lion Broadcasting Co. v. FCC, 395 U.S. 767 (1969).

Smolla, R. 1992. *Free Speech in an Open Society.* New York: Vintage.

Smolla, R. 1994. *Smolla and Nimmer on Freedom of Speech: A Treatise on the First Amendment.* New York: Bender.

Texas v. Johnson, 491 U.S. 397 (1989).

TRAC v. FCC, 801 F.2d 501 (1984).

Turner Broadcasting System v. FCC, 512 U.S. 622 (1994).

United States v. O'Brien, 391 U.S. 367 (1968).

33

Do Journalism Ethics and Values Apply to New Media?

Fred Mann

. . . Being a journalist is what I've always been about. It's how I have always defined myself. Journalism and its enduring values and ethics are very much a part of who I am. I felt the connection decades ago, when Chris Peck and I worked together on the college newspaper. I still feel it today.

But today, in the online world, the challenges to traditional journalistic values and ethics are major. I feel very lucky to have grown up professionally at the *Philadelphia Inquirer,* where values such as editorial integrity, balance, fairness, and accuracy were as ingrained as they were at any other paper on the planet. People like Jim Naughton and Gene Roberts and Gene Foreman made it a religion for us all. And as a result, I really feel like I can carry those values into this strange, new world with as much enthusiasm as anybody.

But it is no easy trick. This game is so new that we really haven't drawn the lines on the playing field yet. There are troubling issues around every corner online. At most every Internet-related conference, the issues under discussion are either business related (as in, how do we make money on the Web? Or who do we cut a deal with to better our position and become the really dominant online player in our market?) Or the issues are technological: who's got the best software for tracking advertising logs, or which is a better way to go with your music clips—Real Audio or Shockwave?

Originally published in *Poynter Research File,* February 22, 1997. Reprinted with permission of the Poynter Institute and Fred Mann.

Editorial issues, when they are discussed at all, are also couched in the context of the latest innovation and coolest new design. Journalistic values and ethics don't usually make it on the radar screen at these conferences. There is some sort of assumption that if we are newspapers and we're going online, well, we'll act like newspapers and try to be fair and balanced and accurate. It's a no-brainer.

But it's not a no-brainer. For me it's a—brainer. Look at the situation here. Just about every newspaper you can think of is going online. Why? Because they are scared not to. Because they've been told they need to. Because they want to protect their franchise as the leading local information provider. And because they hope that there is money in it. Maybe there is. But publishers and newspaper chain CEOs usually are not going into this cheaply. There is hardware to buy and staff to devote. The cost can be high for larger papers.

To run these new operations, most newspapers reach into their newsrooms. Some put their online services under the marketing department or even under advertising. For those of us who come from the newsroom, it can be a shock. You are suddenly publisher of a start-up venture that everyone in your building says is the wave of the future. You are a businessman, a businesswoman, not just an editor. You are expected not just to gather and report and edit the news, like in the safe old days. You are expected to do all that, and turn a profit—soon!

Maybe it's just me. Maybe it's my own coming to grips with the business side of journalism. After all, when an editor becomes a publisher, there are always new concerns to struggle with. And when he becomes *both* editor and publisher, he, by definition, runs into an unhealthy set of demands. But online, it's even stranger for there are few clear boundaries.

Where is the line between advertising and editorial? Many of our sites, mine included, have what we blithely call "sponsored" content. Car reviews sponsored by Toyota. Restaurant reviews linked to an editorial database of local restaurants—but a restaurant can add to an accompanying Yellow Page-style listing of information by paying for a boldface upgrade. Is that a reader service or selling editorial content to the highest bidder? We think we've put on enough safeguards to protect the editorial integrity of our information. But where *we* draw the line is not necessarily where *you* would. We may all subscribe to the same traditional journalistic values, but how you implement them in a world of clicks and links and interlocking databases is not as clear as it used to be.

I attended the Interactive Newspaper Conference in Houston recently, sponsored by that venerable newspaper Bible, *Editor & Pub-*

lisher. During the four-day conference, there was one—count 'em, one—hour-long session on journalistic ethics. And, frankly, it didn't shed much light on anything. The conference did hand out awards (as any self-respecting conference does these days.) A jury awarded three prizes to large newspaper Websites (over 100,000 print circulation.) The big one, for Best Online Newspaper Site, went to Kevin McKenna's excellent electronic publication of the *New York Times*. The second award, for Best Use of Editorial Content Online went—again—to the rather piggish *New York Times*. I was not surprised. I wanted both of those, but I knew we didn't deserve them. The third award, we *did* win. I was shocked and greatly honored. And when I thought about it some, I was pretty puzzled. The category? Best Use of Advertising Online.

That's not an award I had ever aspired to.

It made me wonder: We use advertising to pay the bills. What do other Websites use it for? I accepted with extreme modesty (actually modesty bordering on embarrassment), shook Kevin's hand, had my picture taken, and sat down. Man, wouldn't my buddies in the newsroom be proud of me now?

But the more I thought about it, the more I thought it was okay. Apparently these judges thought that our handling of advertising—of which we have a lot—was appropriate, tasteful, entertaining, and most important, not confusing or distracting from the news content. I took it as validation of our journalistic values. Of course, my ad staff took it as a great marketing ploy to sell more ads.

I go on about advertising because it is the hot button issue for many of us, but the areas of ethical concern online are legion.

Conventional wisdom (and, in this case, pretty undeniable wisdom) says that those companies that partner wisely will ultimately win the game online. Okay. So you go out and form various types of business alliances with other companies. You sign a deal with AT&T because they can give you the Internet access you need to offer to your potential audience. You partner with your major local bank so that you can offer their online banking services on your site and draw a bigger audience and therefore sell more ads. You ally with a major health care provider because you want their doctor database online. You throw in with one of your local major league sports franchises to co-sponsor an interactive game which drives your hit totals and gives the ballclub lots of easy promotional mileage. You even do business with Microsoft because, while they may ultimately devour you, you need their technical support and, Jeez, they'll throw money at anything.

Now that all that is in the works, post some credible business coverage online. Maintain your high standards for impartiality. Make sure your readers remember your impeccable credibility when they read that story about the high-tech war-to-the-death between Netscape and Microsoft which appears right next to your advertising button which says "Powered by Microsoft" on the screen.

I'd love to say that all these scenarios are hypothetical. They're not. They are all real. They are all situations we have faced, with no great sense of consistency—save one: to try to live up to the standards we have set for ourselves in print. Frankly, I don't think we have always succeeded. But we have done fairly well. I look to my colleagues for guidance and for support.

How responsible can you be or do you have to be about information you link to online? Is it your fault if the site you connect with misleads people or offends them? What about the site that links *from* the site you linked *to*? What about giving community groups the tools to post their own information on your Website? It's a great public service. It's a great communication device. It's a great audience builder. Hell, you can probably sell more ads that way. But what if those community groups post bad information? Or libel someone? What if your bulletin boards, like ours, become magnets for the most appalling kinds of hate mongering—stuff that you wouldn't let in your newspaper in a million years—yet your lawyers tell you that you can't censor those boards or you can be held liable for their content?

How do you create a new brand on the Internet? Something that plays off your newspaper credibility, but is much more hip, much more cool and Web-friendly. Can hip and cool also be fair and balanced?

How do you maintain allegiance with the value of completeness when you are busy delivering the personalized news content that online technology allows today? Are there a lot of your users out there who have programmed their searching agents to bring them back daily reports on more than their stock portfolios, baseball scores, travel bargains, and the weather? Think there are a lot of folks who will be exposed to daily feeds about inner-city poverty and suffering in Bosnia? Oh yeah—give me more . . . every hour!

How are we going to maintain accuracy when we are not dealing with two or three or four edition deadlines a night, but rather an edition deadline every minute? Speed and immediacy are critical to success on the Internet. Speed and immediacy are also, as we know, no friends of accuracy, fairness, completeness, and balance. And I know that there is not an online newsroom in the world that has the kind of copy desk and backfield editing resources that their print newsroom has.

Their online staffs don't even have all that many journalists most of the time. Some of my staff came from the newsroom, but others are young Internet jocks, right out of college (or more correctly, out of their sophomore year of college). They make our site go, but they no more identify with traditional journalistic ethics and values than our editors understand Java coding. And in a start-up business, we've got everybody doing a little of everything. Oversight is vitally important, but it's often hard to come by.

The list is endless, and I've gone on too long already . . . [but the following topics need more spirited discussion].

- Sites are tracking their usage on the Web—and then giving that user data to advertisers. How ethical is that?

- Sites are packaging audio music clips with their record reviews. Very cool for the user. But then they are selling the albums online next to the reviews—and taking a cut of the sales price. Is that still so cool?

- We have the capacity to imbed ad links into editorial copy now, and charge for those links. Who, aside from my ad manager, thinks this is a neat idea?

Just for the record, there are some clear ethical benefits to presenting news and information on the Web. With an endless newshole, we can be more complete, we can add more context, we can include more voices, and we can help people more fully understand complex issues. But, also for the record, just because a newshole is endless doesn't mean that we can fill it properly. We still face those wonderful age-old issues of who's going to fill it. And with what? Resource and time pressures don't disappear just because we've moved to the Internet.

[I can't answer all these confusing questions.] I do have one important answer, however—one that may seem obvious to those of you still dealing in column inches and first-edition deadlines, but it is easy to forget when your brain has been taken over by megabytes and server software problems. It is simply this: If we hope to prosper online, it is because, amid the thousands of Websites—from Yahoo! to the two guys in their garage in West Philly—we journalism sites are paid attention to because we have brand recognition that says we are credible sources of information. We are believable. People trust us. And if we let our *new* media concerns about quick profits and business alliances run away with our *old* traditional values, our credibility—and our marketability—will be shot.

Newspapers online have to be more than just newspapers online.

They have to go farther, offer more, connect with a new type of audience in ways that are often more unpredictable and nontraditional and chancy. They have to try new things. Break some rules. Plow some new territory. Do some things that will make their publishers cringe and their newsrooms threaten rebellion.

But in so doing, they cannot—they *must* not—abandon the underlying principles of good, traditional journalism. For if they do, they will be no more trusted than Microsoft and America Online and the other non-newspaper news sources on the Web. And once that happens, newspapers will be battling these strong new competitors on *their* turf of slick presentation and hot new technology rather than content and credibility. And that is a game most of us will lose.

Local markets—local content—is what this global new medium is really all about. That's where the value to the user is, and that's where the advertiser dollars are. These local markets are ours to capture because we have the content and the credibility and the history as the premiere local information providers. To see our newspaper online services grow into real valuable news sources for our readers, and real valuable revenue streams for our companies, we need to keep up technologically, develop smart business plans, create strong and user-friendly content, *and*—the great unspoken—keep our credibility. We do that by living up to our ethics and values—the old-fashioned ones that have served us so well and so long.

34

Without a Rulebook

Dianne Lynch

In February 1997, Fred Mann, general manager of Philadelphia Online, addressed thirty-seven of his colleagues in the auditorium of the Poynter Institute for Media Studies and set the tone for the four-day ethics conference that was to follow.

Online journalism, he said, is a quagmire of conflicting interests and new ethical dilemmas. It raises questions even the most seasoned journalists have yet to consider. "And if I was asked to speak tonight because I could answer all of these confusing questions, well, they screwed up," Mann said. "I can't."

It was his hope, he continued, that the conference would produce some common understandings. "I look to this gathering for guidance and support," he said.

Mann, who oversees the *Philadelphia Inquirer* and *Daily News'* Website (*www.phillynews.com*), may have found both. But what he didn't get was consensus.

Despite long days of heated debate, and the drafting of a set of guidelines for making ethical decisions online, participants left St. Petersburg with more questions than answers:

• Are news sites responsible for the information they link to?

• How does a site remain credible and accurate in the face of minute-to-minute deadlines?

This article originally appeared in *American Journalism Review*, January/February 1998. Reprinted by permission of *American Journalism Review*.

- Are online sites responsible—legally or ethically—for what goes on in their chat rooms?

- Are "cookies" (online tracking devices) and registration requirements an invasion of users' privacy?

- And perhaps most troubling: Is the longstanding church-and-state relationship between editorial and advertising morphing into an overly accommodating partnership?

"We failed to reach consensus on many issues and, in some cases, to even agree on the nature of the problems," wrote participant Anne Stuart, managing editor of *WebMaster* magazine (*www.web-master.com*), in her column on the conference.

[Two years] later, not much has changed.

Web editors around the country say there is little consistency across the profession—even between one situation and another in a single newsroom. And while most journalists contend that traditional values remain relevant online, they disagree sharply about how those values play out in a medium defined by immediacy, interactivity, burgeoning competition, and unflagging pressure to produce revenue.

Such ethical uncertainty has not slowed the rush to cyberspace. AJR [*American Journalism Review*]/NewsLink (*www.ajr.org*) reported in October [1997] that more than two thousand American newspapers publish regularly on the Web, and—despite the one hundred or so publications that abandoned their online enterprises [in 1997]—the number continues to grow.

With 71,000 new users logging on to the Internet every day in 1997 and newspaper readers twice as likely as average Net users to spend money online, the question for most media outlets is not if but how to establish a strong Web presence—though many acknowledge that it is fear of obsolescence rather than enthusiasm that drives their efforts.

But as the online landscape evolves from an unsettled frontier into, perhaps, a commercial boomtown, professional attention remains fixed on technology and economics.

The problem, say some editors and ethicists, is that the online environment changes rapidly and unpredictably. Decisions are made in a culture still uncertain of itself, and the clamor for profits too often drowns out other concerns.

"In the case of new media, people are going one hundred miles an hour, both to get up to speed and to stay ahead of their competitors," says Bob Steele, director of Poynter's ethics program. "We need to ask ourselves, 'How do we make good decisions in an environment that has neither a long journalistic tradition nor an opportunity for reflection?' "

Steele suggests that online newsrooms look to their print counterparts as models. But the very nature of the online audience changes the terrain, argues Doug Manship Jr., new media director of the *Advocate* in Baton Rouge.

Print newspapers adhere to community standards as they make ethical decisions, he says. "Most papers know their readership very well and make editorial and advertising decisions based at least in part on their readers' sensitivities."

But how does an editor gauge an audience that could be national, even international, in scope?

That's just one of the challenges that traditional approaches to ethics may not cover, according to Brooke Shelby Biggs, columnist for Hotwired (*www.hotwired.com*) and producer of the site's commentator page.

"The ideals put forth in the ethics codes still hold true and are very valuable online," Biggs contends, "but this particular medium has so many ingredients that the codes don't take into account. It makes things a lot more complicated."

Biggs argues for a new media watchdog group, a coalition of journalists to serve as a touchstone for the industry. Not a news council, the group would be a "cross-section of representatives of the online community talking about these issues in a more formal way." At minimum, she says, online journalists need a better understanding of their audience and its culture.

The Web community is anti-establishment and skeptical of the status quo. It assumes that information should be free-flowing, unrestrained, and open to interpretation—assumptions that thwart the old media's traditional role as gatekeeper and protector of the public's right to know.[1]

"The people who have been great at communicating information to a mass audience will continue to be great at it," she says, "but they're going to have to be more open and creative about it, even while they're protecting their credibility and authority."

If there is anything about which most editors and observers seem to agree, it's that good ethics is good business. In the increasingly chaotic and fragmented world of online media, newspaper sites have brand names to protect and defend—brand names that set them apart from a ravenous pack of wannabe news providers.

"I do have one important answer," Mann told the ethics conference. . . . "If we hope to prosper online, it is because, amid the thousands of

Web sites—from Yahoo! to the two guys in their garage in West Philly—we journalism sites are paid attention to because we have brand recognition that says we are credible sources of information."

But how do you foster credibility online? Through roundtable discussions, Staci D. Kramer, a freelancer and chair of SPJ's [Society of Professional Journalists] Task Force on Online Journalism, is helping to define issues in new media, ranging from credentialing to copyright to ethics. The organization's traditional code of ethics is a good place to start, Kramer says. Its tenets are direct and clear: Seek truth and report it; minimize harm; act independently; and be accountable.

For trained and experienced journalists, the SPJ values are working assumptions, Kramer says. But that may not be true for the new breed of online publishers and writers. "There is a feeling that the difference between people who were trained as journalists and people using the Internet to act as journalists is that the first group adheres to a common set of ethical guidelines, and the second doesn't feel that it has to," Kramer says.

In addition, independent journalists don't benefit from the institutional checks and balances built into newsroom routines. The daily news cycle sends a story through a series of internal checkpoints before it arrives on a reader's front porch or computer screen. That's not always the case in an environment in which anybody with a computer and a modem can publish.

"Online is different," Kramer says. "But if I'm a reporter, I still shouldn't be printing a story without sending it first through an editor. It can't go directly from me to my computer to the Web, the way it does with so many people who are pamphleteering online."

Kramer says it's important to remember that despite the differences between old and new media, the fundamental issues remain the same. "We need to remember: Common sense doesn't leave the room when online journalism comes in," she says.

Who could argue? But one newsroom's commonsense decisions can depart dramatically from another's, which results in widely varying policies on such fundamental issues as linking, the use of cookies, and advertising relationships. In the forefront—and coming under fire for some of its decisions—is the venerable, traditional, and authoritative *New York Times*.

LINKING

On September 15, 1997, the *New York Times*, in both its print and online versions, featured an in-depth story by reporter Nina Bernstein about the use of electronic data-gathering techniques that have "turned private detectives into a vanguard of privacy invasion." "At a time of growing public alarm over the erosion of privacy by technology and data commerce, electronic dossiers have become the common currency of computer-age sleuths, and a semi-underground information market offers them much more: private telephone records, credit card bills, airline travel records, even medical histories," Bernstein wrote.

The print version of the story named the businesses that provide these services. The online version provided direct links to their Websites.

On October 21, the *New York Times* on the Web (*www.nytimes.com*) carried a story about a new Website devoted to establishing the innocence of convicted killer Charles Manson. Under the headline "Manson Family Web Site: History Rewritten by Losers," the story described the prosecutor's concern that the Website "obviously is sucking in unsuspecting young people who have no idea what a bad person Manson is."

At the close of the story, the *Times* provided links to Access Manson and three other sites espousing his innocence.

The links in these stories probably led readers to less-than-credible organizations or information, acknowledges Rob Fixmer, editor of CyberTimes, the section of the *Times*'s site featuring original material. But, he adds, the *Times* is providing its readers a service, not assuming responsibility for the information at the other end of the click.

"Our job is to share as much information as possible," he says. "We have to have enough faith in our readers that, when we send them to a site, they will make an informed, intelligent decision about what they're seeing."

That doesn't mean the *Times* has no standards for linking, Fixmer adds. He has written guidelines based on the *Times*'s tradition as a family newspaper: no links to sites that "celebrate violence" or present sexual content; no links that promote or extol bigotry or racism.

In addition, when a reader clicks on a link embedded in a story, a "disclaimer" page appears, explaining that the user is leaving the *Times*'s site for destinations over which the newspaper has no control. "In a way, that's a legal disclaimer to the point that we're telling you you're going somewhere that has some affinity to the story," Fixmer explains, "but we don't know what you're going to find when you get there."

The *Washington Post*'s site (*www.WashingtonPost.com*) has adopted a similar approach: a combination of vetting links and informing readers when they're leaving *Post* territory. Staffers make every effort to review links and let readers know what to expect.

Even so, the site posts an "Editor's Note" in the margin of linked pages, reminding readers that their clicks are taking them away from *WashingtonPost.com*. Many sites rarely link to content outside their own pages, a practice some Net users say exemplifies the old media's failure to exploit or understand the unique features of the new medium.

But among sites that do embed links in their editorial content, disclaimers are often touted as a workable solution: They create a safety zone between a site and the rest of the Net, thereby protecting its brand name and credibility.

That's a practical answer but not an ethical one, says Poynter's Bob Steele. "We cannot just say 'Buyer beware,' " Steele says. "That alone does not mitigate against the harm that can come from tainted information."

In his view, sites are ethically responsible for the information they provide to readers, even if that information comes through a link. "I've never liked the word 'disclaimer,' " he says. "It means, 'I do not claim responsibility.' I don't believe that's an appropriate position for a news organization to take."

Steele says there's nothing wrong with warning readers "when we are leading them to something that might alarm them," but, "to say 'disclaim' and wash our hands of it to me seems to be both arrogant and irresponsible."

COOKIES

Click on *www.nytimes.com* and several things could happen:

If you're new to the site, you'll be asked to register. You'll need a user name and password. You'll be asked for your age, your gender, your zip code, and how and where you buy the *Times*; you'll also be asked for income information, but that's optional. And you'll be asked whether you want to receive e-mail about site features and advertisers.

Fill in the blanks and *nytimes.com* is open for business, unless you've configured your browser to reject cookies. Then you'll find yourself back at the registration page, cycling through the same process. Over and over. Until you decide to let the *Times* embed in your home computer a bit of data—commonly called a cookie—that allows it to track where you go on its site.[2]

In short, the *Times*'s policy is clear and unequivocal: No cookies, no access.

In an online collection of replies to frequently asked questions, the *Times* explains the rationale. Cookies are used to save your log-on information. They keep tabs on which of the site's paid services you can access, and they allow the *Times* to track your clicks, either for advertising or editorial content.

So what's the big deal?

Despite the fact that most sites—including the *Times*'s—assure readers that cookie information is used only in the aggregate and won't be sold or provided to other companies, privacy advocates argue that cookies infringe on Web users' right to surf the Net anonymously and privately.

In addition, they argue, many Web users don't even know that cookies exist. They're not sophisticated enough to set their browsers to warn them about cookies, or to delete the files in their hard drives where cookies are stored.

And it's all too easy to imagine scenarios in which cookie data could be used to track a Web user's personal proclivities and site preferences. For example, a Tennessee newspaper filed suit in October claiming that local government employees' cookie files are covered by open records laws; the newspaper wants the files to determine whether city workers have been spending work hours visiting entertainment or adult-oriented Websites.

"If I were to gather this kind of information about a student or colleague, I probably would be guilty of stalking under current law," University of Illinois journalism professor Eric Meyer said in a posting in an online news forum. "Online, we call it intelligent marketing, and we clamor to sign up as part of such networks. Why? Because it's money, and money is in particularly short supply online."

However you spin it, say cookie opponents, using software to track users' Web activities reeks of George Orwell—Big Brother in cyberspace. Except in this scenario, the motivation is profit.

The potential for abuse is there, acknowledges Kevin McKenna, . . . editorial director of the *New York Times* Electronic Media Company . . . "But cookies are not intrinsically good or evil," he says. "It's how they're used. And we use them for good reasons."

The *Times* is highly sensitive to its users' concerns about privacy, McKenna says. That concern prompted the site to post a privacy policy that articulates exactly what it will do with the information it's collecting.

The *Times* is not the only news site to require registration and cookies. The *Wall Street Journal* Website (*www.wsj.com*), which charges an annual subscription fee, also demands that readers provide personal information before accessing its services.

But many other news sites—even those whose editors argue that cookies aren't as threatening as many people believe—are very sensitive to the public's general antipathy toward them, at least for now.

McClatchy's *Nando.net* is one. Executive editor Seth Effron says the staff is still divided on the use of cookies, both within its site and in advertising content.

Christian Hendricks, the site's president and publisher, says advertisers are just trying to measure the effectiveness of their banner ads, not infringing on the privacy of users. But it's a distinction that readers sometimes miss, he says. And that makes cookies as much a public relations issue as an ethical one.

"I actually had someone tell me a cookie knows everything about the user," Hendricks says. "Things like where the user has been on the Web, their credit card numbers, all kinds of things."

Incorrect though that perception may be, it's that kind of public image of cookies that makes them more trouble than they're worth, in his view. "One must remember that a cookie by itself is meaningless," he says. "It's the information that is attached to it in some data bases— and how that information is used—that is problematic."

TRANSACTION FEES

Read a book review at *nytimes.com,* click a Barnes & Noble link, and order the book. You get quick service, the giant bookseller makes a sale, and the *Times* gets a commission.

Is it just good business-or an inappropriate melding of a respected news site's advertising and editorial content? The answer depends upon whom you ask.[3]

Bernard Gwertzman, editor of *New York Times* on the Web, says his staff debated the arrangement and consulted with the Sunday book editor and senior editors at the paper before it was approved. He also ran it by a group of people at "one of those interminable Internet conferences" and found opinions decidedly mixed.

"I wasn't at all sure on this one, either," he admits, "so we had demos, we kicked it around."

There was easy consensus, Gwertzman says, that the *Times* reviews weren't going to pander to the bookseller. But there were two issues to consider, according to McKenna: "The first was our own integrity, which we don't intend to compromise. The second is user perception, which is equally important."

The arrangement's success depends upon the site's ability to convince readers that advertising isn't affecting editorial content, according to McKenna. The *Times* came out of its deliberations convinced that it could strike the balance.

"In the end, I decided it was a service for our readers," Gwertzman says. "We need to explore avenues of revenue since we don't charge for our product, but we need to do it in a respectful way."

Nytimes.com is far from the first or only news site to establish transaction-fee relationships with online vendors. Salon (*www.salon.com*), one of the bestknown Webzines, has a deal with Borders Books, and *Amazon.com* has a growing "associates program" in which it contracts with online publishers who earn up to 15 percent on sales resulting from consumer clicks off their Websites.

But common practice doesn't make an arrangement valid or ethical, say some observers.

SPJ director Kramer says appearances are just as important as reality. "If the *New York Times* can live with the fact that there appears to be a conflict of interest there, they have to realize that somewhere down the road, those appearances may come back to haunt them," she says.

The site's most sophisticated users will assume that the traditional firewall between advertising and editorial content remains intact, Kramer says. "But your ethical responsibility is to program and present information to your broadest audience, not your most sophisticated user," she adds.

In response to suggestions that agreements like the one between Barnes & Noble and the *New York Times* are simply a service to readers, journalism professor Meyer scoffs outright. Under many such arrangements, he wrote in an online posting, news organizations "have an active financial stake" in the topics they cover. He added, "Any way you cut it, however many rationalizations you try to make, coverage becomes an unethical shill for a product."

Most of the editors contacted for this article were more open to the idea that the new medium demands—or at least allows—new relationships with advertisers. After all, they argue, they're providing their products free of charge; the money has to come from somewhere.

"You can't apply the ethics from the old media to the kinds of information and editorial content you'll find on the Web," says

Hotwired's Brooke Shelby Biggs. "And you can't do it in advertising either."

Nevertheless, it's the tension between revenue and readership that most concerns online editors. The challenge is to keep advertisers happy even as a news site maintains its traditional—and ethical—obligations to objectivity, fairness, and credibility.

"What exists in newspapers and what we've got to translate into online is that we're independent and not for sale," says Tim McGuire, editor and senior vice president for new media at Minneapolis' *Star Tribune*. "That means advertising cannot and will not affect coverage. It also means that you must not fool readers about what is advertising and what is news and information."

That doesn't mean sites shouldn't accept transaction fees, McGuire argues. It does mean they need to be honest with their readers about what they're doing. "When you click on that button that takes you to the Barnes & Noble site, the *nytimes.com* site should say, 'You may click to Barnes & Noble and order this book, and when you do, the *New York Times* gets a cut of that,'" McGuire argues.

Even murkier, says McGuire, are sponsorship arrangements in which advertisers actually pay for the presentation of some kinds of editorial content.

"That's going to be a very touchy area," he says. "We need to look at what television has always done and say, 'Can we do this kind of thing in a way that makes it very clear to readers what the role of our sponsors is?'"

Anne Stuart's observation about the state of new media ethics remains as true today as it was a year ago: There's no consensus about whether the Web poses new problems and issues, much less how they should be addressed.

McGuire says the profession needs to relax about the fact that guidelines for online journalism have yet to be written. "Some people forget that it took us a long time to work our way to a firm understanding of newspaper rules," he says. "We're going to have to work our way to a set of rules about online, and they may not be the same rules."

But Jim Willse, editor of Newark's *Star-Ledger* and 1997 chair of ASNE's [American Society of Newspaper Editors] New Media Committee, says the traditional rules and values work just fine, even in the online world. Most of the new situations presented by the Web are practical—not ethical—concerns.

"Most of these issues don't bother me very much . . . ," he says. "You've got common sense, you grew up with good values, you're not going to invite incursions into your editorial integrity. There doesn't seem to be any reason for any great hand-wringing about it."

Publishing the news is basically the same, whether you're doing it once a day or once every fifteen minutes, Willse suggests.

"I don't see any new ethical issues online that are fundamentally at odds with traditional journalism," he says. "I guess I'm just less anguished about these things than some of my colleagues."

NOTES

1. See "NetGain," *American Journalism Review*, November 1996.

2. See "The Cookies Crumble," *American Journalism Review*, July/August, 1997.

3. See "The World of New Media," *American Journalism Review*, December 1997.

Contributors

Akbar S. Ahmed, Pakistani scholar in residence at Selwyn College at the University of Cambridge.

Ien Ang, Professor of Cultural Studies at the University of Western Sydney, Nepean, Australia.

Andrew Belsey, Lecturer in Philosophy and a member of the Center for Applied Ethics, University of Wales, Cardiff.

Leo Bogart, sociologist specializing in mass communication and among the foremost authorities in marketing and consumer psychology.

James Carey, Professor, Graduate School of Journalism, Columbia University.

Ruth Chadwick, Professor of Moral Philosophy and Head of the Centre for Professional Ethics, University of Central Lancashire, Preston, UK.

David Chagall, author of several books, including *Surviving the Media Jungle.*

Louis A. Day, Professor of Communications, Louisiana State University.

George Gerbner, Bell Atlantic Professor of Telecommunications at Temple University, and Founder and President of the Cultural Environment Movement.

Adam Goodheart, senior editor and writer at *Civilization* magazine.

Lawrence K. Grossman, former president of NBC and PBS.

Don Hazen, Director of the Independent Media Institute and former publisher of *Mother Jones* magazine.

Neil Hickey, editor at large, *Columbia Journalism Review.*

Louis Hodges, Knight Professor, Department of Journalism, Washington and Lee University.

Joe Holley, contributing editor, *Columbia Journalism Review.*

Craig L. LaMay, Associate Professor of Journalism, Northwestern University.

Dianne Lynch, journalism instructor at St. Michael's College, Burlington, Vermont.

Fred Mann, General Manager of Philadelphia On-line, the Website for the *Philadelphia Inquirer* and the *Philadelphia Daily News.*

John C. Merrill, Professor of Journalism, University of Missouri, Columbia.

Davis "Buzz" Merritt, editor and senior vice president, the *Wichita Eagle* and leading advocate of public journalism.

Newton N. Minow, Annenberg University Professor, Northwestern University and former Federal Communications Commissioner.

Lance Morrow, University Professor, Boston University.

Sinéad O'Brien, freelance writer and contributor to the *American Journalism Review.*

Adam S. Plotkin, contributor to the *Journal of Mass Media Ethics.*

Carl Sessions Stepp, senior editor, *American Journalism Review,* and teacher, the University of Maryland College of Journalism.

Jacqueline Sharkey, Professor of Journalism, University of Arizona.

Alicia C. Shepard, contributing writer, *American Journalism Review.*

Scott Sherman, a writer whose essays have appeared in such publications as the *Nation,* the *Utne Reader,* and *Lingua Franca.*

Scott Stossel, associate editor of the *American Prospect.*

Jules Witcover, author and reporter for the Baltimore *Sun.*

Dick Wright, political cartoonist, United Features Syndicate.

DATE DUE

GAYLORD			PRINTED IN U.S.A